Property,
Markets, and
Government Intervention

Property, Markets, and Government Intervention

A Textbook in Microeconomic Theory and Its Current Applications

DANIEL ORR
Professor of Economics
University of California, San Diego

Goodyear Publishing Company, Inc.
Pacific Palisades, California

Library of Congress Cataloging in Publication Data

Orr, Daniel.
    Property, markets, and government intervention.

    Includes bibliographies and index.
    1. Microeconomics.   I. Title
Hb171.5.067   33u. i   75-19565
ISBN 0-87620-728-X

Current printing (last digit):

10   9   8   7   6   5   4   3   2   1

Y-728X-9

Printed in the United States of America

The author wishes to thank these publishers for their permission to reprint the
following material:

In Chapter 8:
From "New Hampshire" from *The Poetry of Robert Frost,* edited by
Edward Connery Lathem. Copyright 1923, © 1969 by Holt, Rinehart and
Winston. Copyright 1951 by Robert Frost. Reprinted by permission of Holt,
Rinehart and Winston, Publishers, and by Jonathan Cape Ltd.

In Chapter 18:
From *Literature and Revolution* by Leon Trotsky, University of Michigan
Press, 1960. Reprinted by permission of the publisher.

Lucille Souyer

to LILLIAN N. ORR

One of the great intuitive economists,
and my first teacher.

Contents

CHAPTER THREE

The Individual in Society   36

Part Two

THE IDEALIZED MARKET ECONOMY

CHAPTER FOUR

Demand and Supply: Elements and First Applications   59

CHAPTER FIVE

The Law of Demand   84

CHAPTER SIX

Further Topics in Demand and Consumer Theory   113

)

Part Four

COLLECTIVIZE, INTERVENE, OR . . . ?

Preface

The market system has been an important component of human society for a very long time, and for part of that time—more than two centuries—it has been an object of observation and systematic study. The economic theory that we know today has evolved out of those processes of study and observation.

The goal of economic theory has always been to explain, predict, and interpret the workings of the economy (especially the market exchange part of the economy). Through time, the institutions of property and exchange, like the structure of society, have grown more complex. Increasing complexity has kept economic theorists busy, applying new ideas and new bodies of knowledge (principally mathematical knowledge) to the search for better, more successful, and more intellectually satisfying descriptive-predictive mechanisms. Discrepancies between economic models and the "real world" have been perceived, and have stimulated much effort to comprehend and, if possible, eliminate them.

Discrepancies between economic theory and "reality" have been very important in quite a different area as well. The failure of an economic institution to function in the simple and transparent way that theory says it should has been regarded from time to time to be a *problem* to be solved by "policy-makers" through political-governmental action. Increasingly in recent

years we have seen attempts to reconstruct, reform, or control
the fundamental institutions of property and exchange. Economic theory has been broadened and extended by these attempts at control, in part to make understandable the way new
control actions work, in part to justify and rationalize new control actions before they are taken.

Even though the processes of growth and change in economic theory have not always given the appearance of rapid
progress, theory has remained useful in illuminating the way
the private exchange sector of the economy works and how responses and initiatives by policy-makers can be expected to
influence outcomes.

The preceding statement may be taken as the organizing theme of this book.
In accord with that statement, this book has several distinctive features of content. First, there is a discussion of the ethical foundations of market allocation.
Why is the satisfaction of individual preferences taken to be the goal of the economic activity within our economic system? Is that goal common to all economic
systems? How well does our existing system perform in the service of that goal?
Such questions are seldom investigated in a microeconomics text, yet they are
important in the appraisal of economic performance and the comparison of economic systems. Chapter 3 is a review of nineteenth-century liberal thought regarding the significance of the individual human being and an investigation of
how that thought has affected our economic, social, and political institutions.

Second, while microeconomic theory is presented informally, it is not developed casually. The organization and content of the book reflect a concern to high-
light the analytical processes that are important in evaluation of economic performance. No attempt has been made to review all results on all traditional topics
in microeconomics; but if the main objective has been met, most of the results
that can be presented at a reasonably accessible level and that are of direct rele-
vance to the issue of performance are treated fully here, while other important
ideas are used in passing, rather than given a full-blown development. For example, there is no discussion of revealed preference, but elementary techniques
of that analytical tradition are used in discussion of the substitution effect in Chapter 5; and there is no lengthy exposition of Chamberlin-Robinson imperfect competition, but the salient efficiency implications of that tradition are preserved in
the discussion of free entry with product differentiation in Chapter 11.

A third feature is the particular attention that has been paid to *time*. The time
dimensions of variables, even in static analysis, are made explicit; and the elements of capital theory are brought in for discussion in connection with problems of allocation through time in the face of meaningful intertemporal change.
The careful reader will notice that capital is scarcely mentioned at all until intertemporal analysis is undertaken in Chapter 11; in the earlier chapters that discuss
production theory, inputs are simply designated by number, rather than named

"labor" and "capital." This treatment serves, I hope, to clarify rather than to further obscure the many-faceted concept called "capital."

Fourth, I should mention an issue of style and content. As is true of almost every worthwhile current textbook in general economics and every older book that we still read and remember, the mark of the author—his tastes, interests, and values—is very much upon this book. By inserting myself into this book, I have tried to establish a dialogue with the reader. Much of the material that is treated here is controversial and not a matter of settled scientific consensus. In treating controversial material, I have tried neither to camouflage nor to glorify my own personal values and political outlook; and in chapters that deal heavily in controversial issues, there will be found among the bibliographical notes references to accessible works of different persuasions.

Textbook authors, usually, direct their efforts at a particular well-defined segment of the market, as determined by what has enjoyed success in the past. This book, however, was written with no single audience or market segment, and no "model" predecessor, in mind. Instead, the goal was a book that could, with minor adaptation, be used by either introductory or intermediate students. In intermediate applications, a novelty is the heavy emphasis on the applicability of theory, in the analysis of problems and in the assessment of policy alternatives. For better or for worse, our macro courses have for years integrated policy analysis with Keynesian and neoclassical equilibrium theory; but few micro books have clarified issues and analyzed policy responses with comparable care.

Materials that explore details in greater depth (sometimes with the aid of the calculus), or additional and more specialized topics, which are addressed to a more experienced audience, are treated in asterisked sections or gathered at the ends of chapters in asterisked appendices. If that material is omitted, the experience here at U.C. San Diego indicates that introductory students of widely diverse background and ability can understand and enjoy the text. And by virtue of the organizing theme and topical coverage, the book also is a natural choice for use in business school economics courses (not managerial economics, but courses on the functioning of the economic order, which typically are based upon nonmathematical "intermediate micro" books). Finally, I hope that teachers of courses in "political economy" will find this mixture of value theory and value systems congenial and usable. Part One, Chapter 10, and Parts Three and Four offer a useful core of material for such a course, assuming a micro theory prerequisite.

Many friends and colleagues have read through parts of this book in earlier drafts, and their comments have in the main been useful and encouraging. These include John Bonin, William W. Brown, James Buchanan, John Conlisk, Richard Emmerson, Cotton M. Lindsay, Joyce Pickersgill, Wolfhard Ramm, Richard Schmalensee, and Laurence G. Smith.

Comments from you, the reader, are always more than welcome and will be answered if an answer is called for.

Daniel Orr

Part One

EXCHANGE, PREFERENCE, AND WELFARE

Chapters 1 to 3 constitute Part One of this book. Their purpose is to motivate the reader, and to orient him a bit regarding the later analysis. Chapter 1 defines *property* and *markets,* and examines some of the consequences of those institutions in a context that is familiar to nearly everyone, and appalling to many—the context is the transformation of a rural and agricultural area into suburban housing. Many of the concepts and theories that are analyzed in detail later on are touched upon in Chapter 1. Chapter 2 introduces the reader to an extremely important, yet rather simple idea: that a general increase in happiness and well-being can result from exchange. This idea is introduced in the context of a couple of "toy" illustrations involving very rudimentary societies and social orders. Chapter 3 is a digression into the domains of moral and political philosophy. Its purpose is to explore the philosophic foundations of market allocation; or rather, to present the most persuasive arguments that have been offered by philosophers in behalf of an economic system in which most things of value are privately owned and allocation is accomplished principally through market action.

CHAPTER ONE

Who Took
the Orange Trees
Out of Orange County?

Knowst thou the land where the lemon trees bloom,
Where the gold orange glows in the deep thicket's gloom,
Where a wind ever soft from the blue heaven blows,
And the groves are of laurel and myrtle and rose?

GOETHE (1795)

I am myself and what is around me, and if I do not save it,
it shall not save me.

JOSE ORTEGA Y GASSET (1911)

1.1. SCARCITY IN THE MIDST OF PLENTY

1.1.1. The "Evil" of Economic Development

America has historically been a westward-looking nation. The story of westward migration reached a romantic peak in the decade of the 1840s, when parties in wagon trains forged across the roadless plains, mountains, and deserts to the valleys of the Sacramento or Willamette. Yet the magnitude of that early migration, and its impact on the land and people of America, appears trivial when compared to the migrations that began about a hundred years later. Because of improved transportation, increased job opportunity, and the attractions of climate and environment, immigrants have, since the Depression and World War Two, wrought truly fantastic changes upon the sunny slopes and fertile valleys of

California. Nowhere are the changes more visible or more dramatic than in Orange County.

In 1930, a single two-lane highway wound down the coast of Southern California, connecting the region's metropolis with Mexico. Los Angeles was certainly a major city—a few years earlier, it had passed Detroit to become the fourth largest city in the nation, with a population of just over 1.2 million. However, to the south, the only semblance of a city was at San Diego, where some 150,000 residents basked in the sun beside a spectacular harbor, and devoted themselves mainly to the business of the United States Navy and to the entertainment of visitors from Los Angeles.

The drive between the two cities was an experience: miles of untouched seacoast, thousand-foot hills hugging the shore, and an electric blue sky. On a side trip across the coastal hills that stretch from Newport Beach to Capistrano, one could visit a pristine valley bordered on the east by the mile-high rise of the Santa Ana range. Scattered through the north end of the valley were trees—the orange groves that gave the county its name. The coastal communities of the county were idyllic—Newport Beach, Laguna Beach, San Juan Capistrano, San Clemente—all picturesque, isolated retreats for the vacationer, the artist, the retired. Since then, what has happened?

Freeways, tract after tract of monotonously similar new homes, shopping centers, dragstrips, a major league ballpark, Disneyland, California State University, Fullerton and the University of California, Irvine have all happened. The beauty and seclusion and charm and clear air have been transformed into a mess that is increasingly hard to distinguish from any of the smog-blanketed suburban jungles surrounding Chicago, or Houston, or Washington, or you name the city.

Some numerical evidence may help you to grasp the profound nature of change west of the Santa Ana Mountains. From Table 1.1 we see that in 1930, Orange County was home to 118,674 people. A total of 63,803 acres were planted in citrus trees, which yielded a crop valued at $41.636 million. By 1970, population had surged to 1.420 million (more than a tenfold increase); citrus cultivation declined to 15,360 acres, and the crop value was $12.551 million. If the dollar value of the citrus crop is corrected to reflect general price-level changes, the drop in crop value is far more dramatic—in constant dollars of 1970 purchasing power, the 1930 crop would have been valued at $101.255 million.[1]

There are numerous other counties in the United States that show substantially the same pattern of explosive growth: Fulton (Georgia), Nassau (New York), Arlington (Virginia), Du Page (Illinois), Maricopa (Arizona) are a few

---

[1]The problem of price-level changes (inflation and deflation) over time is not one of the issues that will be examined in this book. However, we do consider some of the theoretical and practical problems entailed in compiling *index numbers* that attempt to measure the impact of price-level changes on the "standard of living." See Chapter 6, Section 6.4.

TABLE 1.1. Population and Citrus Cultivation in Orange County, 1920–1970

Year	Population	Acres in Citrus Cultivation	Citrus Crop Value	Citrus Value 1971 Dollars
1920	61,375	43,500	$11,440,000	$ 23,186,000
1930	118,674	63,803	41,636,000	101,255,000
1940	130,760	76,128	20,969,000	60,709,000
1950	216,224	65,649	32,135,000	54,200,000
1960	703,925	34.453	30,112,000	41,283,000
1965	1,158,000[a]	24,483	17,501,000	22,687,000
1971	1,420,386[b]	15,363	12,551,000	

[a]U.S. Census Bureau estimate.
[b]1970 census.
Source: U.S. Census Bureau; Orange County Department of Agriculture, *Agricultural Crop Reports* (Annual).

that have developed along similar lines since World War Two. All are part of a pattern that is of increasing concern to civic and conservation groups. In the view of such groups, more and more open land is destroyed forever to no good purpose, and in nearly every instance, at the core of the expansion is a great central city, becoming progressively more decayed and dispirited and dangerous.

1.1.2. Scarcity and Change in Orange County

The rhetoric of the concerned reflects the depth of their concern. In Orange County, would it not be better to go on raising oranges? Think of the ravaged beauty, the steadily increasing problem of smog, the annoyance of congestion and crowding! Think of the unemployment and hardship wrought upon the most disadvantaged of socioeconomic groups, the agricultural laborers! Must we continue to rob future generations of their heritage by sacrificing our scenic treasure on the altar of profit? We only do so to benefit the big tract builders and big highway builders, and the cement and lumber monopolists who supply them.

Fortunately, there exists a discipline, economics, that is useful in understanding, explaining, and evaluating processes of change and accompanying conflicts of economic interest like the ones that are unfolding in Orange County. Economics teaches us that a central problem in society is *scarcity*—not enough clean air, or open space, or high-salaried jobs, or beautiful and comfortable homes to make everyone happy. Noneconomists (and indeed, even some who call themselves economists) are continually offering us simple explanations of the observed events in Orange County, explanations which usually run in terms of too many people, or the greed of a powerful and ruthless few. Experience reveals that the attempt to provide comprehensive explanations of complex social events in such simple terms is almost sure to be unsuccessful. Only when situations of conflict and change are approached with some coherent and proven perspective can understanding be expected to develop, and understanding is necessary. Without it, the actions of a concerned citizenry can do harm instead of good.

1.1.3. The Major Objective

The central objective of this book is to explore the ways in which the unfolding events in our society are affected by the general condition of scarcity. We will see how economic analysis can be applied to the tasks of *explaining* and *evaluating* an important class of events—those which are shaped by our response as individuals, and as a society, to the problem of scarcity. Scarcity rears its head in more obvious places and in more poignant ways than we will find in Orange County. We could have opened this book with a discourse on Chicago's West Side black community, or Hazard County, in the Appalachians of Kentucky, and the issue of scarcity would have been more immediate to all of us. But that, in some measure, is the beauty of Orange County as an opening subject—it enables us to see that scarcity is a problem of *competing claims* for goods that exist in limited supply, and to understand that the problem of scarcity is confronted in the wealthiest sectors of society, as well as in the poorest.

What about Orange County, then? Why is it changing in the way we have described? In developing an answer to this question, we must understand the workings of a large part of the *economy*. The economy is a collection of institutions (like banks and labor unions), customs (like dumping waste in rivers, or not working on Sunday), and laws, all of which affect and help to shape the crucial decisions that are made by individuals and groups confronted by scarcity.

How do individuals respond to scarcity? We will assume that everyone who has a stake or a role in the changes that are taking place in Orange County seeks to make himself better off, to enhance his own subjective sense of well-being to the greatest possible extent. Society denies an individual the use of naked force or power in the pursuit of his own interest. It is the essence of a civilized social order that an individual cannot coerce others in order to obtain what he wants. Two important processes—economic and political—are accepted by society as instruments by which individuals can try to move events in directions that they deem best for themselves. Both processes are concerned in important ways with the resolution of the conflicting and competing claims of different individuals for scarce resources.

The most important economic process is one whereby claims are settled through a system of voluntary and impersonal interaction called the *market exchange* process. We will understand better what is going on in Orange County after seeing how the market exchange process affects events there. Our first analytic undertaking, then, will be informally to define and describe the mechanism of market action, with reference to the provision of housing in Orange County.

1.2. THE MARKET MECHANISM

1.2.1. Goods

Economists define a *good* as something that is *wanted* by someone. A particular article may be a good at one time or in one place, and not be a good elsewhere or at a different time. Crickets are wanted by fishermen in Minnesota in August and there they are a good. Crickets invade the farmlands of California's Imperial Valley by the million in August, to drown in swimming pools, plug up drains, or get crushed on the streets and sidewalks of El Centro, Brawley, and Calexico. Crickets are *not* a good in the Imperial Valley, as anyone who tried to sell them there, or give them away, would find out.

1.2.2. Property

"Property is theft," wrote the French philosopher Proudhon, thereby assuring himself the kind of immortality that is reserved for coiners of silly slogans. For no social order is complete without a system of assigning who has the right to use goods, and rules governing the exchange or transmission of those rights. Proudhon's feelings were actually directed against *private* property, an arrangement under which individuals control the use of property, and can freely exchange or bequeath those rights. Private property has had a long and usually honorable role in Western civilization. In the Book of Deuteronomy (the oldest of the Old Testament books) we see that the Law of Israel protects rights of property, in the eighth (don't steal) and tenth (don't covet that which is your neighbor's) commandments. In addition the Law specifies how property shall be used (see Deut. 22:8–9, or 24:19–25, for example), protected (Deut. 22:1–4; 23:15–16; 23:24–25; or 25:13–16), and transmitted (Deut. 21:15–17). Similar provisions are to be found in the even older Code of Hammurabi, which bound ancient Mesopotamia c. 1700 B.C.

Throughout recorded human history, then, individual human beings have been accumulating, using, exchanging, and disposing of property. Moreover, for as long as private property has been codified, there have been provisions in law that have restricted its use, exchange, and disposition to maintain some traditions and protect some interests.

We can identify two alternatives to the private property system. The first is to leave unspecified the rights to control and use some goods. This alternative is still observed at times; nobody "owns" the whales of the oceans, and yet they are used (on a catch as catch-can basis, with hunters from Japan and the Soviet Union doing most of the catching).

The second alternative is collective or government ownership of property. Under that system, officials of the State (either elected or self-appointed) control the accumulation, use, and disposition of some classes or types of property. We will discuss such "public ownership" or collectivist arrangements at length in Chapter 18.

The extent to which private property is entrenched among English-speaking peoples is seen in the fact that ownership rights are almost never denied to people. A convicted murderer can own, control, and dispose of property (but by imprisonment he may be denied its use). Slaves were denied the right to own some kinds of property (notably land) in the early nineteenth-century U.S., but emancipation gave that right to them; and even in the South, during the post-Reconstruction period of intense anti-Negro feeling, no serious move ever was made to deny property ownership on grounds of race.

The topic of property is a fascinating one. How did ownership rights in North American lands become established between 1600 and 1920? By what method or rationale does the Soviet Union lay claim to the vast emptiness of Siberia, when hundreds of millions of Chinese are crammed into their comparatively tiny adjacent homeland? What establishes the claim of Kuwait to control the vast reservoir of petroleum wealth upon which that nation rests? Why did European Jews educate their children so intensively during the nineteenth century? All these questions are answered in terms of property rights, how they are asserted and defended, and how they may be breached. Our purpose here, however, is not to deal in depth or extensively with that topic. We want to see that property is a fundamental institution of our social order, and has been for millennia, and further, to appreciate that every social organization has "property"—in that it must assign the rights to control and use things.

1.2.3. The Market

An important analytical abstraction of economists is the *market,* where rights of ownership and use of goods are exchanged. The market of economic analysis transcends its concrete real-world namesakes, such as the New York Stock Exchange, the Chicago Board of Trade, or your neighborhood A&P, Bohack, Safeway, Kroger, or Piggly Wiggly. To the economist, a market is best described as a collection of potential *buyers* and *sellers* of a good that is well-defined in terms of the problem under consideration. Each of the potential buyers will consider purchasing the good from one or more of the sellers in the group; and each potential seller is willing to make some of the good available to one or more of the potential buyers. What do we mean when we talk about a good being "well-defined in terms of the problem under consideration"? We mean that whether or not a definition is adequate for analytical purposes will depend on the question that is asked. For some studies, "transportation" may be adequate as a definition of a good. For another study, "automobile" may be an adequate definition; and in yet other cases, it may be necessary to define "automobiles with wheelbase less than 96 inches'' (compact cars) and ''automobiles with wheel-base greater than 174 inches'' (luxury cars) as different goods.[2]

1.2.4. Price, Supply, and Demand

Economists have found it fruitful to focus on the role of *price* in studying the way that markets bring about a resolution of the competition among buyers to obtain the good, and among sellers to part with the good. It is the usual view that, other things being equal, if the price of a good rises, buyers will respond by demanding less of the good, and sellers will respond by supplying more of it. *Quantity demanded,* the total quantity willingly purchased per unit of time, and *quantity supplied,* the total quantity willingly offered for sale per unit of time, are both viewed as *functions* of the good's price. These functions are called *demand* and *supply.* Figure 1.1 shows the hypothetical behavior of buyers and sellers in a market that is important to the present discussion—namely, the market for "housing" in Orange County. Along the horizontal axis, the quantity of housing per unit of time is measured. The unit of measure is square feet per month. Along the vertical axis, price of housing is measured, in cents per square foot per month. The demand curve, labeled *D,* is drawn with negative slope: at the high price of 50 cents per square foot per month, the small quantity of 150 million square feet per month would be demanded. At the low price of 20 cents per square foot per month, a total of 900 million square feet per month would be demanded.[3] Symmetrically, the supply curve *S* in Figure 1.1 is positively sloped, reflecting the greater willingness of builders to make housing available at high prices, and the pressure that high prices put on occupants of existing housing to move elsewhere. At prices of 50 cents and 20 cents, the quantities supplied are 600 million square feet, and zero, respectively.

In Figure 1.1, the only price at which there is no pressure for change is 40 cents per square foot per month. At that price, total quantity demanded per month equals total quantity supplied; the housing market is *cleared* or *in equilibrium* at that price. In any market, the price of the good will adjust until the mar-

---

[2]"Transportation" might be an adequate characterization of the good in a study of how households spend their incomes. In studying the effect of the price of gasoline on automobile purchases, it would be advantageous to examine car purchases by size category.

[3]A word on the quantity unit is in order. Some goods, like sugar, are bought and used up. The unit of quantity measure for the sugar market would be, simply, pounds or tons per month. Other goods, conspicuously exemplified by housing, are not used up, but instead yield a flow of services. In fact, the good we are discussing is not housing, but rather the *use of* housing by renters or owners. In Figure 1.1, the quantity of 900 million square feet per month demanded at a price of 20 cents is not "consumed," to be replaced every month with new housing; it is the amount that owners and renters would want to occupy if the purchase price and rental rate throughout the market area averaged out to 20 cents per square foot per month. Incidentally, this example affords another illustration of our earlier remark that the definition of a good depends on the purpose of analysis. For some analytical purposes it would be desirable to distinguish between rental housing and owner-occupied housing.

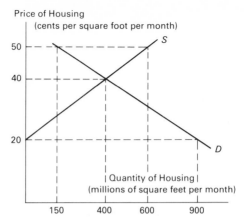

FIGURE 1.1.   Hypothetical demand and supply curves for housing in orange county.

ket is cleared. *Clearing will occur as a result of higher prices bid by buyers if quantity demanded exceeds quantity supplied; or lower prices asked by sellers, if quantity supplied exceeds quantity demanded.*

1.2.5. Factors Affecting Demand and Supply

A number of important considerations will determine the demand for housing in Orange County (the shape and position of the demand curve). For example, the price of housing elsewhere in Southern California will affect the number of people who search for a place to live in Orange County. If for some reason housing becomes relatively cheap in the San Fernando Valley, in the north of Los Angeles, then many Los Angeles commuters will choose to settle there instead of in Orange County. This leaves a smaller group of potential purchasers or renters to bid for housing in Orange County; and the demand curve for housing will shift as shown in Figure 1.2, from *D* to *D'*. A lower price of housing elsewhere means a reduced demand for housing in Orange County. It is not necessary that *all* potential buyers or renters of Orange County housing have the choice of settling in the San Fernando Valley; if *some* potential Orange County buyers have that choice, then the price of San Fernando Valley housing will affect the demand for Orange County housing.

A second factor that affects the Orange County housing demand is the income of the population of potential residents. The higher that income, the greater the amount available to spend on housing, and the higher the housing demand. A drop in income will lead to a demand shift like the movement from *D* to *D'* in Figure 1.2.

Finally, the weather, atmosphere, and climate of Orange County will affect the demand for housing there. As the county becomes more smoggy relative to other nearby areas, the more likely it is that at any given housing price, a potential resident will choose to settle elsewhere, or that a current resident will move

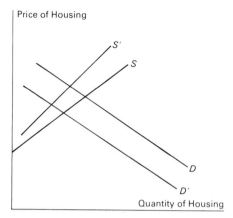

FIGURE 1.2.   Shifts in supply and demand curves, illustrating reductions in supply and in demand.

elsewhere. An increase in smog in Orange County can also cause a demand shift like the *D* to *D'* shift shown in Figure 1.2. In general, the *alternatives* confronting residents and potential residents will be decisive in determining how strongly they value the prospect of life in Orange County.

A similar story may be told about the potential suppliers of housing—the owners of homes already built, and the developers and builders. If development work in San Diego to the south or the San Fernando Valley to the north is expected to pay off better than new housing for Orange County, then the resources necessary to provide new housing are more likely to be used in those other areas. If the price level for housing in Orange County is low relative to housing prices elsewhere, then owners are not as likely to be induced to sell out in favor of moving elsewhere. Thus, housing prices elsewhere will affect the supply of housing in Orange County, as well as the demand. An increase in prices elsewhere will reduce supply, just as it increases demand. Such a supply shift is shown in the movement from *S* to *S'* in Figure 1.2.

The cost of resources used in providing housing also will affect the housing supply. Higher resource prices lead to a supply reduction, like *S* to *S'*.

Having touched upon the way that the market is cleared, and the main factors that affect housing supply and demand, we take a look at the important part that market action plays in the development of Orange County.

1.3. THE EFFECTS OF DEVELOPMENT

1.3.1. The Benefited and The Injured

When you want to know *why*, ask: *who gains?*

That Sicilian proverb, freely translated, leads us into a consideration of why

Orange County is developing, and how the forces that produce development work through the market process. Obviously, to repeat a contention of the conservationists who deplore events in Orange County, highway contractors and tract builders do reap significant financial benefits from the great stimulus that development affords to their lines of activity. They in fact stand among the groups most obviously benefited. However, on the basis of the supply and demand analysis that we just completed, we may conclude that the largest group to realize financial benefits from development, in terms of the number of persons involved, is composed of Southern California renters and home buyers. A part of this group benefits in a direct and obvious way—they rent or purchase in Orange County, and their decision to live there reveals that they regard it as superior to any alternative living site they can afford. But people moving into the San Fernando Valley, forty miles to the north, also benefit from the availability of housing in Orange County. This is a result of the fact that some people who settle in Orange County would otherwise have bid up housing prices in the San Fernando Valley.

We see, then, that home buyers in Southern California as a group are made financially better off by development. Does it follow in a symmetric way that home *owners* and especially home *sellers* are made financially *worse* off? There are two effects of development to consider in answering this question.

1. First, anyone selling an old house finds himself in competition with the sellers of new houses. The price received for the old house is lower than it would be if no new houses were available. If somehow all other aspects of development could continue, but the supply of new houses could be cut off, then sellers of old houses would be able to get much higher prices.[4]

2. But second, there are other aspects of development that we cannot ignore: new roads transform once-inaccessible outlying areas into places from which people may easily commute; and better schools, hospitals, and shopping facilities develop. These aspects of development increase the value of old houses in the developing area.

Thus, we cannot judge *a priori* whether development leads to higher or lower values of existing housing, because the depressing effect of competition from new housing works against the enhancing effect of the better services that are made available in the area in the course of development. In the case of Orange County, the prices of older houses have risen dramatically over time. The question of interest is: would they have risen even *more* in the absence of development? If the answer to that question is yes, then owners of old houses would have been better off financially if development had been avoided.

---

[4]Without new houses as competition, sellers of old houses would have a measure of *monopoly power,* and would be able to get higher prices. Monopoly effects are very important in economics and will be discussed at length later on in this book (Chapter 11).

Another large group that benefits from Orange County's development consists of businessmen who serve the residents of the new housing in the County, and employers who operate establishments within commuting distance. The incomes of businessmen are significantly increased; and the employers find that their task of attracting new employees (and hanging onto old ones) is made easier by the availability of more (and consequently cheaper) housing in the vicinity of their operations.[5]

Fairly large groups, then, are benefited (but only in a small way, in some cases) by the development of Orange County. Who is made clearly worse off?

As a first instance, it is tempting to point to the agricultural laborers who had previously derived a substantial part of their livelihood from picking in the citrus groves. Their array of employment alternatives is reduced; they are forced farther afield and to compete more vigorously to find jobs. It follows that their incomes are reduced and they are made worse off, *if they all continue to work as agricultural laborers*. What other occupation could they turn to? For one, the new houses will predictably have gardens, and where there are gardens there are jobs for nurserymen and gardeners. These lines of work require different and more diverse skills than do fruit picking; and they require some *physical capital* (equipment used to produce a good or service: tools, spray equipment, mowers, and a truck are capital to a gardener). However, by apprenticeship to men already in these trades, and by frugality (or perhaps a lucky borrowing opportunity) the requisite skills and equipment can be acquired by some of the more fortunate among the former pickers.

What signals light up to indicate that new workers will be rewarded in these new lines of activity? Do the builders and developers, with great foresight, anticipate the future "needs" of their customers for gardening services, and seek to provide an adequate supply of gardeners in advance? By what mechanism are gardening and nursery services made available? The answer is "the market provides": in this case, markets for ornamental plantings and garden care. When new homeowners begin to install and tend their landscaping, their demands are felt as higher prices for plantings and gardening services. New nurseries are opened in the area, and gardeners take on helpers who are enabled to learn the trade. This all happens because it has become profitable.

Thus, it is not clear *a priori* whether development will benefit or injure the agricultural laborers of Orange County. If the effect of suburbanization is to increase the demand for "unskilled" or "semi-skilled" workers, the farm workers may be made better off as a group. If, instead, job opportunities are reduced by the change from citrus ranch to suburb, the agricultural workers are injured (displaced geographically, and subjected to lower income).

---

[5]Cheaper than what? Than housing was in the years before the new construction began? No. Cheaper than housing *would be* now in the absence of new construction. The proposition that more housing means cheaper housing is equivalent to the proposition that the demand curve for housing is negatively sloped: see if you can figure out why.

What about long-term, old-time residents of Orange County? Development subjects them to smog, congestion, and reduced natural beauty. Are they clearly injured? We have already seen that any property they hold within the county may rise in value owing to development activity, and to the extent that this happens, the wounds of urbanization are in part compensated by financial benefits. But for many, no solace is to be had from market processes. In the face of an increasingly less pleasant environment and higher rents, they may feel compelled to move on.

That brings us to a very interesting concerned group, the orange growers. Interesting, because they are faced with strong pressures to relocate or find a different livelihood; but at the same time the value of their land is growing rapidly. Economic pressures on the fruit growers stem from two sources. One is the market (higher prices can be obtained if they wish to sell their property), and the other is political in nature. With suburbanization, land values rise,[6] a reflection of the fact that land is now quite desirable for use in housing, as well as for its current use, agriculture. As the value of a grower's land rises, in a very real sense it becomes more *costly* for him to continue producing fruit on it. For by persisting as a fruit grower, he passes up an *opportunity* to sell out and thereby obtain a sum of money sufficient to increase his economic well-being greatly. As an alternative to continued fruit farming in Orange County, he could sell his valuable grove, use a part of the proceeds to buy a similar grove in northern San Diego County, and have considerable money left over.

But consider the case of a sentimental grower, who is so devoted to his own home, land, and way of life that no reasonable price can induce him to move, even just down the road to San Diego County. The high price he could get for his land will not induce him to move; but he almost certainly will feel that second type of pressure accompanying development, the one that comes from collective (or political) action. As land values rise, county and municipal real estate taxes will rise also, in order to pay for all those public services—such as schools, streets, and sewers—that are made necessary by population growth. One consequence of the higher taxes is to force the sentimental grower to stop growing fruit on land that is highly prized for housing development. And so he finds that the value of his property has increased as a result of adjacent suburban development. The array of alternatives open to him has also increased; but the alternative that may be most precious to him—that of remaining where he is—becomes less and less feasible with time, owing to higher and higher taxes.

Finally, we should ask about the effects of development on the most interesting group of all—ourselves, the ordinary citizens—the people who have no economic stake in Orange County, but drive through from time to time perhaps; or who used to enjoy the abalone diving near Dana Point, having spent numerous weekends there in quieter times. Nearly all of us prefer orange groves to smog

---

[6]Land values rise, in fact, *in anticipation* of suburbanization, through the activity of *speculators*. The role of speculators is widely misunderstood; it is examined at length in Chapter 14.

and billboards, and so the process and result of development seems a horror story. What recourse do we—the casual, or mildly interested, or totally engaged bystanders—have whereby we can make our preferences felt? Without property rights in the county, our only recourse is political. We can advocate laws and statutes to be directed at such problems as pollution of air and water, and the size and placement of billboards along public highways. Additionally, we bystanders can hope that the county and its municipalities will enact ordinances to stipulate building standards; design streets and highways to prevent avoidable traffic chaos; and provide for public parks and beaches. We can further hope that all these state and local laws, statutes, ordinances, and provisions will do some good in terms of the purposes for which they are conceived. But to keep the land as we may remember it, we can do virtually nothing.

1.3.2. Indirect Effects of Development: An Example

To illustrate how pervasive and widespread the effects of market action are, suppose (as is true) that the newer areas of Orange County are virtually all white in terms of the racial composition of residents. Does the development of Orange County then have any positive impact on the welfare of excluded ethnic groups such as blacks? We must recognize that if blacks are excluded arbitrarily on grounds of race, then they will feel less well off: injured by being excluded, and being told that their freedom of choice is restricted. But even if some minorities are totally excluded from the newer areas, the development of Orange County will convey some *economic* benefit to members of the excluded group. The benefits will be the result of an indirect process, in which *all* housing in Southern California becomes somewhat cheaper, as people respond to the available new housing in Orange County. Fewer whites will be *competing* with blacks (bidding against them) for housing in Los Angeles, because some whites will elect to buy or rent in Orange County. The reduction in the number of whites bidding against blacks means that blacks will pay less for housing in Los Angeles than they would have to pay if Orange County were not being developed. The benefits of Orange County development would be more significant for blacks if exclusion were not practiced; but even if blacks are excluded or feel excluded from direct participation, the market process conveys to them some measure of indirect benefit from Orange County development. The market process conveys a benefit, in the form of lower housing prices in other nearby locations, even to groups of people who suffer the injury of exclusion. Stated more abstractly: one need not be a potential trader in a particular market in order to benefit from the action of that market. This is true because markets affect each other: a change in the price observed in one market can affect the price that will prevail in another market. This is the same point that was made earlier when it was asserted that buyers of housing in the San Fernando Valley derive some small benefit from Orange County development.

1.4. ECONOMIC ANALYSIS AND PUBLIC ISSUES

1.4.1 The Economic Order and Resource Allocation in Orange County

Earlier, it was suggested that scarcity is central to the process of change in Orange County, and consequently to understand such a process, economics—the study of man's organized response to scarcity—is a useful aid. As we saw in the previous section, a small knowledge of how market processes and political processes work enables us to recognize the good and bad effects of change, and to identify the parties to whom these costs and benefits accrue. But economic analysis is useful not only because it helps us understand the nature of processes like the development of Orange County; it also makes possible a comparison and evaluation of proposed alternative responses to "problems" that are seen to arise out of such processes. It is flatly impossible to evaluate objectively whether a given set of allocative choices is good or bad from the standpoint of society as a whole; an individual will typically judge the alternatives by their impact on his own self-interest, and on what he considers to be the public welfare. Economic analysis offers guidance in the evaluation of how one's own interests are affected, and how the "public interest" is affected. Economic analysis discloses the impact of events on the various parts of society.

The question, then, that is central to an understanding of our organized response to scarcity is: *how are resources allocated?* That is, what use is made of resources? This question can be enlarged by asking several additional questions: *what* goods are produced? *By what means (how)* are they produced? *To whom* do the goods go, and who benefits from their production in the stipulated manner? When answers to these questions are available, some judgment is possible on whether or not the outcomes of allocation processes are "good," according to the subjective criteria or values that an individual employs in gauging goodness or badness.

The allocative choices in Orange County are clear—more housing, less agriculture; more organized (and costly) recreation, less tranquil contemplation; more employment, less open space. We note that there is more money to be made from housing, organized recreation, and employment than from agriculture, whittling, and open space. This fact may underlie the occasional charges of "sellout," "anything for a buck," or even less flattering characterizations of developers and those who acquiesce in development. Later on in this book, we will want to take a look at the fact that there is more money in the new allocative choice than in the old, and ask: what does it signify, in terms of what is good or bad, that the total value of all money incomes is increased by development? For the time being, we only note that those who have property rights or political power are seen at this early stage of discussion to be almost sure beneficiaries of change, while the "little guys"—the fruit pickers and the nostalgic bystanders

—may come out holding the short end of the stick. Judgment regarding the justice of that outcome, and the reasons for it, must be deferred until some sharper analytic tools have been forged.

1.4.2. The Spirit of Intervention

We must be careful to avoid dismissing as sentimentalists all those individuals who express dismay over Orange County's development. The foregoing remarks came close to suggesting that all critics are people who long only for "what was" when they view "what is." Nostalgic or sentimental observers are numerous and vocal, but they aren't the most important critics of the development process. Another group (let us call them interventionists) look at "what is," and instead of marking down unpleasant events as inevitable consequences of "progress," they speculate on ways of achieving progress with less destruction of such valuable goods as clean air and natural landscape. The criticisms that interventionists offer take several forms: (1) there are aesthetic as well as economic and technical dimensions to efficient operation. Thus, highways shouldn't slash through hills, even if routing them around entails longer travel times for highway users. (2) Individuals should be compelled to consider common aspects of their own private property—aspects that affect the well-being of many people in subtle ways. Thus, a Main Street men's clothing salesman should not locate a thatched-roof replica of Shakespeare's birthplace next door to a starkly modern glass-and-steel bank office, even though such a choice would be extremely appropriate as a setting for the sale of men's tweeds. (3) Individuals who control the use of resources are greedy and myopic. The result is that too much is spent in advertising the new houses built by a handful of developers in Orange County. The houses that get built aren't actually needed, and the consequence of the whole process is that we use up the precious resource of open land without due concern for the needs of future generations.

As we will see, some interventionist criticisms have substantial merit. A problem associated with those criticisms is: how can they be made effective? Is there any hope that our customary methods of resource allocation can accommodate the criticisms? Will that accommodation be made spontaneously through the actions of individuals if a sufficiently large part of the population can be educated to understand the critics? Or will it be necessary to change the allocation process, as, for example, by more direct government control, in order to effect the recommended reforms? Many people who would like to see a better outcome from the processes of allocation suggest that direct government participation in the allocation process is necessary if a better outcome is indeed to be obtained. Their view should not be accepted without careful consideration of alternative possibilities: it often turns out that government involvement in the processes of allocation is neither necessary nor beneficial.

It must be recognized that intervention is a process that can lead to general and widespread harm unless it is intelligently justified, designed, and carried out. An important lesson was taught during the 1960s: good will and problem-solving zeal are not sufficient in and of themselves to assure a better society. To perceive a problem, and to be willing to undertake its remedy, is not enough. It is further necessary to know what we are doing if intervention is to result in benefit. In forecasting the benefits that may be realized from government involvement in allocation, it is interesting to trace the effects of existing government policies. When we do this, we often find that effects differ significantly from what is intended. Programs and policies intended for social betterment may work in the opposite direction. To consider only one example: the highway construction program, conceived as a device that contributes to the convenience of the population at large, is in fact an important contributor to the problem of smog. In recent years we have witnessed the passage of government anti-smog programs, in response to a problem that is as severe as it is only because of earlier government programs. It may be worthwhile to wonder in advance what unanticipated secondary effects will arise out of the anti-smog programs.

1.4.3. A Look Ahead

Orange County embodies and reflects many of the important problems facing contemporary society. We have sketched some of the ways in which private and government actions there have brought about changes that are simultaneously enriching and dismaying. The problems that are perceived in Orange County are felt almost everywhere, and the tools of economic analysis that are used in understanding those problems can be useful in understanding and evaluating other troublesome issues. The use of natural resources, the provision and acquisition of education, the provision of defense against foreign attack, and changes in the income and wealth levels of individuals over time—these are but a few of the issues we will look at.

There is concern among many critics that our economy, which relies heavily on private action in response to individual preferences and profit opportunities, cannot respond adequately to so bewildering and seemingly unrelated an array of problems unless some guiding or controlling intelligence is exercised to make it work properly. Our task is to see how the economy functions, and to try to judge how well it functions. We will examine some of the more popular and important proposals for economic change that are propounded by social critics; and we will try to evaluate whether the proposed changes will in fact bring about more efficient and equitable allocation of our economic resources. But before these undertakings, we must obtain deeper understanding of the problem of scarcity, and a firm grasp on the tools of economic analysis which are so useful in the study of our response to that problem.

APPLICATIONS AND EXTENSIONS

1. Draw a diagram similar to Figure 1.2, but interpret the diagram as a description of the market for candy. What units of measure are appropriate along the horizontal (quantity) axis? Suppose a process is developed whereby ice cream can be made much more cheaply out of emulsified soybean oil: what will the effect be on the demand for candy? Suppose that for some reason affecting Cuban agriculture, the price of sugar drops to half its current level: what effect will be observed on the supply of candy?

2. This question is difficult, and offers a test of your economic intuition. Suppose oranges could be grown nowhere in the world except Orange County. As a consequence, suppose every suitable square foot of land in Orange County has been devoted to orange cultivation continuously since 1925, and the largest achievable orange crop has been obtained every year since then. Under those circumstances, would population growth and urban development in the Southern California area have led to higher orange prices, or not?

3. What reasons can you think of for the proposition that demand curves are negatively sloped (higher prices of a good lead to a lower rate of consumption of the good within the economy)? Can you think of exceptions to the proposition: of instances in which an increase in a good's price leads to a permanently higher rate of demand for the good? (Chapter 5 is devoted to this important proposition; don't be surprised if your views in response to this question undergo a change after reading Chapter 5.)

4. Do you agree that
   (a) without scarcity there would be no competition?
   (b) if we could eliminate competition among individuals, scarcity would disappear?
   Are the statements (a) and (b) equivalent to each other, or are they inconsistent, or neither?

5. Do you find it credible that market processes will provide unskilled farm workers with other jobs, like gardening and plant nursery work, as suggested in this chapter? Over what period of time do you think displaced workers might become re-employed: a week? a year? two generations?

6. Do you agree with either diagnosis given below? If so, what remedy can you suggest?
   (a) "Zoning laws and other ordinances governing land use offer little or no protection against the misuse of property in order to obtain personal gain: the laws are easily manipulated by property owners who seek only to serve their own objectives."
   (b) "Zoning laws are a barrier to free use of property; they prevent the best use of resources, and are a detriment to social welfare."

7. In sixteenth-century France, a tax was placed on the size and number of *windows*. What effect do you suppose this tax had on architectural fashion?

8. Do you agree or disagree with the statements below? Do you see any difference between them?
   (a) "A man's home is his castle. If he wants to raise oranges on trees in his back yard, nobody should be allowed to stop him."
   (b) "A man's home is his castle. If he wants to raise hogs in pens in his back yard, nobody should be allowed to stop him."

CHAPTER TWO

Exchange and the Economic Problem

The greatest meliorator in the world is selfish, huckstering trade.

EMERSON (1870)

2.1. METHODS AND MOTIVATION IN RESOURCE ALLOCATION

2.1.1. Threats, Exchange, and Status

Chapter 1 illustrates the fact that individuals are engaged in a type of "competition," in which each person exercises some claim on the scarce resources of Orange County. Economics is concerned with the rules and processes of that competition: it is the study of man's organized response to the central problem of scarcity. In this chapter, a more formal analysis of the response to scarcity is developed. It is occasionally suggested in books like this one that scarcity is a problem that has affected all societies at all times. This claim may be excessive; but certainly scarcity as it is discussed and analyzed by economists is a problem in all modern societies, and our response to it is a worthwhile topic of serious study.

In an attempt to establish some degree of order, and thus to increase our understanding of competition and other social processes, the economist Kenneth

Boulding has identified three types of social relationship.[1] These are

1. Threat.
2. Exchange.
3. Status-determined.

All three are to some degree important in economic behavior, in the processes of competition among individuals for scarce resources. The threat relationship ("You give me what I want, or I'll see to it that you're sorry you didn't") was once far more important than it is today. In feudal society, much more of society's allocation was in response to direct or implied threat than we now observe. Today, residual pockets of allocation by threat remain: teenage hoodlums extort lunch money from younger schoolmates in school lavatories; the crime syndicate controls all baby diaper service in a major city and warns others not to compete; the Department of Defense predicts dire consequences if a desired appropriation is refused by the Congress. In the picture of the donkey driver who dangles a carrot in front of his beast, but who also is ready to whack the animal with a stick, a threat relationship is embodied in the stick.

The carrot, certainly, is the exchange relationship—"You give me what I want, and I'll do something nice for you in return." In human affairs, exchange, blessedly, has gone a long way toward replacing the threat as the pre-eminently important instrument of allocation. This is a good development, because exchange offers benefit to *both* involved parties. Participation in a pure exchange relationship (one not backed up by some implied threat) is entirely voluntary, and entirely based on the prospect of gain.

Status-determined (or as Boulding calls them, "integrative") relationships are illustrated by the parent who sacrifices to educate his child, the soldier who dies for his country, the church member who tithes, the donkey driver who insists upon driving (instead of being driven by) his beast. Because of the great role-defining importance of status, we are not at all surprised to observe any of those examples; but it would be news indeed to find a child supporting a parent, or a church paying regular sums out to its members.

It seems almost unnecessary to remark that many if not most allocative decisions are based on a mixture of all three types of relationship: in this regard, the man in the cart with carrot and stick is by no means unique.

Because of its great extent and importance, and because of the captivating aspect of mutual benefit, economists have focused on exchange, almost but not quite to the exclusion of the two other relationships, in their study of allocation. Thus, the main theme of this book is the exchange process and how it works. But there will be many secondary themes, also, that deal with *intervention,* or the intrusion of government into the allocation process. Intervention frequently replaces exchange relationships with status-determined ones, and occasionally with threat relationships. We will want to investigate the reasons for and effects of intervention.

[1]Kenneth Boulding, *Economics as a Science* (New York: McGraw-Hill, 1970).

2.1.2. The Postulate of Self-Interest

Regardless of which relationship he chooses to focus on, but especially when he is dealing with the exchange relationship, the economist's analysis of response to scarcity will usually rest on a basic postulate or proposition. The proposition is

> Any individual who engages in a competition for scarce resources is motivated by self-interest.

It is important to distinguish what is, and what is not, implied by that proposition. It does not assert that all people are "selfish" in the sense that the well-being of others is of no concern to any individual. However, it may well be the case that the preponderant majority of individual members of the human race look to their own health, safety, comfort, and pleasure as being in the first order of priority. There is room in the analysis for selflessness and commitment to the service and elevation of others—that type of behavior can be and is explained in terms of personal pleasure derived from being of service, from satisfying a sense of duty. Nor does the proposition assume that people seek a maximum of wealth or power—leisure and solitude can be goods in the analysis of response to self-interest. After all, these are important goods in real life. Nor does the theory overlook the possibility that the wealthy may engage in acts of private charity, or that all members of the society may collectively vote to tax away a part of higher individual incomes to support poor people. All of this behavior can be comprehended in the traditional theoretical framework of the economist.

Economic theory *does* assume that all behavior, even apparently random or habitual behavior, works as though it were purposeful, with the purpose being to make an individual feel as well off, on his own terms and by his own standards, as he can possibly be.

A frequent misrepresentation of the self-interest hypothesis involves "economic man," a calculator of the monetary costs and benefits of every action. The behavior pattern assumed in economic theory does not necessarily involve such conscious computation, any more than an expert knowledge and constant explicit application of the laws of ballistics is necessary for success in playing baseball. Uncalculated, habitual, or "instinctive" action can serve self-interest, and economic theory assumes that behavior patterns that fail to do so will adapt; that is, they will be supplanted by patterns that do serve self-interest, even if the self-serving patterns are only accidentally learned and unconsciously adopted.

2.2. THE DEFINITION OF COST

In service of self-interest, *choice* among alternatives is constantly necessary. Exemplifying the types of choice are more leisure, or more work; more expenditure on housing, or a larger and more powerful automobile; and production of wheat, or production of flax. Choices are made among *production* alternatives and *consumption* alternatives. In consumption, a dollar spent toward obtaining a season ticket for football leaves a dollar less to spend on concerts, or other forms of entertainment; and indeed, a dollar less for *any* good. The choice of football tickets removes *opportunities* for other pleasure-giving consumption expenditures. The pleasure sacrificed from the most satisfying of the foregone alternatives is a part of the *cost* of the football ticket choice; and only if the pleasurable benefits accruing from a season of football exceed the pleasure from the sacrificed alternative is the choice consistent with maximum service to self-interest.

Similarly, choices are made in production. A producer of soap can, by making relatively minor changes in his equipment, produce paint instead. A part of his *cost* of producing soap is the return he passes up by not producing paint, or any other alternative product that may be more profitable than paint. His total cost of soap production is composed of (a) direct costs, such as cost of materials, wear and tear on buildings and equipment, and selling costs (advertising); and (b) costs of foregone opportunity, such as the net revenues passed up by not producing paint, or shoe polish, or whatever the most profitable alternative to soap happens to be. The decision to produce soap serves the producer's self-interest only if the returns from producing soap are greater than the returns he would realize had he adopted another of his output possibilities.

The economist's concept of cost, then, is quite subtle, because *opportunity costs* are a recognized part of the total. It will be shown in the following that opportunity cost is a very important concept for the analysis of choice. A few more examples will help to clarify and fix the concept of opportunity cost in the reader's mind.

1. The proprietor of a new hotdog stand finds at the end of his first year of operation that his returns were $4200. He averaged sixty hours work a week during the year. He had resigned his long-time job as an assistant librarian, a job that would have paid him $2.25 per hour for a forty-hour week had he held onto it; and further, he could have sold hotdogs at the stadium and arena at various sporting events throughout the year, and averaged twenty hours a week; that supplementary job would have paid about $1.75 per hour, on the average. His combined earnings would have been in excess of $6200 had he elected the outside employment opportunities instead of running his own hotdog stand. Thus his *returns* from self-employment in the hotdog stand (proceeds less all costs) were *negative*, and on the order of $2000 for the year.

2. A sociologist's wife asked her husband how much a candy bar cost. The sociologist said "twenty cents." An economist was asked the same question by his wife. He replied "the cost of that candy bar is the pleasure foregone by giving up the most pleasurable twenty cents' worth of alternative consumption; *plus* one and a half ounces of presumably unwanted body-weight, and slightly greater chances of tooth decay." (Some economists speak in a very precise, but stilted, way.)

3. A president of the United States asked how much an all-volunteer military, with salaries sufficient to attract adequate manpower, would cost. An economist answered that the costs are *negative:* the value of output that society loses by ran-

domly drafting its military is greater than the tax savings from the low salaries made possible by the draft. A volunteer and competitively salaried military would attract personnel whose alternatives in civilian employment are less interesting and remunerative; and also less valuable to society.

This fundamental concept of *opportunity cost* underlies the most famous of all analytical apparatuses of economics—supply and demand analysis.

2.3. SUPPLY AND DEMAND IN A VERY RUDIMENTARY "SOCIETY"

2.3.1. Two-Person Exchange with Fixed Endowments

In Chapter 1 the market for housing in Orange County was described, and supply and demand in that market were hypothetically constructed. In the remainder of this chapter, we will use successively more complicated and ''realistic'' models, in order to show how markets work in much greater detail than was provided in Chapter 1. It will be seen that the concept of opportunity cost, as discussed in the preceding section, is very important in evaluating whether market activity leads to good or bad outcomes (as judged by the individuals who are affected by those outcomes).

Two convicts, Phil and Dave, share a cell. Each is given a weekly ''indulgence packet'' containing twenty cigarettes and five ounces of chocolate. An economist would call the contents of that packet the *resource endowment* of the convict. In this simple first example, that endowment is not affected in any way by the market process; it is imposed by the prison authority. Phil is a nonsmoker and is reluctant to become a smoker; he gives Dave all twenty of his cigarettes, and receives an ounce of chocolate in payment. Both convicts enjoy their revised indulgence packets more as a result of the trade. To Phil, the cost of giving up twenty cigarettes is low, and is more than offset by the ounce of chocolate he receives. To Dave, the pleasure lost by not consuming an ounce of chocolate is not a high cost, compared with the pleasure gained from twenty additional cigarettes. Phil would willingly give up all twenty of his cigarettes for a quarter-ounce of chocolate, but he would rather use the cigarettes himself (burn them to drive away mosquitoes, or learn to smoke) if Dave refused to come up with at least that quarter-ounce of chocolate in exchange. The difference between the ounce Phil actually receives and his quarter-ounce *reservation price* is Phil's *gain from trade*. Dave would willingly give up an ounce of chocolate for only five cigarettes, the fifteen additional cigarettes that Dave actually receives in excess of his reservation price constitute his gain from trade.

Apparently, a wide range of exchange rates: eighty cigarettes per ounce of chocolate at one extreme, five per ounce at the other, *could* have prevailed in the cell of Phil and Dave. Why was the figure twenty chosen? We don't know, and can't tell from the information given. As more traders enter into the process of exchange, the range of possible exchange rates will be narrowed down, and hence the question becomes less important.[2] The process of trading will tend toward some single rate of exchange as the number of traders is increased, and the rate of exchange that emerges will clear the market.

2.3.2. Two Goods, Many Traders, No Production

Suppose Phil and Dave are sent to an isolated work camp with four other convicts. The same indulgence packets continue to arrive for each prisoner containing twenty cigarettes and five ounces of chocolate, but the scope of trade is expanded by the increase in the size of the group. To see what the outcome will be, we need information on the tastes and preferences of all the prisoners. This information is summarized in Table 2.1; it shows how many cigarettes each prisoner would offer per ounce of chocolate (if sign is plus) or demand (if sign is minus) at different rates of exchange (ounces of chocolate per cigarette). Convicts I and II are our acquaintances, Phil and Dave; the other four men are new in the analysis, and are labeled III through VI, respectively.

Now, the rates of exchange in the left-hand column of Table 2.1 are nothing more or less than *prices:* different possible prices of an ounce of chocolate in terms of cigarettes. (The same information could have been expressed as different possible prices of a cigarette in terms of ounces of chocolate.) Each column represents the willingness of one of the convicts to give cigarettes in exchange

TABLE 2.1.   Excess Supply of Cigarettes in Convicts' Six-Person Exchange

CIGARETTES PER OUNCE OF CHOCOLATE	I	II	III	IV	V	VI	Sum
				PRISONERS			
120	0	−600	−480	−600	−360	−600	−2640
80	+20	−400	−280	−360	−160	−400	−1580
40	+20	−160	−120	−80	−40	−200	−580
20	+20	−60	−40	−30	−10	−100	−220
10	+20	−20	−10	0	0	−50	−60
5	+20	−5	0	5	10	−22.5	+7.5
2	+20	2	4	8	12	−8	38
1	+20	5	10	6	8	−1	+48
2/3	+20	10	15	5	6	0	56
1/2	+20	20	20	4	5	0.5	69.5
1/3	+20	20	20	4	5	1	70

[2] Actually, to prove that under reasonable conditions more traders will result in a narrowing of the possible terms of trade is not difficult. But to specify conditions under which a *single* rate of exchange will be determined in a market with a *finite* number of traders is very hard indeed. This is a question that has fascinated abstract economic theorists since it was first posed by F. Y. Edgeworth (an immortal economic theorist) in 1881.

for one ounce of chocolate in response to different possible prices. The columns are the *convicts' individual demand schedules* for chocolate. For example, if the price were ten cigarettes per ounce of chocolate (shown in the fifth row of Table 2.1), convict IV will not engage in exchange, convict III will give up an ounce of chocolate to obtain ten cigarettes, and convict VI will give up five ounces to obtain fifty cigarettes. Convict I would offer to give up all twenty of his cigarettes to get two ounces of chocolate, and convict II would offer two ounces of chocolate in order to obtain twenty additional cigarettes. In the right-hand column marked SUM, the total excess supply of cigarettes among the six convicts is recorded. That excess supply varies with price. At high chocolate prices (when many cigarettes must be given up per ounce of chocolate), a large negative total excess supply, or large *excess demand* for cigarettes, is recorded. This reflects the fact that at high chocolate prices, chocolate would be very *costly,* in the sense that much pleasure is lost by giving up the cigarettes necessary to obtain one ounce of chocolate, as far as most of the convicts are concerned. Every additional ounce of chocolate obtained at the high price means substantial opportunity cost, and hence the demand for chocolate is low. But a high chocolate price is equivalent to a low cigarette price; hence the demand for cigarettes is high at high chocolate prices.

The total excess supply of cigarettes recorded in the right-hand column is plotted in Figure 2.1. The graph shows that at some price near six and a quarter, excess supply will be zero. Only when excess supply is zero do we find a workable balance, or *equilibrium;* everyone who wants to give up cigarettes will ob-

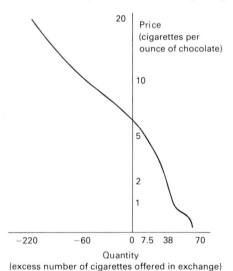

FIGURE 2.1.   Excess supply of cigarettes in convicts' six-person exchange (logarithmic scale on both axes).

tain sufficient chocolate so that he is satisfied with his exchange; and everyone who wants more cigarettes and less chocolate similarly can trade away chocolate, and feel agreeably compensated by the cigarettes he obtains. We cannot assert that there will always be only one price that clears the market, but for the case we are discussing, Figure 2.1 is drawn as if there were only one. From Table 2.1 we see that a price of ten is too high, and a price of five is too low. That range is considerably narrower than when Phil and Dave alone were trading: recall in that case, anything *above* eighty was too high a price, and anything *below* five, too low.

2.3.3. Many Goods, Many Traders, Production

The next natural step in the analysis of exchange is to stipulate that goods do not come from outside the trading society, but rather originate within it. Further, we want to relax the condition that the resource endowment of each individual is fixed in advance, as it was in the case of exchange among prisoners. The problem involving production and variable endowments is the central one to be analyzed in this book, and we will want to examine it at some length. The core of our analysis of this central question is found in Chapters 4 to 8.

It is easy to envision how a society of six prisoners can arrange exchanges for two goods. It is less easy to see how a society, by an essentially similar process of exchange in the service of individual self-interest, can arrange for the production of many different goods, or to see how it is determined in the society how the goods that are produced will be distributed for use among the various individual members of the society. Another simple fable will help to clarify the important analytical issues. It will illustrate how the problems of production and distribution are solved by exchange, just as the story of the convicts illustrated gains from trade and the movement toward an equilibrium exchange rate in a many-person trading group.

2.4. SUPPLY AND DEMAND IN AN ISLAND PARADISE

2.4.1. The Setting

Envision a group of people who live in isolation on a never-never island in some benign latitude. This island contains resources that can be used to sustain the group. Some of these resources, like fresh water, edible plants, shellfish, and other forms of sea life, are *renewable*. That is, they are of such a nature that if the people exercise reasonable care in their use, supplies of these resources will be perpetually available. Other resources, including, let us suppose, a small stand of slow-growing, straight-grained, large trees are *exhaustible*, at least from the perspective of the present generation of the group. Finally, the group is endowed with an important resource, human knowledge and skill.

Let us suppose that survival would be no issue, even if the people on the island were to muddle around independently of each other, avoiding open force in their interpersonal relationships, but not cooperating or coordinating effort in any meaningful way. Everyone would scrape along without immediate danger from hunger or thirst, and with adequate protection against the weather. Can we then say that this society is confronted by scarcity?

We can. At the very least, there will be *competition* for use of the trees, as each individual (or family unit) perceives the desirability of having a boat, a rack for drying fishnet, a loom on which to weave Tapa cloth, and other wooden articles. Cutting all the trees immediately might satisfy all the desires of everyone for a short period of time, but leave a large problem for the future. Or, suppose one individual finds that the island clams are an excellent fertilizer for yams, a food of which he is inordinately fond. His clams-into-yams agricultural technique causes a change, such that it is no longer possible for everyone to gather an ample clam dinner in a short period of time. As these two instances of trees and clams illustrate, scarcity can manifest itself in the problems of how to use exhaustible resources, and how to husband renewable resources. Scarcity, as we are using the term, is a problem in any instance where there is not enough of a good to satisfy all the claims that compete for use of the good. (In this regard, the agricultural land of Orange County, viewed in Chapter 1, is precisely similar to the trees on our island.)

2.4.2. Specialization and Exchange

Now suppose that one of the islanders, in experimenting one day with a length of hollow cane, discovers that he can make music. He finds that he cannot spend as much time as he would like in composing and performing on his flute—time is scarce, and work for survival is time-consuming. Can an arrangement be found whereby he can devote more time to his music and still survive? This question can be broadened, and we can ask: can the islanders find an arrangement, perhaps by "cooperating" with each other, so that everyone can have a better life from access to a wider array of more useful and beautiful things, without using the island's resources up at a rate that jeopardizes the future availability of the resources? An affirmative answer is found in a cooperative relationship, called *specialization and exchange*. Our musician, for example, can exchange a serenade for a breakfast, and a concert for a new roof on his hut. If the group of islanders is large enough, and wealthy enough, the musician may find it possible to devote his full time to music. But if the group is very small, or if the members of the group have barely enough to sustain themselves, then less frequent call will be heard for the musician's services, and he will find it necessary to supplement his earnings from music by other activity.

If everyone in the society[3] specializes and exchanges, *more* goods will be available for everyone. Net-makers and menders, fishermen, farmers, shellfish gatherers—all develop special skills by intensive practice of their occupation, and all design and use special equipment which makes their work faster, easier, and more comfortable. The process of specialization contributes to *efficiency:* it makes larger amounts of all goods available from a given expenditure of human effort and the island's resources.

2.4.3. The Problem of Determining Resource Use

Specialization and exchange open avenues for betterment, but the development of these processes does not mean that there are no further issues for an economist to investigate. He will also want to know how the island society controls the use of resources, and how well that job is being performed.

The island society may grow concerned over the possibility of resource exhaustion. Or it may be that the net-mender and the farmer both feel that their services are not sufficiently appreciated or adequately rewarded. To alleviate concerns, avoid disputes, and oversee the problem of providing a livelihood for everyone, the islanders elect a master coordinator (MC). It is the job of the MC to see to it that the correct amounts of all goods are being produced, that terms of exchange between specialists are fair, and that everyone is contributing his share to the island society.

The MC makes decisions that serve his own ideas of equity and propriety. He *dictates* or *imposes* output quotas and rates of exchange that will prevail in the society. This procedure is seen to work very well for some purposes—his feeling that the dwindling stand of trees should be saved means that none are cut, and he even succeeds in getting new ones planted. However, it soon appears that his output quotas and rates of exchange do not mesh very well. The clam digger, for example, finds that after meeting his quota, he has many clams left over every day, because at the MC's imposed rates of exchange, clams are not much desired by other people.[4] At first, the clam-digger quietly throws away his excess clams, but soon he protests that there is waste. The MC, a reasonable man, looks for better exchange rates and more reasonable quotas, but he finds that everything he tries leads to difficulty—excess production here, shortages there, people standing idle with quotas too small to keep them busy somewhere else.

The MC concludes that the control of output quotas and exchange rates is not enough to make the economy work well—he insists that he must be given the

---

[3]With interdependence and cooperation, we can justify calling the islanders a society.

[4]In other words, the MC chooses a set of exchange rates and quotas at which there is a large *excess supply* of clams: return to Section 2.3.2 and refresh your grasp of this concept.

power to impose quotas for the use of goods, also, or else he will be unable to manage. The people conclude that this is an unreasonable power to grant, and the search begins for a better way of coordinating.

A new MC is elected, who has promised to proceed democratically. His method, which he dreamed up after reading a leaflet written by a group of Berkeley student political activists that floated in to the island one day, is to invite everyone to vote on how much of everything will be produced. Voting continues until a feasible mixture is chosen—that is, until an output mix approved by everyone can be produced without danger to the island's resource base. But some of the outputs that are requested by vote put an excessive burden on some individual specialists, and those specialists fail to meet their output quotas. When they are threatened with penalty, they comment to good effect on the irony of using discriminatory coercion to make a democratic process work effectively. Other voting schemes are tried, and all run into the same kinds of problems that plagued the dictated solutions of the first MC. No system of balloting seems to yield the right amount of all goods, and acceptable compensations to all individuals, perhaps because every individual except the musician votes to consume a lot of everyone else's output and to produce very little of his own.

2.4.4. A Price System

Finally, a third MC assumes responsibility for economic activity on the island. His approach seems to be very indirect. He restores the old system of barter, but collects information on rates of exchange among individual producers. He finds that fishermen are giving five Totuava for a net and demanding twenty large yams for a single Totuava, so he advises the yam-grower to trade for a net before trading for the fish, because the net-maker will exchange a net for thirty yams. The yam-grower, after collecting this information from the MC, finds that his *price* per Totuava is only six yams (thirty yams → one net → five Totuava) instead of twenty yams. The net-maker and the fisherman are not made worse off in this transaction, and so all applaud the new arrangement; indeed, on one occasion or another, everyone finds himself benefited in a similar way.

The new arrangement has developed in a way that is convenient for everyone. Instead of spending the time required to make all the exchanges with each other necessary to obtain maximum advantage, individuals then begin to bring the goods they produce to the MC, and he makes the exchanges. It is found convenient for the MC to give people *markers* for the goods they bring in. These markers can be used to make exchanges at later times. Sometimes the MC gives people markers in exchange for goods that are not yet ready for sale. The net-maker, for example, has seen a bargain in cord fiber that he needs. the MC credits him with markers on Tuesday for the promise of delivery of the net on Friday. Fewer markers are paid by the MC to the net-maker on Tuesday than would have been offered on Friday for the completed net—but that is acceptable to the net-maker, since the bargain on rope fiber might not still be available on Friday.

The arrangement is not perfect. Specialists still find that the goods they produce often seem too "cheap"—too few markers are forthcoming from the MC. On one occasion, a fertilizer packer who worked on Seagull Ledge asserts that he is being exploited—"Here I stand, after shoveling this stuff all day, and what do I get? A lousy six markers!" The MC, in reply, gently suggests that he look over the prices of other goods, to find a pleasanter and more rewarding occupation in producing goods that seem high-priced.

A problem arises in connection with the nonrenewable resource, the trees. The MC finds it necessary to suspend the cutting of trees, because people have been cutting at a frantic pace. When the MC asks why, several people reply, "I may not need wood right now, but if I wait until I do need wood, the trees may all have been cut by other people." Finally, the MC hits upon a very sound plan: he assigns trees to individuals as owners. Every man can cut the trees with his own initials carved in them at any time he wants, but he cannot cut trees belonging to anyone else. It is decided also that owners of trees can sell cutting rights to other people, with the terms of sale to be a matter of private agreement between the owner and the cutter. Each person, by virtue of this arrangement, has *property rights* in some trees, and each person can use or preserve trees in the manner that he sees as best.

The third MC, then, has hit upon an organizational form whereby goods production is made responsive to the desires of the individuals in the community. Individuals can regulate the type and amount of effort they put forth, with consequences that affect their incomes—the number of markers that they receive. There is still grumbling, dissatisfaction, and complaint; but the type of waste that accompanied the first MC's efforts has been eliminated; apparent injustice can be explained by the third MC to the satisfaction of all but the most relentlessly self-pitying individuals in the society; and alternatives can always be found for individuals who really feel themselves to be badly occupied or inequitably treated.

2.4.5. The Island Paradise and The Society at Large

Parables can be useful pedagogical devices. They deliberately put aside the complexity of a real-world situation, and thereby focus on some central point, question, or issue. In that respect *models,* which are devices that scientists use, are like parables. It would be a mistake to push farther with the island parable, although there are many more points that can be made with its help. At the present time, however, the reader doesn't have a sufficient grasp of analytical technique to appreciate more elaborate stories of life in the island society. The parable has helped with a central purpose of this chapter, which is to sharpen our appreciation of the economic problem:

> Conflict arises because the resources of society are not sufficient to meet the goals of society's several individual members, and that conflict must be resolved. Resources must be apportioned (allocated) among society's individual members.

That same problem was seen as important in the more immediate, real-world setting of Orange County (Chapter 1). For the time being, no further inferences or morals should be drawn from the parable—although the acute reader will note that the contrast drawn between the approaches taken by the first MC and the third MC is not very flattering to the former. That contrast will be explored in a more systematic way in Chapter 18, when the question of central planning is considered.

2.5. MUTUAL INTERDEPENDENCE AND THE CIRCULAR FLOW

The parable of the Island Paradise suggests that if a society takes advantage of the gains that can be obtained from exchange, a high degree of *interdependence* is created among the individuals of the society. This fact of mutual interdependence is even greater in a modern contemporary economy. We can begin to appreciate the full extent of that interdependence when one small part of the whole ceases to function in the expected way. New York City offers numerous telling examples of the extent to which we depend on each other: the garbage collector's strikes of 1967 and 1975, the great power failure (which gripped the entire Northeastern United States) of 1965, the teachers' strike of 1968, plus occasional minor irritations like newspaper strikes, transportation system strikes, and water shortages—all serve to point up the extent to which the orderly and habitual patterns of existence so dear to most of us depend on our ability to count on the continuing "cooperation" of others.

We can represent the interdependence of allocation decisions in a market exchange economy by use of a device called a *circular flow* diagram, Figure 2.2. Even in so simple a diagram, some fundamental ideas are portrayed: *productive services* are compensated by *input payments;* these payments are exchanged for *goods* and *services,* and goods and services are portioned out or allocated by use of a system of *prices.* Every individual functions in two roles: as a producer, he collects payments for the productive services he provides, and as a consumer he uses those proceeds to buy goods and services. In the activity of production, certain people (businessmen) who want to make profits organize and direct the use of productive services in making goods, and they later sell those goods to be consumed.

The prices of goods and services, and the input payments, are more than a recompense for providing goods or productive services, however. The prices also serve as signals which help to regulate the mixture of goods and services that flow through the system. When individuals desire more bacon or fewer aprons than are being produced, they bid *more* for available bacon, less for available aprons; producers of bacon find it worthwhile to apply more resources to bacon production, while the resources used to produce aprons are less highly

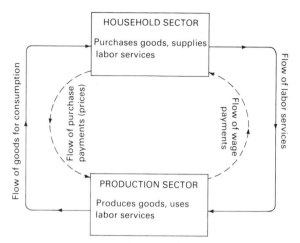

FIGURE 2.2. The simplest circular flow depiction of economic activity.

rewarded than before, and they tend to move out of the production of aprons. This important flow-regulating role of prices is not shown explicitly in Figure 2.2.

There is a similarity between this simple circular flow representation of an economy at work, and the hydrologic cycle: rain falls, seeps into the ground, emerges from springs into a river, flows into the sea, is evaporated, condensed, and the cycle begins again. In its simplest representation, the hydrologic cycle is a reminder that water flows do not *originate* in rainfall or springs, to disappear once and for all into the ground or the ocean. Similarly, the circular flow of economic activity is a reminder that goods do not originate in production for the sole purpose of profit-making. Rather, goods are produced for use in consumption to sustain and motivate workers, who turn out other goods, which are used in consumption to sustain—and so on. Even in the simplest version of Figure 2.2, circular flow analysis can help us to avoid some important misconceptions. It may be contended, for example, that the general standard of living would be greatly increased if all wages were doubled by passing a law. But standards of living within society are related to the flow of *goods* into consumption; goods consumption always is eventually limited by goods production capacity; and hence, higher wages may only permit consumers to bid up goods prices. Scarce resources will impose an effective upper limit on society's capacity to produce goods; *total* output will not increase in response to higher prices once the "full use of resources" limit is reached. Figure 2.2 has the virtue of focusing on the important relations that must always hold between money flows and the flows of physical goods and services.

Having established the character of response to the economic problem in a private exchange economy, where allocation rests heavily on the voluntary and self-interested actions of individuals, and having seen the circular flow that arises in such an economy, we are in a position to proceed with a detailed analysis of how such an economy works. Before that undertaking, we want to analyze the basis for organizing economic activity to serve the goal of satisfying individual preferences, and to survey the role of collective action, through the mechanism of government, in an economic system that is organized with that goal in view. There are practical and philosophical issues that arise when we talk about government's role in the economy. The practical issues are investigated from time to time throughout the book. The philosophical issues are the main subject of Chapter 3.

APPLICATIONS AND EXTENSIONS

1. "The illustration involving exchange between two convicts illustrates the most important drawback of our reliance on market exchange processes. There is only one fair and just rate of exchange between chocolate and cigarettes, and the two convicts are not likely to find that rate by their bargaining and dealing." Do you agree? If so, what do you take to be the basis for deciding a "fair" price? Is it any easier to decide on a "fair" wage for airline pilots in society at large than it is to decide on a "fair" rate of exchange between the two convicts?

2. Suppose the six convicts had exhibited an inclination to consume *more* cigarettes as the price of cigarettes rose, and *more* chocolate as the price of chocolate rose. (Out of boredom, or with their judgment warped by confinement, they find satisfaction in consuming those goods which their fellow prisoners value most highly.) Under these circumstances, prepare a supply and demand analysis similar to that of Table 2.1. Will an equilibrium be found in exchange if their desire for goods rises with the price of the goods?

3. Considering opportunities foregone, what is the cost to an individual student of his college education? Does this cost differ between two students, one of whom attends a private university and the other a public university? What is the cost to society at large of an individual's college education? Does the cost to society differ between providing the education in a private or a public university?

4. In the parable of the island paradise, no mention was made of the possibility that one individual might *hire* another individual: the net-maker, for example, might hire two apprentice laborers. Do you think that if this omission were rectified, the message of the story would have to be altered in any important way?

5. In an economy with five goods and no money, how many *prices* would be recorded? If money is created in the society, as happens in the island paradise when the third MC introduced "markers," how many prices would be recorded? Do the two situations, with and without money, differ in any fundamentally important way, apart from the number of prices that are recorded?

6. In the island paradise, suppose that after the third MC has organized a price system, a "shortage" of yams is observed. Which of the following statements is true?

    (a) The price of yams has been set too low compared to the prices of other goods.

    (b) The economy of the island is out of equilibrium.

(c) If the relative price of yams is appropriately adjusted, fewer people will feel it worthwhile to grow yams after the adjustment.

7. Suppose that the third MC mischievously declares that all goods are worth twice as many markers after midnight March 31 as they were before that time. What effects would be observed in the society?

CHAPTER THREE

The Individual
in Society

Liberty is not a means to a higher political end. It is itself the
highest political end.

LORD ACTON (1907)

3.1. CONTROVERSY AND VALUE JUDGMENTS

3.1.1. Sources of Controversy in Economics

Much of what you will read in this book, or in any introduction to economics, is
controversial, a subject of honest disagreement among qualified observers.
Sometimes the center of disagreement is trivial—a question of what should be
emphasized in an analysis. Occasionally, disagreement runs much deeper. At
different times, and among different observers, disagreement has centered on at
least five important and highly interdependent questions:

1. What is the current *state* (position and condition) of the economy?
2. How do we best describe and analyze the *workings* of the economy?
3. What economic *goals* are *desirable?*
4. How *well* is the economy performing in light of these goals?
5. What economic *policies* (actions on behalf of the whole society) will be beneficial?

The first question, regarding the state of the economy, is one of measurement
and observation. It is not a trivial task to identify the institutions and procedures,

and to record or estimate the numerical information, which adequately characterize the state of the economy. Government and private agencies report price-
level changes, employment rates, commodity prices, and other "indicators" of
where the economy is; and universities teach courses on the institutions and laws
that shape and regulate private commerce. Keeping track of all the indicators and
remaining current on all the relevant institutions and laws is a big job, and it requires skill to judge what information is important in these areas. There is often a
great deal of controversy as to what the state of the economy actually is, especially when important policy decisions are at issue. For instance, there is always
a significant time delay in reporting the rate of unemployment (the percentage of
the labor force that can't find work). That delay is the source of considerable uncertainty as to how well policies designed to combat unemployment are actually
working, and hence, as to what further should be done. As a second example,
the relative income shares of the richest ten percent of the population and the
poorest ten percent are not known with any precision. Yet another highly controversial question about the state of the economy: is the economy predominantly *competitive* or *monopolistic?* Competition, as we shall see, is an
economic attribute that is believed to be of great importance, but that is impossible to measure directly. And available information that may bear on competitive performance is difficult to evaluate and interpret.

Question 2 asks how the workings of the economy can best be described and
explained. There are both observational and theoretical sides to this question. To
illustrate the observational issues, consider the fact that although it is a widely
accepted popular view that *price discrimination* against blacks exists in most
housing markets—that is, black people pay more than white people for a given
quality of housing—until a few years ago, that proposition had never been
affirmed in any conclusive study. In fact, there existed a number of studies
which suggested that the alleged price discrimination did *not* exist! Apparently,
the source of confusion on this question of price discrimination by race was observational: it centered on the way data are reported by the Bureau of the Census. Data are computed and reported for each *census tract.* A census tract is a
small urban or large rural area, with an average population in the neighborhood
of 10,000. Housing expenditures are estimated from information obtained by
taking a sample of the individual residents in each tract; those expenditures are
reported as averages per tract. When average housing expenditures are compared for different census tracts (with correction made for differences in quality
of housing), it emerges that expenditures per family are no higher in predominantly black tracts than they are in predominantly white tracts. These data,
which compare average quality-corrected expenditures across different tracts,
conceal an extremely significant effect: nonwhites who live in a racially mixed
neighborhood pay far *more* than they would for an equivalent dwelling in an all-
black neighborhood; and whites who live in racially mixed neighborhoods pay
far *less* than they would in an all-white area. This effect doesn't show up clearly

in census tract data, but when *households* are compared, as in a recent study in New Haven, Connecticut, the differences in expenditure by race are clear.[1]

The process of theorizing is an attempt to understand the working of the economy. In building theoretical models, it is necessary to separate the essential features, which are operative in nearly all cases and at nearly all times, from the features that are peculiar to individual instances and which have no general importance. In this process, there is controversy as to what is and what is not a reliable aid to greater understanding. For example, much analysis in economics proceeds on the assumption of exact functional relationships between variables—the relation between supply of housing and price of housing that was used in our informal examination of Orange County (Chapter 1) or the relation between price and excess demand in exchange among prisoners (Chapter 2) being cases in point. If those relationships change rapidly over time, then much of the analysis that rests upon them may be untrustworthy. Certain economic variables, such as prices, incomes, and purchased quantities of goods, are alleged to be related, or to move relative to each other, according to specific rules. There is often controversy regarding the way the relations are structured. In recent years, significant attention has been devoted to *testing* different specifications of important economic relationships; these tests apply modern mathematical techniques of statistical analysis to data gathered through observation of the economy. However, much remains to be accomplished in this direction; few if any significant controversies in economic theory have been cleared up to the satisfaction of all competent observers by this process of statistically analyzing economic data.

The response that any individual will offer to question 3, on the desirability of different alternative economic goals, will in large measure depend on considerations of political belief, or ideology. Whenever ideology enters, controversy is not far behind; and the responses that economists offer to question 3 are no exception. Perhaps the most interesting and engaging item of ideological controversy among economists centers on the issue of equality versus liberty, in instances where those two abstract social objectives are found to be in conflict, as they frequently are. Consider, for example, the problem of providing manpower to the armed forces in a time of national crisis. The *classical liberal* views compulsion as one of the greatest evils in society, and so he advocates a volunteer military, with salaries sufficiently high to attract an adequate rate of enlistment. The *progressivist egalitarian,* a different type of liberal, regards a volunteer army as a scheme that shifts a disproportionate share of the risk of death onto the poorer classes; only a conscription system that ignores considerations of income can provide equality of treatment according to his definition, and will be acceptable to him. Thus, conflict over goals leads to disagreement on issues.

---

[1]For a report on the New Haven study, see A. Thomas King and Peter Mieszkowski, "Racial Discrimination, Segregation and the Price of Housing," *Journal of Political Economy,* 81 (May–June 1973), 590–606.

These first three questions (What is the state of the economy? How does the economy work? What should our economic goals be?) are interrelated in various obvious ways and also in more subtle ways. The way an individual answers the second and third questions will affect whether or not a particular item of information about the economy interests him. On many occasions we see that the personal ideology of an individual determines his description of how the economy works. This tendency is particularly noticeable among people who have no training in economics. Moreover, an individual's personal ideology, and his resulting view of appropriate economic goals, may be affected by his perception of the state of the economy—his exposure to the "facts of economic life," as he sees them. Karl Marx is not the only person whose views have been shaped by the shock of seeing the misery of the poor of his society. Marx's work illustrates the way the processes of observation, goal-advocacy, and theorizing may be heavily entwined in the careers of practicing professional economists.

The extent of interdependence among observation, theorizing, and goal-advocacy is seen clearly when the subsidiary questions, 4 and 5, are considered. (Questions 4 and 5 are subsidiary in a logical sense—it is necessary to know the state, workings, and goals of economic activity before policies can be prescribed in response to question 5, or evaluations of performance can be offered, in response to question 4.)

Question 4 asks how well the economy is working. One widely discussed measure of the economy's performance, called *efficiency,* will be discussed throughout this book. Efficiency can be assessed in terms that will be found acceptable by different individual observers whose values differ widely. However, even if there is agreement among those observers on the question of efficient operation, there may be strong disagreement on issues that call for explicit value judgments. One such issue is the welfare of the population. Because the assessment of welfare is controversial, there will be disagreement regarding the best policies to improve welfare. (Such policies are the subject of question 5.) Thus, every evaluation of welfare is bound to reflect opinions regarding what is desirable; and while it is possible for an economist to offer policy advice as a disinterested professional or technician, in service of goals that he may not personally endorse, it is more common to find that he is a strong advocate for the predicted *outcome* of his advice. When a Republican replaces a Democrat in the White House, a new group takes over the offices of the Council of Economic Advisors, even though the economic analysis that is used in those offices doesn't change much.

3.1.2. The Scientific Outlook and Moral Values

It is a well-established contemporary tradition in economics that discussion can be usefully separated into two categories. The economist can speak about what *is* as a scientist or a professional; that is, he can speak on *positive* issues. Alternatively, he can prescribe the objectives that he feels *ought to be served,* and when he does, his advice is *normative.* It is the usual view that positive statements are deductions from a *science* of economics, while normative statements go beyond the science of economics, into the controversial and exciting realms of political, social, and moral philosophy. Or put in simpler terms, positive statements are "value-free" while normative statements are "value-based" or "value-serving." In that usual view of things, it is felt that as economics becomes more highly developed as a science, controversy with regard to positive issues will occur less and less frequently, but controversy with regard to normative questions will continue because of the inevitability of conflict among the value systems of different individuals.

There is considerable appeal in that positive-normative dichotomy, and it has been a very constructive outlook, because it has fostered acceptance of the attitude that there is a body of economic theory which can and should be subjected to scientific method, so that theory evolves into a closer approximation of objective truth.[2]

Despite the generally constructive impact of the distinction between positive and normative analysis, there has been some dissent and disagreement as to whether it should be preserved. Some students, especially in recent years, have accused economists of ignoring the world's evils, and of hiding behind the pretext of a positive outlook in their work (much like the stereotyped and probably nonexistent nuclear physicists of the 1940s who did research on nuclear weapons, without concern for how their work would be used). Other observers find normative overtones in the most benign positive statements: the economist who analyzes a simple problem by using supply and demand analysis is accused of the political act of advocating the capitalist system by his choice of analytical tools. Such extreme mistrust of attempts to separate positive from normative analysis is misplaced; yet the critics do have a point, because the line that separates "value-free" from "value-based" statements is not as simple to find as the positive-normative dichotomy asserts it to be. In the view of some observers, values enter in a significant way into statements about what *is,* even into some statements that are straightforward deductions from economic theory. There is no objective way whereby it can be established that those individuals are wrong: if a person finds a value judgment in a statement, and can argue coherently why he finds it, one cannot refute his argument by pointing out that the statement is a deduction from theory.

In fact, to be useful and applicable, any economic theory must analyze the customs and institutions of one or more particular societies, or speculate on the

---

[2]The questions: What is science? Is there "objective truth" to be discovered? If so, by what methods does the search for truth proceed? are but a few of the important and absorbing issues discussed in the philosophy of science. The most influential and important figure in shaping our views regarding these questions is the contemporary philosopher, Karl R. Popper. A useful introductory discussion is found in the first essay of his *Conjectures and Refutations* (New York: Basic Books, 1961).

effects of change in customs or institutions. Economics textbooks tend to focus, understandably, on the institutions of English-speaking countries. Thus, American (or British, or Canadian) customs, priorities, procedures, and beliefs must underlie the analysis, because they have shaped the institutions that are being analyzed. Economic institutions evolve: they are a product of historical experience, and of a philosophical outlook about the good life and the good society. So, while it is true that the general economic problem of organized response to scarcity is one that is encountered at all times and in all societies, it is also true that the analysis in much of contemporary economics owes its content to the dominant ideology or political philosophy of the society to which the analysis applies. It is not necessary to search far for an example of the effect of ideology on economic analysis. The supply and demand analysis that has been taught throughout America, England, and Western Europe for more than a century is based on an important initial premise: *the preferences of individuals should play an important part in decisions about allocation.* That premise is much less widely held in the Soviet Union, and so the many interesting (to us) deductions and predictions yielded by supply and demand analysis are viewed to be of little interest or importance in that nation.

3.1.3. Values and Controversy: The Subject of This Chapter

This chapter attempts to describe and to evaluate the more important among the ideological tenets that have helped to shape the American economy. By considering questions of ideology explicitly, we will see that much contemporary controversy regarding economic policy can be resolved *only* on ideological grounds. Our understanding, in certain important areas, of what the state of the economy is, and how the economy works, is not adequate to provide us with more "scientific" prescriptions for action. As with all other contemporary textbooks, the main thrust and aim of this book is to understand what *is*. Especially, we want to understand how the market exchange system really works: how it affects other matters of vital concern, and in turn responds to them. But in attacking that question, areas of real ignorance can be identified, and in those areas, the "fundamental philosophical view of the nature of man and society"—in short, the ideology that currently dominates in our thoughts—will be a most important guide to action. Thus, ideology, which in itself is a matter of controversy, is a guide to action for settling controversies in economic policy. For that reason, an understanding of the historical impact of ideology on the economy, and a clarifying background on contemporary ideological controversy, is worthwhile.

We now turn to the philosophical issues raised by the two institutions of *private property* and *voluntary exchange via the market process;* these two institutions are important among the ones that shape and direct the search for a solution to the economic problem in America and much of Western Europe.

3.2. INDIVIDUALISM AND ECONOMIC ORDER[3]

3.2.1. A Warning

Economics as it is taught today bears the mark of a number of influential think-ers. Most of the men whose work has been distilled in contemporary textbooks are long since dead; but the moral, social, and political philosophy that guided their thought can still be discerned in contemporary economic thought. What are those central philosophical tenets that have helped to shape our important economic institutions? How have these tenets endured for so long? What is to be gained from an investigation of their specific nature? Later in the book we will ask: what challenges have been issued to this long-established way of looking at economic life? On what bases do the more important challenges rest? As we pro-ceed, the issues of political ideology that have an important bearing on economics will be brought forth for explicit discussion.

There is a danger in investigations of this type. Words of highly favorable (or sometimes unfavorable) connotation must enter the discussion, because alterna-tive terms of neutral impact are hopelessly long-winded. Words like liberty, equality, security, welfare, freedom—these must be carefully defined, and the issue of their relationship to the economic order of a particular society must be considered on its own merits. It is not sufficient to assert that an economic order is adopted with the goal of achieving some good condition (liberty, efficiency), or to assert that a particular policy is designed to act against a bad condition (poverty, degradation of human life). The value of choices and actions must ul-timately be judged on how well they serve specific objectives, and on how valid or legitimate the objectives themselves are. In that kind of evaluation, confusion caused by catch-phrases and loaded words is regrettable, and an effort must be made to avoid it.

3.2.2. The Individualist Precept

The eighteenth century saw the systematic exploration and analysis of an idea called liberty. At the time it was first seriously analyzed, in ancient Greece, lib-erty was thought to be the legitimate aspiration of a few select members of soci-ety. The major political philosophers of the eighteenth century, by contrast, saw liberty as the legitimate aspiration of every man, not just members of an elite. Political and ecclesiastical tyranny and absolutism were vigorously challenged, and the right of every man to seek fulfillment of his own innate and unique vir-tues and talents was upheld.

These intellectual currents swirled in many directions, and divergent mainstreams of thought have emerged out of them. In France, Rousseau, Saint-Simon, Comte, and others contributed to the analysis of liberty, ironically, at a

---

[3]The section heading is borrowed from F. A. Hayek: see his book of that title (Chicago: Univer-sity of Chicago Press, 1948).

time and in a nation that knew little of liberty from first-hand experience. In Britain, Locke, Hume, Smith, and others were articulating the philosophical foundations of freedom, in a nation in which liberty was a substantial reality. It is interesting and significant that these British philosophers and their disciples were instrumental in laying down the foundations of economics even as the discipline is taught and practiced in much of the world today.

Both traditions, British and French, emerged from an *individualist* philosophy. The basic ideas of that philosophy are that (1) all values have their basis in the experience of individual human beings; (2) goals of the individual are the ends of social processes, and so society exists only as a means of serving individual goals and resolving any conflict among those goals that might arise; (3) within the context of formal social processes, all individuals are treated as equals.[4]

These basic ideas constitute what we will call the *Individualist Precept*. While both traditions agree on the validity of these basic ideas, and both nations have tried to implement them, the two traditions disagree sharply on the type of social order that is best calculated to contribute to their fulfillment. They also disagree on the meaning of ''equality,'' and hence on the interpretation of the third basic idea.

3.2.3. Evolutionary Individualism: Great Britain

Despite the strong advocacy of the Individualist Precept, the British individualist tradition, into the nineteenth century, remained skeptical about the potency of the human intellect. There was never the suggestion that any individual, if left to his own devices, could design a social Utopia. There was no feeling that man, working by himself or in a group, would ever succeed in consciously designing a workable society in the way, say, that he could build a workable and predictable sailing ship. Skepticism about the possibility of social planning prevailed in the British tradition. The British writers expounded the view that liberty, in a properly structured society, gives individuals the opportunity to experiment, to make mistakes, and to learn. If better social arrangements were sought by one individual, the outcome of his search was believed not to be predictable or knowable in advance. On the contrary, the value of freedom in such a search for new ways of doing things was seen to come from the fact that, despite the fallibility of each individual searcher, progress would result from the winnowing of each man's contribution. Thus, if social institutions are chosen which allow the maximum benefits to be realized from the free play of individual searching, the product will be a society in which the total contribution of all individuals will transcend the

---

[4]In Britain, as in France, the existence of a monarchy and hereditary titles of nobility has been a source of social tension. To the extent that privilege has been preserved through this institution, the individualist precept has been violated. The eighteenth-century Irish politician and philosopher Edmund Burke is remembered as one who struggled hard to reconcile his individualist outlook with his feelings of affection toward tradition, including the tradition of the peerage.

understanding or capability of any individual. The character and content of this British view is worth attention. Individualism does not deny man's need of society; less does it assert man's great power of intellect. What it does assert is that no other rules of social organization are as likely to yield progress as is the rule: let each man seek for himself, according to his own knowledge and belief about what he can accomplish.

With regard to the problem of economic organization, the British tradition attached great prospect of benefit from the two institutions of *private property* and *free market exchange*. An order in which individuals are substantially free to act in the service of their own self-interest was seen to lead in the direction of economic abundance and social benefit. A small but important economic role was reserved for the State: enforcement of contracts; regulation of currency; prevention of coercion (from all sources, foreign and domestic); and provision of services (such as streets and great libraries) "which, though they may be in the highest degree advantageous to a great society, are, however, of such a nature, that the profit could never repay the expense to any individual or small number of individuals."[5] Individual actors in the economic drama were subject to the rule of law; and the impartial enforcement of the law was seen as the most important part that the State should play.

Thus, a system of market allocation, when structured so that no man has the power to coerce his rivals or fellow traders, best serves the elusive objective of social good—where the efficient use of resources to produce an abundance of popularly demanded goods is viewed as an important element contributing to that good. Because individuals are free under a market form of organization to strive for their own gain, many new goods will be introduced, and many new ways of producing goods will be discovered. But equally importantly, the market system protects each individual best against greedy abuse by his fellow man.[6]

3.2.4. Rationalist Individualism: France

The French tradition, in contrast to the British, is heavily influenced by Rousseau's view of the "noble savage"—the pre-lingual individual man, uncontaminated by contact with a society that fosters egotism and selfishness. It was a tenet of the French tradition that societies that evolved spontaneously must have

[5] Adam Smith, *The Wealth of Nations,* Book V, Ch. 1, Part II.

[6] ". . . the main point about which there can be little doubt is that [Adam Smith's] chief concern was not so much with what man might occasionally achieve when he was at his best, but that he should have as little opportunity as possible to do harm when he was at his worst. It would scarcely be too much to claim that the main merit of the individualism which he and his contemporaries advocated is that it is a system under which bad men can do least harm. It is a social system which does not depend for its functioning on our finding good men for running it, but which makes use of all men in their given variety and complexity, sometimes good and sometimes bad, sometimes intelligent and more often stupid." F. A. Hayek, "Individualism: True and False," in *Individualism and Economic Order* (Chicago: University of Chicago Press, 1948), pp. 11–12.

a corrupting influence on man; but nonetheless a good society can be designed by the exercise of human intelligence.

This tradition rejected the economic institutions, based on voluntary association, that evolved in Britain; instead it was believed that a rationally planned and sanely structured economy could be built in the service of the same individualist ends that inspired Smith and the British thinkers in his tradition. The planned economy is a central idea of the French individualist tradition. Human intelligence made a planned economy a workable prospect. Furthermore, the inequities that were seen in the older feudal order were attributed to private ownership of productive resources, so that it was held that state ownership of productive resources should accompany planning. Moreover, the French tradition attached a far different meaning to the word ''equality'' than did the British. In Britain, equality meant something akin to equal protection of the law: no person should be granted privilege, or benefit from protection not based on rules equally applicable to all persons. The French tradition assigned the opposite meaning to equality: each citizen was to be made as well-off economically and politically as every other citizen.

Two divergent economic traditions, then, have emerged from a basic philosophical commitment to individual liberty. One view sees mankind as capable of planning an orderly and beneficial society, and is not reluctant to impose the benefits yielded by planning on all men; the other view holds that the full effects of any action cannot be foreseen, and hence progress cannot be mapped out in advance, but must instead be found in trial and error. In this second view, man must be given the maximum leeway, consistent with the rights of other men, to experiment and to innovate.

3.2.5. Individualism and Selfishness

For more than two hundred years, contention has raged over the legitimate scope and applicability of the Individualist Precept. Some of the controversy has been the outgrowth of simple misunderstanding, as exemplified in the questions: is not the Individualist Precept mere selfishness, elevated to the level of principle? Has man no duty to his fellow man, and no right to expect help from his fellow man in time of need? In reply to these questions, it can be stated that the Individualist Precept *tolerates* the most pathologically selfish individuals, so long as their selfishness is not injurious in some meaningful way to other people. A man who buys up a fine vintage of wine, or the world's supply of Degas paintings, and orders his acquisition destroyed in the event of his death, might be permitted to carry out his eccentric plan without interference in a society with a strong commitment to the Individualist Precept. However, the man who attempted to buy up his community's entire supply of diphtheria serum in a time of emergency would very quickly be stopped by agents of the law in the interest of the common good. What, then, determines whether or not an action is contrary to the common good? Some would argue that the work of Degas (or Caracci, or Picasso—tastes do vary) is more important to humankind than is diphtheria serum during an emergency. In point of fact, what they are saying is that they would *prefer* to lose lives (even their own, perhaps) rather than lose the work of some master artist. Crucial, then, is the question of how widely shared that preference is. If most of the society's individual members shared an intense feeling for the importance of Degas' work, that work would not go unprotected. In any case, where it is suggested that society should interfere with individual human action, the act of interfering itself must be viewed as an evil, if the Individualist Precept is acknowledged. In such cases, the choice for society is between two evils: abridging individual action, or bearing the consequences of the individual action if it is not abridged.

We see, then, that the issue of selfishness is a bit of a red herring. Persons are permitted displays of egocentricity as long as they are not viewed as harming others in a meaningful way by their actions; symmetrically, other persons of charitable inclination are permitted to engage in crackpot schemes and to make absurd proposals in the interest of helping mankind as long as their activity does not coerce or otherwise meaningfully infringe upon the liberty, dignity, or privacy of other individuals. *The Individualist Precept is not a statement of how man should behave in society; it is a statement about the limits that society can justify imposing on its individual members.* In actuality, far from encouraging narrow selfishness, the individualist outlook may, by its emphasis on the ultimate worth of the individual person, make man more appreciative of and sensitive to his fellow man.[7]

3.2.6. The Normative Importance of the Individualist Precept

A more interesting basis from which to consider the validity of the Individualist Precept is found in the questions: is there some higher good in society that bears on the society at large, and not on its individual members? That is, can we find something in a society (in the culture, perhaps), some manifestation that can be called good, but that cannot be attached or assigned to some particular individual, or to all members of society *as* individuals? This question can be rephrased

---

[7]In Ashley Montagu, *The Humanization of Man* (New York: Grove Press, 1964), this elementary confusion, which equates individualism to selfishness, is compounded and amplified into a full-blown tirade of astonishing scope. In that book we learn that individualism is a doctrine that man exists outside of (or independent of, or above) society; that individualists exist only for themselves; that individualism engenders a thirst for security in the human psyche that can be quenched only by succumbing to a totalitarian government (Nazi Germany is mentioned as the natural outcome of unfettered individualism); and many other frightening "facts." Such observations are not merely ignorant and incorrect, they are also beside the point. To repeat: the Individualist Precept is concerned with the issue of society's attitude on the question of the importance of its individual members, as that attitude is manifested in law and custom, and *not* with the attitudes of individual men toward their roles in the various social groups to which they belong at any moment in time. The first issue is, of the two, the one that is important for questions of political and economic organization. It is also the issue to which the individualist writers of the British liberal tradition addressed themselves.

in a more explicitly *normative* form, as an inquiry about things as they *should be:* is it legitimate to accept the goals and feelings of individuals as the only criteria on which any evaluation of social arrangements will be based? Or is there an identifiable purpose of the society, the State, the group, or the race which should be considered as being above or equivalent to the purpose of its component individuals? In the twentieth century, the most conspicuous example of anti-individualist thought was in Nazi Germany. Can other less oppressively structured anti-individualist or holistic movements find thoughtful advocates and large followings over long periods of time?

The scope of the Individualist Precept is not usually questioned as a part of the subject matter of economics. It is nonetheless an important question to economists, because the Individualist Precept is an important underpinning of traditional political economy; it also has been important in shaping economic institutions, and thus has had a direct bearing on the content, applicability, and importance of economic theory. The analysis that will be developed in this book employs the Individualist Precept as an important criterion by which economic arrangements and outcomes are judged.

Throughout history, views contrary to the Individualist Precept have been routinely accepted, and by observing those views, we can get a feeling for the importance of the Individualist Precept in shaping our own contemporary social and economic life. A striking compilation and analysis of such anti-individualist views, as expounded by some of the most important political philosophers in the history of Western thought, has been provided by Karl R. Popper. Consider this view, which Popper has pieced together, in translation, from the writings and lectures of the nineteenth-century German philosopher, Hegel:

> The State is the Divine Idea as it exists on earth. . . . We must therefore worship the State as the manifestation of the Divine on earth, and consider that, if it is difficult to comprehend Nature, it is infinitely harder to grasp the Essence of the State. . . . The State is the march of God through the world. . . . The State must be comprehended as an organism. . . . to the complete State belongs, essentially, consciousness and thought. The State knows what it wills. . . . The State . . . exists for its own sake.[8]

The summary message of such a view would seem to be: you have no importance except as a tool to be used at the will of those who rule in The State. A more direct contradiction to the Individualist Precept would be hard to find.

As an exercise in speculative thought, ask yourself: what would economic life be like in a nation that is organized in accord with the views quoted above?

---

[8]K. R. Popper, *The Open Society and Its Enemies* (London: Routledge and Kegan Paul, 1945), Ch. 12. The passages translated here from Hegel's own writings are referenced by Popper in Note 8 to Chapter 12. (For the sake of completeness, we should point out that a number of scholars have accused Popper of unfairness in his use of such quotations, which portray Hegel as a totalitarian thinker. However, we are interested in the above quotes because they offer a striking example of anti-individualist thought, not because they necessarily reflect Hegel's own thought.)

Would there be free exchange of goods? Rights of property ownership? Choice of vocation or occupation?

We turn now to a consideration of the troublesome issue of equality, and the legal traditions that have directed our approaches to that issue.

3.3. EQUALITY AND THE LAW

3.3.1. "Good" versus "Bad" Laws

The classical notion of liberty, which influenced the British tradition of Smith, Hume, and others, stressed freedom of the individual from arbitrary restraint or coercion. An individual who threatens to harm another in order to make the threatened individual behave in a desired way is practicing coercion. There are degrees of coercion. Blackmailers and nagging spouses are to different degrees coercive; society may choose to protect its members by law from blackmailers, while tolerating nagging spouses as a lesser evil than the coercion that would result from a system of laws which regulate the details of husband-wife relations. The law itself is inevitably coercive in its effect on someone, and hence, in a society that takes the avoidance of coercion as a serious goal, laws are to be passed only when some greater evil thereby is avoided.

The slogan "That government is best which governs least" is often attributed (we can hope erroneously) to Thomas Jefferson, and is frequently offered as a summary of the Individualist Precept. Certainly, this is an indefensible proposition when taken at its face value; it is the *reductio ad absurdum* of the Individualist Precept. A less catchy version, but one more faithful, might read "That government is best which reserves the power of coercion to its own use; and uses that power of coercion only to avoid greater evil than the evil which attends its exercise, and always uses the power of coercion impartially, according to clearly predefined rules." But who on earth could or would remember such a characterization of good government?

There are several points to note in that revised individualists' characterization of good government before its phrasing is forgotten.

First, good laws reserve the power of coercion for use by the State. Individuals cannot within the law administer punishments, or levy taxes, or appropriate the property of others, but the State can.

Second, good laws always are directed against some substantial evil. A law preventing the sale of milk on Sunday may be defined as good if (a) the society accepts that such an act is mortal sin, and (b) further accepts that the entire community is incriminated if one of its members commits such an act. The law is good, because it enables the society to spare all its members the agony of damnation. However, if either of the conditions (a) or (b) fails to hold, then the law is at best an exercise in paternalism, and at worst a meddlesome intervention in the rights of individuals to engage in private contract.

Third, good laws are impartial. Even if the community can justify to itself the *general* prohibition of some activity, such as selling milk on Sunday, there is no righteous way to prohibit that activity to arbitrarily designated individuals. Even if you can accept "No person shall . . ." you cannot condone "No Negro shall . . ." unless you are willing to tolerate privilege (rights reserved by law to a politically powerful minority) or discrimination (rights withdrawn by law from a politically weak minority). Equal treatment before the law is an article of the British individualist tradition not only because it conforms to a particular abstract notion of justice but also because it is believed (based on observation of human behavior) that where equal treatment is once violated, workable social order will tend to be replaced by a scramble for privilege.

Fourth, the law is not applied retroactively, and if its meaning is unclear, there is recourse to the courts for clarification. This point is troublesome in some contexts: for example, the Nuremberg Trials following World War Two convicted highly placed Nazi officials for *obeying* the laws and administrative commands of wartime Germany. Were the convictions based on a retroactive imposition of new laws? Or were they, as they were stated to be, justifiable on the ground that a higher moral law forbids certain acts, even if those acts have the temporary sanction of existing law?

Finally, and here we perceive some validity in the standard version of the slogan "best equals least," the power of law is used only sparingly, because to apply that power is in itself evil, because it is coercive.

In application to economic life, the law of Britain and other nations in the British tradition fostered a system of free exchange. Both parties usually enter into an exchange voluntarily (without coercion); and if either finds the exchange arrangement not to his liking he is free to terminate it, or not to engage in it in the future. Coercion in an exchange system *can* arise if one party to an exchange has no choice of trading partner while the other has a wide choice (monopoly); or if one party deceives the other as to the real nature of the goods being exchanged. However, such coercive possibilities were judged by the earlier individualists to be rare; and hence no need was seen for the State to intrude as a matter of course in the exchange process. Only in instances where monopoly or deception appear to be clear dangers does the State intervene to prevent coercion through the mechanism of exchange.

3.3.2. Liberty, Equality, and Security

The slogans of France's revolutionary proletariat notwithstanding, liberty and equality often are not compatible goals. In Britain, before the Industrial Revolution, an enormous gulf separated the "haves" from the "have nots," and the capitalist economic order that evolved during the Industrial Revolution did not suddenly and dramatically eliminate those differences. We have no reliable information on the incomes of individuals who lived during that period, but we do know that the emergence of a market economy and the industrialization of the nation most certainly improved the conditions of life for the poorer classes.[9] However, these changes in economic organization did not suddenly lift the poor to an equal economic footing with the rich, because the rich were also benefiting most handsomely from the newly developing economic system. A constant companion everywhere to the remarkable progress of this era was a noticeable inequality that persisted despite that progress.

In the eyes of some writers, this inequality was itself felt to be coercive: the rich could hire the poor or not, as they chose; the poor could work for whatever rich man would hire them—or starve. Other people, including many of the rich, and many intellectuals, became so enamored of the emerging pattern of economic gain that they resisted any attempt to tamper or interfere with the workings of an unregulated exchange economy. The "Social Darwinism" of the nineteenth century decreed that famine in Ireland might be a proper object for the attention of private British charity, but not for British government policy. According to that doctrine, the Irish proved their unfitness by their inability to feed themselves. In contrast to the remarkable and visible gains from industrialization, the persisting squalor, and such practices as child labor, appeared to be the more conspicuous and intolerable, and pressure on the State to interfere and provide remedy built up steadily. Testimonials like "Liberty without equality is a name of noble sound and squalid meaning"[10] accumulated, and widespread sympathy developed for the view that in the absence of minimal comfort, there could be no enjoyment of liberty. The firmly entrenched tenet of equal treatment before the law acquired an odious connotation to some observers, and the view was put forth that economic inequality demanded *unequal* treatment, with the poor receiving preference. The crushingly powerful and oft-quoted ironical phrase of Anatole France denounced the traditionalist argument for equal treatment: "[Observe] . . . the majestic equality of the law, that forbids the rich as well as the poor to sleep under bridges, to beg in the streets, and to steal bread."[11]

Various movements throughout the world—Marxism-Leninism and British Fabian socialism being the most important examples—crystallized a desire for equality into policies for the abolition of unregulated exchange and the abolition of private ownership of productive equipment. It was felt that the State, as a sen-

---

[9]Hayek, in *Capitalism and The Historians* (Chicago: University of Chicago Press, 1954), examines the widely held erroneous belief that the lower classes were somehow happier and better off before the Industrial Revolution than after.

[10]L. T. Hobhouse, *Liberalism* (London, 1911). The danger of slogans like this can be seen by anyone who pauses to ask: But what about equality without liberty?

[11]Anatole France, *Le Lys Rouge* (Paris, 1897), quoted in Hayek, *The Constitution of Liberty* (Chicago: University of Chicago Press, 1960). It is well to understand precisely what the quoted passage means. It does not demonstrate that the rule of law is meaningless; it does point out that a part of mankind was (and is) living under such acute deprivation that adherence to the rule of law does not assure the deprived of a decent life.

sitive representative of all people, could regulate economic life in the direction of greater equality, so as to make the fruits of liberty available to everyone.[12]

To this day, the controversy between those who favor equal treatment—the classical liberals—and those who favor intervention in order to establish greater equality of income—the progressivist egalitarians—continues. The issues can be laid out along the following lines.

1. Both sides in the controversy claim that the objective of social organization should be to enable individuals to fulfill their own goals, aspirations, and potential.

2. Classical liberals see this objective being achieved by adherence to the Individualist Precept. They further point to the outcomes of collectivist or socialist experiments as evidence that we do not know how to *build* a free, progressive, and fulfilling society; the best we can do is to avert the coercive interference (by private individuals and the State) that prevents a liberal society from emerging spontaneously from private relations. Equal treatment before the law is an essential condition; without it there develops privilege or discrimination, and there is no experience in history on which to base a hope that the wealthy and politically powerful will use their power to benefit the politically weak in the long run.

3. The progressivist egalitarians see the classical framework as excessively burdensome, in terms of the degree of inequality that can be expected to result from it. There is a growing skepticism on the part of many members of this group concerning the ability of the State to impose sound policies—they too are aware of the lessons of socialist experimentation. Some of them show a far more pronounced willingness to rely on private market allocation wherever possible than they would have expressed in the 1930s, or even the 1950s. But they remain committed to the view that some significant additional interference with private ownership and market processes is necessary, in the name of equality.

3.3.3. Four Articles to Guide and to Judge Allocation

That controversy keeps the economics profession stirred up over the appropriate scope of market action, and the corresponding appropriate extent of interference by the State. A shifting accord, based on political compromise, is reached in practice between advocates of more intervention and advocates of greater reliance on private mechanisms. Agreement across a wide spectrum of political views should be possible on all of these articles:

1. The Individualist Precept is valid. That is, there is no "welfare" in society, other than the welfare of each of its individual members. Society and the State have no legitimate goals, except as those may be goals of its individual members. No in-

---

[12]That view, with heavy emphasis on minimal security for everyone, to be achieved by the direct action of the State, has come to be known as the "liberal" view. Those who adhere to the classical liberal view, embodied in the Individualist Precept, have come to be known as conservatives; yet many of them continue to refer to themselves as liberals. The confusion in terminology is great, but there can be little confusion regarding the conflicting ideas and goals of the two "liberal" groups. For purposes of clear identification, I have named this second view the *progressivist egalitarian* view.

dividual exists solely as the means whereby another individual achieves greater satisfaction: within the context of social processes, all individuals are viewed as equals.

2. Liberty, in its classical definition as absence of coercion, remains a social good of high standing. Action taken by the State almost always has coercive aspects, and so the resulting benefits must be clear to justify action by the State.

3. Certain State action is clearly appropriate for

    a. Prevention of significant coercion by private individuals

    b. Enforcement of exchange contracts

    c. Provision for defense from outside attack

    d. Regulation of the monetary system

    e. Provision of "beneficial but unprofitable" goods, such as sewers, highways, libraries, etc.[13]

    f. Assurance of some level or degree of security to all individuals in the society.[14]

4. A guiding principle to the State, as it considers whether to take an action to affect allocation, should be: *any action that reduces both liberty and equality should be avoided.*

There will be differences of opinion on how these articles apply in specific circumstances. For example, two individuals who subscribe to all four articles might disagree over the specific question as to whether or not there should be a law that establishes a minimum wage. On that question, economic analysis can help: under widely applicable circumstances, the minimum wage can be shown to reduce both liberty *and* equality (see Chapter 16, Section 16.4.1). Or there might be disagreement over a (hypothetical) proposal to require that all businesses must hire a number of Negro workers, until the black-white ratio is the same in their workforces as in the community at large. The gain in equality might offset the implied loss of liberty in the eyes of one observer, but not to another. On this issue, economic analysis can contribute further understanding as regards the likely impact of such a measure on economic efficiency. But there is no violation of the fourth article in this policy; it may be judged that the gain in equality justifies the encroachment on liberty. Objection to such a measure, if it is to be voiced, will be on the ground that "equal opportunity" is crudely measured by conformity to a quota, and is brought about by unequal or preferential treatment before the law.

That question of equal protection versus equal opportunity is perhaps the source of sharpest division between the classical liberals and the progressivist

---

[13] See the footnote 5, p. 24, and the related text.

[14] On this point, even those observers who hold very strictly to a classical liberal position offer little dissent. For example, F. A. Hayek, in *The Constitution of Liberty* (Chicago: University of Chicago Press, 1960), p. 302 observes: "the state provides . . . a uniform minimum for all who are unable to maintain themselves and endeavors to reduce unemployment as much as possible by an appropriate monetary policy [that is, by regulation of the monetary system, as provided in Article 3-d: author] . . . any further provision required for the maintenance of the accustomed standard should be left to competitive and voluntary efforts."

egalitarians. A decision as to the wisdom of measures like the employment proposal just discussed must rest on the judgment of society's individuals, or rather on the judgment of their elected representatives.

Many policies of government can be usefully criticized on the ground that they violate the fourth article. Farm price-support programs, tax preference and other measures affecting the petroleum industry, and even much of the public support of higher education—all carry the danger of reducing both liberty *and* equality.

3.4. THE INDIVIDUALIST PRECEPT IN ECONOMIC THEORY

3.4.1. Surviving Institutions

Many of the institutions that govern resource allocation in contemporary American society reflect the vigor with which the British individualist tradition has persisted in this country. The same is true, but to a significantly lesser degree, in Great Britain itself. Among these contemporary institutions are (1) extensive private ownership of property, (2) relatively free exchange of goods and services, and (3) relatively free movement of people and goods within the nation. An elaborate structure of law defines and protects these traditional institutions. Note, however, that qualifying words lurk in the list: "extensive" and "relatively." The economic theory that this book transmits and uses in large measure ignores those qualifying words: in our *theoretical* view of the economy, terms like "completely" private ownership or "perfectly" free exchange would be more descriptive.

All theories resort to simplification and abstraction so that people who use them can obtain useful explanations and predictions. Economic theory, in its most ambitious and cohesive form, attempts to describe a nation's market economy as a mechanism, to identify the ways in which the forces of self-interest are reconciled within that mechanism and to enable a systematic evaluation of the results or outcomes that are a product of the mechanism. In this *general equilibrium* form, economic theory assumes full private ownership and perfectly free exchange, because that treatment greatly simplifies the analysis, but those assumptions are also consistent with the view that the Individualist Precept is a fundamental part of the social order. Moreover, most economic decisions in the contemporary United States are made by individuals, and most exchange is between private persons;[15] these are further reasons to employ an individualistically oriented theory to describe and explain the processes of allocation, and to serve as a standard by which performance is judged. The economic theory of general equilibrium treats as ideals those institutional arrangements that pro-

---

[15]In the legal sense of the word *person*. A corporation or bank is a person, as long as it is not an agency of government.

vide for the maximum exercise of individual preference; constructed in that way, the theory gives useful insight into the workings of markets, and it may be useful as a standard or benchmark by which actual economic arrangements and performance can be judged.

In addition to this work of wide scope and lofty ambition in general equilibrium analysis, economic theory has found wide practical application in evaluating the functioning of component parts of the economic order. This *partial equilibrium* approach is especially useful for investigating the effect of changes in such economic arrangements as the tax laws or laws governing the employment of workers. Partial equilibrium analysis also can be a useful aid in predicting what the consequences of economic development will be (in places like Orange County).

As economic performance is judged, whether with the assistance of general equilibrium or partial equilibrium analysis, one important consideration in the process of judgment is usually whether the preferences of individuals are well-served by the existing or proposed economic order.

3.4.2. Government in a "Hierarchy" of Allocation Decisions

The articles to guide allocation which were just stated assign an important role for the State to play in economic life. Article 3 specifically concedes the necessity of government action to prevent coercion, enforce contracts, arrange for the national defense, regulate the monetary system, provide some services of a particular type that would otherwise not be available in adequate quantity, and assure some minimal level of economic security. With the passage of time and the acquiescence of the electorate, the American State has assumed a much broader array of economic functions than is assigned in Article 3. Especially since 1930, government has become an increasingly important factor in economic life. Government now makes a wide variety of decisions concerning the creation and disposition of material wealth.

First, governmentally directed allocation decisions take precedence over some (but not all) of an individual's own personal choices. The ideal envisioned and crudely implemented in the tax law is that the individual's first obligation is to provide the "necessities of life" for himself (and his family); after that provision is made, some part of his remaining income is taxed away and allocated by the government. He then allocates the part of his income that is not absorbed by taxation, primarily through market exchange.

Second, many market exchange contracts among individuals are regulated and constrained by the State. It is illegal, for example, to contract to provide alcoholic beverages to a minor, or marijuana to anyone; and if you wish to sell haircuts or medical services, you may be required by the State to obtain a license, which is sometimes difficult to do. General equilibrium theory, with its emphasis on market allocation and the accommodation of individual objectives, has not been extended to take these large allocative and regulatory roles of the government into account. However, other theories have been developed which can be used to analyze government-directed allocation. These are theories of *macroeconomics,* and are directed at important questions of the *level* and *stability* of economic activity within the whole nation. In the usual treatment of these questions, taxation and government expenditures are important variables. Taxes and expenditures are seen to affect the level and stability of aggregate economic activity, which by law[16] and custom are concerns of government. Tax collections and expenditures by the government are in part consciously regulated to meet this concern. Those topics and theories are not covered in this book.

Other activities have been designated for government direction, and hence they have priority over the activities that remain in the realm of individual choice. Among the more important centrally directed resource allocation decisions, not specified in the articles of Section 6, are those involving

1. Education.
2. Welfare (such as medical care for the aged, public medical clinics, and lunches for school children).
3. Transportation (including maintenance of river channels, canals, and harbors; subsidization of all domestic airlines; and construction and maintenance of highways).
4. Provision of miscellaneous goods (electricity, mail delivery, insurance, weather forecasts, and protection against floods and fires, just to name a few).
5. Space exploration, and the support of scientific research and development.

The breadth and pervasiveness of governmentally directed resource allocation activity is suggested in this partial listing, and further attested by the fact that in 1969, governmental expenditures at all levels—federal, state, and local—amounted to about one-third of the value of all the goods and services produced in America; by 1976, that fraction had increased to well over 40 percent.

APPLICATIONS AND EXTENSIONS

1. Suppose you own a house in a fairly classy seaside town. It is proposed that further "development" (the building of new houses) be curtailed in your town. What economic effect will that proposal have on you if it is adopted?

2. Same question, but this time suppose you own a vacant lot, not a house. Do you see a sense in which the proposal would "take" property from you in the second case, and "give" it to you in the first case?

---

[16]The Employment Act of 1946 explicitly charges the federal government with maintenance of high levels of employment and stable prices through the use of widely discussed policies, some of which involve manipulation of tax rates. The income tax cut of 1964 (and the tax surcharge of 1968) are examples of legislation enacted in the attempt to discharge the responsibilities specified in the Employment Act.

3. A community enacts a law which is intended to prevent the building of "ugly" houses. An elected architectural control committee must pass on all plans before building can begin. Do you approve of such a law?

4. Similar question, but this time the intent is to prevent the showing of "unsuitable" motion pictures: an elected committee must approve any film that is shown in town. Do you approve?

5. Same question, but this time the community seeks to curtail the publication of "dangerous" ideas. Should a community be empowered to elect a committee whose role is to prevent the publication of dangerous ideas?

6. "It is far better that ten thousand criminals go unpunished than that one innocent person suffer punishment." Do you agree? What are the tradeoffs that are implied in that statement between liberty and security?

7. "The life of every individual human being is infinitely precious to society." Do you agree? If so, why haven't you devoted all your money and energy to the abolition of automobile transport, which kills about 50 thousand people a year in the USA?

BIBLIOGRAPHICAL NOTE

A readable popular chronicle of how collectivism is rooted in the French individualist tradition is found in the early chapters of Edmund Wilson's *To The Finland Station* (New York: Doubleday-Doran, 1940). Alexis de Tocqueville, a Frenchman who embraced the British version of individualism, presented a justly renowned analysis of the American experiment which still bears careful reading, *Democracy in America* (Paris, 1835). This book is especially useful on the issue of equality versus liberty. A contemporary popularization of the British tradition which offers a number of interesting economic policy prescriptions in that tradition is Milton Friedman, *Capitalism and Freedom* (Chicago: University of Chicago Press, 1962). Karl R. Popper's *The Open Society and Its Enemies* (London: Routledge and Kegan Paul, 1945) is a study of the intellectual foundations of anti-individualist political movements.

The major sources to consult are the works of Friedrich Hayek, perhaps the most important contemporary authority on our subject. Three works: *The Counter-Revolution of Science* (Chicago: University of Chicago Press, 1955), *The Constitution of Liberty* (Chicago: University of Chicago Press, 1960), and *Individualism and Economic Order* (Chicago: University of Chicago Press, 1948) are absorbing and lucid treatises of the highest order of scholarship. The second is of especial importance.

More recently, a major contemporary philosopher has sought to show that the British tradition can be interpreted to support more explicitly egalitarian ends: John Rawls, *A Theory of Justice* (Cambridge, Mass.: Harvard University Press, 1971). Rawls' book has stimulated much fresh discussion of these issues. Perhaps the most significant response that Rawls' work has evoked is from his departmental colleague at Harvard, Robert Nozick. *Anarchy, State and Utopia* (New York, Basic Books, Inc., 1974) offers a "classical liberal" commentary on Rawls' egalitarianism. Finally, we must mention an excellent analysis of the contemporary British economy, also viewed from a classical liberal perspective: Samuel Brittan, *Capitalism and the Permissive Society*, New York, Macmillan & Co., 1973.

Part Two

THE IDEALIZED
MARKET ECONOMY

Three ideas were developed in Part One. First, the problems that can be illuminated by economic analysis are real and important. Second, the market system offers responsive means of coordinating the choices and preferences of individuals. And third, the reliance on a market system has ethical, as well as technical dimensions. Here in Part Two, the workings of markets will be explored in much greater detail. The goals are (1) to learn how competitive markets work, (2) to develop some skill in the analysis of problems which involve the application of market (supply and demand) analysis, and (3) to obtain a perspective on the question of how the market system affects "social welfare."

Chapter 4 contains a discussion of the fundamentals of competitive market equilibrium, and several illustrations of fairly realistic and important problems than can be better understood when supply and demand analysis is applied.

Chapters 5 and 6 are a deeper investigation of demand. Chapter 5 contains a theoretical analysis of how the choice behavior of individuals can result in market demand curves that are negatively sloped. Elements of a "theory of consumer behavior" are involved in developing that relationship between market demand and individual choice. Chapter 6 discusses several important and interesting topics in demand theory and consumer behavior. These are reviewed for two reasons: first, because they provide a firmer grasp of how economic theory is structured, and second, because the topics covered are intrinsically interesting either as intellectual exercises or as approaches to important issues.

Chapters 7 and 8 are devoted to a thorough discussion of supply relationships. Chapter 7 contains a treatment of an important institution, the business firm, and an important development in social organization that accompanies market exchange, the division of labor. Chapter 8 treats the theory of production and market supply. Chapter 9 extends supply and demand analysis to cover cases that involve more than one period of time in a meaningful way. Chapter 10 is a review of thought on the question: how does a market system affect the welfare of society's individual members?

CHAPTER FOUR

Demand and Supply: Elements and First Applications

As scarce as truth is, the supply has always been in excess of demand.

JOSH BILLINGS (1865)

When the well's dry, we know the worth of water.

BENJAMIN FRANKLIN (1738)

Markets, market equilibrium, and the incentive effects of price changes were introduced informally in Chapters 1 and 2. These ideas all will be developed in a more careful and formal way in the next few chapters. In this chapter, market supply and market demand relations will be further analyzed, and the workings of markets will be shown to be important in understanding a variety of problems and issues.

4.1. CHOICE, DEMAND, SUPPLY

4.1.1. Choices and Self-Interest

Every individual in society functions in two economic roles: as a producer and as a consumer. Much of the activity of producing and consuming is channeled through exchange relationships: the machinist or physician or cherry picker sells his skills and efforts either directly to consumers or to an employer, who uses those skills and efforts in combination with other valuable things to produce goods that are sold to consumers. The wage that is obtained, either as a salary from the employer or as a payment that the consumers make directly, is the reward obtained for productive effort in an exchange system. That wage, in turn, is expended on goods and services produced by other people. Satisfaction through consumption is obtained by exchange.

It is worth noting that large amounts of productive effort and consumption enjoyment occur outside the confines of the exchange system. When a woman as mother cares for her sick child, or as housewife polishes her silverware or irons her husband's shirts, she is producing just as surely as if she were drawing a wage; but her productive efforts are occurring within the status-determined (intregrative) system, not the exchange system. Similarly, the sick child, or the other members of the household to whom she ministers, are consumers of her service. And she in turn may derive consumption value from her activities, in the form of pleasure from her relations with other members of her household.

Economics pretty much limits its domain of study to exchange processes. In the study of those processes, the postulate of self-interest, as discussed in Chapter 2, has been found to be useful and illuminating; it has helped to explain much of what we observe to take place in exchange. That postulate asserts, quite simply, that individuals who engage in exchange seek out production and consumption opportunities that leave them feeling as well or better off than any known alternative. Individual choices are directed by the motive of obtaining higher satisfaction.

We will have the opportunity in the next few chapters to develop and critically review theories of how individual choice operates and how it affects the mechanisms of demand and supply. In this chapter, we will take a broad view: we will not worry in detail about individual choice behavior; but we will invoke the postulate of self-interest in developing demand and supply analysis in a preliminary and rather crude, but nonetheless useable, form.

4.1.2. Price Signals in the Circular Flow

In an exchange system, changes in the rate of exchange are the signals that regulate the flows of different types of activity. Suppose, for example, that the participants in an exchange system learn that oats are a more nutritious and palatable cereal than barley. They substitute oats into their diets to replace barley (an act that serves their self-interest as individuals). The economy-wide impact of their individual decisions is to increase the demand for oats and diminish the demand for barley. There will be a "shortage" of oats and an "oversupply" of barley. To ration the suddenly more popular oats, owners of oats will raise the oat price. To sell the suddenly less popular barley, owners of barley stocks will lower the barley price. Grain growers will notice the rise in one price and the drop in the other, and will perceive that oat growing is now more profitable, and barley growing less profitable, than before. They will grow less barley and more oats. Thus, the price adjustments in barley and oats serve as signals that regulate the amounts of those two grains that flow through the exchange system.

Production and consumption decisions are affected by relative price changes. In the simple drama we just reviewed, a change in *taste,* which arose out of new information about nutrition, led to a change in the relative prices of two cereal grains. We could equally well have talked about a change in availability being the important force in producing change. Suppose a new high-yield strain of oats is developed: then the cost per bushel of producing oats will decline, relative to the cost of producing other grains; supplies of oats will increase and oat prices will fall to induce people to consume this suddenly cheaper and more abundant grain.

In the circular flow of economic activity, then, price changes regulate the amount of different activities that take place, in response to changes in taste and changes in opportunity. A drop in a good's price (compared to the prices of other goods) is a signal that either (a) fewer people want to consume the good than before, and so less of it should be produced, or (b) the good can be produced more abundantly than before without using any more resources, so more of it should be consumed. These changes which lead to a fall in price are a reduction in demand (Figure 4.1) or an increase in supply (Figure 4.2).

4.1.3. General Interdependence Among Prices

It is important to re-emphasize, however, that the price signals in an exchange system do not operate independently of each other. The change in oat demand or

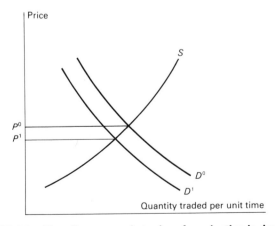

FIGURE 4.1.   The effect on market price of a reduction in demand.

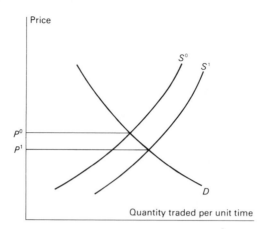

FIGURE 4.2. The effect on market price of an increase in supply.

supply affects oat prices; that change in turn affects the prices of other foodstuffs, natural fibers, and forest products. The demand or supply of any goods for which oats is a substitute in consumption or production will be affected by the oat price change; and the resulting changes in the prices of those directly affected goods will lead to further changes within the circular flow system, affecting the markets for goods which are themselves not importantly affected by oat prices.

The full effects of any change in taste or production opportunity, then, cannot be easily measured, or even explicitly described. However, in theorizing about the workings of the market exchange system, we can readily capture the effects of price changes in full generality. We only need to note that the price of any good will have an effect in the market for every other good. In many cases, of course, the effects will be so small that they will be unmeasurable. We can then write the supply and demand relations in any market in this general form:

$$D_j = D_j(P_1, P_2, ..., P_j, ..., P_N)$$
$$S_j = S_j(P_1, P_2, ..., P_j, ..., P_N)$$

where D_j is the quantity demanded of the jth good (measured in units per unit interval of time), S_j is the quantity supplied of the jth good per unit of time; and the functions $D_j(\cdot)$ and $S_j(\cdot)$ tell us that those rates of supply and demand depend on the prices of all N of the goods and services traded in the market system. (All labor services of different distinct types are counted among the N goods.) A similar pair of relations can be defined for all of the markets $1, ..., N$. The exchange system is *in equilibrium* if (and only if)

$$D_j = S_j \qquad\qquad j = 1, 2, ..., N,$$

i.e., the N prices must be such that quantity supplied equals quantity demanded in all markets.

4.1.4. Demand Relations: Substitutes, Complements, and Inferior Goods

How do the N different prices affect the quantity demanded of any particular good? Consider the demand for fly swatters, for example. Keep in mind that among the $N - 1$ other goods that are traded in the system, some will be *substitutes* for fly swatters: when the price of insecticide or screening goes down, the number of fly swatters demanded should also decline, because those goods are substitutes for fly swatters. When the rental rate on vacation cabins in the north woods goes down, the number of fly swatters demanded should increase, because a fly swatter is necessary for survival in a north woods vacation cabin. Fly swatters and vacations in the north woods are known as *complementary* goods: they tend to be consumed together. (Other less farfetched examples of complementary goods are cameras and film, tea and sugar, pancake flour and syrup.)

When the price of a good changes, the demand for a substitute good moves in the same direction, and the demand for a complementary good moves in the opposite direction (when the price of film increases, the demand for cameras can be expected to decline).

Other prices of goods which are neither substitutes nor complements, but which affect the demand for fly swatters, are the wages of workers who are also the consumers of fly swatters. What happens to the demand for fly swatters when general wage levels in the society go up? We can't tell in advance; it is necessary to study behavior. People may buy more fly swatters because the rise in wages makes them wealthier, and hence better able to afford more; or they may buy fewer fly swatters because at high income levels more elaborate and expensive methods of insect control may supplant the use of fly swatters. If an increase in income within the society diminishes fly swatter sales, then the fly swatter is an *inferior good*. If the increase in income stimulates those sales, then it is a *normal good*.

Finally, a rise in the price of any good is usually expected to diminish the sales of that good. When the price of fly swatters rises *relative to the prices of other goods,* we expect to observe a reduction in fly swatter demand.

4.1.5. Supply Relations: Substitutes, By-Products, and Productive Inputs

As with demand, the supply of fly swatters will respond to changes in the prices of other goods. If the resources used in fly swatter production can equally well be used in producing children's beach toys, then a higher price for beach toys will tend to diminish the supply of fly swatters. Resources will be taken from fly swatter production and used to make more sand sifters.

Finally, an increase in the good's own price is expected to cause an increase in the quantity of the good that is supplied.

Among the N traded goods, there also will be some that are *inputs* into the production of fly swatters. When the price of a productive input (like wire or plastic mesh) rises, the supply of fly swatters always declines.

Sometimes goods are produced in complementary pairs: one good is said to be a *by-product* of the other. When the price of beef rises owing to a demand increase, leather output also tends to increase, for example.

4.2. DEMAND AND SUPPLY CURVES

4.2.1. The Standard Diagrammatic Form

It has long been the standard practice in economics to focus on the relations that exist between the quantities of a good supplied and demanded, and the good's own price. This has been done for a variety of reasons. The full gamut of relations with prices of all goods is simply too much to try to comprehend systematically; the good's own price is seen as being, usually, the single most important variable in producing an equilibrium in the good's market; and in many applications a useful understanding can be obtained without trying to work out all the various effects that result from changes in the markets for other goods.

We have already seen how supply and demand diagrams look, and we have observed an application in which they are used. The process of equilibration through price adjustment has also been discussed (see Chapter 1, Section 1.2.3). The standard supply and demand diagram embodies the hypotheses that *quantity demanded decreases and quantity supplied increases when the good's own price increases*. These hypotheses are important: if they fail to hold true, the market system may function in strange ways, as we shall see shortly. Much of the advanced theory of demand and supply, in fact, is concerned with an investigation of precisely the questions: How sure are we that demand curves are negatively sloped? How sure are we that supply curves are positively sloped?

The standard supply and demand analysis does not exclude from consideration the effects of other prices on the equilibrium of a good's market. The effects of other prices in supply and demand analysis are explored in the next section.

4.2.2. Shifts in Demand and Supply Curves

Our purpose in this section is to clarify an important difference, between (1) a change in a good's own price, which is the *result* of a shift in demand or supply; and (2) a change in another variable (such as the price of another good), which affects demand or supply, and which is the *cause* of a shift in demand or supply.

The demand for automobiles will depend on the price of automobiles, on the prices of substitutes like train rides and other means of transportation and recreation, on the prices of other consumer goods, and on the tastes and preferences of the community. The supply of automobiles will depend on the price of automobiles, the prices of other goods that could be supplied from the resources used to make automobiles, and on the manufacturing techniques available for producing automobiles. In a supply and demand diagram, *only the price of automobiles is explicitly included from the list of variables that influence supply and demand for automobiles.* It would be useful and correct to include other variables explicitly in the analysis, but unhappily, functions are hard to draw and to read in more than two dimensions. Hence the influence of the other crucial variables is represented in a very simple way: when one of those variables changes, the result is a shift in either the supply curve, the demand curve, or both. If the price of rail transport drops as a result of the development of a new lightweight nuclear engine, then the demand for autos will shift downward, or to the left. If the price of gasoline rises as a result of political tension in the Middle East, then the demand for automobiles will also shift downward. If the total income of the community increases, the demand for autos will shift upward, assuming that the automobile is a normal good.

The full process of equilibration after an event like the development of that hypothetical nuclear railway engine is complicated. The first effect is on the supply of railway passenger service: it shifts to the right because that service is now much cheaper to provide. The drop in the price of train rides is felt in other markets: automobiles, for example, where demand shifts downward and the price of automobiles falls as a result. The drop in automobile price will, in turn, have an effect on the demand for train rides: that demand will shift downward, and the price of train rides will fall still more. Such adjustments will affect *all* markets to a greater or lesser degree, and as each market adjusts, the price change influences all other markets anew. Only with time will these "shocks" caused by the process of adjustment dampen out, and their influence die down. There is an issue, indeed, as to whether such dampening down ever does occur. Some analysts have argued that an economy is continually vibrating, with all markets perpetually out of equilibrium; and some have seen a definite tendency for these vibrations to become very large and troublesome—wide swings in price and output, leading to what was once popularly called the *business cycle.* It would be a move to a separate topic, albeit an important one, to look into those issues here. For present purposes, we want to grasp firmly the classification:

In any market

a. a change in price is *caused by* a shift in supply, or demand, or both;

b. a change in another variable (such as a price in a different market) *causes* a shift in supply, or demand, or both.

If these classifying rules are understood, there will never be the kind of confusion that is exhibited in this made-up quotation: "There is no point in subsidizing the construction of housing for the poor. When that housing becomes available at low prices, demand for it will increase, and the price will be bid right back up again to nearly its present level."

If we sort carefully through that statement, we see that it says

a. a subsidy will cause the supply curve to shift so that more housing is supplied at any price (correct);

b. the resulting drop in price will cause the demand curve to shift to a higher level (incorrect);

c. the effect of the two shifts is to cancel out any good that might result from the action.

In a corrected version, we would have (b) the resulting drop in price induces a greater quantity demanded, which can be sustained out of the increased supply; and (c) the effect of the housing subsidy is to make a larger quantity of housing available at a lower price than would otherwise be observed (Figure 4.3).

The elementary confusion between a shift in demand or supply (which *brings about* a change in price) and the change in quantity supplied or quantity demanded (which *accompanies* the change in price) is a source of much error in economic analysis. It has been argued in Congress, for example, that programs to pay for medical training cannot work: the subsidy will increase the supply of medical care, and lower the price, but the lowered price will simply increase the demand, which will drive the price of medical services right back up, and nobody will be better off than before. That argument also is confused, because the subsidy causes a shift in the supply curve and leaves the demand curve unchanged (Figure 4.3 again). The new equilibrium E^1 will occur at a price that is lower than the old equilibrium E; and the increase in quantity between E and E^1 represents a clearcut gain to the subsidized consumers of medical services.

4.2.3. Slopes of Demand and Supply Curves and Market Stability

The points labeled E and E^1 in Figure 4.3 are *equilibrium* points. If the supply and demand functions are S and D, and the quantity Q^0 is supplied to the market

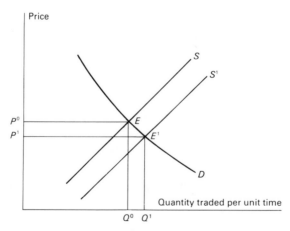

FIGURE 4.3. The effect of a subsidy is to increase supply, as from S to S¹, and to reduce price.

and the price P^0 prevails, then there will be no forces tending to produce any change in the market; that is why we call the point E an *equilibrium* point.

An interesting problem is uncovered when we ask: how do we know that a shift in supply of the type shown in Figure 4.3 will actually result in a lower price and greater output? What *adjustment process* assures that buyers and sellers will perceive the change in equilibrium, and will respond by "moving to the new equilibrium"? For the sake of concreteness, we will discuss that question in application to a hypothetical supply shift in the fly swatter market.

After a shift in supply from S^0 to S^1 (Figure 4.4), the quantity $\bar{Q}$ is offered at the price P^0, instead of Q^0 as before. Demand, however, has not changed. Hence there is a "gap" between the greater number of fly swatters supplied per period, $\bar{Q}$, and the number per period demanded, Q^0. That gap is called *excess supply* (or more customarily, *excess demand,* with the understanding that excess demand can take negative values as well as positive values.) With negative excess demand, the amount $\bar{Q} - Q^0$ is added to the inventories of fly swatter producers in each period. That undesired buildup of inventory holdings acts as a signal to the producers of fly swatters: they attempt to get rid of excess holdings by cutting the price of their product, and they attempt to avoid future buildups of fly swatter inventory by cutting back on their rate of output. The effect of these two adjustments is to move toward the new equilibrium E^1, when the quantity Q^1 sells at a price P^1.

Similar patterns of adjustment could be depicted for a reduction in supply, or for an increase or reduction in demand. If the excess demand that results from any such shift is negative, suppliers' inventories will build up, and they will respond as we described. If the resulting excess demand is positive (as with a reduction in supply or an increase in demand), then inventories will be depleted.

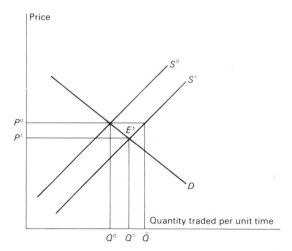

FIGURE 4.4. The excess supply, or negative excess demand $(\bar{Q} - Q^0)$, exerts a downward pressure on price and output.

Temporary shortages will cause an upward pressure on price, a cutback in the rate of demand, and an increase in the rate of supply. (In some markets, of course, there are no suppliers' inventories of finished goods awaiting sale, the market for medical services being a good example. In those cases the need to adjust is felt because of the rate at which the available service capacity is utilized. Long lines at a clinic are a signal to add more doctors if possible; lots of idle time in the clinic is a signal to release doctors to go elsewhere.)

To summarize, then: if any price and output other than the equilibrium combination prevails in a market, "forces" will be set in motion that tend to restore the equilibrium. We emphasized suppliers' adjustment to excess demand in the preceding discussion; that behavior constitutes the "force" that restores equilibrium.

The *stability* of equilibrium also can be analyzed in terms of the response of market price to excess demand. If there is a positive excess demand, price will rise. If there is a negative excess demand, price will fall. With supply and demand curves conventionally drawn, as in Figure 4.5, equilibrium will be *stable:* prices above P cause negative excess demand, and prices below P cause positive excess demand, and in either case, adjustment will be back to P.

Suppose, however, that the supply curves are not conventionally sloped, as in Figures 4.6 and 4.7. In 4.6, the price-adjustment mechanism will work properly: any price above P^0 will induce a negative excess demand. However, in Figure 4.7, a price *below* P^0 induces a negative excess demand; and the resulting drop in price is a movement away from, rather than toward, equilibrium. (At P^1, excess demand is negative, so price adjusts downward, say to P^2. But at P^2, the excess supply is even larger, and when price drops again, movement is even farther from equilibrium.) Figure 4.7, in which the supply curve is "flatter" than the demand curve, exemplifies a case of unstable equilibrium when the market price adjusts to excess demand.

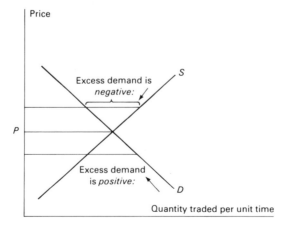

FIGURE 4.5.   Excess demand and price-output adjustments when demand and supply curves are conventionally sloped.

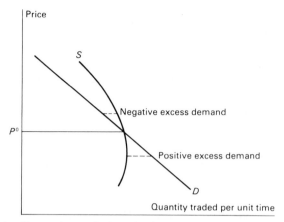

FIGURE 4.6. **Excess demand with a backward-bending supply curve: price and output adjustments will be toward equilibrium.**

A similar analysis could be conducted of markets in which both demand and supply are positively sloped. The outcome of that analysis would conform to this rule:

> When supply and demand have slopes of the same sign (positive or negative), the process of adjustment to excess demand will indicate that the equilibrium is stable whenever D lies to the *left* of S above the equilibrium price.[1]

FIGURE 4.7. **Another "abnormal" supply curve. This time excess demand is of the wrong sign, and adjustments will be *away from* the equilibrium price P^0.**

---

[1]This analysis of the stability of equilibrium in terms of excess demand was originated by Léon Walras, a worthy French economist, in 1875. An alternative adjustment system, with slightly different stability implications, was invented by Alfred Marshall, an English great, in the 1880s. See exercise 11 at the end of this chapter for details.

The question we have just investigated, of whether or not equilibrium is stable, is an important one. If a market system is to do a good job of conveying information to producers about what consumers want, and to consumers about what producers can make cheaply and well, then it must not be susceptible to the kind of instability that we saw in Figure 4.7. In an unstable market, the signals are perverse; an increase in demand leads producers to supply less, rather than more. Their resource-use decisions go in a direction contrary to the desirable one.

4.2.4. Elasticity

Elasticity is a *dimensionless* measure of response between any pair of related variables. Consider the demand curve for coal, for example. The curve depicts a relationship between the price of coal and its rate of purchase by users (quantity demanded). Figure 4.8 shows a demand curve. At the price P, the associated rate of coal purchase is Q. At the lower price $P - \Delta P$, the rate of purchase is higher: $Q + \Delta Q$. We see, then, that from the point (P, Q) a change in price of $-\Delta P$ is associated with the demand response ΔQ. The price change relative to the original price is $-\Delta P/P$, the demand rate change relative to the original output rate is $\Delta Q/Q$. If the *ratio* of these two relative changes is taken, we obtain the *price elasticity of demand:*

$$\eta = \frac{\Delta Q}{Q} \div \frac{-\Delta P}{P} \quad .$$

Elasticity is a *dimensionless* measure of response, because it is independent of the units in terms of which the two variables are measured. In this respect, elas-

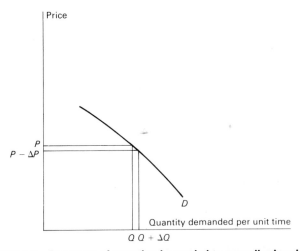

FIGURE 4.8.   Response of quantity demanded to a small price change.

ticity differs from the slope of the demand curve. The demand for coal, if price is in dollars and quantity in tons, will be steeper than a curve that depicts the same demand, but along which price is in dollars and quantity in hundredweight. The elasticities of these two representations of the demand relationship, however, will be the same.

The *total revenue* collected on the sale of a good is price per unit multiplied by quantity sold. As demand curves are usually drawn, quantity and price are inversely related: the greater the quantity, the lower the price that will result in the sale of the entire quantity.

It is useful to know how total revenue is affected by a change in the quantity offered for sale, given the price change that accompanies it. In Figure 4.9, a simple straight-line demand curve is drawn. We see that when the available quantity is greater than Q^i, total revenue is zero because nobody is willing to pay a positive price for a good that is so abundant. At the other extreme, if quantity sold could be restricted in an attempt to get price up as high as possible, the maximum price that could be realized on any transaction would be nearly P^i. But if price were set at exactly P^i, quantity sold would be zero, and again total revenue would be zero. Somewhere between the extremes of selling zero output at a high price and selling a large output at zero price is a price-quantity combination which leads to the highest attainable revenue.

The maximum-revenue combination in Figure 4.9 occurs at the output $Q^i/2$, or half the output at which the demand curve intersects the quantity axis. (In any case involving a straight-line demand curve, it will be true that revenue will be at a maximum when the quantity sold to buyers is half the intercept value of the

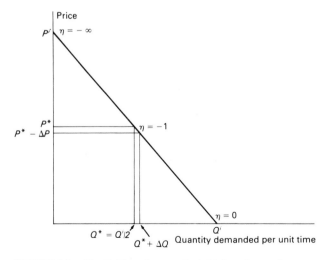

FIGURE 4.9. Elasticities along a straight-line demand curve.

demand curve. In the special case of the straight-line demand curve, then, if output is less than $Q^* = Q^i/2$, an increase in output results in an increase in revenue. If output is greater than Q^*, a reduction in output leads to an increase in revenue.)

Examining our definition of elasticity, we see that at the point $(0, P^i)$, elasticity takes an unboundedly small value: the formula is

$$\eta = \frac{\Delta Q}{0} \div \frac{-\Delta P}{P^i} = -\infty$$

at that point. At the point $(Q^i, 0)$, we see that

$$\eta = \frac{-\Delta Q}{Q^i} \div \frac{\Delta P}{0} = \frac{-\Delta Q \cdot 0}{\Delta P \cdot Q^i} = 0$$

and hence elasticity at that point is zero. At the point (P^*, Q^*), we see that

$$\eta = \frac{\Delta Q \cdot P^*}{-\Delta P \cdot Q^*} = -1$$

because $P^*/Q^* = -\Delta P/\Delta Q$.

Those calculations illustrate the relations between demand elasticity and total revenue. Total revenue takes on its maximum value at a point where the price elasticity of demand equals -1. If price elasticity is less than -1 (if it takes values like -17 or -1.216), then total revenue can be increased by a *cut* in price (or an increase in output). Demand is said to be *elastic* in that range. If elasticity is greater than -1 (if it takes a value like $-.6$), then total revenue can be increased by an *increase* in price (or a reduction in output). Demand is said to be *inelastic* when elasticity is in the range $(-1, 0)$.[2]

We could have defined supply elasticity equally easily, but that concept will have no application in this book. Other useful concepts are *income elasticity* of demand:

$$\epsilon = \frac{\Delta Q}{\Delta I} \cdot \frac{I}{Q}$$

where I is income; and *cross-elasticity of demand* between two goods

$$\eta_{1,2} = \frac{\Delta Q_1}{\Delta P_2} \cdot \frac{P_2}{Q_1}$$

These respectively measure the responsiveness of quantity demanded to changes in income and changes in the price of another good.

---

[2]Some discussions are careless about the sign of demand elasticity. They take it for granted that all demand curves are negatively sloped, and so the minus sign can be understood to be present in all cases. If elasticity takes a positive value, the demand curve is positively sloped.

4.3. SUPPLY AND DEMAND ANALYSIS: EXAMPLES AND APPLICATIONS

4.3.1. Demand Elasticity and Transit Fares

The response of revenue to changes in output and price, which demand elasticity measures, is important in a variety of applied contexts. For example, it can be seen that it may be unwise for a municipal mass transit system to change its fares, even when the system starts to lose money as a result of higher costs. Suppose the transit system authorities are advised that taxpayers are tired of seeing the system operate at a loss, and they raise fares. A fare increase will not produce the desired effect if the demand for the service of public transport is elastic: the higher price will lead to a lower total revenue. The transit authority, then, faces a quandary: if it raises fares, many passengers will adopt other means of travel; so many will do so, in fact, that the revenue receipts after the fare increase will be lower than before.[3] With elastic demand, the transit authority would obtain an increase in the revenue received by *lowering* fares: a large increase in the number of passengers would more than offset the reduced take from each passenger. Why are fares not always cut as long as demand is elastic? There might be high costs associated with providing transit service to additional passengers: costs of obtaining new equipment and the staff to operate and maintain it. These costs might be so high, in fact, that they would more than offset the gain in revenue. The transit system, under those conditions, cannot be operated except at a loss: higher price means lower returns (unless decisively large cost savings result from the smaller number of passengers); and lower price means higher costs and hence no gain in returns.

A similar example: in years of bad harvest, the price of strawberries is high; but when harvests are good, the "bottom falls out of the market" and strawberries can be purchased very cheaply. This phenomenon is easy to comprehend: the demand for strawberries is inelastic over the observed range of outputs, and a low quantity available means that higher revenues are obtained when a bumper crop is marketed. That same elasticity effect is observed in the world coffee market, which explains a policy occasionally followed by the government of Brazil: in some years, a large part of the coffee crop is destroyed to avoid "spoiling the market," as would happen if the entire crop were offered for sale.

4.3.2. Price Fixing: Agriculture

During the 1950s and early 1960s the agricultural price-support program was a favorite example of how *not* to conduct a government program. The problem that Congress and the administration were trying to solve, simply stated, was

---

[3] And, incidentally, problems of automobile congestion will probably be made worse.

that many farmers suffered very low incomes: in bad crop years, yields were small, and though prices were high, total sales revenues were low. But for high outputs, demand is inelastic, so that in good years, the large quantities produced drove market prices down, and once again total sales revenues declined.

Government's response to the problem of low and fluctuating farm incomes was an attack on the fluctuation of farm prices. In several heavily produced commodities, including wheat, corn, and cotton, minimum prices were established under the guise of a commodity storage program. The program provided that growers could leave their crops in government storage areas. The federal government paid the support price on receipt of the crops. By repaying that minimum price at a later time, farmers could take their crops out of storage and sell them on the open market, which would be sensible action should market prices rise above the support price. But if market prices remained below the support price, there was no incentive for the farmers to reclaim the goods. After a term in storage, ownership of the stored goods permanently reverted to the government.

The effect of such a program can be seen in Figure 4.10. The support price P is above the market-clearing price P^*; the government buys the quantity $(Q^S - Q^D)$ at the price P. The quantity Q^D is sold on the market at the price P. The outlay $P(Q^S - Q^D)$, plus any costs of storage, are the costs of the price-support program to the government.

An alternative farm subsidy plan was considered in the 1940s, and rejected by Congress. That plan, also illustrated in Figure 4.10, called for the sale of *all* output at the market-clearing price, but the difference between the market price and

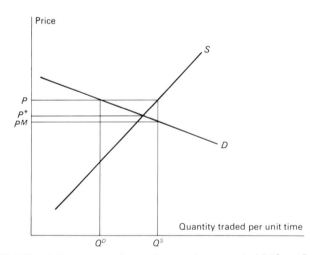

FIGURE 4.10. **Price support via purchase and storage: hold $Q^S - Q^D$; or via direct subsidy: let Q^S clear the market with a subsidy of $P - P^M$ on each unit sold.**

the support price would be paid directly by the government to the farmers. The quantity Q^S that the growers would provide in anticipation of the support price P would have resulted in a market-clearing price of P^M. In Figure 4.10, the outlay on the modified plan, $Q^S(P - P^M)$, is considerably less than the outlay on the purchase and storage plan that was actually adopted, $P(Q^S - Q^D)$. In addition, the modified plan involves no costs of storage. (However, under other demand and supply conditions, such as those shown in Figure 4.11, the modified plan could be more costly than the actual plan.)

The purchase and storage plan that was actually adopted eventually backfired in a small way on its proponents. Large government inventories, built up at times of low demand, were used to keep price *down* to the support level, long after market demand had grown to a level like D^1 (Figure 4.11). The amount $A - Q^S$ was supplied (mainly to foreign buyers) out of inventories in each period, until stockpiles were exhausted. Hence, in the later years of the 1960s, the purchase and storage program in a small way led to a reduction in farm incomes, because the surpluses that were accumulated earlier were liquidated by the government, and price was kept down to the level P.

4.3.3. The Problem of Unequal Farm Incomes

One problem with the purchase and storage support program that was perceived very early was that it worked overwhelmingly to the advantage of big farmers. Tied as it was to output, the program rewarded the owners of large, fertile landholdings and new and efficient machinery. The program was much less beneficial to poor farmers of backward technique working small and infertile plots and producing small crops. Indignation began to grow at the spectacle of some

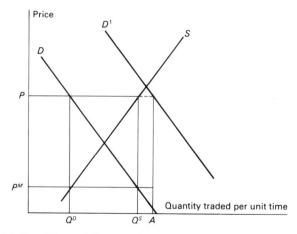

FIGURE 4.11. Effects of the two support schemes with less elastic demand and supply. Effect of selling out of storage after a shift upward in demand.

farmers (including a number of congressmen) taking literally hundreds of thousands of dollars per year in price-support payments, while the typical low-income farmer got very little. In 1959, a crusading Senator from Delaware (a state with few large farms) took steps to end the abuse. He introduced a bill in Congress to prohibit the collection of more than $35 thousand per year in price-support revenues by any one operator. That satisfying exercise in righteousness, unfortunately, had no effect whatever: big operators continued to benefit as before, and small operators were affected not at all.

The reasons why the Senator's law was ineffectual are easy to understand with the help of supply and demand analysis. There are two "categories" of output that are eligible for purchase and storage at the support price P: (1) the entire output of "small" growers, who market *less* than $35 thousand worth of the commodity annually; and (2) the first $35 thousand worth of the output of each "large" grower. There is one "category" of output *not* eligible for purchase and storage: the output of a "large" grower *in excess of* his first $35 thousand worth. If the Senator's program was to have the effect of helping small growers more than large growers, or reducing the expense of the program to the government, it was necessary that the output eligible for support be *less* than $Q^S - Q^D$ (Figure 4.12). If in fact *more* than $Q^S - Q^D$ were eligible for support, then the support program, plus normal market demand Q^D, would enable *all* growers, large and small, to obtain a price P on *all* of their output.

Consider what would happen if the total output that is eligible for support had been *less* than $Q^S - Q^D$. For concreteness, suppose the maximum payment to an individual grower had been set at $15 thousand instead of at $35 thousand. In that case, the total quantity of output eligible for support might have been a (Figure 4.13) and the quantity $Q^S - a$ would have been ineligible for support. The a units would sell at the support price P, and $Q^S - a$ units would sell at the lower market price P^M. The total reduction in support payments,

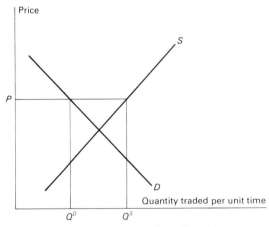

FIGURE 4.12. Excess farm output $(Q^S - Q^D)$ with support price at P.

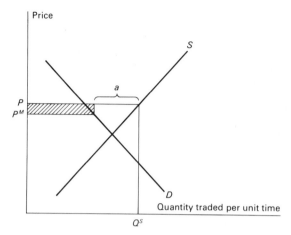

FIGURE 4.13. **Effect of restricting the amount of output eligible for support to *a*: *P* is obtained for those *a* units of output; the remaining $Q^S - a$ units sell for P^M.**

equal in value to the area of the shaded rectangle (Figure 4.13), represents reductions in incomes of the large farmers (where in our example, a "large" farmer is one who sells more than $15 thousand worth of product).

Thus, a bill that had all the trappings of a serious attack on profiteering at government expense turned out to be ineffectual. The reason: insufficient care was taken to measure the relevant economic variable, excess supply at the support price, even though a ready estimate of that variable could have been obtained by examining past quantities of the commodity that the farmers left in storage.

Farm price-support programs are still a part of the law, and limitations on the amounts that individual farmers may receive are also still in force. But the support prices have not been increased for some time; and the growth in world demand for farm products, plus the inflationary policies of governments, have combined to move market prices well above support prices for most commodities.

4.3.4. Price Fixing: Labor Markets

A second area in which market price has often been mistrusted is in the markets for the productive services of individuals, the "labor markets." In these markets some sellers lack the skill to render valuable productive services. As a consequence, the wages that those individuals earn do not correspond to our notion of a decent existence. If the low productivity of some individuals is the chief source of difficulty, then a law that prohibits employers from offering wages below some minimum level will operate directly *against* the interest of those individuals who need help. The pattern of treating symptoms emerges in this case— *problem:* low productivity; *symptom:* low incomes; *policy response:* declare low wages to be illegal.

No enterprise will knowingly continue to use productive inputs that cost more than some alternative input. If a firm must pay its floor sweepers $5 per hour, it will invest heavily in mechanical floor-care equipment, throw away its brooms and dustpans, and lay off many of its sweepers. If it must pay an elevator operator $5 an hour, it will install automatic elevators. When wages are market-determined, and there is no legal minimum, the incentive for these substitutions is reduced. In Figure 4.14, the number of man-hours of unskilled labor demanded has the same negative slope as any market demand curve, and for the same reasons: as price falls, more and more ways are found to substitute the increasingly less expensive input into the production process, just as consumers find more and more ways to substitute less expensive goods into consumption.

If by law the wage rate cannot fall below W_{min}, unskilled labor will be substituted for, until $M* - M^D$ man-hours in unskilled jobs are eliminated. Meanwhile, M^S man-hours are offered and are ready for use at the wage W_{min}. Hence, not only is labor less in demand than at the market wage, but schoolboys and others outside the labor force are attracted by the promise of a high minimum wage into job search that often proves futile, and the apparent rate of unemployment is thereby increased.

A good rule in examining any legislative proposal is to ask: who benefits from the proposal? Who pays for those benefits? Demand and supply analysis suggest that the minimum wage imposes a burden on workers whose wages are low because their productivity is low. It is less obvious, but nonetheless true, that minimum-wage legislation *helps* relatively privileged groups, like high-income workers who run the machinery that replaces unskilled labor, the engineers who design the machinery, and the capitalists who make the machinery.

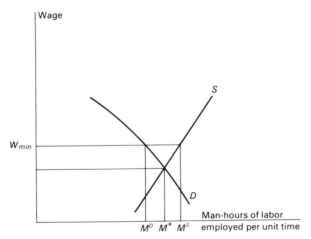

FIGURE 4.14.   **A minimum wage above the market wage increases supply and reduces demand for labor services.**

The effects of minimum-wage legislation can also be viewed from a regional perspective. It has always been true that the minimum wage has served to protect workers in heavily industrialized, highly unionized and high-wage areas of the nation from emerging competition in the rural South, an area to which industry occasionally has moved in the past, in response to the attraction of lower costs in general and lower labor costs in particular. By closing off access to low-priced labor, the minimum-wage laws discourage "flights of capital" such as characterized the textile industry in its movement from New England to the rural South in the 1930s. In one view, that blockage is "good"—it enables Northern union members to go on earning a "decent, living" wage. In an abstract economist's view, the laws constitute a barrier to resource flows in response to price signals—and hence, a barrier to efficient operation. And the socially concerned individual can point to people who are deprived by the laws of the opportunity to improve their own lot in life—the Southern laborers who eagerly offer themselves for "exploitation" at a "substandard, inadequate" wage. The eagerness of the Southerners to earn those low wages is a good illustration of the relativity of judgment on such questions as what constitutes an "adequate" wage.

4.3.5. The Incidence of a Commodity Tax

Suppose the government, for one reason or another, decides to impose a tax on some good, such as liquor, cigarettes, or perfume. How will the tax be paid? Will consumers pay it in the form of higher prices, or will producers pay it in the form of reduced sales and lower profits?

In Figure 4.15, S^0 and D are market supply and demand for the good in the absence of taxation. When the tax is imposed, a fixed sum is collected by the government on every unit produced. For concreteness, suppose the good is cigarettes, and the tax is twenty-five cents per pack. Then every pack of cigarettes sold must bear a stamp, sold by the state to the producer for twenty-five cents. When the stamp is affixed to the pack, the cost of the pack rises by twenty-five cents. The quantity that was offered for $\$P^0$ before the tax is offered for $\$(P^0 + .25)$ after the tax is imposed.

The effect of the tax, then, is to shift the supply curve upward from S^0 to S^1, as illustrated in Figure 4.15, where S^1 differs from S^0 by the amount of the tax. With supply at S^1, the new equilibrium price will be at P^1.

We see that consumers now pay P^1 instead of P^0 per pack, but producers now receive $(P^1 - T)$ instead of P^0 per pack. The tax, then, is borne in part by the consumers, in part by the producers.

If the demand curve were sloped more or less steeply, the apportionment of the tax between consumer and producer would be different. If the demand curve were vertical, for example, the consumers would pay the entire tax. If the demand curve were almost horizontal, the producers would pay almost all of it.

Occasionally, legislators present two arguments in favor of taxes on "bad" items like cigarettes and liquor. First, they tell us, the tax will cut back the rate of use of the "bad." And second, it will generate nice revenues for the state's treasury (usually estimated by multiplying the proposed tax by the current rate of consumption). As we see in Figure 4.15, the higher the revenue receipts are, the less the cutback in consumption will be, and *vice versa*.

4.3.6. Public Higher Education: Some Provocative Questions

The list of issues to which supply and demand analysis can be applied is large. For example, consider the effects of subsidy (in the form of tax financing) of higher education: ask who pays and who benefits, and see if there is any formal difference between public university students who are the offspring of high-income families, and the wealthy farmers who were seen in Section 4.3.2 to benefit most handsomely from agricultural price-support programs. In the one case, wealthy farmers are the beneficiaries of the price-support programs that lead to higher food prices and higher taxes. In the other case, high-income students receive tax-financed benefits, with taxes collected from both high-income *and* low-income tax payers.

It is often suggested that society benefits directly from the financing of universities by tax revenues. That suggestion is certainly valid if higher education would disappear entirely if there were no public universities; but private institutions can and do fill the desired role, so the suggestion has no substance. Conceded, there is a problem that many able students would be denied a university education without some sort of subsidy; but it is far from necessary to found and

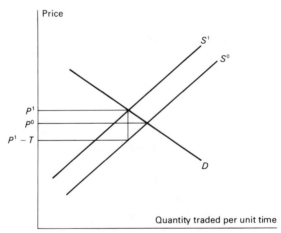

FIGURE 4.15. **An excise tax is like a negative subsidy: it shifts supply downward from S^0 to S^1.**

support universities in order to provide that subsidy. The issue of public support for deserving students can and should be separated from the issue of state-owned and state-run universities.

4.4. FEATURES OF THE ANALYSIS

What common themes can be found in the foregoing applications of economic analysis?

1. Economic incentives—higher returns for producers, more desirable kinds of employment for workers, and more preferred patterns of consumption for consumers—are powerful, and always operative. The *law of demand,* which states that less of a good or activity will be used as its cost increases, is a convenient and usually an accurate way of representing how economic incentives work.
2. Policy design is a subtle and difficult art. If the nature of a specific problem is misunderstood, nonproductive or even counterproductive actions may be taken in the attempt to remedy a bad situation.
3. Persons or groups affected by an economic policy will act to make that policy work to serve their objectives.

How can economic policies and institutions be designed to avoid problems and pitfalls? A difficult question. But economic analysis can help in avoiding costly and nonobvious mistakes.

In Chapter 5, we will explore the main *theoretical* justification underlying the "law of demand," which was stated in the preceding paragraph, item 1.

APPLICATIONS AND EXTENSIONS

1. Suppose the price of gasoline is observed to rise. What effects would you expect to see if you observe
   (a) the average size of automobiles produced
   (b) the number of automobile miles traveled per year
   (c) the demand for urban transit services
   (d) the rate of search for new sources of petroleum by producing firms like Standard and Gulf?
2. "The energy crisis will lead to the construction of smaller, better-insulated homes." Explain why. Is it necessary that a law governing the size and construction of homes be passed in order to produce that desired effect?
3. In 1870, substantially more than half the nation's energy supply came from burning *wood,* in stoves, fireplaces, steamboats, and locomotives. Today, less than one percent comes from that source. Why?

4. Suppose that grade A (large) Valencia oranges sell for $40 per hundredweight in New York, and grade B (medium) Valencias sell for $25. Suppose transportation costs from Orange County to New York are $5 per hundredweight.

   (a) What, given the indicated New York prices, do you think the prices are in Orange County?

   (b) Consider the *ratio* of Grade A to Grade B oranges consumed in the two places. Where would you expect to find that relatively more Grade B oranges are consumed? Why?

5. Leopards are among the threatened species of world wildlife. To preserve these superb animals, concerned groups have brought pressure on people to stop buying (and thereby stop the manufacture of) leopard-skin clothing. In the absence of any property rights in leopards, that pressure may help to preserve the species. But suppose that property rights in wild leopards could easily be established. Would you expect that the pressure to stop harvesting them would increase or reduce their chances for survival?

6. Suppose that the demand for a good vanishes entirely: take horse-drawn buggies as an example. Suppose further that a government program of buggy purchases is instituted to "preserve employment in this important industry, and enhance social welfare."

   (a) Do you think that social welfare would in fact be enhanced by such a program? Clarify your answer in terms of the way resources are used to serve individual preferences.

   (b) Are you aware that some important industries are or were kept afloat by precisely such programs? Examples include watchmaking, shipbuilding, and aircraft manufacture.

7. For more than two decades, quotas were imposed on the importation of petroleum and petroleum products into the U.S. Trace the effects of the import quota on (1) the U.S. market price (2) the rate of consumption of U.S. reserves (3) the vulnerability of the U.S. to future "oil blackmail." Does the argument "quotas are necessary in order to protect our domestic production capability" make sense to you? That argument constituted a central part of the rationale for quotas.

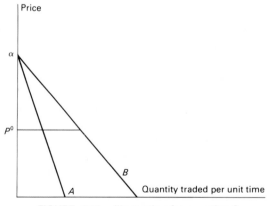

FIGURE 4.16.   Illustration for question 8.

8. Consider the demand curves A and B (Figure 4.16). Use the definition of elasticity to determine whether the price elasticity of A is greater than or equal to the price elasticity of B at some price $P = P^0$. Let the formulae for these curves be:

$$P^A = \alpha - \beta^1_q \qquad\qquad P^B = \alpha - \beta^2_q$$

where $\beta^1 > \beta^2 > 0$.

9. A nation's *current balance of payments* may be defined as the total value of goods sold to foreigners, less the total value of goods purchased from foreigners, during some time period (e.g., one year). *Devaluation* is a reduction in the number of units of foreign money that is required to buy a unit of the devaluing nation's money.

   (a) Suppose a new rate of exchange is announced between the British pound and the U.S. dollar: instead of £1 = $2.40, the rate is £1 = $2.20. Who has devalued, the U.S. or Britain?

   (b) If the U.S. dollar is devalued relative to the British pound, will Scotch whiskey cost U.S. drinkers more than before, or less?

   (c) Show that if foreign demand for a nation's exports is inelastic, and the domestic demand for foreign goods is inelastic, then a devaluation will lead to a smaller balance of payments.

10. Calculate the formula of a demand curve whose elasticity is exactly -1 for *every* price.

11. (Marshallian Stability Analysis.) In Figure 4.5, page 68, we interpret the supply curve S to indicate the "reservation price" of suppliers for different rates of output. (Thus, to get the output rate Q^1, price must be *at least* P^1, to get Q^2, P^2, etc.) The demand curve indicates prices that will *clear the market* of different quantities. (Thus in the diagram, if Q^1 is offered, the market clears at P^1, at Q^2, P^2, etc.)

   The Marshallian Stability Test: *If the market clearing price exceeds the suppliers' reservation price, then output will be increased. If the suppliers' reservation price exceeds the market clearing price, then output will be reduced.*

   (a) Verify that if S and D are "normally sloped," then equilibrium will be stable, according to the Marshallian test.

   (b) Verify that in the market shown in Figure 4.6, page 69, equilibrium is *not* stable, using the Marshallian test.

   (c) Verify that in the market shown in Figure 4.7, page 69, equilibrium *is* stable, using the Marshallian test.

CHAPTER FIVE

The Law
of Demand

Man's chief difference from the brutes lies in . . . the number
and in the fantastic and unnecessary character of his wants,
physical, moral, aesthetic and intellectual. Had his whole life not
been a quest for the superfluous, he would never have established himself as inexpungably as he has done in the necessary.

WILLIAM JAMES (1896)

The task undertaken in this chapter is to convey a deeper understanding of the
theory of consumer demand. In Chapter 2, "toy" examples were developed
from hypothetical small-scale societies, and Chapter 4 examined some of the
simpler issues encountered in the real world. A critically important condition
was assumed to hold as those examples and analyses were presented: *the
quantity of a good demanded decreases as its price rises (relative to the prices
of other goods)*.

That condition is important in the context of those simple examples, because
if it fails to hold, the exchange process might not reach an equilibrium; price
changes might not bring about equality between the excess demands of some
traders and the excess supplies of the remaining traders. That problem of equilibrium's stability was reviewed in Chapter 4, Section 4.2.3.

Because the slope of a demand curve is such an important factor in theory,
economists have developed a *theory of consumer behavior* in an attempt to discover whether or not negatively sloped demand curves can reasonably be viewed

as a "law"—that is, as a condition that can be expected to hold at all times and in all markets.

Until around 1915, it was routinely taken for granted that if individuals do in fact seek to maximize the satisfaction that they derive from the goods they consume, then all demand curves will be negatively sloped. Before that time, theorists had studied the effects that positively sloped demand curves might have; and the possibility was recognized that there might be a positively sloped demand curve for some important basic foodstuff in a poor society (see Section 5.3.5). Finally in 1915, a rigorous formal analysis of negatively sloped demand curves was provided; that work, which was done by a Russian economist and published in an Italian journal, was not widely known among English-speaking economists until almost twenty-five years later.[1] That investigation has, through time, come to be recognized as the cornerstone of the theory of consumer behavior.

We will trace through that theory of consumer behavior in this chapter, for several reasons. First, the results that will be obtained are interesting in and of themselves. Second, the formal analytic procedures developed here can be used in modified but recognizable form throughout economic theory; and it is worth mastering those procedures in the context of demand theory, because they can then be used with little effort in other important contexts. Third, this analysis can be a source of insight into the way that economic theorizing proceeds. Once the student has acquired that insight, he can step back from the issues that are being examined at a theoretical level, and he can critically consider the process of theorizing itself.

5.1. INDIVIDUAL PREFERENCES AND OPTIMUM CHOICE

5.1.1. Analytical Assumptions

In the first five sections of this chapter, a geometrical apparatus will be developed which is very useful in illustrating the major propositions of the economic theory of consumer behavior, and which, in fact, has historically been useful in deducing some of those propositions. The apparatus incorporates one assumption about the world that is made in order to simplify the task of presenting the analysis geometrically; and it embodies several further assumptions about the behavior of individuals and workings of markets.

Assumption I (Analytical Simplification): There are exactly *two goods* in the world.

By this assumption, it becomes possible to represent different *goods bundles*

[1]E. Slutzky, "On the Theory of the Budget of the Consumer," *Giornale degli Economisti* (1915), translated and reprinted in G. J. Stigler and K. Boulding, eds., *AEA Readings in Price Theory* (Homewood, Ill.: Richard D. Irwin, 1952).

as points in a two-dimensional diagram, as shown in Figure 5.1. For concreteness, suppose the two goods are called "food" and "warmth" (we could equally well call them I and II, or A and B; the designation is not too significant. All that matters is that we must be able to specify quantity dimensions per unit of time so that we can measure the rate of use of each good. We must also be able to agree that the goods can readily be exchanged among individuals. We might have difficulty in designating the two goods as "security" and "pleasure," for example, because of the conceptual problem of measuring or exchanging quantities of these two sentiments.)

The point A in Figure 5.1 is a goods bundle containing a_1 units of food and a_2 units of warmth (measured in calories or BTUs per time period—no problem). A consumer who obtains the goods bundle A will consume a_1 units of food and a_2 units of warmth per unit of time (per month, say). By such a representation, any point in the area above and to the right of the two axes, and along either axis, is a bundle containing non-negative quantities of the two goods and denoting non-negative rates of consumption of the two goods. That area, then, is the *goods space* of our two-good world. Point B contains b_1 units of food and no warmth; the origin, point 0, contains no units of either good. A point such as C, which contains negative quantities, and hence negative rates of consumption of a good, is given no interpretation at this stage of analysis. It is simply ruled out as a possibility.

The assumption that there are only two goods in the economy is a relatively innocuous one. All of the results that are developed with the aid of this assumption can be generalized, and shown to hold when there are many goods, except that in more advanced texts it is seen that there are results which pertain to *complementarity* between goods (automobiles and gasoline are complementary; so

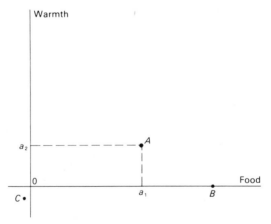

FIGURE 5.1.   In a world of two goods, *A* and *B* are *goods bundles* (points in
             goods space).

are sugar and coffee), and those results cannot be derived from an analysis that assumes only two goods. In our two-good world, the goods must be substitutes, they cannot be complements.

Assumption II (Existence of an Ordering):   Every individual, when confronted by a *choice* between any two goods bundles, can state (or will reveal) which bundle he prefers, or whether he is indifferent between them. Only three possibilities exist: the first bundle is preferred to the second; the second is preferred to the first; or the two are regarded as equally desirable (in which case, the individual is said to be indifferent between the bundles).

The important point to notice in connection with this assumption is that each individual can rank all possible bundles: no matter which pair of bundles in the goods space is compared, anyone can express preference for one or the other; or indifference between the two. For example, in comparing the bundles A and B of Figure 5.1, a particular individual might choose A. His neighbor might be indifferent. But both individuals must have a ranking of the two suggested possible bundles.

Assumption III (Desirability of More Goods):   If a goods bundle is changed by adding more to at least one of the goods, then every individual will rank the bundle more highly after the change.

According to this assumption, the goods bundles that lie in the shaded area in Figure 5.2 (or on the boundary lines of the shaded area) must be ranked more highly than the bundle A, because all of them contain more of at least one of the goods than does A. Any movement away from the origin is a movement toward more highly ranked goods bundles.

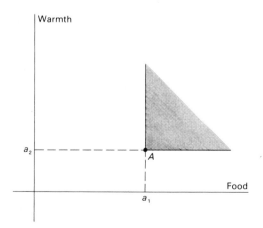

FIGURE 5.2.   The shaded area and its boundaries contain goods bundles that are preferred to A.

Assumption IV (Consistency of Preferences): If *A, B,* and *C* are any three goods bundles, and if an individual has ranked them so that *A* is not preferred to *B* and *B* is not preferred to *C*, then *A* cannot be preferred to *C*.

This condition, called *transitivity* by mathemeticians and logicians, is understandably required if the preference ordering of an individual is to have any reliable analytical significance.[2] For as analysts, we want to be able to treat preference in much the same way as we treat an ordering on sizes or weights. The job of a tailor would be confusing if he is told to make suits for three customers, and he is further told

Mr. A's measurements are all ten percent larger than Mr. B's
Mr. B's measurements are all six percent larger than Mr. C's
Mr. C's measurements are all three percent larger than Mr. A's.

The tailor would undoubtedly conclude that a joke was being played, and give up. Preference is certainly not as immutable as the relative sizes of three grown men, and an individual who is in the process of changing his mind about what he prefers might be observed to violate Assumption IV. However, the job of predicting or analyzing consumer behavior when preferences do not change is sufficiently interesting and difficult, so we will insist on dealing only with cases that satisfy the consistency condition of Assumption IV.[3]

5.1.2. Indifference Curves

The goods space can be ''partitioned'' or ''separated'' in a useful way, in accord with the preferences of a particular individual. The first step is to choose an arbitrary goods bundle, say bundle *A* in Figure 5.3. The second step is to identify all the goods bundles that are equally valued to *A*, according to our individual's ranking. These bundles are represented by the curve labeled *I(A)* in Figure 5.3. Then all bundles on or above *I(A)* are preferred or equally valued to *A*; while *A* is preferred to all bundles below *I(A)*, bundles that lie between *I(A)* and the origin. The curve *I(A)* is an example of an *indifference curve:* it is a collection of bundles among which the individual has no preference.

For the time being, we will assume that there is *at least* one indifference curve that passes through every point in the goods space; and we will further assume that the curves are continuous (no gaps or breaks) and convex (bowed outward in the direction of the origin). From the assumptions of the previous section, we

[2]Recently, highly abstract work has been undertaken by economic theorists to develop consumer theory *without* transitivity. Alternative conditions can be found that make it unnecessary to assume transitivity.

[3]Two more assumptions will be made shortly. In addition to those two, still other assumptions are, strictly speaking, necessary, but their importance is not easy to make clear in an informal analysis, and so they will be omitted from the present discussion. In Chapter 6, Section 6.5, a sufficient set of assumptions is used to derive ''indifference curves'' in a rigorous manner. At this stage we will proceed on the basis of Assumptions I–IV, with V and VI to follow shortly.

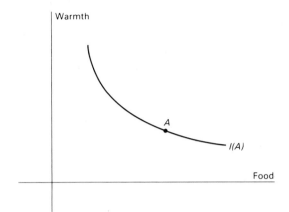

FIGURE 5.3. *I(A)* is the *indifference curve* through *A:* the set of goods bundles that are neither preferred to *A* nor less preferred than *A*.

can deduce two important properties of these curves: first, they are always negatively sloped at every point; and second, there can be *no more than* one indifference curve through any point.

Negative slope. If indifference curves were not negatively sloped everywhere, there would be intervals in which Assumption III is violated. For suppose we have an indifference curve with an interval of positive or zero slope, beginning at point *A* (Figure 5.4). If the indifference curve is positively sloped, as shown, it will pass through points *A* and *C*. This implies that the consumer is indifferent between *A* and another bundle, *C*, which contains more of both goods than does *A*. But that would violate Assumption III, and so there can be no indif-

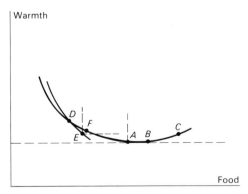

FIGURE 5.4. **Indifference curves must be negatively sloped and cannot intersect, or the assumption that goods are desirable cannot hold.**

ference curve connecting A and C. By a similar argument, there can be no indifference curve connecting A and B, because B contains more food and no less warmth than A. Indifference curves cannot be positively sloped, nor parallel to either axis of the diagram. They must be negatively sloped throughout their lengths.

Only one indifference curve through any goods bundle. If the goods bundle D had two curves passing through it, as in Figure 5.4, then we would have the conditions: D is not preferred to E, and F is not preferred to D. However, F contains more of both goods than does E, and consequently F must be preferred to E. Thus, if indifference curves intersect, as they do at D, we violate either the consistency Assumption IV, or the value-of-more-goods Assumption III. We conclude that indifference curves cannot intersect: there is at most one indifference curve through any goods bundle.

Convexity. In addition to Assumptions I to IV, we have assumed that indifference curves are convex. The convexity of an indifference curve needs further discussion, because it implies something interesting about the structure of individual preferences. In Figure 5.5, we note that A and B are two goods bundles on the same indifference curve. In bundle A, food is *relatively abundant* compared to B. That is to say, the amount of food held per unit of warmth is greater at A than at B. We ask: what is the maximum amount of warmth that an individual will give up to get one more unit of food? He will give up an amount which, with the added unit of food in exchange, leaves him on the same indifference curve he started from. The bundles A' and B' identify the moves from A and B which leave the individual as well off, but with an additional unit of food in each case. Food is relatively less abundant at A, compared to B; and because it is the individual will give up more warmth to get an additional unit of food when he is at A, compared to when he is at B. The convexity of the indifference curve, then, is a consequence of

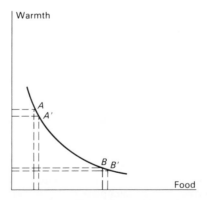

FIGURE 5.5. When food is relatively scarce (as at A), more warmth will be given up to get additional food than when warmth is relatively scarce (as at B).

Assumption V (Rate of Substitution):   Along any indifference curve, the more abundant the first good is relative to the second, the more of the first good that will be voluntarily given up in exchange for one unit of the second.

In the economist's jargon, the *rate of substitution* increases with relative abundance along the indifference curve.

Assumption V strikes most people as reasonable, and convexity follows directly from Assumption V. But convexity is not only a reasonable property, it is an enormously convenient one, as well; how convenient will be appreciated in some part before the reader finishes this chapter.

5.1.3. The Individual's Preference Ordering (Indifference Map)

Figure 5.6 depicts several indifference curves. It is sometimes called an "indifference map." For some analytical purposes, an indifference map is a useful way to represent an individual's preferences. In Figure 5.6, the curve $I(B)$ contains goods bundles that are more highly valued than those lying along $I(A)$. Any bundle along $I(A)$ will have an interval of $I(B)$ lying in the more-of-both-goods region above and to the right of it, hence any $I(B)$ bundle must be preferred to any $I(A)$ bundle. In general, in comparing the individual's ranking of goods bundles along two indifference curves, the curve that lies farther from the origin will contain the preferred bundles.

An indifference map, then, is a selection of a few indifference curves that partially depict the structure of an individual's preferences. Examples of indifference maps for two individuals with drastically different tastes are shown in Figures 5.6 and 5.7.

The indifference map is not a full representation of the individual's preference ordering, however. Between any two curves shown, there will be many goods

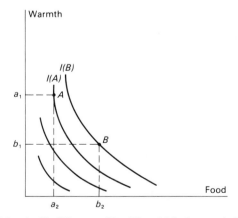

FIGURE 5.6.   An "Indifference Map" in which the goods bundle *B* is preferred to *A*.

bundles, each lying on its own indifference curve. It of course is impossible to depict the full and complete preference ordering, in which every goods bundle is precisely located relative to every other one, by means of geometry.

5.1.4. The Income Constraint

According to Assumption III, a consumer will always prefer goods bundles containing more of both goods. But what determines how much of both goods he can obtain? That will depend on the resources he has at his disposal, which he can use to acquire the two goods. Economists call the flow of goods the individual's *income:* hence, the individual's consumption rates of the two goods are limited by his income. An individual's income can be measured most simply in a two-good world by his goods endowment. In the example of exchange among prisoners (Chapter 2, Section 2.3), every man had the same endowment of chocolate and cigarettes. In the less restrictive analysis that will be developed in this chapter, different individuals can have different endowments; but as we will see, gains from exchange can still be realized.

In Figure 5.8, let E be the endowment bundle of the individual we are observing. Many individuals engage in a process of exchange, some giving up warmth to get more food, others giving up food to get more warmth. We will suppose that the equilibrium rate of exchange among those individuals is two units of warmth per unit of food: at that rate of exchange, the market is cleared. Also at that rate of exchange, the individual whose endowment is E could exchange away all his warmth and move to the point A, or he could exchange away all his food and move to the point B; or he could exchange away some warmth and move to a point between E and A; or he could exchange away some food and move to a point between E and B. The line connecting A and B is the individual's *income constraint* line. It passes through his endowment point E, and its

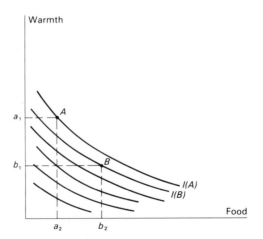

FIGURE 5.7.   Another individual's indifference map. He prefers A to B.

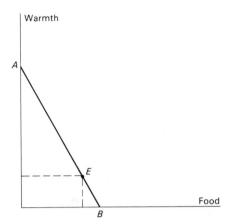

FIGURE 5.8.   An individual's endowment *E* and the exchange rate between the goods determines the position of the income constraint line *AB*.

slope shows the rate at which food and warmth are traded when the exchange process is in equilibrium. The individual can obtain any goods bundle on or below his income constraint line, but goods bundles above that line are not accessible or available to him: he ''can't afford'' bundles above the line.

The important point to notice is that the income constraint line is determined, in this two-good world, by the individual's goods endowment, and by the equilibrium rate of exchange between the two goods. The representation of the income constraint as a straight line reflects an important assumption:

Assumption VI (Competitive Exchange):   The equilibrium rate of exchange between goods is not measurably affected by the exchange decision of one individual.

If the market rate of exchange varied in response to the amount of food or warmth that our individual offered to exchange, then that fact would affect the choices open to him: the line *AB* in Figure 5.8 would not accurately represent his available choices. Assumption VI, then, implies that an individual buyer does not bid up the price of a good as he increases his consumption of the good. (Of course, if *all* consumers decided to purchase more food and less warmth, then we do not expect the rate of exchange between the two goods to remain unchanged.) If the exchange decisions of single individuals have no effect on market prices, the exchange process is said to be *competitive,* and the exchange rates are said to be competitively determined. Hence, Assumption VI could be stated in the compact form ''market exchange rates are competitively determined.''

5.1.5. The Consumer's Optimum Choice

The problem that the individual consumer seeks to solve, then, can be represented in Figure 5.9. He wants to find the most highly preferred goods bundle

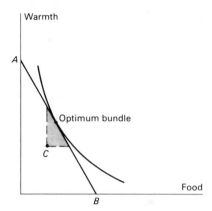

FIGURE 5.9. The bundle *C* cannot be optimal because bundles with more of both goods are attainable.

he can afford; that is, he must choose from the bundles that lie on or below the income constraint line. Somewhere along the line there is a goods bundle which surpasses every other bundle he can afford in the satisfaction that it yields him. We call this the *optimum choice* goods bundle. We know that the optimum choice bundle will not be found *below AB,* for every bundle like *C* is dominated by other attainable bundles in the shaded triangular area above *C* (Figure 5.9). Those bundles contain more of *both* goods than does *C.*

Furthermore, as long as the indifference curves are convex and do not contain any flat intervals that have the same slope as the income constraint line, there will be only one optimum choice bundle. (Figure 5.10 illustrates the possibility of *many* optimum choice bundles if indifference curves have flat intervals.)

If indifference curves are smooth and have no flat intervals, then the optimum choice goods bundle must be found at a point where an indifference curve

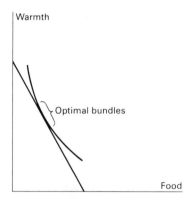

FIGURE 5.10. **Many bundles could simultaneously be optimal if indifference curves had "flat" intervals.**

touches but does not cross the income constraint line; and there can be only one such point, because the indifference curves are convex and nonintersecting. If the curves were not convex, or if the possibility of intersection of curves were not ruled out, there could be more than one optimum choice, as shown in Figure 5.11. A and B would be optimum choices if the curves were not required to be convex.

5.1.6. Summary and Criticism

Under a set of explicit assumptions, we have seen how a single best-attainable goods bundle is "discovered" by an individual consumer. The position of that bundle will depend on (1) the individual's preferences, (2) the individual's income, and (3) the market rates of exchange between the goods.

Even a hasty reading will disclose that the foregoing discussion is *not* concerned with the question of how consumers draw up their budgets. Nor does it attempt to prescribe how consumers *should* spend their incomes. Rather, it shows that a set of assumptions can be specified, from which it can be deduced that an individual's demand for the various goods available in the economy will depend only on his preferences, his income, and the exchange rates (or relative prices) of all goods. Economists have always focused on the importance of preferences, incomes, and prices in discussing how individuals behave; and the theory described in Sections 5.1.1 through 5.1.5 indicates a way in which those variables can be made the principal components of a theory of choice.

It is worthwhile pausing to consider what the theory cannot and does not do in the form in which it has been presented here. There is no hope that the theory will yield useful information on how preferences are formed, or can be changed; and there is no hope of evaluating whether preferences are "good" or "bad." The analysis cannot cope successfully with individuals whose preferences fluctuate rapidly; and it is also of doubtful value if relative prices or incomes are

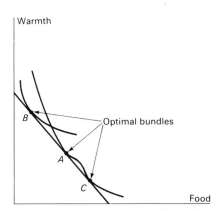

FIGURE 5.11.   Multiple optima could occur if indifference curves were non-convex or intersecting.

changing rapidly. Finally, of course, the theory may be very unsuccessful if either of the Assumptions II (existence of an ordering) or IV (consistency of preferences) should fail to hold; and the theory will require substantial modification if any of the other assumptions except I (two goods) fails to hold.

The theory, then, cannot answer some interesting questions, and it is derived from some restrictive assumptions. Is it a useful device or, as some critics contend, an idle game? Every economist must answer that question for himself. In my own view, the theory of consumer choice is useful in illuminating how, under explicit conditions, individuals will respond to market exchange opportunities, and how they will benefit from those opportunities. There is undoubtedly much room for improvement in the theory, and when those improvements are made, they will be welcomed and incorporated into the analysis. For the time being, the theory whose rudiments are presented here is the best tool that we have available for predicting individuals' responses to market opportunities.

Predictions about individuals' responses to market opportunities will be derived from the theory, in the remainder of this chapter.

5.2. TWO-PERSON, TWO-GOOD EXCHANGE AGAIN

5.2.1. The Edgeworth Box

With the aid of indifference curve analysis, the gains that result from exchange can be shown clearly.

In Figure 5.12, indifference maps are presented for two individuals who, like the prisoners in Chapter 2, are the only traders in a society. The point *a* identifies the initial endowment of Trader A; point *b* shows the endowment of Trader B. (Points *a* and *b* are the goods bundles that Trader A and Trader B, respectively, possess before any exchange takes place.) In order to explore and illustrate the possibility of gain from exchange, these two indifference maps are superimposed on each other in a particular way.

1. Rotate the map of Trader B until the origin is in the upper right-hand corner instead of the lower left-hand corner (Figure 5.13). B's quantities of food and warmth now are measured leftward and downward, instead of rightward and upward.

2. Superimpose B's map on A's in such a way that (i) B's food and warmth axes are parallel to A's, and (ii) B's endowment point *b* lies on top of A's endowment point *a* (Figure 5.14). The points *b* and *a* coincide at the point labeled 0 in Figure 5.14.

By this construction we obtain an *Edgeworth Box,* named after F. Y. Edgeworth, an immortal economic theorist who lived in late Victorian England.

The dimensions of the Edgeworth Box measure the quantities of the two goods that are available for exchange within the two-man economy. The height of the box is equal to the combined initial warmth endowment of Trader A and

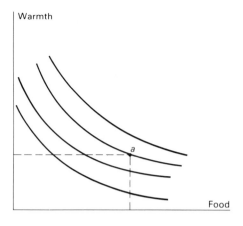

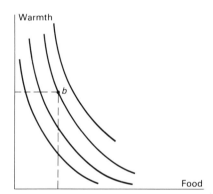

FIGURE 5.12. Trader A's preference ordering and endowment.
Trader B's preference ordering and endowment.

Trader B; the width of the box shows their combined initial endowment of food. The effect of an exchange is to move the two traders away from point 0 to another point within the box. The dimensions of the box are not changed by exchange: the same total amounts of both goods are available to be consumed by the traders after exchange, but the holdings of each trader do change. Suppose, for example, the traders move to the point C (Figure 5.14). Trader A gets w units of warmth, and gives up f units of food in exchange. The move from 0 to C, then, involves a rate of exchange of w/f: this rate of exchange is measured by the slope of the line connecting 0 and C.

Exchange must result in a move from the initial endowment point to some point that lies within the shaded region of Figure 5.15. That region is bounded by the indifference curves that pass through 0: $I(a)$ is Trader A's curve through 0, and $I(b)$, Trader B's curve. Trader A will resist any suggestion of a trade that involves a move to a goods bundle that lies between $I(a)$ and the origin of his indif-

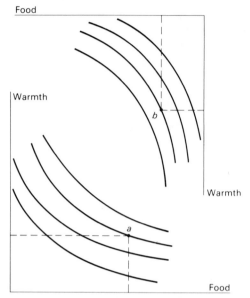

**FIGURE 5.13.   Trader A's preference ordering and endowment.
Trader B's preference ordering and endowment.**

ference map; the bundle 0 on *I(a)* is preferred to any bundle lying below *I(a)*. Similarly, Trader B will resist any suggestion that they move to a bundle lying *above I(b)*—between the origin of his indifference map and *I(b)*. The shaded area contains all trades from 0 that are potentially agreeable to both traders: trades lying outside the shaded area would leave one or the other of the two traders feeling less well-off than before trade.

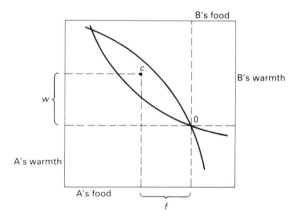

FIGURE 5.14.   An "Edgeworth Box" for Traders A and B.

5.2.2. The Contract Curve and the Pareto Condition

Is it always possible for two individuals to realize gains from exchange in two commodities? The answer, clearly, is no. There are endowments which have no trades associated with them that are potentially agreeable to both traders. These endowments occur where one of the indifference curves of Trader A is tangent to an indifference curve of Trader B. As we see in Figure 5.15, any move away from a tangency point like α takes one or both traders to a lower indifference curve. The move to γ makes both traders worse off; the move to β makes Trader B worse off.

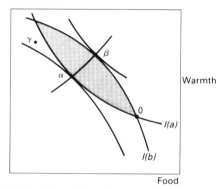

FIGURE 5.15.   The region of mutually beneficial exchange.

Divisions (or allocations) of the two goods which are characterized by tangency between the traders' indifference curves are so important that they are given a name: they trace out what is called the *contract curve*. If the indifference curves of the two traders are smooth and convex, and have no flat intervals, there will be exactly one point of tangency on every indifference curve of either trader, and the contract curve will be as shown in Figure 5.15.

If the two traders begin with goods endowments that don't lie on the contract curve, gains from exchange are possible, and bargaining or trading can continue to the mutual benefit of the two traders until the contract curve is reached. In Figure 5.15, successful trading will take the two traders from 0 to one of the points on the contract curve between α and β. Without further information there is no way to predict the point on the contract curve at which the process of exchange will terminate. We do know that if the traders are going to reach the contract curve after only one trade, it is necessary that the exchange rate be equal to the common slope of the indifference curves at the point on the contract curve to which the move is made, as shown in Figure 5.16. If, as in Figure 5.17, the traders move from 0 to a point like A or B, where the tangency condition is not satisfied, then further exchange will be of mutual benefit.

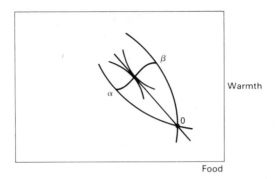

FIGURE 5.16.   An exchange to the contract curve in one step.

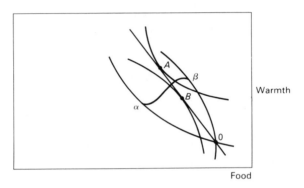

FIGURE 5.17.   An exchange rate that does not arrive at the contract curve.

The property that holds only along the contract curve—that exchange offers no prospect of gain to both traders—has been an important criterion in judging whether or not resources are allocated *efficiently*. The term "efficiently" here has a very specific meaning which can be illustrated in the context of a two-person, two-good exchange. If greater satisfaction for one of the traders can be obtained from a reallocation of available goods, and the other trader is not made worse off by that reallocation, then the initial allocation is inefficient. Only when neither trader's condition can be improved without injury to the other is the allocation of resources *efficient*. The condition of efficient allocation, that no reallocation can yield improvement for some without injury to others, is called the *Pareto Condition*, after the major Italian economist who indicated its importance. In more general settings, with more numerous traders, and with production of goods as well as their exchange, the Pareto Condition is the criterion for judging whether resource use is efficient. Later on (in Chapter 10), we will give careful attention to the question of how helpful the Pareto Condition is in judging whether or not resources are allocated well, from the standpoint of the welfare of society's individual members.

*5.3. THE SLOPE OF INDIVIDUAL DEMAND CURVES

5.3.1. Money

In the text of this chapter, the discussion of market exchange focused on a world of two goods. In such a world, there is only one consequential price—namely, the rate of exchange between the two goods. In a world of many goods, there would be difficulty in keeping track of the exchange rates for all possible pairs of goods, and so the society contrives a single "good" in terms of which the values of all other goods are measured. In the parable of the island paradise in Chapter 2, that good was called "markers"; in more conventional settings it is called *money*. The rate of exchange between a good and money is the good's price.

Money can be introduced as a third good in our two-good food and warmth world. We assume that money doesn't enter into the individual's preference ordering: no matter what his holdings of food, warmth, and money are, he would just as soon have the best combination of food and warmth that an extra dollar can buy as have the extra dollar itself. The preference ordering, then, is assumed to be unaffected by the introduction of money; it can be represented as an ordering over the two goods, food and warmth, just as in Section 5.1.3. Money enters the analysis in a convenient and meaningful way through the income constraint line. If the individual's endowment is received in the form of money, instead of in the form of food and warmth, then he can spend his money to buy those two valued goods. If the amount of the individual's money income is M, and prices of food and warmth are P_f and P_w, respectively, then the individual can afford to buy M/P_f units of food if he uses his entire money income to buy food; or M/P_w units of warmth if he uses his entire money income to buy warmth; or he can buy any combination of food and warmth lying on or below the line connecting the points M/P_f and M/P_w. In Figure 5.18 let the point B be at the distance M/P_f from the origin, and let the point A be at the distance M/P_w from the origin. Then the constraint line determined by the individual's money income, M, is as shown in Figure 5.18. The position of the constraint line is determined by the individual's money income (his endowment) and the prices of the two goods. As in the analysis which did not include money explicitly, his optimal choice goods bundle will depend on those variables, and on his preference ordering.

5.3.2. The "Law" of Demand

We are now ready and able to make the concept of a demand curve more precise, and to see in more detail why demand curves are usually drawn with negative slope.

According to the theory of consumer behavior, the rate at which an individual purchases a good is determined once his optimum goods bundle is chosen; and

*The material in this section may be too advanced for some introductory coverage. The summary in Section 5.3.7. is accessible and should be read.

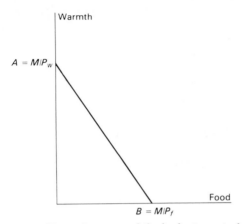

FIGURE 5.18.   Money income and the budget constraint line.

that bundle will depend on his preferences, his income, and the prices of all goods in the economy. The individual's demand curve for a particular good is obtained by holding his income, and the prices of all other goods, at a fixed level; and observing how his purchases of the good in question will vary in response to changes in the price of the good.

The reason for paying special attention to the effect of changes in the good's own price is that price adjustments are seen to be of central importance in the process of achieving market equilibrium. Price adjustments do the bulk of the work in bringing about the necessary equality between quantity supplied and quantity demanded. Hence, the way quantity demanded responds to changes in price must be of paramount interest.

It is commonly assumed, as in Chapters 1, 2, and 4, that the total amount of a good purchased by all buyers will be inversely related to the good's price: as price rises, total purchases decline. If it could be deduced that every individual buys less of a good when its price rises—if every individual's demand curve for the good were negatively sloped—then the total purchases by all individuals would certainly be inversely related to price. As a theoretical exercise, then, we will see whether the "law of demand" can be deduced from our theory of consumer behavior, as a proposition about the purchase behavior of a single individual. The "law" was stated by a great economist:[4]

> There is then one *Law of Demand,* which is common to all demands, viz. that the greater the amount to be sold, the smaller will be the price at which it will find purchasers. . . .

Notice that Marshall states the "law" as an empirical proposition: his phrasing in effect says: "we have never seen or observed a positively sloped demand curve

[4]Alfred Marshall, *Principles of Economics,* 3rd ed. (London, 1895), p. 175.

for a good, and we never expect to see one.'' As an empirical proposition, the
"law" may be valid. However, as we shall see, it *cannot* be deduced from our
theory of consumer behavior. Nonetheless, the attempt to deduce it from consumer theory is worthwhile, because in the attempt we discover important relationships among the variables which affect an individual's consumption behavior—namely, his income and the prices of goods.

5.3.3. Income Effects

Recall that the income constraint line separates the goods space into two parts: a
set of attainable goods bundles and a set of unattainable goods bundles. We first
observe what happens to the set of attainable goods bundles as income changes.
An individual whose income is M can afford M/P_f units of food per unit of time,
or M/P_w units of warmth (Figure 5.18). The income constraint line is the line
connecting these two quantities; the individual can afford any goods bundle on
or below that line.

Now suppose his income increases from M to M', as in Figure 5.19. He can
now afford more of both goods: his income constraint line is the line connecting
M'/P_f and M'/P_w. When the income constraint line shifts outward from the origin,
the individual's ability to purchase goods, or his *real income,* increases. Any outward shift in the income constraint line enables the individual to consume more of
either good (it increases his real income); an inward shift means he can no longer
consume as much as before of both goods (it reduces his real income). If the income constraint line is parallel to its original position after it shifts, then the relative price of the two goods, P_f/P_w, is unchanged.

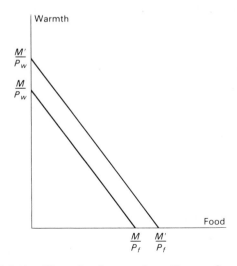

FIGURE 5.19.   Effect of an increase in real income from M to M'.

The adjective ''real'' is used to remind us that an apparent gain in income may not be what it seems: if, for example, the individual's money income M *doubles* to $2M$, but the prices also double from P_f and P_w to $2P_f$ and $2P_w$, then the individual is neither worse off nor better off than he was before the change: his real income is unchanged, because his income constraint line does not shift.

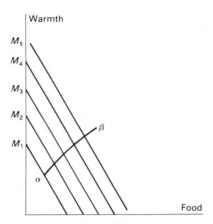

FIGURE 5.20. An income-consumption curve, both income effects positive.

Suppose, in Figure 5.20, the income constraint line is the one labeled M_1, and the individual's optimum goods bundle is the point α. We observe what happens when real income increases to higher levels M_2, M_3, and so forth; as illustrated in Figure 5.20, the increases in real income occur with no change in relative prices. The goods bundles that are chosen as income increases determine a curve, called the *income consumption curve*. The income consumption curve can take one of two interesting shapes. If the individual consumes more of both goods as his income increases, then the curve traces a path like $\alpha\beta$ in Figure 5.20; or if he consumes less of one of the goods when his income increases, a path like $\alpha\beta$ in Figure 5.21 is traced. As seen there, less warmth is consumed with further increases in income beyond the level M_5. In Figure 5.20, both goods are *normal* goods for the individual depicted. The income effect on the consumption of both goods is positive. In Figure 5.21, warmth is an *inferior good* for the individual at income levels above M_5. Above M_5, the *income effect* on the consumption of warmth is negative. When more income leads to a lower rate of consumption, the good in question is said to be *inferior*.

5.3.4. Substitution Effects

Another interesting shift in the budget line is brought about by a change in the relative prices of the two goods. Suppose the money price of food falls, but the money price of warmth remains unchanged (Figure 5.22). The income constraint line shifts outward from M_1 to M_2 as shown. This shift means not only that rela-

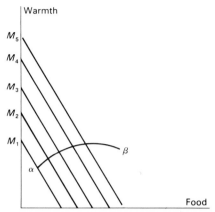

FIGURE 5.21.   An income consumption curve, with negative income effect on warmth beyond the income level M_5.

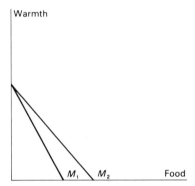

FIGURE 5.22.   A rise in real income due to a drop in the price of food.

tive prices have changed; *it also means that real income is greater, because the set of attainable consumption bundles is unambiguously larger.* (The set is expanded to include all the consumption bundles above M_1, and on or below M_2.) We have already seen how an individual's consumption responds to changes in income; we now are curious as to how his consumption changes when relative prices change, *but real income is unchanged.* To investigate that issue, we must find a way to depict a change in relative prices which does not at the same time mean a change in real income. To meet that goal, an arbitrary judgment is rendered:

> When the price of one good falls, relative prices change, and the consumer's real income increases. Suppose his money income is reduced after the price falls, in such an amount that, at the *new* relative prices, he can just afford to buy the consumption bundle that was his optimum choice at the *old* relative prices. Then the price reduction and the money income reduction, taken together, are said to leave the individual at the same real income level as before the price reduction.

In Figure 5.23, the move from M_1 to M_2 is the effect of the price change. A parallel shift downward from M_2 to M'_2, so that the income constraint line passes through α, the optimum choice consumption bundle before the price change, leaves relative prices at the new level, but real income at the old level.

How, then, does purchase behavior change when relative prices change but real income is unchanged? That question asks: where will the optimum choice consumption bundle be found if the income constraint line shifts from M_1 to M'_2 (Figure 5.23)?

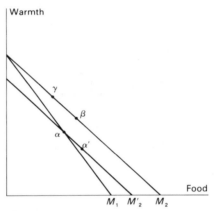

FIGURE 5.23.   Real income and relative price components of a change in food price.

By simple chain of reasoning, it can be shown that when the price of food falls, and the real income gain which results from that drop is offset by an appropriate reduction in money income, then the quantity of food consumed must increase.

The point α was the optimum choice bundle on M_1. It follows that α is preferred to any bundle on or below M_1. After the individual adjusts to the change in relative prices that is represented by the shift from M_1 to M'_2, his optimum choice bundle must necessarily lie along M'_2. But bundles along M'_2 that contain less food than does α all lie below M_1; and the individual's choice before prices changed revealed that he preferred α to all bundles on or below M_1. Hence the new optimum choice bundle must lie along M'_2 to *the right* of α, and it must contain more food than α does.

That analysis underlies this important proposition: *when the relative price of a good falls, but real income remains unchanged, then the rate of consumption of that good must increase.*

That proposition is interpreted in terms of substitution among goods in response to relative price changes with income held unchanged. When a good becomes relatively cheaper, it is substituted into preferred goods bundles. The proposition is often stated in the compact form: *the substitution effect of a change in price is negative.* (*Negative* because a *lower* price implies a *higher* rate of consumption: price and consumption move in *opposite* directions.)

5.3.5. The Total Effect of a Price Change

When the price of a good changes and there is no offsetting change in money income, the change in an individual's optimum goods bundle is composed of the income and substitution effects discussed in the preceding two sections. In Figure 5.23, the income constraint line shifts from M_1 to M_2 as a result of a drop in the price of food. The optimum goods bundle shifts from α to β. As shown, the individual's rate of food consumption increases. But it also is possible that the optimum goods bundle can shift to a point such as γ, with less food consumption than at α, when the price of food falls.

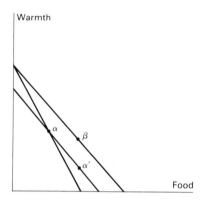

FIGURE 5.24.   An inferior good (food) with negatively sloped demand.

Look at the price change and the individual's response to it, as a two-part process. First, measure the pure substitution effect of the change by taking away the appropriate amount of money income, as discussed in the preceding section. The consumer's optimum response will be a move like the one from α to α' in Figures 5.23, 5.24, and 5.25. From the analysis of the preceding section, we know that α' always lies to the right of α. Second, restore the money income that was taken away in moving the individual from α to α'. If food is a normal good, as illustrated in Figure 5.23, then the move will be to a point β, which lies to the right of α'. For a normal good, both the (negative) substitution effect and the (positive) income effect act to increase the good's consumption when the good's price falls.

But suppose food is an inferior good. Then Figures 5.24 and 5.25 illustrate the possible outcomes. Because food is assumed to be inferior, the optimum goods bundle that is chosen after the compensating income change is restored, β, will lie to the left of α'. In Figure 5.24 this negative income effect is smaller in magnitude than the substitution effect. Figure 5.25 depicts the case in which the income effect is larger in magnitude than the substitution effect. *Only for a good that is inferior can a lower price result in a lower rate of purchase. Moreover, it is also necessary that the income effect that results from the change in the price of that good be numerically larger than the substitution effect,* as is shown in Figure 5.25.

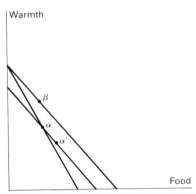

FIGURE 5.25. An inferior good for which the demand curve will be positively sloped (food).

If the income effect of a good's price change is large, purchases of the good must account for a significant portion of the individual's total purchases. It is not likely that there are presently enough individuals in countries like Canada, England, or the USA who show large enough negative income effects in the demands for certain goods so that the *total* demand for those goods (the demand of all individuals) will violate the law of demand. Alfred Marshall, whose statement of the law was quoted on page 102, suggested that wheat may have been such a good for many people in nineteenth-century England; later writers have suggested that potatoes were such a good in eighteenth- and nineteenth-century Ireland. However, no clear case of such a good has ever been conclusively established; the purchase, price, and production data are all too sketchy for the two suggested instances (English wheat and Irish potatoes) to verify that there are or have been instances in which demand indeed does increase when price goes up, or decrease when price goes down.

5.3.6. Aggregation and Market Demand Curves

The market demand schedule is obtained by summing all individual demand schedules. As in Figure 5.26, this summation is done in a horizontal direction: we find the *total quantity demanded* at any price by adding the *quantities demanded by each individual* at that price. The simple construction of market demand as the sum of individual demands at different prices is based on the hypothesis that the individual demands are *mutually independent*—that is, the

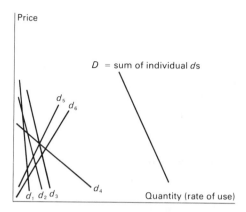

FIGURE 5.26. Construction of the market demand curve D from the demand curves of all individual traders.

amounts purchased by individual A do not depend on individual B's purchases, and this independence holds across all individuals in the society. The assumption that demands are mutually independent, incidentally, is not a trivial one. Independence implies the complete absence of any emulative ("keeping up with the Joneses") behavior. Effects of that type simply cannot be comprehended in the standard analysis that has been presented in this chapter.

The demand summed across all individuals is most important to the study of how the market handles the job of resource allocation. If the aggregate quantity demanded diminishes when price increases, then a higher price cuts down the rate of use of the good; price changes have the expected rationing and incentive effects. If that *market* demand curve for a good is to be *positively* sloped, it is necessary that (a) the demand curves of some individuals be positively sloped, and (b) those individuals "outweigh" those others who have negatively sloped demand curves. In Figure 5.26, individuals 5 and 6 have positively sloped curves; but individuals 1 to 4 "outweigh" them: D, the market demand curve, is negatively sloped. We see that D can have the conventional negative slope, even though the demand curves of some individuals may be positively sloped.

5.3.7. Critical Summary of Results on the Laws of Demand

The law of demand, which states that demand curves are negatively sloped, originated in armchair observations of the world by nineteenth-century economists. Because the law is of great importance to an economist's view of how market processes work, a great deal of attention has been devoted to the process of substantiating the law. The theoretical exercise presented in this chapter, which is based on a theory of individual consumer behavior, indicates that there may be occasions when the law of demand does not hold, even if all conditions assumed in the theory of consumer behavior do hold. However, those conditions which the theory indicates to be necessary for positively sloped demand curves are thought unlikely to be observed widely.

Other sources of support for the law of demand can be found. Casual observations of behavior, of the type favored by nineteenth-century economists, can be invoked in support of the law, and in fact constitute the most persuasive argument in favor of the law in the view of many economists. We observe, for example, that when a civic authority raises the price of water, the *per capita* rate of water use within the city invariably declines. When the price of butter rises relative to other goods, the *per capita* consumption of butter declines. Instances of this type can be multiplied many times, and contrary instances, in which higher price leads to higher consumption, are (1) much less common and (2) readily explained on the grounds of change in income or some other important variable that has an opposite effect from price.

Everyone is aware that the scientific method reflected in these armchair empirical exercises is not of high quality. Some unsympathetic observers go so far as to dismiss such exercises as mere sociology, and not proper economics at all. Since about 1930, great effort has been devoted to careful statistical studies of demand, using the techniques of *econometrics,* the statistical analysis of economic data. The methods of econometrics have been developed in conjunction with their application: a very serious literature of econometric theory now exists, and the topics in that theory have been developed for the most part in response to needs that arose out of empirical investigations of economic theories. Very few published econometrics studies of the demand for specific goods have suggested that demand is a positively sloped function of the good's price. The first section in the next chapter describes at an elementary level some of the difficulties that have been encountered and surmounted in empirical work on demand.

Based on the totality of available evidence, most economists look upon the law of demand not as an inviolate and literal law, but as a very useful and reliable working hypothesis. Economists are called upon to predict the effects of various important changes in the economy, and in making these predictions, most economists will proceed in full confidence that demand curves slope downward.

How would we interpret our findings if in fact empirical investigation disclosed that the law of demand is violated by many different goods at many different points in time? It would probably be a mistake to conclude that those goods all are inferior, as defined in Section 5.3.3, although we learn there that a good must be inferior to violate the law of demand. Instead, we would probably call into question the entire system of deduction that led to the "normal versus inferior" goods classification. That deductive system rests on several important hypotheses about behavior: individuals make their purchase decisions in a way that is systematic, not random; more of a good is preferred to less; preferences do not change rapidly or frequently through time; the preferences of different individuals are independent of one another. If the law of demand were found to be widely violated, underpinnings of our theory of consumer behavior would necessarily be called into question, for that theory is principally a device for rationalizing the law of demand. Alternatively, we might well wonder whether the total demand for a good can be viewed as a simple sum of individual demands for the good: positively sloped demand curves could occur if individuals were slavish imitators of their neighbors, or of the Beautiful People, like Ms. Jacqueline Lee Bouvier Kennedy Onassis and her chums.

APPLICATIONS AND EXTENSIONS

Supply and demand analysis originated from a desire to analyze real-world problems and to "comprehend reality." The theory of consumer behavior is by contrast far less directly practical and empirical in its aim. It was developed as a theoretical edifice, with motivation provided by the desire to see whether anything could be deduced about the slope of a demand curve from "laws of optimum choice." Can an individual who behaves "rationally"—i.e., in conformity with some system of axioms or postulates—be expected to show regularities in his choice behavior that can be interpreted as leading to negatively sloped demand curves for all goods?

Because of this difference in aim, consumer behavior theory does not lend itself as readily to problem solving as does supply and demand theory. Hence the poverty of this section on applications and extensions.

1. Suppose an individual's preference ordering over the two goods, food and warmth, can be represented numerically by the equation

$$SV(F, W) = afw^2$$

where SV is his subjective valuation of any bundle containing food and warmth, f is the amount of food in the bundle (measured in pounds per week), w is the amount of warmth in the bundle (measured in equivalent hundredweight of bituminous coal per week), and a is a constant, $a \neq 0$.

(a) If $f = 10$ and $w = 27$, and the amount of f more than doubles to 22.5, by how much can w decline without leaving the individual worse off?

(b) Suppose an individual's maximum satisfaction is obtained when he expends his entire income on $10 f$ and $27 w$. Now suppose his money income doubles, but the prices of f and w are unchanged. Given the subjective valuation,

$$SV(F, W) = afw^2$$

will he increase his consumption of food by more than his consumption of warmth, or *vice versa*?

(c) Now suppose the same conditions hold as in (b), but

$$SV(F, W) = kf^{1/2}w^{1/2};$$

i.e., subjective valuation is now proportional to the square root of both F and W. Which increases in larger proportion now when income doubles?

(d) Same exercise, except

$$SV(F, W) = lf^{1/3}w^{2/3}.$$

BIBLIOGRAPHICAL NOTE

Numerous sources on the present topic may be found. Somewhat less compressed treatments are in R. T. Gill, *Economics: A Text With Included Readings,* 2nd ed. (Pacific Palisades, Ca.: Goodyear, 1975), and in R. G. Lipsey and P. Steiner, *Economics* (Evanston, Ill.: Harper & Row, several editions). An advanced, mathematically explicit treatment is K. G. Kogiku, *Microeconomic Models* (New York: McGraw-Hill, 1971). The modern version of consumer theory was introduced into popular currency by two significant books of the 1930s and 1940s: J. R. Hicks, *Value and Capital* (New York: Oxford University Press, 1939) and P. A. Samuelson, *Foundations of Economic Analysis* (Cambridge, Mass.: Harvard University Press, 1947).

An extremely useful book for the mature advanced student is S. Bowles and D. Kendrick, *Notes and Problems in Microeconomic Theory* (Chicago: Markham Publishing Co., 1970).

Almost every source that the reader will consult on this topic (including all of the above except for the 1966 edition of Lipsey and Steiner) develops consumer theory via a discussion of the archaic and somewhat misleading topic of "utility." That topic is covered from an historical point of view in Chapter 6, Section 6.2.

The question of positively sloped demand curves is dealt with in a readable and absorbing paper: G. J. Stigler, "Notes on the History of the Giffen Paradox," reprinted in Stigler, *Essays in the History of Economics* (Chicago: University of Chicago Press, 1965).

CHAPTER SIX

Further Topics
in Demand
and Consumer Theory

The difficulty in life is the choice.

GEORGE MOORE (1900)

The purpose of this chapter is to set forth two topics of general interest and importance, which are covered in the first two sections, and to discuss three additional topics of more specialized interest, which can be skipped by readers who prefer not to consider more advanced material at this point and which are covered in Sections 6.3 to 6.5.

6.1. EMPIRICAL STUDIES OF DEMAND

The earliest inferences by economists of the law of demand cannot be dated precisely, but we do know that they were based on intuition and personal introspection. Later, crude observations of the *qualitative* effects of relative price changes were made and these tended to conform to the intuition that quantity demanded is an inverse function of price. Such studies of qualitative effects can be conducted "from the armchair": they involve very little in the way of data gathering or careful analysis. Such studies have long had an honorable place in the search for economic knowledge; they are certainly superior to a purely introspective and subjective view of the world as evidence in support of a proposition about economic behavior.

The period between roughly 1890 and 1925 was an extremely active one in the development of a new mathematical science called *statistics*. That science showed the way the mathematical theory of probability can be used to judge the reliability of propositions like "other things being equal, the demand for sugar in Britain will decline as the price of sugar increases." Beginning around 1910, statistical theory was applied in interesting ways to questions that concern economists. Around 1930 those applications became sufficiently frequent and important to warrant separate recognition as *econometrics*, the statistical theory and actual practice of empirical economic research.

Very early, research workers in econometrics learned that it is a tricky task to estimate a demand curve. Actual quantity and price data can be collected in two basically different ways: observations of one particular market can be made at different (and preferably regularly spaced) points in time—this is a process that gives a *time series* of data. Alternatively, geographically separate markets can be observed during one single time interval; that kind of observation yields a *cross section* of data. In either case, price will depend not only on quantity purchased, but on other prices, incomes, and the tastes and preferences of individuals who patronize the observed market. Taste differences in a cross-sectional study can be extremely important. It clearly would be foolish to observe both vegetarian India and sausage-loving Austria in a single study of the demand for pork; but more subtle differences in preference between states, or communities in the same state, may go undetected, and can upset the analyst's results. Over long periods of time, taste differences can also be important in a time series study. Unfortunately, it is an inherent limitation of statistical analysis that small numbers of observations yield results that are far less reliable than large numbers of observations; hence, the tempting solution to the problem posed by changes in taste, which would be to limit the process of observation to short periods of time or to markets in a small number of similar communities, is likely to be a poor one, because too much usable information is lost by reducing the number of observations.

Another basic problem confronts empirical research on demand. It is possible that observed transactions are not equilibrium transactions. If an observation is made when a market is not in equilibrium, the observed price-quantity combination would not necessarily lie on the demand curve. In Figure 6.1, suppose supply shifts from S_1 to S_2. During the time when buyers are adjusting to this shift, the market is observed to be operating at the point A. (Such a rate of operation could occur because buyers may think the price P_A is a temporary low one, and they may seek to "stock up" on the good, not realizing that in fact price is due to fall even farther.) If a reliable estimate of the demand curve is to be obtained when numerous market positions like A are recorded, it is necessary that the observed data points lie around the demand curve throughout its length. If, for example, the observations that are collected during adjustment lie primarily below the demand curve after a reduction in supply, and primarily above the demand

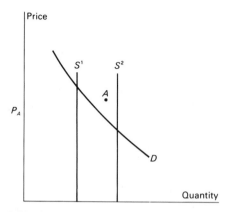

FIGURE 6.1.   A hypothetical observation of price and quantity when the market is temporarily out of equilibrium due to supply shift from S^1 to S^2.

curve after supply has increased, and if several supply shifts occur during the time that observations are taken, then the estimated demand curve will be steeper than the true curve.

Where statistical theory is most helpful is in separating the effects of the several variables which influence the price and quantity demanded of a particular good: the activity in markets for other goods (represented by the prices of those goods), and the incomes of the population served by the market. The most common and soundest approach to the empirical study of demand is to take time series observations on price, rate of purchase (quantity), and the several other important determining variables, and to estimate *both* the demand and supply curves for the market.

It must be made clear why demand and supply relationships should be estimated together and taken explicitly into account. We ask: why is a simple curve, fitted to price and quantity observations, *not* an adequate estimate of demand?

Suppose that a simple visual fitting technique is used to draw a curve through the scatter of points shown in Figure 6.2. A curve of good fit that passes through these observations will have a positive slope. However, it is not legitimate to conclude on that basis that the demand curve is positively sloped. Over the period during which the data were collected, variables that influence demand may have been much more rapidly and widely fluctuating than were variables that influence supply. The supply relation would then have been the more stable of the two, the series of data observations would have lain along the supply curve, and the simple fitted curve would be a much better estimate of supply than of demand.

Figure 6.3 uses an extreme example to show the difficulty with fitting demand curves by simple techniques. The demand curve shifts in every period, while the

FIGURE 6.2.   A "scatter diagram" of observed transactions: prices and quantities.

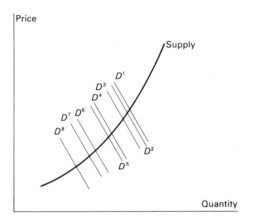

FIGURE 6.3.   Shifts in demand may generate observations that lie along the supply curve.

supply curve remains stable. The result is a set of points that lie along the supply curve. It is imperative to see how much the two curves move; variables other than price and quantity must be brought into the analysis for that purpose. In a properly conducted study it is specified in advance which variables affect demand and which affect supply. In that specification, it is necessary that complete overlap be avoided: some variables that affect demand must be excluded from the list of variables affecting supply, and vice versa. From changes in those variables, it is possible to estimate the amount of movement in supply and demand curves, and to estimate both relationships, supply and demand.

6.2. NUMERICAL REPRESENTATIONS OF A PREFERENCE ORDERING: "UTILITY FUNCTIONS"

6.2.1. Utilitarianism: A Ghost from the Past

Indifference curves represent an individual's *ranking* or *ordering* of the goods space. A curve through the goods bundle x identifies all of the goods bundles that are equal in desirability to x, in the view of the individual; and the curve permits the identification of preferable and less desirable bundles as well. Because the curves cannot intersect, there is no reason why we can't assign a number to each indifference curve and use those numbers to represent the place in the individual's ordering that is occupied by the goods bundles along the curve. Thus, in Figure 6.4, the curves are marked with numbers, and the larger those numbers are, the higher in the individual's preference ordering are the goods bundles on the curve.

There is no obstacle to this numbering scheme, if the individual's preferences satisfy the Assumptions in Chapter 5 (Section 5.1.1); or the Axioms of this chapter (Section 6.5). And a numbering system is easy to construct: if we draw a straight line outward from the origin into the goods space, as shown in Figure 6.4, that line will intersect every indifference curve exactly once; the distance to the origin from its intersection with the line can be the number assigned to every indifference curve.

Such a numerical representation of the preference ordering may be very useful in some applications. It is easy to compare two numbers to determine which is the larger; and many of our techniques of mathematical analysis are useful only if some explicit numerical representation of preferences is available. For reasons that are understandable only after some review of the history of

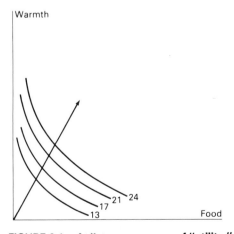

FIGURE 6.4.   A distance measure of "utility."

economic ideas, numerical representations of preference orderings are called *utility functions*.

In the middle nineteenth century, when individual choice behavior was first carefully studied by economists, the utilitarian philosophers were heavily influential. In their view, the pleasure or pain that one individual feels can be measured and compared to the pleasure or pain of another individual. The pleasure, or *utility*, derivable from a goods bundle, by their reckoning, is measurable in the same way that height, weight, or temperature are measurable. Their view of measurement implies not only that people can make a ranking of goods bundles, as we have assumed; it implies that rankings can be specified in terms of numbers which convey a great deal of information. To a utilitarian, if the goods bundles α, β, and γ have utility numbers 1, 2, and 4 attached to them by some person, then that person gains twice as much pleasure by substituting γ for β as is gained when β is substituted for α. The pleasure or "utility" that the individual derives from the goods bundle is an inherent property of the bundle, and can be measured not only in terms of "greater than" (preferred to) but also in terms like "twice as great as" or "forty percent greater than."

Modern theorists have rejected the idea that goods have an inherent property called "utility." Whereas a utilitarian would say "γ is preferred to β because it yields twice as much utility," a modern theorist would say "Since γ is preferred to β, a higher utility number must be assigned to γ than is assigned to β." Utility is the force that shapes preferences, in the eyes of the utilitarian; utility is simply a quaint name that is attached to the numerical ordering that was derived from and is consistent with preferences, to the modern theorist. Because modern theorists view utility numbers as simple numerical orderings, they reject the idea that the utility gains realized by one individual can be compared to the utility losses suffered by another, which result, say, from a transfer of income.

Suppose in Figure 6.5 an income transfer moves Mr. A from the indifference curve marked 400 to the curve marked 375; and Mr. B from the curve marked 550 to the curve marked 800. A utilitarian philosopher would say that Mr. B's gain of 250 is greater than Mr. A's loss of 25; hence the transfer should occur. A modern theorist would argue that Mr. B gains and Mr. A loses, all right, but magnitudes or intensity of gain and loss cannot be measured and compared. To the modern theorist, the only significance of the numbers attached to Mr. B's curves is the fact that 800 is greater than 550. The numbers 1.004 and .95 would equally well have served to label the curves: 1.004 is greater than .95, just as 800 is greater than 550.

6.2.2. Marginal Utility

In utilitarian discussions, and in some modern discussions, the idea of *marginal utility* appears. The marginal utility of a good to an individual can be defined as the individual's gain in utility resulting from obtaining an additional unit of the

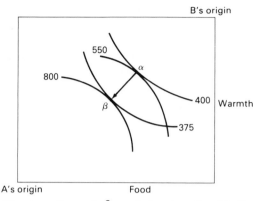

FIGURE 6.5. **The move from α to β results in a transfer of both goods (income) from A to B. B's numerical "utility" increases from 550 to 800, while A's declines from 400 to 375.**

good, or more properly (with the modern interpretation of "utility," and in terms of the calculus), the rate of change in the individual's numerical preference ordering with respect to the good. Utilitarian theorizing had continued for some time before the idea of marginal utility became established, and the discovery of that idea was a very important one. It made possible the resolution of Adam Smith's famous paradox of diamonds and water:

> Nothing is more useful than water: but it will purchase scarce anything; scarce anything can be had in exchange for it. A diamond, on the contrary, has scarce any value in use; but a very great quantity of other goods may frequently be had in exchange for it.[1]

This passage is vague: will a year's supply of water to a great city purchase "scarce anything?" Will a thousandth of a milligram of diamond dust bring "a very great quantity of other goods . . . in exchange for it?" Despite its vagueness, however, Smith's comment offers a nice application of an important idea. The idea is that the prices of goods are proportional to the marginal utility of the goods to the purchaser. That idea did not become firmly established in economics until around 1870, nearly a century after Smith wrote. Let's explore that idea, and see how it resolves the paradox of water and diamonds.

If an individual already consumes an abundance of water, he is unlikely to be willing to pay a great deal for an additional gallon per month. The marginal utility of that gallon of water to him is low; he will pay only a low price to obtain it. The same individual may own no diamonds; the pleasure he will obtain from having a half-carat diamond is best known to himself, but if that pleasure is sufficiently great, the marginal utility of a diamond is great, and he willingly pays a high price for it. In these simple terms, the paradox vanishes. In the

[1]Adam Smith, *The Wealth of Nations* (New York: Random House, 1937), p. 28.

analysis, notice how an important point emerges: the marginal utility of a good depends on how much of the good the individual already holds.

In Figure 6.6, the price of diamonds per carat is seen to be high, and the price of water per gallon, quite low. The individual's optimum choice goods bundle is at the point α, where his income constraint line is tangent to an indifference curve, denoted $I(\alpha)$.

The slope of the income constraint line is $-P_d/P_w$, the ratio of the price of diamonds to the price of water. (The slope is

$$-Q_w/Q_d \, ,$$

but that is equal to

$$-M/P_w \div M/P_d \, ,$$

and that in turn is equal to $-P_d/P_w.$)

Now consider the slope of the indifference curve at the point α. Suppose a small quantity of water is taken away from the individual: call that quantity ΔW. How much additional diamonds, ΔD, must the individual be given to leave him feeling neither worse off nor better off than he felt at the point α? Obviously, the ΔD that moves him back to the indifference curve $I(\alpha)$ is the required amount. Figure 6.6 shows this change, "enlarged" in the inset.

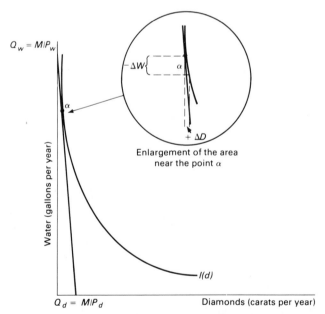

FIGURE 6.6. Illustration of Smith's "Diamond-Water Paradox," showing the relation that must hold between prices and "marginal utilities" for any optimum choice goods bundle.

Suppose we denote the gain in pleasure that the individual experiences per unit increase in diamond consumption when he is at the point α as

$$MU_d(\alpha),$$

which we read "the marginal utility of diamond consumption at point α." Similarly, $MU_w(\alpha)$ is the gain in pleasure that results from a one-unit increase in the rate of water consumption when he is at the point α. If a reduction in water consumption by ΔW and an increase in diamond consumption by ΔD leaves the individual on the same indifference curve $I(\alpha)$, then it must be true that

$$-\Delta W \cdot MU_w(\alpha) + \Delta D \cdot MU_d(\alpha) = 0, \tag{1}$$

and therefore that

$$\frac{-\Delta W}{\Delta D} = -\frac{MU_d(\alpha)}{MU_w(\alpha)}.$$

But $-\Delta W/\Delta D$ is the slope of the indifference curve $I(\alpha)$ at the point α, if ΔD is chosen small enough.

At an optimal choice goods bundle, the slope of the indifference curve is equal to the slope of the income constraint line. When we set these two slopes equal, we find that

$$\frac{-MU_d(\alpha)}{MU_w(\alpha)} = \frac{-P_d}{P_w},$$

and thus

$$\frac{MU_d(\alpha)}{P_d} = \frac{MU_w(\alpha)}{P_w}.$$

For an optimal choice consumption bundle, the ratio of "marginal utility" to price is equal across all goods. Thus, if the marginal utility of diamonds is great relative to the marginal utility of water, we can expect the price of diamonds to be high relative to the price of water.

How can the modern theorist justify using a concept like marginal utility when he has explicitly rejected the idea that utility numbers have any concrete significance beyond a mere ordering? The way the concept is used in modern theory does not attach any of the strong implications of measurability or comparability to the concept of utility that were imputed to it by the utilitarian philosophers. The formula (1), in fact, is simply the definition of an indifference curve; and the marginal utilities of the depicted goods are never used in the modern analysis to denote anything more than the slope of the indifference curve. In that application, *any* pair of numbers that yield the same ratio will do: 4/5, or 20/25, or 1.70/2.125. In the modern theory, "marginal utility" is a terminological, not a conceptual holdover from the earlier days.

*6.3. INDIVIDUAL DEMAND CURVES
FROM INDIFFERENCE MAPS

This section contains an exercise in geometric manipulation, which apparently illustrates how an individual's demand for a good can be deduced from his indifference map, if that is known. Actually, the exercise is not a demonstration of how demand curves are constructed or obtained at all; rather, its purpose is to demonstrate the terms under which a logical consistency exists between the indifference curve analysis of consumer theory and the law of demand. There is, after all, no prospect whatever of knowing an individual's indifference map but not knowing his demand curve for one of the goods. The exercise, if taken at face value as a demonstration of how to go from indifference maps to demand curves, is pointless, since it can never be applied.

As usual, it is convenient to assume that there are two goods. The price of one of the goods is changed, and the individual's purchase response is observed. In Figure 6.7, M_1, M_2, . . . are income constraint lines associated with successively lower prices of one of the goods, food. The money price of the other good, warmth, remains unchanged. The individual's money income also remains unchanged. The heavily drawn curve labelled $\alpha\beta$ in Figure 6.7 is called the *offer curve*. It connects all of the optimum choice goods bundles which are associated with the different possible prices of food. From the income contraint lines and the offer curve, sufficient information can be deduced to construct the individual's demand curve for food.

To obtain a point on the demand curve, pick out one of the income constraint lines, such as M_1 in Figure 6.7. The price of food is obtained from the knowl-

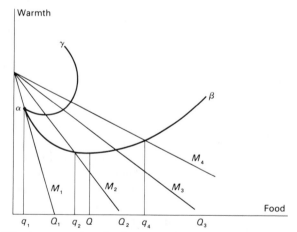

FIGURE 6.7. **Income constraint lines associated with different food prices; optimum quantity responses on the offer curve** $\alpha\beta$.

*The material in this section may be too advanced for some introductory coverage.

edge that Q_1, the intercept of M_1 at the food axis, is equal to money income divided by the price of food. Thus P_1, the food price associated with M_1, is given by

$$P_1 = M_1/Q_1.$$

The food component of the optimum choice goods bundle on M_1 is q_1 in Figure 6.7. Hence, when the price of food is P_1, the quantity of food that the individual uses is q_1.

Numerous price-quantity pairs can be determined, each one beginning with a different income constraint line, and the individual's demand curve for food is simply a plot of the prices and associated quantities like q_1, q_2, and q_4, thus determined.

A couple of interesting points can be deduced from this exposition of the relation between demand curves and indifference maps. First, expenditure on food increases in response to lower food prices within the range where the offer curve is negatively sloped. The distance between the offer curve and the horizontal axis is proportional to the expenditure on *warmth*. That expenditure *declines* when food prices drop, so long as the offer curve is negatively sloped; and hence, expenditure on food must be increasing within that interval. In Figure 6.7, then, the demand for food is elastic when quantity is less than Q; it is inelastic for all quantities greater than Q. Second, if the demand curve for food is positively sloped, the offer curve must be backward bending, as the curve $\alpha\gamma$ is in Figure 6.7.

*6.4. THE PROBLEM OF INDEX NUMBER DESIGN

Through time, the relative prices of goods are likely to change, and individuals are likely to alter their consumption behavior in response. Furthermore, general changes in the level of *all* prices can occur. One cause of a general change in prices can be assigned to the authority who is responsible for controlling the supply of money in the economy; if he allows that supply to expand at too rapid a rate, the price of money may fall relative to all other goods: the purchasing power of money declines.

With a hodgepodge of price and output changes occurring from one period of time to the next, it becomes difficult to keep track of the economic well-being of the various individuals of the community. To determine whether an individual is, by his own standards, better off economically today than he was yesterday would be easy, if we knew the individual's indifference map. If in Figure 6.8 α is yesterday's goods bundle, then he is better off if, and only if, today's bundle lies above the indifference curve $I(\alpha)$. However, we do not know how to locate the indifference curve $I(\alpha)$, and hence we are forced to base our conclusions about relative well-being through time on more ambiguous indicators.

Consider, for example, this suggestion: if an individual spends more today

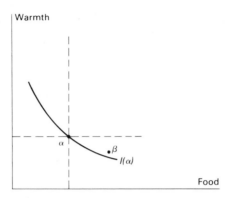

FIGURE 6.8. Base-period consumption α and current-period consumption β, illustrating the difficulty of comparison.

than he did yesterday, he is better off today. In light of the possibility that general increases in price are possible, that suggestion appears naive. If all prices double, and expenditure increases by ten percent, an individual is clearly consuming fewer goods; and according to our assumptions about preference, he is therefore less well off.

A less naive suggestion is: if an individual's *real income* increases, then he is better off. To estimate the value of real income, an attempt must be made to correct for the changes in price that occur through time. *Price index numbers* are compiled, one for each time period, which are intended to correct or ''deflate'' prices to a common basis. The total value of an individual's money income in a given year then can be divided by that year's index number, and the resulting value can be compared to values in other years. These corrected values of income are taken as the basis for judging the direction and magnitude of changes in his real income through time.

Price index numbers, including the ones that are used in the U.S., have certain important conceptual shortcomings which will be explored in this section.

In calculating index numbers, a *base period* is arbitrarily selected from the distant or recent past. The base period is the time against which all previous and subsequent periods are compared. The purchase price of a carefully chosen bundle of goods is recorded for the base period. That bundle is usually chosen to represent a typical or average consumption pattern. The purchase price of the bundle is given by

$$p_1^0 \cdot x_1 + p_2^0 \cdot x_2 + \ldots + p_n^0 \cdot x_n \equiv \sum_{i=1}^{n} p_i^0 \cdot x_i$$

where the subscripts indicate the specific goods contained in the bundle (there are n of them); and the superscript ^{0} indicates that the prices $p_1^0, p_2^0, \ldots, p_n^0$ of the n goods are recorded as of the base period. The quantities $x_1, \ldots, x_n$ are amounts supposedly consumed by a "typical" household. Those amounts are assumed not to change through time. To draw a comparison between the base period and some later period, called the current period, the sum

$$p_1^1 \cdot x_1 + p_2^1 \cdot x_2 + \ldots p_n^1 \cdot x_n \equiv \sum_{i=1}^{n} p_i^1 \cdot x_i$$

is calculated: the superscript 1 is taken to indicate that prices are recorded as of the current period. The sum

$$\sum_{i=1}^{n} p_i^1 \cdot x_i$$

is the purchase price of the same typical goods bundle in the current period. The ratio of the goods bundle purchase prices in the two periods,

$$\sum_{i=1}^{n} p_i^1 \cdot x_i \Big/ \sum_{i=1}^{n} p_i^0 \cdot x_i \equiv P_1$$

is the *price index* of the current period. If prices are unchanged between the two periods, the price index is $P_1 = 1.00.$[2] If the weighted average of prices—the total price of the goods bundle $x_1, \ldots, x_n$—declines, then the price index will be less than 1.00, and so forth. *To see what happened to an individual's real income, we simply divide his current-period money income by the current period price index.*

Price indices are sometimes used to find out what happened to the total value of a nation's output, correcting for price changes. Suppose that in the current period, N goods are produced in the economy, in the volumes $x_1^1, x_2^1, \ldots, x_n^1$, and suppose those goods exchange at prices that prevail during this period, $P_1^1, P_1^2, \ldots, P_1^n$. The total value of output in the current period is

$$\sum_{i=1}^{N} p_i^1 \cdot x_i^1$$

To compare the value of output in the current period to the value of output in the base period, the calculation

$$\left(\sum_{i=1}^{n} p_i^1 \cdot x_i^1 \right) \Big/ P_1$$

is made. The result of the calculation is, approximately, the value of output in the current period, in terms of base period prices. If that output value (which is also called real gross national product, or real GNP) increases, it is inferred that economic activity has increased; and some observers tacitly or explicitly suggest that the nation's economic welfare has also increased.

[2]Index numbers frequently are multiplied by 100 before they are reported. Thus, a price index of 155 means that prices have risen by 55 percent since the base period. We will *not* carry that 100-multiple around in the following discussion.

The goal of index number calculations, we must keep in mind, is to enable judgments about changes in economic well-being within the society through time. As a more modest goal, the numbers should at least enable us to form a judgment about how the "cost of living" has changed through time. To see the shortcomings of the index numbers for both purposes, we observe what the numbers would imply in a simple world of two goods.

In Figure 6.9, the indifference map of an individual is drawn. M^0 is the individual's income constraint line in the base period, and α is his base-period optimum goods bundle. If his income constraint line shifts outward in an unambiguous way between the base period and the current period, as to M_1' or M_1'', we judge that his economic welfare has increased. (In accord with the Individualist Precept [Chapter 3, Section 3.2.2], we assert that the individual is the judge of his own well-being; his economic well-being is taken to rise when he moves to a more highly preferred goods bundle; and shifts like those to M_1' or M_1'' unambiguously enable the individual to move to a more highly preferred bundle.)

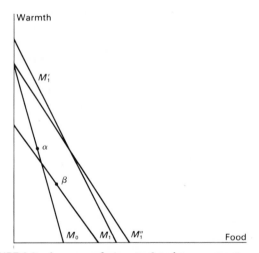

FIGURE 6.9.   Is a move from α to β an improvement or not?

When a shift is to an income constraint line like M_1 in Figure 6.9, it is difficult to judge whether an individual is better off or worse off economically than before. He chooses the goods bundle β. Because we don't know his indifference map, help is needed to decide whether he has gained or lost by the move from α to β. Our verdict will always involve elements of arbitrariness and possibly, error.

We take α, the optimum choice bundle of the base period, as the goods bundle that is used in calculating an index. The quantities of the two goods contained in that bundle are α_1 and α_2. The individual's expenditure in the base period, then, is

$$\sum_{i=1}^{2} p_i^0 \alpha_i .$$

If he purchased that same bundle in the current period, his outlay would be

$$\sum_{i=1}^{2} p_i^1 \alpha_i .$$

We calculate the current period index

$$\Lambda_1 \equiv \sum_{i=1}^{2} p_i^1 \alpha_i \Big/ \sum_{i=1}^{2} p_i^0 \alpha_i \tag{2}$$

and obtain the current period real income, by dividing the expenditure in the current period by this index:

$$\sum_{i=1}^{2} p_i^1 \beta_i / \Lambda_1$$

where β, the optimum choice bundle of the current period, contains quantities β_1 and β_2 of the two goods. If expenditure in the current period, corrected for change in prices, exceeds expenditure in the base period, then real income is said to have risen. That is, if

$$\frac{\displaystyle\sum_{i=1}^{2} p_i^1 \beta_i}{\Lambda_1} > \sum_{i=1}^{2} p_i^0 \alpha_i , \tag{3}$$

real income is judged to have risen. The inequality (3) can be rewritten

$$\frac{\displaystyle\sum_{i=1}^{2} p_i^1 \beta_i \cdot \sum_{i=1}^{2} p_i^0 \alpha_i}{\displaystyle\sum_{i=1}^{2} p_i^1 \alpha_i} > \sum_{i=1}^{2} p_i^0 \alpha_i$$

or more succinctly,

$$\frac{\displaystyle\sum_{i=1}^{2} p_i^1 \beta_i}{\displaystyle\sum_{i=1}^{2} p_i^1 \alpha_i} > 1. \tag{4}$$

The inequality (4) tells us that if β costs more than α at current period prices, then real income has risen.

Geometrically, the expenditure quantity

$$\sum_{i=1}^{2} p_i^1 \alpha_i$$

can be represented by drawing an income constraint line, sloped to represent current period prices, through the base period goods bundle α (the broken line of Figure 6.10). If that line lies above β, it is asserted that there has been a reduction in real income; if that line is below β, as in Figure 6.10, it is asserted that real income has increased.

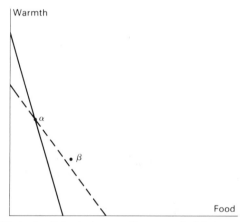

FIGURE 6.10.   Price index test (Laspeyres): β is better than α.

As we see in Figure 6.11, the first of those assertions can be incorrect, but the second cannot. In panel (1), the goods bundle β which is judged inferior to α is actually preferable to α. In panel (2), β is judged preferable to α. There is no way that it can be inferior: if it lay below $I(\alpha)$, as the bundle γ does, it wouldn't be the optimal choice goods bundle along its income constraint line. Thus: if our index number calculation asserts that there has been an increase in the real income of an individual, we can be confident that his real income has indeed increased; if the calculation indicates a decrease in his real income, we cannot be sure what has happened.

It can be easily seen in a two-good world that if the index

$$\Phi_1 \equiv \sum p_i^1 \beta_i \Big/ p_i^0 \beta_i$$

is used, instead of the index in equation (2), then there is ambiguity when an increase in real income is indicated, but no ambiguity when a decrease is indicated. The only confusing cases that remain, then, are those for which the first index Λ_1, called the *Laspeyres' index,* signals a decrease in real income, and the index Φ_1, called the *Paasche index,* signals an increase. Recall, however, that in practice,

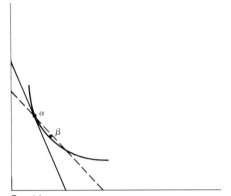

Panel 1

Price index test (Laspeyres): β is "really better" than α, but the index says α is better.

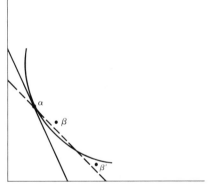

Panel 2

Price index test (Laspeyres): β is said to be better, and there is no way it can be worse.

FIGURE 6.11. Price index test (Laspeyres): β is said to be better than α, and there is no way it can be worse.

Price index test (Laspeyres): β is "really better" than α, but the index says α is better.

indices are calculated by reference to arbitrary "representative" goods bundles, and not by reference to the actual bundles consumed in the two periods, α and β. That fact makes the availability of the Laspeyres' and Paasche alternatives less helpful in reducing uncertainty about what index number calculations actually tell us.

Index numbers offer information about welfare changes only when they are applied to an individual. The individual must satisfy our axioms of preference (Section 6.5 of this chapter). The tastes of the individual must be unchanged between the base period and the current period. The array of available goods must be unchanged between the two periods. The goods bundle that is compared between periods in formulating the index must be meaningful in terms of the individual's preferences: it should not contain large numbers of goods that he would never consume at any price. When any of these conditions fails, the index number becomes nothing more than an indication, perhaps a crude indication, of change in the general level of prices through time.

*6.5. THE AXIOMS OF PREFERENCE AND THE EXISTENCE OF INDIFFERENCE CURVES

Chapter 5, Section 5.1, presented a rather sketchy description of the way in which indifference curves are derived from assumptions about individual choice behavior. Because a complete and satisfactory treatment of that topic requires some mathematical apparatus, it has been deferred until now. Some familiarity with the differential calculus is required to follow the arguments of this section.

Notationally, α, β, γ, and δ are goods bundles in a two-good world, and the symbol $\aleph$ denotes a relation between a pair of goods bundles that is called "not preferred to." The sentence

$$\alpha \; \aleph \; \beta$$

is read: "the goods bundle α is not preferred to the goods bundle β." A set of axioms or assumptions defines the tastes and describes the choice behavior of individuals. The first three axioms define properties of the relation $\aleph$.

Axiom I (Completeness of the Relation $\aleph$): If α and β are any pair of arbitrarily chosen goods bundles, then either $\alpha \; \aleph \; \beta$ or $\beta \; \aleph \; \alpha$, or both.

Axiom II (Reflexivity of $\aleph$): for any goods bundle α, it is true that $\alpha \; \aleph \; \alpha$.

Axiom III (Transitivity of $\aleph$): For any three goods bundles α, β, and γ, if $\alpha \aleph \beta$ and $\beta \aleph \gamma$, then $\alpha \aleph \gamma$.

To establish the fourth axiom, it is necessary to know what is meant by the *size* of a goods bundle. If α_1, α_2 are the quantities of the goods in the bundle α, and β_1, β_2 are the quantities of the goods in the bundle β, then β is *not larger than* α if

$$\alpha_1 \geqslant \beta_1$$
$$\alpha_2 \geqslant \beta_2.$$

That is, α must contain no less than does β of both goods; β is *smaller than* α if $\alpha_1 > \beta_1$, or $\alpha_2 > \beta_2$, or both.

Axiom IV (Monotonicity of $\aleph$): If α and β are any two goods bundles, and β is smaller than α, then $\beta \; \aleph \; \alpha$, but it cannot hold that $\alpha \; \aleph \; \beta$.

We next define a relation that is derived from the basic relation $\aleph$.

If $\alpha \; \aleph \; \beta$ and $\beta \; \aleph \; \alpha$, we write "$\alpha \, \mathfrak{Z} \, \beta$," which is read "$\alpha$ and β are equally preferred."

Axiom V (Continuity of ℜ): If α ℜ β and β ℜ γ, and if a continuous curve is drawn in the goods space connecting α and γ, then there must be at least one point on that curve, called δ, satisfying the condition δ ℑ β.

Axiom V can be illustrated in our world of two goods (Figure 6.12). The goods bundles α, β, and γ are ranked in ascending order of preference. A continuous curve is drawn between α and γ. The points δ and δ' on that curve satisfy the conditions δ ℑ β and δ' ℑ β.

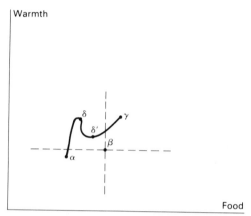

FIGURE 6.12. Illustration of Axiom V.

We now define an *indifference class*.

The indifference class of the goods bundle α, denoted $I(\alpha)$, is the entire set of goods bundles β such that β ℑ α.

It now can be proved that the indifference class of a goods bundle has three important properties: (1) it exists and is not empty; (2) it is a continuous curve; and (3) it is negatively sloped.

1. Existence. The indifference class $I(\alpha)$ exists and is non-empty. By axiom II, and the definition of ℑ, we have that α ℑ α: hence $I(\alpha)$ exists and contains at least one goods bundle, α itself.

Before turning to the continuity property, we must know that the *goods space* is the set of all possible consumption bundles, i.e. every point in the food $=$ warmth diagram (Figure 6.12) that contains nonnegative quantities of both goods; and a *ray* is a straight line through the origin into the goods space.

2. Continuity. The indifference class $I(\alpha)$ must intersect any ray in the goods space exactly once. There must be at least one intersection, for observe in Figure 6.13 that the ray passes through the two shaded areas "northeast" and "southwest" of α. By Axiom V there must be at least one point on the ray, call it β, satisfying the condition β ℑ α. But there can be no more than one such point. Suppose that both β ℑ α and β' ℑ α. Then, by Axiom III and the definition of ℑ, β ℑ β'. But that would violate Axiom IV, since $\beta' > \beta$. Thus, any point like β in

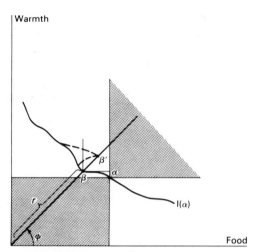

FIGURE 6.13. **The indifference class $I(\alpha)$ cannot "bend back," as shown in the hypothetical broken path. Along the ray of angle ϕ, β is the only point in $I(\alpha)$.**

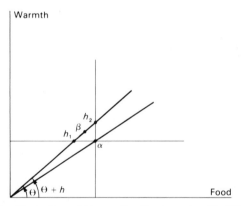

FIGURE 6.14. **Illustration of the continuity property of indifference curves.**

the indifference class $I(\alpha)$ can be identified or located by (a) the angle ϕ between the ray that passes through it and the horizontal axis; and (b) the distance from the origin to the point (i.e. β has well-defined polar coordinates).

The indifference class is continuous. In Figure 6.14, let Θ be the angle of the ray through the point α, and let β be the point in $I(\alpha)$ along the ray with angle $\Theta + h$. (We have just seen that there will be exactly one such point.) By Axiom IV, β must lie between the points h_1 and h_2. Now let the angle h be decreased; h_1 and h_2 both go to α, and they "squeeze" β between them. Thus, at the limit $h = 0$, $\beta = \alpha$. That limit satisfies the condition for the continuity of $I(\alpha)$ at α, and the same argument holds for every point in $I(\alpha)$. We thus are justified in calling the indifference class $I(\alpha)$ an *indifference curve*.

3. Negative Slope. The indifference curve $I(\alpha)$ is negatively sloped. By Axiom IV, the indifference curve through α cannot intersect the shaded regions, or the boundaries of those regions, in Figure 6.14. Because it is confined to the unshaded regions, it is negatively sloped in the neighborhood of α.

All of the useful properties of indifference curves, except for convexity, are established by the preceding arguments. To define convexity precisely: if α and β are *any* two points on the curve, and if the chord (straight line) connecting α and β lies above the curve everywhere, then the curve is convex. Convexity follows directly from the last of our axioms:

Axiom VI (Convexity of Indifference Curves): If α and β are on the same indifference curve, and if the good on the horizontal axis is scarcer at α than at β, then the indifference curve is more steeply sloped at α than at β.

To repeat: this section is intended to close some of the loopholes that were left open in Chapter 5, Section 5.1. Readers interested in formal analysis should note that the proof of continuity of indifference curves that is presented here does not apply directly to preference orderings on more than two goods. Some fixing up is necessary if these results are to be extended to many-good worlds.

BIBLIOGRAPHICAL NOTES

The material on estimation of demand curves is covered in much greater depth in any good econometrics text. One good elementary one is L. R. Klein, *Introduction to Econometrics* (Englewood Cliffs, N.J.: Prentice-Hall, 1962). The growth of economic theory out of utilitarian philosophy is briefly reviewed by George Stigler, "The Development of Utility Theory" in his *Essays in the History of Economics* (Chicago: University of Chicago Press, 1965); and Paul A. Samuelson, *Foundations of Economic Analysis* (Cambridge, Mass.: Harvard University Press, 1949), Ch. VII. The derivation of demand curves from preference orderings was, as far as I know, first done by J. R. Hicks in *Value and Capital* (New York: Oxford University Press, 1939). Hicks doesn't quite spell out the operation, but the method is implicit in his second chapter.

Finally, the material in the final section of this chapter is closely based on D. B. Bushaw and R. W. Clower's excellent *Introduction to Mathematical Economics,* (Homewood, Ill.: Irwin, 1957), now out of print. For a more comprehensive treatment, and less restrictive axiom systems, see D. W. Katzner, *Static Demand Theory* (New York: Macmillan, 1970), a mathematically advanced book.

CHAPTER SEVEN

Business Firms and the Division of Labor

GLORIOUS OPPORTUNITY TO GET RICH

We are starting a cat ranch in Lacon with 100,000 cats. Each cat will average twelve kittens a year. The cat skins will sell for thirty cents each. One hundred men can skin 5,000 cats a day. We figure a daily profit of over $10,000. Now what shall we feed the cats? We will start a rat ranch next door with 1,000,000 rats. The rats will breed twelve times faster than the cats. So we will have four rats to feed each day to each cat. Now what shall we feed the rats? We will feed the rats the carcasses of the cats after they have been skinned. Now get this! We feed the rats to the cats, and the cats to the rats, and get the skins for nothing.

ANONYMOUS (1875)

7.1. "SYMMETRY" BETWEEN SUPPLY AND DEMAND

In the last three chapters a simple but important idea was developed: if for any reason the *relative price* of a good falls, then the rate of use of the good by individuals will usually increase. Here, an important related problem is taken up. This chapter investigates the way that relative prices affect decisions to provide, or supply, various goods. It will be seen in symmetry with the results obtained regarding demand, that a higher relative price will usually evoke a greater willingness on the part of individuals to provide the good, or relinquish their holdings of it. This similarity of motivation that exists between supply and demand is greatest in a simple exchange economy, with fixed endowments of all goods (see Chapter 2, Section 2.2). In such an economy, quantity supplied and quantity demand are indistinguishable. Figure 7.1 illustrates in the familiar context of two goods and two traders that in an exchange which leads to equilibrium, (a–a') is the Good II quantity supplied by Trader B (and demanded by Trader A); (b–b') is the quantity of Good I supplied by A and demanded by B.

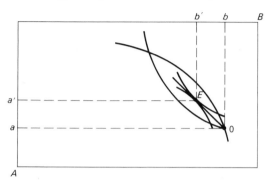

FIGURE 7.1. **"Supply" and "Demand" in a simple two-person exchange with no production.**

If the processes by which goods are created and supplied rested on the same simple considerations of taste and preference as the processes by which goods are demanded, there would be little more to say on the subject of supply. "Supply" would simply be a symmetric part of the act of exchange; the goods "supplied" by one party of the exchange are "demanded" by the other party, and vice versa, as in the simple box diagram analysis of Figure 7.1. In an idealized world, where knowledge of the future is free and exchange transactions consume no time or effort, we can imagine individuals creating things which bring satisfaction, pleasure, or comfort, and trading those things for the similar creations of other people when such exchange is seen to be mutually advantageous. However, the day is past (if it ever existed) when goods were crafted predominantly at the initiative and discretion of individuals; and in order to discuss the supply side of the market intelligently and with insight, we must understand the technology of production and the role of business firms; and we must look into the economic forces that underlie the development of the business firm as an important institution in the economy. The first and most important reason why business firms have arisen is a technical one; important gains in efficiency can be realized by *specialization*.

7.2. SPECIALIZATION AND THE DIVISION OF LABOR

An important idea of long standing (developed at length in the eighteenth-century writings of Adam Smith) is that gains can be realized by organizing production activity as a sequence of specialized steps. With specialized organization, manual skills can be refined, and special tools and equipment can be designed for each task in the production process. The result of simplifying the individual jobs and providing special equipment will be an increase in the rate of output.

The productivity gains from this *division of labor* have always been easier to illustrate and exemplify than to analyze; economists have always taken it for granted that physiologists and psychologists could explain the origins of the gains. Familiar examples are (a) modern assembly-line operation, in which each worker has a very narrowly defined specialized task; (b) football coaching, in which one man is responsible for tutoring defensive backs, another for offensive interior linemen, a third for quarterbacks, and so forth; and (c) modern physics, in which one man does high-energy physics, another plasma physics, a third quantum theory, and so forth. In fact, the division of labor extends to and affects almost every line of human activity including the family. Three recognizably important questions will now be considered: (1) What are the sources of the gain that is realized from the division of labor? (2) What determines how far division of labor will be carried? (3) What offsetting faults have been alleged regarding the division of labor?[1]

7.2.1. Where do the Gains Come From?

As has already been mentioned, the gains that come from specialized operation are not too well-understood. Some of those gains can be attributed to the physical nature of man—he learns by doing, and repetition develops coordination and facility. Another source of gain is in a better ordering of the worker's physical environment—with division of labor, there is less need for any worker to move about or to change tools. Specialization in labor is usually accompanied by the invention and use of productive equipment which itself is specialized to a simple task. The introduction of such special equipment may in turn lead to additional specialties, each one related to some phase of construction, installation, or maintenance of that equipment. We should be careful to avoid the view, however, that the machines ''cause'' or ''are the reason for'' the division of labor; it is even an exaggeration to say that division of labor is made possible by the machines. In a society that had only rudimentary hand tools, like the ''Island Paradise'' of Chapter 2, we would expect to encounter a division of labor; specialized tools are not a precondition. On the contrary, it would seem that ideas for the kinds of machines that can be developed are suggested by the search for more efficient ways to divide labor. The precise pattern that the division of labor will take will depend in part on the productive equipment that is available; but the tendency to specialize in production precedes the introduction of specialized productive equipment.

---

[1]This question has a strong ideological flavor; because it would interrupt the flow of the economic analysis at this point, its discussion is deferred (Chapter 10, Section 10.5).

Our findings on this first question, then, are in part negative: the gains from specialization do *not* come solely from the provision of specialized equipment.

7.2.2. What Limits the Extent of Specialization?

Known techniques of production impose a limit on specialization, but in addition, the demand for output (the rate of sale that can be achieved at market-determined prices) will play an important part in shaping the extent of specialization. Goods for which there is little demand at prevailing market prices (like racing sulkies or Givenchy gowns) are not produced by elaborate, highly mechanized processes involving the skills of many specialists, at least, not by comparison to "comparable" goods like bicycles or J. C. Penney frocks. This is the essence of Adam Smith's famous dictum that "the division of labor is limited by the extent of the market." Smith's statement should not be confused with the (false) converse proposition that the extent of the market is limited or determined by the division of labor. A technology of supply that involves significant division of labor will be uneconomical unless a large scale of operation can be sustained: that is, unless there is significant demand, there will be little division of labor in the production of a good. Keep in mind that the availability of a division-of-labor technology does not assure that significant demand for a good will be forthcoming. Nor, conversely, does it follow that the market for a good will be small because division of labor is avoided in production of the good, although this rather muddled idea sometimes seems to be widely current.[2]

Specialization is of further importance because it offers an answer to the question: why do we have business firms? Specialization brings up the need for coordination, and the need for coordination has brought about a heavy reliance upon peculiar organizations called business firms to organize production. Business firms have much in common with the central planning authorities of socialist states: both firms and planning bureaus are mechanisms that reduce the scope of market exchange in the process of resource allocation.

7.3. THE FIRM

7.3.1. Market Organization of Production Processes: The Rejected Alternative

People tend to take familiar things for granted, so few people can be expected to wonder why business firms exist. In Chapter 3 we offered the proposition that

---

[2]Note the text's use of an example of a good—a famous couturier's dresses—which is popularly assumed to owe its value to the fact that it is individually handcrafted instead of mass-produced. The reader should note that the market for this "style good" is small because its price is high (relative to other kinds of clothing); and because the market is small, the good is individually handcrafted. It is *not* the case that reliance on handcrafting necessarily implies a high price and hence a smaller market. The issue can be clarified by asking whether Paris originals, if made by a highly mechanized process but sold in lots of one, would sell for a lower price than their handcrafted counterparts. There is no reason to suppose they would sell for less, and good reason to suppose that they would cost more.

much in the way our economy is organized rests on an individualistic outlook; and throughout we have argued that market exchange processes serve an individualistically oriented society very well. Why, then, is production not entirely a market-directed process? We can envision an economy in which every step in the production of every good is accomplished by market action—a worker buys some goods to work on, then sells his output to a man at the next higher stage of production for still more processing. The worker need not own the equipment that enables him to perform his chosen task most effectively; an owner of such equipment could rent it to the worker at a market-determined rate. Under such an arrangement there would be no worker-employer relationship, no person concerned with the problem of how production processes should be structured, and no problem of negotiating terms or conditions of employment.

The first important drawback of such extensive reliance on "market" organization is the heavy demand it would impose on the ability of the economy to transmit information. Every time an individual processed a batch of materials, he would be faced with the problem of finding another individual to take the batch for further processing. Over time, of course, the problem of learning whose tastes in productive activity meshed with one's own would be solved; and we would expect individuals who "fitted together" well in the production of a good to form tacit or explicit contracts to take up and pass on a particular volume of work. Thus, the first obstacle to market organization can be overcome, but in surmounting that obstacle, some of the freedom of action that individuals would have in a fully market-directed regime would be given up. A second obstacle then appears—the contracts to purchase and to deliver, which span the work in process between raw materials and finished goods, are bound to break down if consumer tastes shift in an important way. In a world of uncertainty, shifts in taste (with a resulting breakdown of contracts) is always a possibility. Thus, each independent operator must wonder: how large a batch of goods can I safely contract to handle? Every individual will assess the future in his own way, and if each person decides a different amount should be produced, the smooth working of the market system is impaired: contracts for purchase and delivery become very difficult to arrange. The individual producers of a good might try to *insure* against changes in consumer taste that result in the drying up of demand for the good they help to produce. Such insurance arrangements would be much like employment insurance, in which a worker buys a guarantee that part of his salary will continue until six months after he loses his job. An underwriter could probably be found who would sell guarantees to individual producers that they will receive a minimum level of income for a specified period.

By the time an individual has established continuing relations with a small group of fellow workers, and has signed over a part of his proceeds in exchange for an assured income level, he has moved a long way from our initial picture of self-determination limited only by impersonal market forces. He has given up a degree of control over what he will do and how extensive his activity will be; and he has accepted bounds on what his returns will be as well. He in fact has done something very much like an individual does who goes to work for General Electric, or IBM, or Procter & Gamble—he has become the employee of a firm: in effect, if not in name.

There is another kind of insurance workers will find to be desirable. Suppose the final product fails owning to worker negligence. If the worker sells his services directly to the final consumer, then any legal redress the consumer may have will be directly against the worker himself. As an employee of a firm, the negligent worker can be fired, but his accumulated personal wealth cannot be confiscated to compensate the consumer for any loss that may have been sustained. That compensation for loss is payable by the firm. Thus, the firm is a liability insurance agent for the worker as well as an unemployment insurance agent.

(It should be noticed that this liability insurance role extends in an important way to the customer, as well as to the worker. A customer who purchases from a firm has greater assurance of being able to secure compensation for any loss he may sustain. It is easy to find and to sue a firm; it might be next to impossible to find and to sue a negligent worker who was involved in a chain of market transactions for goods at intermediate stages of completion.)

7.3.2. The Firm: A Traditional View

The foregoing discussion may well indicate why firms emerge in a market economy. Firms economize on transmission of information, and they offer some degree of protection against uncertain events that would otherwise depress the incomes of workers. Few if any other benefits can be provided by the central and arbitrary direction of the firm that cannot as well be provided by the diffuse and taste-directed mechanism of the market. In economic theory, the organizer and dictator of the firm's activity is called the *entrepreneur* (enterpriser). The entrepreneur obtains productive equipment for the firm, either out of his own wealth or by borrowing. He directs the firm's activity, and signs contracts with labor which protect workers to a large extent against income fluctuation. Because his reward is obtained by keeping that which is left over out of the firm's sales proceeds after workers and lenders have been paid, his goal is to make the firm's returns through time as high as possible. The job he faces in maximizing these returns has at least two highly interdependent important parts: *market forecasting*—he must decide what he should produce on the basis of what can be sold profitably; and *production organizing*—he must decide how resources should be organized at any given point in time, and through time.

The traditional view of the firm, with the entrepeneur at the helm, is somewhat anachronistic. If that view has any model in history or reality, it is an early nineteenth-century English proprietorship. Two of its assumptions have been pointed to by numerous writers as patently false: first, a single individual (or unanimous group) is assumed to set the firm's goals, make its decisions, and bear its risks. And second, the goal underlying the activity of the firm is assumed to be the highest level of return that can be obtained by legitimate means—or, as it is usually stated, the highest "profits" that can be obtained. A large and inconclusive literature exists on the questions (a) How important is the fact that under the modern corporate form of organization, a firm's owners seldom have any role in its operating decisions? (b) How "realistic" is the assumption of returns-maximization as the common goal of those who make decisions in the firm? (c) If the returns-maximization assumption is unrealistic, what alternative, more realistic assumptions can be indicated? (d) How would alternative, more realistic assumptions about ownership, control, and motivation affect the analytical theory of the firm?

We should note that neither of the questioned assumptions in any way affects the foregoing analysis of why firms exist. Both, however, especially the second, play an important part in shaping our subsequent analysis of how firms operate; they are important in the traditional analysis of market supply decisions. It is, then, necessary to recognize the existence of questions about the structure and goals of a firm, and further to recognize that these questions may be important. We will take the view that firms behave *as if* a single intelligent decision-maker is responsible for all choices, and seeks to find the highest level of returns. We take this view for several reasons. (1) It is analytically tractable: it leads to simple formulations of firm behavior. (2) It is the only view of the firm that has been offered so far which yields useful and empirically testable predictions about firm behavior. Finally, (3) it is consistent with the crude fact that firms which are not profitable frequently do not survive, and hence, some continuing concern for profitability can be expected within the firm. None of these defenses is an adequate or sufficient ground for rejecting a "superior" theory of the firm: one that is easy to understand, can be made to yield useful predictions, and is more descriptively appealing in the bargain. However, unfortunate though it may be, no such superior theory has yet been developed; in fact, there is little to show for the past substantial effort that has been invested in the search for superior theories.

7.4. ORGANIZING, FINANCING, AND MEASURING THE SUCCESS OF A BUSINESS

7.4.1. Proprietorships and Corporations

In order for a beginner to understand the workings of the market system, he or she should master the elements of economic theory; but moreover, he or she should acquire some knowledge about our economic institutions. The purpose of this section is to provide some extremely important institutional material from the fields of law, accounting, and business finance. We want to know: in terms of the law, what is a business firm? Where and how does a firm get the *liquid capital* necessary to begin and to continue its operations? What techniques are used to measure the income that is generated by the activity of the firm?

To some economics students, institutional material is terribly dull stuff, while to others, it's a breath of fresh air from the real world after all that indigestible theory. However regarded, this material is essential to a grasp of such diverse topics as the way income is divided between rich and poor and the reasons why business firms merge with one another; hence it is worth the time and effort that we allocate to it. We begin with a discussion of proprietorships and corporations, the two different legally recognized forms of organization that firms can have.

A firm is an organization that produces and sells goods or services. Under the law, a firm has many of the important attributes of a person. It can own property, sign contracts, engage in lawsuits, own patent rights, or go bankrupt. Firms can merge with other firms, which is a bit like getting married, or they can "spin off" other firms, an act analogous to having children. Anyone can found a firm. In some states or locales, it is necessary to register as a business establishment, and in some trades it is necessary to have a license. But for the most part, it is as easy to start a firm as it is to buy an automobile or get married.

The question of a firm's ownership and organizational form is absolutely crucial. Small firms that are wholly owned by single individuals are called *proprietorships* or (if there is more than one owner) *partnerships*. A proprietor can borrow money, sign legal documents, and employ people in the name of the firm. If anything goes wrong with the firm, the proprietor is wholly responsible. For example, if the proprietorship's delivery van runs over a pedestrian, the proprietor is sued (even if someone else was driving), and if the law awards a large settlement in favor of the pedestrian, the proprietor may lose the full amount of his personal wealth; he may have to sell his home and his wife's jewelry to pay the settlement. Or, if the firm fails, the proprietor may have to sell his car and house in order to pay the firm's debts. The same legal stipulations hold for a partnership: partners are personally liable for the debts of their firm.

Corporations are organized rather more intricately. A corporation must have a charter from a state before it may open up for business. (The states all permit each other's corporations to do business; it is not necessary for a corporation to be chartered by every state in which it operates.) Ownership shares in the corporation are sold: these shares are called *stock*, and the individuals who buy the shares, thereby becoming part owners of the corporation, are called *stockholders*. The principal difference between being a stockholder and a proprietor is in the fact that a stockholder's liability is limited to the amount of money he "put into the firm"—the amount of his stock purchase. Thus, when a corporation goes bankrupt, no stockholder's personal belongings can be confiscated to cover the debts of the firm. Typically, the ownership of corporations is diffuse: there are many stockholders. It is not unusual, however, for major stockholders to own a fairly large portion of the firm's stock, and some corporations are without any question controlled by single individuals or families.

A corporation is governed by a board of directors; members are elected by stockholders. These directors may be, but need not be, important holders of the firm's stock. The board in turn hires an administrative staff for the firm: a president, vice-president, and so on. Organization of management, and allocation of responsibilities and functions of these officers, are decided upon within the firm. Management decides in practice what shall be produced by the firm and how, subject to the advice and consent of the board. When major "policy" changes are undertaken, as in the introduction of entirely new products, it is customary to seek the board's approval before proceeding. To that extent, the elected representatives of the firm's owners maintain a degree of control over the firm's activity. Otherwise, management has a fairly free hand in deciding what shall be done in the firm. Occasionally, management operates in a way that displeases the holders of a significantly large part of the firm's stock; these stockholders can then try to force a reorganization of the firm by electing a new board of directors which in turn reorganizes the management. Naturally, the better the firm's performance has been relative to that of other firms, the less likely a reorganizing effort is to succeed: stockholders will vote for the status quo if the firm's earnings have been good. We turn to a simple illustration of the way earnings are measured in a firm.

7.4.2. The Measurement of Earnings

Suppose a firm is organized to produce some useful good, like fingernail clippers. For some reason, a founder believes that high returns can be earned from a production of that good, and he takes out a corporation charter. His charter permits him to issue a specified number of shares of stock. He may use his personal funds to buy a part of that stock. The rest of the stock is sold to friends, or to the general public at large through a brokerage house, a firm that specializes in arranging the purchases and sales of stock of other firms. A price per share is worked out with the brokerage house. The brokers may underwrite the stock issue—that is, guarantee a particular price per share; if they can sell the stock for more to the public, they keep the difference.

The money obtained from the initial stock issue is the firm's *liquid capital*. Liquid capital is used to rent or purchase plant and office space, productive equipment, and raw materials to begin production. Workers and managers are hired, and production begins.

Goods are produced, stored, and eventually, sold. Cash flows into the firm as proceeds of those sales, and is added to the firm's liquid capital. Periodically, the firm presents a record and evidence of its performance to its stockholders and other interested parties in the form of an *income statement*. An income statement tabulates the total proceeds from sales of the firm's output; deducts the cash outlays for labor, materials, and selling effort incurred in producing goods and generating sales; makes allowance for the cost of maintaining the plant and equipment used in production, and deducts that amount; and reports the difference as net income, as in Table 7.1.

Let's pause to examine each category in that income statement. Sales revenue, of course, is the dollars taken in by the firm from customers. The total may include promises to pay, as well as cash paid: it is very common to receive payment for goods sold a few days after the goods are shipped. The expenses, apart from depreciation, are fairly obvious items which measure cash outlays: for our manufacturer of nail clippers, the materials will be steel, lacquer, and packaging; wages are the payment to everyone engaged in activity that contributes to production; and rents are in payment for office space, factory space, and warehouse space used, but not owned, by the firm. Depreciation is not a cash outflow, but rather an estimate of the extent to which productive capital owned by the firm is "used up" in production. There are many misconceptions about the nature and purpose of depreciation: some people view it as a deduction from sales revenues sufficient to recover the purchase price of the asset, or as a fund in which the replacement cost of assets is recovered. However, depreciation is neither of those things: it is simply an indication (to management, owners, and others who are interested in the firm) of the size of the decline in the productive potential of the firm's capital.

On the basis of that operating income, taxes are levied against the firm. Because the firm is a corporation, the federal corporation income tax is charged. That tax is levied at a rate of 22 percent on the first $25,000 of income, and at a rate of 48 percent on all income above that amount. The remainder, operating income less taxes, is called the firm's *profit*.

That profit is used in two ways. *Dividends* are payments to the owners of stock; they are the owners' share of profit. *Retained earnings* are kept within the firm. Dividends are a drain on the firm's liquid capital, and retained earnings conserve liquid capital. A firm that is in need of liquid capital, for the purposes

TABLE 7.1. Simple Version of an Income Statement for a Hypothetical Business Firm

FINGERSHREDDER, INCORPORATED
Income Statement
Year Ending June 31, 19XX

Sales Revenue		$7,465
Less: Cost of Goods Sold		
Materials	$2,210	
Wages	1,340	
Rents	1,400	
Depreciation	1,350	6,300
Gross Margin		$1,165

of repairing equipment, embarking on an advertising campaign, paying bonuses to managers, or whatever, will tend to cut down its dividend payments and increase its retained earnings.

The main departures from realism in this very simple picture of the income-generating process are: (1) The firm in reality may produce more or less than it sells in any given period; inventories of finished goods are used as sources to feed excesses of sales over production, and vice versa. (2) There may be significant selling costs (advertising) involved in merchandising the firm's output. These costs are charged against the firm's gross margin; the difference is called the firm's *operating income*. (3) Nonoperating income from the sale of assets, or from other sources (returns, perhaps, on securities owned in the name of the firm), can occasionally arise, and is subject to taxation. (4) Government is concerned with the way a firm measures depreciation, because the greater the amount of depreciation, the lower the firm's earnings are, and the smaller the amount of income tax that is collected from the firm. Because of this governmental concern, the actual methods of taking depreciation have very little to do with the ideal described above: the amount of depreciation actually charged may not be a realistic representation of the change in the value of potential output from the depreciated asset.

The accounting concepts of expense and income are not the same as the economic concepts of cost and profit. An economist would emphasize that the resources used in the production of nail clippers might each individually have been used in some other application. The returns that could have been realized in its most favorable alternative application are taken to be the proper measure of the cost of each resource. Thus, the accountant's operating income, which, except for depreciation, is composed of cash receipts less cash payments, differs from the measure of profit that an economist would propose, because it ignores opportunities foregone. (But as we will see later, under the equilibrium conditions of theoretically perfect market competition, that difference is nil. If every input's price is equal to the value of its marginal product, there are no discrepancies between prices paid by firms for inputs and the opportunity costs of using those inputs.)

7.4.3. Retained Earnings and Dividends

An owner obtains a share of the firm's earnings from dividends, and the firm protects its liquid capital by retention of earnings. However, there are other effects from the split between dividends and retained earnings—effects that are felt by both the owners and the managers of the firm—and these effects must be explicitly considered. Insofar as management is concerned, earnings retention may make it possible to avoid borrowing (through the issuance and sale of *bonds*) or issuing new stock in order to obtain liquid capital. That may simply serve to make the conduct of the firm's day-to-day operations easier; or it may make it possible for the firm to expand or diversify its operations without seeking new stockholders or lenders.

Insofar as the stockholders are concerned, the retention of earnings has three effects: first, it reduces the amount of dividend income that the stockholders receive from the firm in the current period of time. Second, it increases the firm's *future* earning prospects. (To see this, consider the alternative of having the firm borrow funds. In future periods, the firm will be committed to pay out interest on those borrowings, and that interest would reduce the income available for distribution or retention in future periods.) Third, it makes the stockholder's income stream more uncertain. The stockholder, as an owner of the firm, has a claim on the firm's earnings in the current period. The retained portion of those earnings to which he is entitled is not paid out to him as dividends. Instead, they stay within the firm and are put to work. Because those earnings will be productive, the value of the firm's stock shares will probably rise in anticipation of higher future earnings. The rise in share values gives the stockholder an opportunity to sell his shares at a higher price; he can realize what is called *capital gains*. The amount of capital gain that results from the retention of earnings in the firm may be much more than the stockholder would have received as dividends had the earnings not been retained in the firm, or it may be much less, or it may be the same amount. There is no way to know in advance how large the price change of each share will be. In effect, by retaining its earnings, the firm gives each shareholder a lottery ticket on each share of stock that is held. The price of the ticket is the amount of earnings per share retained in the firm. The payoff realized on the lottery ticket is the size of the resulting capital gain. Different shareholders have different attitudes toward this practice of converting ordinary dividend income into capital gains. Some will prefer the more uniform and predictable stream of earnings that dividends can provide, while others, hoping for a larger return, will be attracted by the higher future income possibilities afforded by retained earnings.

Regardless of how an individual may feel about the predictability of his earnings from stock ownership, however, the tax laws convey benefits to individuals who take their income in the form of capital gains. If a shareholder has owned stock for at least six months before he sells it, he is taxed on the gains he realizes from its sale at only half the rate he would pay on dividend income, under the present federal income tax laws.

What are capital gains, precisely, and how do they differ from ordinary income? Ideally, the goal in defining and measuring capital gains is to distinguish regular and readily anticipated income flows from occasional and unpredictable changes in the value of asset holdings. The reasons for seeking such a distinction are somewhat bogus; they are based in part on historical misconceptions regarding the nature of capital and factors that influence the consumption of individuals; and in part on ancient English traditions and laws governing the inheritance of property. With the passage of time, the distinction between capital gains and "ordinary income" has become firmly entrenched, but legal definitions of capital gains have fluctuated. Individuals who sell any good or asset for more than its purchase price usually call the resulting gain a capital gain, and not income. Business firms may not count the proceeds of their "customary stock in trade" as capital gains; thus, our fingernail clipper manufacturer would not be eligible to declare the income from any transaction involving the sale of clippers as a capital gain (though he could legally declare the proceeds of the sale of a truck or a factory as a capital gain). What is important, however, is that shareholders may count any rise in price between the time they buy stock and the time they sell it as a capital gain, and they will pay less tax on that sort of income as long as the two transactions are at least six months apart.

The tax laws are the major reason, and perhaps the only reason, why the distinction between capital gains and other income is preserved. People who obtain large proceeds by buying and selling assets like land or stock are understandably keen to see the distinction (and the lower tax rates) continued.

With this background material in hand, we turn to a more formal and theoretical examination of how firms operate, with the goal of understanding how supply decisions are made, and the major economic forces that affect supply decisions.

APPLICATIONS AND EXTENSIONS[3]

1. Suppose that a well-coordinated "team" of workers produces a certain known output. If one (randomly chosen) worker is taken off the team, output declines. That decline in output is a measure of a worker's marginal product (denoted MP).

    Next suppose that total output exceeds $MP \cdot n$, where n is the number of workers, as long as production is properly organized. Does the entrepreneur (the individual in charge of organizing workers) earn anything under these circumstances?

2. Now suppose individual workers' productive efforts cannot be directly measured. (They may put in time on the job, but perform in a slack way.) When one worker on the team slacks off, team output declines. What methods of monitoring or incentive systems can you imagine that might successfully combat a tendency of workers to slack off under these circumstances?

3. If it is true that organization and coordination enhances productivity, is that a further reason to expect business firms to organize and hire workers on a contractual basis; or can the benefits of coordination be expected to emerge from an arrangement in which workers are tied together by the kind of hypothetical market relations described in Section 7.2?

[3]The following questions are suggested by Alchian and Demsetz; see the Bibliographical Note.

BIBLIOGRAPHICAL NOTE

The question of why firms exist received its standard treatment by R. H. Coase, ''The Nature of the Firm,'' reprinted in G. J. Stigler and K. Boulding, eds., *AEA Readings in Price Theory* (Homewood, Ill.: Irwin, 1952). A recent interesting treatment of the same topic is A. Alchian and H. Demsetz, ''Production, Information Costs and Economic Organization,'' *American Economic Review* (1972).

The material on organization forms, tax laws, etc. is a distillation of information customarily covered by business school courses in accounting, finance, and business law.

CHAPTER EIGHT

Production Decisions, Cost, and Market Supply

Do you know,
Considering the market, there are more
Poems produced than any other thing?
No wonder poets sometimes have to *seem*
So much more businesslike than businessmen.
Their wares are so much harder to get rid of.

ROBERT FROST (1923)

8.1. REAL COSTS AND THE PRODUCTION DECISION

Here we begin a formal theoretical analysis of the process of production in the firm. Our goal is to understand how the mechanism of market supply works, according to economic theory. Throughout this chapter, we will deal with producers whose individual resource-utilization decisions have no impact on resource prices: we will, in other words, assume that resource markets are *competitive*.

Consider an asparagus grower, who uses fertilizer, land, water, and labor in cultivation of his crop. Suppose he holds the usage rate of the first three of those productive inputs constant, but adds successive hours of his own labor to the cultivation of asparagus. The data in Table 8.1 are a hypothetical record of his experience.

In asparagus culture, the value of additional units of labor input is measured by the pounds of asparagus output that result if those units are added. The third

TABLE 8.1.

Man-Hours of Labor Input Per Week	Pounds of Asparagus Output Obtained at Harvest	Output Gain (Marginal Physical Product)
0	0	
—	—	
15	250	—
16	270	20
17	294	24
18	320	26
19	350	30*
20	378	28
21	402	24
22	419	17

*MPP increases up to this point, declines beyond it.

column of Table 8.1 shows *marginal physical product* (the extra units of output obtained from the marginal, or additional, hour of labor that is applied each week). Several rules can be suggested for determining when to stop adding man-hours of labor input to asparagus culture in the illustrated case. We might consider: "add no more labor when the marginal physical product stops increasing," or "continue adding labor until the marginal physical product becomes negative" as possibilities. But neither makes sense if the farmer is motivated by a desire for higher returns. As a third possibility, consider the rule "stop adding labor when the returns obtained from an additional man-hour per week in asparagus culture are outweighed by the returns obtained from the man-hour per week applied in some alternative pursuit." This last prescription offers a sensible guide. Suppose, for example, that the returns to the farmer from an hour of labor in asparagus cultivation exceed the returns from an hour in strawberry cultivation. Then the farmer would rather devote the hour to work on asparagus instead of strawberries. How can the returns in the two cases be compared? If information on marginal physical product in the cultivation of both crops is available, and if the selling prices of both crops are known, then the farmer can compare the dollar returns from the additional hour spent in cultivating asparagus to the returns that result from spending that hour on strawberries. From that comparison he can judge where the additional hour of labor is best allocated. These dollar returns from an additional hour of labor are called the *value of the marginal product* of labor.

In Table 8.2, we see that when 21 hours per week are spent on asparagus and 17 hours per week are spent on strawberries, an additional hour spent on asparagus has a value of $5.10, or $1.50 more than is realized from another hour of labor spent on strawberry culture. It follows that the man-hour should be allocated to asparagus rather than strawberries, if these are the only two crops being considered for more intensive cultivation. Indeed, the farmer would be well advised to give up an hour of strawberry cultivation and apply the hour to asparagus. In doing so, he sacrifices output worth $4.80 (the cost of moving from 17 to 16 hours per week of strawberry cultivation) and gains output worth $5.10 (the value of moving to 22 hours from 21 hours in asparagus).

TABLE 8.2.

ASPARAGUS (.30/LB)				STRAWBERRIES (.60/QT)			
Man-hours per week	Output (lb)	MPP	VMP	Man-hours per week	Output (qt)	MPP	VMP
21	402			16	320		
22	419	17	$5.10	17	328	8	$4.80
23	432	13	3.90	18	334	6	3.60
24	441	9	2.70	19	339	5	3.00
25	448	7	2.10	20	343	4	2.40
26	454	6	1.80	21	344	2	1.20

VMP: Value of marginal product
MPP: Marginal physical product

In theory, this type of calculation applies to the problem of allocating *all* productive resources among *all* competing uses. In simple terms, the calculation tells the producer that returns and costs of any resource application must be compared at the margin. If returns exceed costs as a result of expanding some line of activity slightly, then that activity should be carried out more extensively. The output at which costs are no longer less than returns at the margin is the point at which further expansion of the activity should cease. If returns nowhere exceed costs the activity should not be carried out at all.

Real (opportunity) costs.   With the foregoing illustration in hand, let us now ask: what is the cost of devoting an additional man-hour to asparagus culture? To an economist the cost is, simply, the returns that could be realized from the next most rewarding use of the resource—in our example, the returns from cultivating strawberries for an additional man-hour. This idea of real cost permeates economic analysis, and when economists talk about "cost," they always are referring to the concept just illustrated. *The cost of an activity (or good) is the greatest value or satisfaction foregone by choosing to engage in that activity (or obtain that good).*

What if agricultural laborers can be hired at $2.50 per hour, and their marginal products are as shown in Table 8.2? Certainly it will pay the farmer to intensify the cultivation of both asparagus *and* strawberries; in fact, Table 8.2 tells us he should hire additional labor up to the level of slightly over 24 man-hours in asparagus cultivation, and just under 20 man-hours for the strawberry bed. In this case, the "opportunity cost" *to the farmer* is measured by the *wage* he must pay to the workers brought in. As with the problem of allocating his own time, the farmer will hire additional labor as long as the value of the marginal product of labor, from sale of the crops produced during the additional man-hours worked, exceeds the price that he must pay to obtain those man-hours. That is to say, in general, resources are applied in production as long as the value of their marginal product exceeds their cost. In the case of the farmer discussed here, if only his own labor is available, the cost of using that labor in asparagus cultivation is the value of output foregone by not cultivating something else. (Possibly, he may value an additional hour of leisure more highly than the value of his marginal product in cultivating *any* crop, in which case the rule tells him he should spend less time, rather than more time, in cultivating his crops.) In general, then, optimal resource-use decisions must satisfy the conditions

$$\text{VMP}_{i,j} = w_i \qquad \begin{array}{l} \text{all inputs } i = 1,2,3,\ldots, m \\ \text{all outputs } j = 1,2,3,\ldots, n \end{array} \qquad (1)$$

In this shorthand statement, $\text{VMP}_{i,j}$ is the value of the marginal product obtained by applying the input numbered i to the output numbered j. w_i is the opportunity cost of an additional unit of the input numbered i. The rule must hold for all m inputs and all n outputs (where m and n are the numbers of input goods used and output goods produced by a producer).

This prescription may not be directly helpful as a guide to action, because it requires that the producer have precise knowledge of the productivity of additional units of input (as in column 3 of Tables 8.1 and 8.2). Even if the rule is not easy to apply consciously, however, it remains important as a tool of analysis. The analysis assumes that the marginal product rule will be implemented crudely by trial and error, if not precisely by rational calculation. At the very least, gross violations of the rule will be noticed and corrected, thereby bring actual practice into closer conformity with the rule's prediction.

Two important questions are to be considered now that the concepts of *marginal productivity* and *real cost* have been spelled out. First, we want to investigate how a supply decision is made by producers. Cost is important in such a decision. Second, there is the question of what imposes a limit on the size of individual firms. Cost is an important element in the conventional answer to that question, too.

8.2. THE FIRM'S OUTPUT DECISION

8.2.1. Cost and Production

The comparison of costs to returns at the margin, which was seen to determine the farmer's employment and allocation of labor, can also be seen to underlie the output decision of a firm. Just as a farmer will continue to hire additional labor as long as the returns per man-hour exceed the wage rate, so a business firm will continue to increase the output of its product, as long as the sum of all costs of making and selling an additional unit of output is less than the revenue received from its sale. The business firm measures the opportunity cost of additional output units in precisely the same way that the farmer measures the opportunity cost of an additional unit of his own time in application to asparagus culture. The firm is conscious of the revenue to be realized from the different possible applications of the various resources it uses in production. A firm that cans asparagus is passing up the chance to can pears; over a long enough period of time the firm could even conceivably switch over and make shotgun shells or baby furniture instead of canning asparagus. Only if asparagus canning brings higher returns to the firm than the many other pursuits it could engage in will the firm continue putting asparagus into cans. An economist would say that the costs exceed the returns to asparagus canning if the firm could direct its resources into some other line of activity that brought higher returns.

The firm's resource-use decisions will determine its rate of output. What conditions will be satisfied when output is optimized? For simplicity, consider a one-product firm. It can be shown[1] that when every input resource is used at the rate where the value of its marginal product is equal to its price to the firm, then it will also be true that

$$P = MC: \tag{2}$$

the price the firm receives for its output equals marginal cost, the cost of producing an additional unit of output. Thus, if the rule (1) governing the use of inputs is obeyed, the rule (2) will characterize the firm's output decision. We focus in rule (2) on the one-product firm because that case is simplest analytically. If cost is properly defined, however, the same result applies for each product of a multi-product firm; straightforward generalization to situations involving many products is always possible.

Consider what happens if the rule (2) is violated. Suppose a firm produces less than the output at which $MC = P$ (Figure 8.1). The cost of producing an additional unit from the low output h is MC_h; that cost is less than the price P at which the additional unit could be sold if it were made. Hence a clear gain of $P - MC_h$ would be realized on the additional unit if the firm produced $h + 1$ units instead of h. Gains of that kind are sacrificed whenever price exceeds marginal cost for the chosen rate of output. A different type of loss is entailed if production continues beyond the point where price equals marginal cost. In Figure 8.1, at the high output rate H, the firm could save MC_H dollars by cutting its output back to $H - 1$ units; and the firm would lose P dollars by selling one unit less. Hence, a gain of $MC_H - P$ dollars is obtained if output is reduced by one unit when price is *less than* marginal cost.

The returns-conscious firm, then, will always seek the rate of output at which

[1]As, for example, in Appendix III of this chapter.

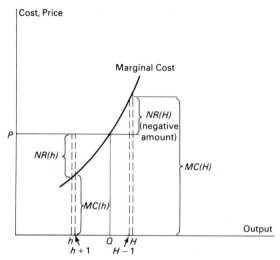

FIGURE 8.1. Losses of net revenue when output is too small *(h)* or too large *(H)*.

price and marginal cost are equal. Only at that output rate is it not possible to earn higher returns by changing the rate of output. Hence, the marginal cost curve tells us the quantity that the firm will supply at different prices: in Figure 8.1 we know P; we see that at the output Q marginal cost is just equal to P; hence Q will be supplied when market price is P. (All this depends, we must remember, on the condition that the firm does not believe a change in its own output rate will affect market price.)

To discuss *how* cost behaves when input uses vary and output changes, it is necessary to develop some modest technical apparatus, which we turn to now.

8.2.2. Production Functions

A firm's *production function* indicates the maximum amount of output that it can produce from any specific combination of productive input quantities. For example, the hypothetical data on asparagus production in Table 8.1 could be deduced from the production function of the farmer. His usage rates of several productive inputs—labor, seed, land, fertilizer, etc.—are "mapped into" (or are functionally related to) different rates of output.

Production functions can be represented in various ways, but most generally as mathematical formulas. For a simple example, if a firm has only one output y and two inputs x_1 and x_2, its production function has the implicit-form representation

$$y = F(x_1, x_2),$$

which we read "the rate of output is a function of the input usage rates."

A production function of a firm with one output and two inputs can easily be graphed: Figure 8.2 shows how. The curve labeled $y = y^0$ shows the various different combinations of the inputs x_1 and x_2 that will yield the output rate y^0, if those inputs are used according to the best known techniques of production.[2] Such a curve is called an *isoquant*.

8.2.3. The Minimum-Cost Input Mix

Cost of production will depend on input prices and on the productivity of the inputs in the chosen mixture. *Any given output rate is achieved at minimum cost when it is not possible to spend a dollar more on one input and thereby save more than a dollar by buying less of the other input.* Suppose the firm wants to produce output at the rate y^0 at minimum cost (Figure 8.2). That output rate can be produced with the input rates (a_1, a_2); i.e., at the point a; but it will not be economical to produce it that way. Total expenditure on the purchase of inputs can be reduced with no loss of output by substituting input 1 for input 2 in the production process. Continued substitution in that direction will yield additional gains until a point of tangency is reached, between the expenditure line through the chosen input combination (E is the expenditure line through the point a) and the production isoquant. At the point (x^*), that tangency condition is satisfied.

Why does this tangency condition indicate the lowest-cost input combination for production at a rate of y^0? Suppose the condition is violated, as it is when the input combination is at point a. From the point a, one unit of input 2 can be given up. The price w_2 of the unit of input 2 will be saved. If the full saving w_2 is used to purchase input 1, w_2/w_1 units of input 1 will be purchased (where w_1 is the price of input 1): the move will be to the point labeled b. But to maintain output at y^0, it is not necessary to add so much input 1: it is necessary to move only to the point labeled c. At c, the total cost of producing is lower than at b (because less of input 1 is used); it is therefore also lower than at a.

Only at x^*, where tangency holds, is the opportunity for this kind of saving not present.

The slope of the output isoquant through any point like a or x^* is equal to the ratio

$$\frac{-\Delta x_2}{\Delta x_1} = \frac{-MPP(x_1)}{MPP(x_2)} \tag{3}$$

This is easily seen. In Figure 8.3, let a small change in inputs be made from the point x: Δx_1 units of input 1 are added, and $-\Delta x_2$ units of input 2 are given up. If the change in inputs causes no change in output from y^0, it must be true that

$$\Delta x_1 \cdot MPP(x_1) - \Delta x_2 \cdot MPP(x_2) = 0. \tag{4}$$

---

[2]The similarity to the indifference curve diagrams used in the analysis of consumer preferences should be clear. In preference analysis, different levels of satisfaction were attached to various combinations of two goods consumed; in production analysis, different rates of output are associated with various rates of use of two productive inputs.

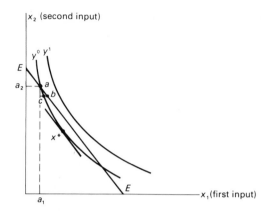

FIGURE 8.2. Two output isoquants, y^0 and y^1, for a simple two-input production process.

The quantity of input 1 added, multiplied by the rate of change of output in response to that increase, must equal the quantity of input 2 subtracted, multiplied by the rate of change of output in response to that reduction. The slope indicated in (3) follows immediately from the constant output rule (4).

The convexity (downward-bowed shape) of the output isoquants plays an important part in production analysis, and requires comment. Observe what takes place as a series of moves is made "down" an isoquant, y^1 in Figure 8.3, for example. The rate of output is maintained constant, but the input mix changes, with more x_1 and less x_2 used at each move. Convexity of the isoquant means

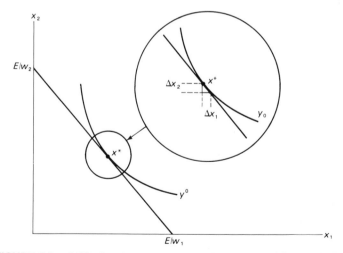

FIGURE 8.3. Achieving the output y^0 for the minimum outlay on input resources. The marginal physical product ratios must be equal to the reciprocal of the resource price ratios.

that in order to maintain the specified output rate of y^0, at each move *more* x_1 must be used for each unit of x_2 given up than was needed at the preceding move. In symbolic terms, as the input usage ratio x_1/x_2 increases, the marginal physical product ratio $MPP(x_1)/MPP(x_2)$ declines.

At the point x^*, the slope of the expenditure line is $-w_1/w_2$. The slope of the production isoquant is $-MPP(x_1)/MPP(x_2)$. From the fact that these two slopes are equal, we deduce

$$\frac{-w_1}{w_2} = \frac{-MPP(x_1)}{MPP(x_2)} \quad \text{or} \quad \frac{MPP(x_1)}{w_1} = \frac{MPP(x_2)}{w_2} \tag{5}$$

The ratios $MPP(x_i)/w_i$ are the additional units of output per additional dollar expended on each input, and these ratios must be equal, or otherwise the output objective can be achieved more cheaply by increasing expenditure on the input with the larger-valued ratio, and reducing expenditure on the input with the smaller-valued ratio. If the output isoquants are convex (as drawn in Figure 8.3), then the marginal productivity-to-price ratio condition (5) is *sufficient* as well as necessary for cost minimization; there will be *only one* input combination yielding minimum cost, and that input combination will satisfy the ratio condition.

8.2.4. Adjustment Costs and Fixed Inputs

The foregoing discussion of production functions lays the groundwork for an approach to the question: how does cost change when output changes? In approaching this important question, economists recognize that inputs may not be equally cheap to alter in the rate of their use. To change some inputs, like plant and equipment (or "physical capital"), requires considerable planning and effort by the firm. The usage rate of some other inputs can be adjusted quickly and virtually without cost. Inputs in the first category are called "fixed." *The essence of "fixity" lies in the high cost of adjustment that is met when the usage rate of fixed inputs is changed rapidly.* Variable inputs on the other hand can be altered in rate of use at virtually no additional cost.

Because fixity differs among inputs, the firm seldom changes its output rates instantly. Instead, such changes typically are worked out over time. In a simple two-input production process, the more variable of the two inputs is first adjusted in its usage rate. At this stage, the output adjustment process is in the *short run*. In the *long run*, both inputs have been adjusted to the new output program. In Figure 8.4, the *short-run output adjustment path* of the firm is labeled *SRA*. It is drawn under the assumption that x_1 is the variable input and x_2 is held fixed at x_2^0. In Figure 8.4, suppose every output increase, from y^0 to y^1, from y^1 to y^2, etc. is of the same size.

The increases in the variable input x_1 which are necessary to bring about these equal changes in output get larger and larger: to move from y^0 to y^1, there is an increase from x_1^0 to x_1^1; from y^1 to y^2 the increase is from x_1^1 to x_1^2, which is larger

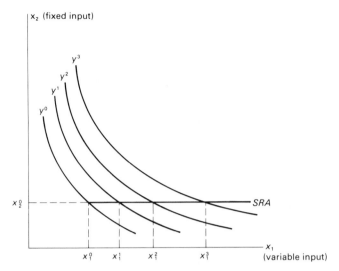

FIGURE 8.4. **The short-run adjustment path *(SRA)* in a simple two-input, one-output production process.**

than the preceding increase; and in moving from y^2 to y^3, a still larger increase in x^1 is necessary. Thus, there are *diminishing returns* in the use of x^1. Diminishing returns is an important topic and we turn to it in Section 8.2.6.

8.2.5. Fixed Costs or Sunk Costs?

In 1974, the governor of California signed a bill providing that a one-half cent increase in the state sales tax would be levied, and the money collected would be used to subsidize the Bay Area Rapid Transit system (BART). BART, it seems, had fallen on hard times and there was concern that it might fail outright. The governor explained the additional support was necessary so that the several hundred million dollars expended earlier on BART would not be wasted.

The governor was articulating a common but mistaken idea. The idea is so common, in fact, that it is given a name: "the sunk cost fallacy."

Money expended in the past on BART was spent in anticipation that the system would be socially useful: people would want to use it. When that expectation was not fulfilled, the earlier expenditure was simply a mistake. Past mistakes seldom can be redeemed by present expenditures of the same type. The loss of the earlier investment in BART occurred when anticipated passenger traffic failed to materialize. That loss is not avoided or diminished by a failure to acknowledge it, or by an effort to spend more to keep the system running. Those added expenditures, in fact, only add to the ultimate size of the total loss— *unless* additional expenditures can stimulate passenger traffic.

Other examples of the "sunk cost fallacy" are easy to find. "We've already put two years into this rotten relationship. If we break up now, those years will have been wasted." "I know camellias won't grow in Minnesota. But I spent thousands of dollars to have those plants sent here from Mississippi, and I'm not going to skimp now on a nurseryman to care for them while they freeze to death." "I've already spent a ton of money on the transmission of this car of mine. I simply can't afford not to get it fixed now that it's broken down again."

In all cases, individuals are reflecting on past actions involving nonrecoverable costs and using those actions as a guide to current decisions. The difference between *sunk* costs and *fixed* costs should be clear. Fixed costs stem from past actions that constrain current choices because they are currently unavoidable. Sunk costs *are* currently avoidable: or at least, an *addition to* sunk costs can be avoided.

8.2.6. Short-Run Production Cost and Size of Firm

In many production applications, a time-honored economic hypothesis will be found to hold true. The *law of diminishing returns* predicts the outcome of a simple conceptual experiment. Suppose the usage rate of all but one input is fixed. Then, *as the use of that one varying input is increased,* the law of diminishing returns predicts that *a level of output will be reached at which the rate of output increase slows down and never increases again.* The law is illustrated numerically by the earlier example of the asparagus grower (Table 8.1), and graphically in Figure 8.4. In Table 8.1, we saw that the changes in output per man-hour increase up to the nineteen-man-hour input rate, at which point diminishing returns set in—additional man-hours of labor begin to yield smaller increases in output.

If we have diminishing returns in a simple two-input production process, then the *short-run marginal cost* of output must increase as output increases as shown in Figure 8.5. For the short-run marginal cost is the cost of obtaining additional units of output while increasing the usage rate of only the variable input. When

FIGURE 8.5.   The short-run marginal cost of production.

diminishing returns set in, the gain in output per unit of variable input decreases. Thus, each additional dollar expended on the variable input yields less output than the previous dollar of variable input expenditure, and so marginal cost increases with increases in output.

Increasing marginal cost, resulting from diminishing returns, decisively limits the ability of the firm to expand its output in the short run, in the simple two-input case that is analyzed here. Suppose, however, that the firm uses many inputs. With many inputs, the diminishing returns "experiment" calls for one input to be varied and the others to be held fixed. However, adjustment costs may be low enough on several of the inputs so that they all can be varied instantaneously. In such cases, conditions concerning the form of the production function can be stipulated which imply that marginal cost is an increasing function of output. An investigation of those conditions is necessarily more mathematical than is consistent with the level of this book; so they will not be presented here.

We will assume that a firm cannot economically expand its output rate indefinitely in the short run while some of its inputs remain fixed. That assumption is equivalent to the law of diminishing returns in the case of a firm with a two-input production process. For cases involving several inputs, plausible general conditions serve to assure the same increasing pattern of marginal cost in the short run.

8.3. THE GEOMETRY OF COST

Short-run adjustment processes have been defined as ones involving changes in the usage rates of some, but not all, productive inputs. In the long run, all inputs are adjusted.

In the two-input case, the firm will be in long-run equilibrium only at some point satisfying the condition

$$MPP(x_1)/w_1 = MPP(x_2)/w_2, \tag{6}$$

assuming (as we do throughout this chapter) that the input prices w_1 and w_2 are not changed when the firm changes its purchase rate.

The points satisfying the condition (6) lie along the long-run output adjustment *(LRA)* curve in Figure 8.6. The firm's long-run total cost of operation can be determined from that *LRA* curve. Each point on *LRA* indicates a relation between a rate of output (read from the isoquant passing through the point) and input usage rates which yield that output at a minimum cost (read from the coordinates of the point). This information suffices to determine the *long-run total cost of production*. For example, the output y^3 is optimally produced by using the input combination x_1^3, x_2^3. The total cost of producing y^3 is $w_1 x_1^3 + w_2 x_2^3$: the input quantities multiplied by their prices. The total cost of any output rate can be computed in a similar fashion, and plotted as in Figure 8.7; there, the total

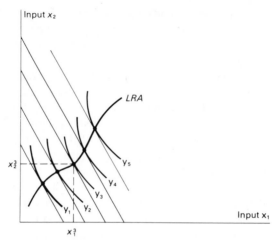

FIGURE 8.6. The long-run adjustment (LRA) path for a one-output, two-input production process.

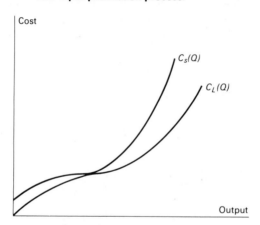

FIGURE 8.7. Total cost of production in the long run and the short run.

costs incurred at various possible rates of output, when all inputs are optimally adjusted to the output rate, are shown in the curve $C_L(Q)$.

The short-run total cost function $C_S(Q)$ is calculated in much the same way, but from the *SRA* curve of Figure 8.4. $C_S(Q)$ shows the total cost associated with different outputs when one input, physical capital, is held fixed. The short-run function that is drawn in Figure 8.7 is associated with one particular holding of the fixed input. If the firm held a different quantity of physical capital, then a different configuration of $C_S(Q)$ would emerge. Any capital holding leads to a short-run curve that is tangent to $C_L(Q)$; the point of tangency is farther to the right, the greater the firm's capital holding.

Marginal costs of production in both the long run and the short run can be obtained from the total cost curves $C_L(Q)$ or $C_S(Q)$. Marginal cost at any output is the *slope* of total cost at that output. The value of the expression $\Delta C_S(Q)/\Delta Q$ gives short-run marginal cost as a function of output Q, and $\Delta C_L(Q)/\Delta Q$ gives the long-run marginal cost function. Occasionally there is confusion between marginal cost (the concept just discussed) and cost per unit, or *average cost.* Average cost is computed as a function of output, for short-run or long-run operation, by dividing the relevant total cost curve by the rate of output: long-run average cost is $C_L(Q)/Q$, and short-run average cost, $C_S(Q)/Q$.

Two important relationships must hold between average cost and marginal cost:

1. For any output at which average cost is neither increasing nor decreasing, average cost and marginal cost must be equal.
2. For any output at which marginal cost is less than average cost, average cost must be falling; and for any output at which marginal cost is greater than average cost, average cost must be rising.

A "typical" or representative configuration of average and marginal short-run costs is exhibited in Figure 8.8. The point *a* corresponds to a point of inflection on the short-run total cost curve $C_S(Q)$; the point *b* corresponds to a point at which the tangent to $C_S(Q)$ is also a ray (passing through the origin of the diagram).

8.4. THE SIZE OF THE FIRM IN THE LONG RUN

If rising short-run marginal cost is in fact encountered in most production activities, then a large expansion in the firm's output will be very costly in the short run. On the other hand, in the long run, when all of a firm's productive inputs

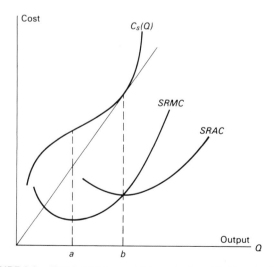

FIGURE 8.8. Total, average, and marginal cost in the short run.

can economically be varied in use, what is there to prevent firms from growing indefinitely large, by simply adding more of *all* productive inputs? When all input usage rates are increased, there is no barrier to growth from diminishing returns; or in any event, that barrier does not operate as it does in the short run. What, then, if anything, puts a limit on the size a firm can attain when it is free to add to any and all of its input usage rates?

Surprisingly, there is a fair amount of controversy over that question among professional economists. In the opinion of some observers, there is no limit on a firm's size, short of the full extent of the market for the goods that the firm produces. As they see it, the natural state of affairs is for all shoes to be produced by one shoe producer, all ice cream and cheese by one dairy corporation, and so on. That most goods are produced by several or many firms is, according to these observers, a historical accident; they believe that as time passes, most of the firms will tend to grow larger. That belief in an historical tendency toward *monopoly* (one seller of a good) is not borne out by direct evidence, as we will see in Chapter 11.

Those who believe that firms can grow indefinitely large may be influenced to hold that view by numerous available analyses of production cost, as measured in actual business enterprises. Economists have gathered data on the costs of production in firms of different size which produce the same good, and have plotted those data as shown in Figure 8.9. A typical pattern emerges from these studies: up to some critical size level, costs of production per unit of output steadily fall as output increases. Once the critical size is reached, the cost of production per unit of output has little or no tendency to change with further increases in the firm's rate of production. This kind of empirical evidence (evidence obtained by observing the real world) leads some observers to conclude that there is no tendency for average or marginal costs to rise in the manner

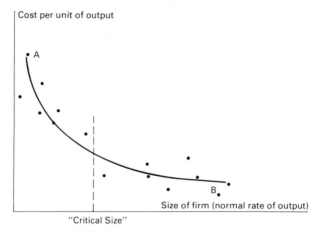

FIGURE 8.9. A hypothetical but typical long-run average cost curve, depicting the accounting data of a cross section of producers.

shown in Figure 8.8 when plant and equipment can be varied, and hence there is no reason why firms should not grow to an indefinitely large size in the long run.

How reliable is evidence of the type displayed in Figure 8.9? Is it justifiable to conclude that as a general proposition, firms never need stop growing? In answer to those important questions, several points may be raised:

1. Empirical work on cost frequently focuses entirely on cost of production, and thereby ignores two important components of the cost of serving a market: these are *selling cost* (advertising, promotional activity, and salesmen's commissions) and *transportation cost,* the cost of making a product available over a wide geographic area. There is certainly reason to believe that both of these components of cost per unit of output will increase as the rate of output increases.

2. Cost comparisons between large-sized and small-sized firms, of the type shown in Figure 8.9, may conceal the fact that the product mixes of large and small firms may tend systematically to differ. As a hypothetical example, suppose Figure 8.9 represented an investigation of the production costs of fifteen steel manufacturing firms. The "small" firms, like A, might concentrate heavily on the production of wire, while the "large" firms, like B, concentrate heavily on the production of steel sheet. If the per-ton cost of sheet is significantly lower than the per-ton cost of wire, then any comparison that concludes that B is "more efficient" than A because it produces a ton of steel more cheaply, is highly misleading.

3. The cost data upon which Figure 8.9 is based are compiled by accountants, who employ a variety of measuring and reporting rules which do not capture the idea of opportunity cost very well. Appendix II suggests ways that accounting procedures and differences in the history of firms tends to undermine the reliability of empirical evidence concerning the absence of increasing cost.

It is apparently a fact of life within organizations that planning and centralized control become increasingly difficult as the size of the organization increases. That fact may bear on the question of viable firm size. Firms respond to profit opportunity signals, and up to a point, centralized coordination and direction of that response pays off with lower cost, as discussed in Chapter 7. However, size brings complexity to the firm, and as size increases, complexity affects the smoothness and purposiveness of coordination and control. Hence, a phenomenon akin to diminishing returns may be operative within the firm in the long run, as well as in the short run. In the long run, the firm's capacity to manage and to coordinate is an input that can not be augmented. The central intelligence necessary to manage and coordinate cannot be perfectly extended by adding *more* managers: at some point some single individual or committee must bear responsibility for all decisions, and as the firm expands, a size will ultimately be reached at which that coordinator's ability to function successfully is diminished. Thus, even in the long run, ability to grow profitably is limited. The markets for most goods will be sufficiently extensive so that we will not expect to find that one firm can supply the whole market economically.

If Figure 8.9 is a valid representation of reality—that is, if long-run costs in fact decrease in such a way that single firms can profitably supply an entire market—then the traditional economic theory of supply is in need of updating.

For the theory assumes that markets will typically accommodate numerous firms that can all operate within the market profitably. In continuing our discussion of supply, we will assume that for many production situations involving many different goods and services, cost considerations will not rule out the possibility that many suppliers will remain profitable, even in the long run.

We conclude this discussion of the size of firms with a note regarding terminology. Figure 8.10 shows long-run average cost curves for two different firms. Firm A displays constant long-run average cost. If Firm A economically increases its output by increasing each of its inputs in the same proportion, then Firm A also displays *constant returns to scale*.

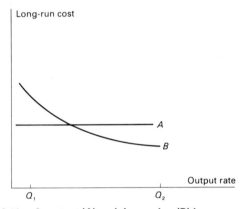

FIGURE 8.10.   Constant (A) and decreasing (B) long-run average cost.

Suppose Firm B, which displays declining unit costs over the interval of outputs q_1, q_2, also increases its output by increasing each of its inputs in the same proportion. Then B is subject to *increasing returns to scale*.

Returns to scale pertains to the way in which output changes in response to *equiproportionate* input changes. If each input usage rate is increased by k percent, and the output rate thereby increases by more than k percent, then we have a case of increasing returns to scale. Associated with increasing returns to scale will be declining average cost of production, as shown for Firm B in Figure 8.10. It is, however, possible to have decreasing average cost and *not* have increasing returns to scale: the optimal pattern of output adjustment in the firm will lie along the *LRA* curve (Figure 8.6); and there is no reason to suppose that movement along that curve will typically involve equiproportionate shifts in the rates of input usage.

The terminology "increasing (or decreasing) returns to scale," however, is frequently indiscriminately used instead of the correct term "declining (or increasing) long-run average cost".

Finally, care should be taken to avoid confusion between returns to scale and the law of diminishing returns. The latter calls for one input to be held fixed, while the former calls for all inputs to change in the same proportion.

8.5. FIXED COSTS AND SUPPLY IN THE SHORT RUN

Some of the difficulty of altering the rate of use of fixed inputs comes from contract commitments. For example, the firm may have a one-year lease agreement
with the owner of a warehouse, or a six-month lease on a fleet of vehicles. Contractual commitments are particularly binding when an output reduction is desired; there simply is no inexpensive and convenient way to reduce the usage of
the inputs provided by contract.

Other inputs, which are not bound to the firm by contract, may nevertheless
be troublesome to use at a slower rate in short periods of time. The firm's owned
plant, for example, may be difficult to sell off on short notice: buyers for such
facilities may not be numerous.

The costs of inputs to which the firm is bound in the short run are called *fixed
costs*. These are costs which the firm cannot avoid, no matter whether it produces or not. The costs associated with variable inputs will account for all of the
cost variation resulting from output rate changes: these are the firm's *variable
costs*. In Figure 8.11, the fixed component of cost is indicated by the intercept of
the short-run total cost curve $C_S(Q)$. Average cost *(AC)*, average variable cost
(AVC), and marginal cost *(MC)* are plotted together in Figure 8.12. Average
fixed cost is the difference between *AC* and *AVC*.

The firm will choose its output rate to maximize its returns. It will therefore
(as explained in the discussion surrounding Figure 8.1) produce at the output rate
at which price equals marginal cost.

Suppose, however, the $P = MC$ output lies *below* average cost. If the firm
produces at a point like *A* in Figure 8.12, the average cost of each unit sold exceeds the price received. *However, a part of that average cost cannot be
avoided, regardless of whether or not the firm produces anything.* At the point
A, the market price received by the firm exceeds the *avoidable* costs of produc-

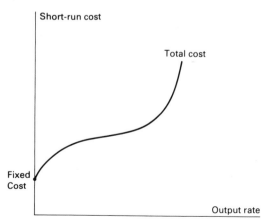

**FIGURE 8.11. Fixed cost as a component of total production cost in the
short run.**

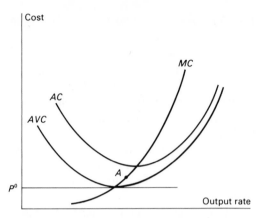

FIGURE 8.12.   Marginal cost, average variable cost, and average cost.

ing each unit, *AVC*. As long as *avoidable* costs are covered, it will pay the firm to continue producing, even if production is unprofitable. Thus the short run supply curve of the firm is the marginal cost curve above its intersection with *AVC*: at prices below the price P^0, no production will occur.

However, through time contracts will expire and buyers will be found for capital goods; and each time such an opportunity presents itself, the firm will have to review the decision as to whether it should continue to produce, or fold. The expiration of a contract in effect reduces average fixed cost and shifts average variable cost upward.

8.6. MARKET SUPPLY

Market supply varies over time periods of different length. The short run marginal cost schedules of supplying firms, when added horizontally, constitute short run market supply; similarly, long run marginal cost curves of supplying firms determine market supply in the long run. Horizontal summation involves adding the different quantities supplied at different prices of the produced good; the supply response of one firm does not depend on the output decisions of other firms (unless the other firms' output decisions cause a change in the cost of the first firm, as could happen for example, when the price of an input rises as all firms increase their outputs).

How does market supply adjust to changes in market price? From an initial market equilibrium at *A* (Figure 8.13), suppose a shift in market demand from *D* to *D'* occurs. The price rises to the level at point *B* as a result of adjustment along S_S, the short-run market supply curve. As firms adjust their input usage through time, they move aggregate supply to the point *A'* on S_L, the long-run market supply curve. If there are no further changes in demand (shifts in the demand schedule), and no changes in input prices or productive technique (which can

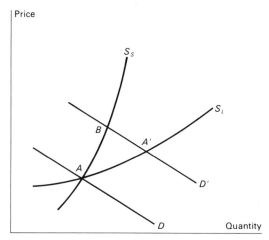

FIGURE 8.13.   Market equilibrium in the short run and the long run, after an increase in demand.

lead to shifts in the supply relationship), the point A' will be an equilibrium point in the long run. That is, when the quantity and price indicated by the point A' are reached, there will be no forces operative to produce further changes. At any other point, buyers would want to take more or less than is offered at the price, or firms would want to adjust their productive input mixes, and further changes will ensue.

"The" short run supply response of an individual firm is, of course, a simplification. Contractual commitments and differences in the difficulty of adjusting usage rates of different inputs will mean that there will be many different cost patterns incurred by a firm before it fully adjusts to changed market conditions. Even more heroic is the abstraction that occurs in extending the idea of "the" short run to the market, for in identifying a short run market supply curve, an aggregate across many different firms, each quite possibly responding at different rates, is represented by a single curve. Thus, the analysis of supply response should not be taken as a faithful depiction of reality. The analysis does, however, do a tolerable job of pointing out an important consideration: namely, that supply doesn't adjust instantaneously to changes in market conditions.

*APPENDIX I
MORE ABOUT PRODUCTION FUNCTIONS

The production function

$$y = \phi(x_1, \ldots, x_n)$$

is said to be *homogeneous of degree k* if

$$a^k y = \phi(ax_1, \ldots, ax_n);$$

that is, if the uniform expansion or contraction of every input by the proportion a leads to an expansion of output y by a proportion a^k. The case of *linear homogeneity* ($k = 1$) implies that when all inputs are changed in the same proportion, output also changes in that same proportion.

A production function that is homogeneous of degree $k = 1$ implies constant returns to scale. If it is homogeneous of degree $k<1$, returns to scale are increasing; $k<1$, declining.

The *elasticity of substitution* between two productive inputs tells us by what proportion input 2 can decline when input 1 increases, without any change in output. In a production function of two inputs, $y = \phi(x_1, x_2)$, the expression for elasticity of substitution between the inputs is

$$\frac{P}{\theta} \cdot \frac{d\theta}{dP}$$

where P is the marginal physical product ratio:

$$P = \frac{\partial\phi/\partial x_1}{\partial\phi/\partial x_2} = \phi_1/\phi_2;$$

and θ is the input usage ratio:

$$\theta = \frac{x_2}{x_1}.$$

Figure 8.14 illustrates θ and P for the input combination x_1^0, x_2^0.

The greater the numerical value of the elasticity of substitution, the flatter will be the production isoquant. When the inputs are perfect substitutes, the isoquant is a straight negatively sloped line, and $dP/d\theta = 0$ for all θ. The elasticity of substitution along a straight-line isoquant is infinite.

Next, we note one particular *explicit* form of production function that has been used widely in empirical economic research. The *Cobb-Douglas* production function has been applied in estimating the productive potential of firms—and nations. Its form is

$$y = Ax_1^\alpha x_2^\beta$$

where y is the rate of output, A, α and β are coefficients to be fitted empirically, and x_1 and x_2 are the quantities of labor and capital respectively that are used per unit of time. The Cobb-Douglas function is homogeneous of degree $\alpha + \beta$.

*APPENDIX II
ACCOUNTING DATA AND EMPIRICAL COST RELATIONSHIPS

In Section 8.2.6, the law of diminishing returns was invoked to support the proposition that supply curves are positively sloped, even in the long run. As indicated in the discussion in Section 8.4, the argument is a weak one, in the view of many professional economists. Their mistrust of the argument may be well justified. However, some of that mistrust is based on empirical results like those described in Section 8.4, and comparisons of accounting reports for different firms may be a very misleading way to compare costs of operations in those firms. An example is presented here to develop these points.

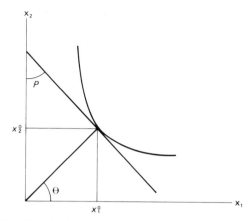

FIGURE 8.14. **The elasticity of substitution is computed from p and θ, as illustrated here.**

In 1956 Alfy bought three lakeside cabins, which he rents to vacationing fishermen and skiers. He paid $8000 each for them, and now rents them for $100 per week, with an average occupancy of thirty weeks per year. His overhead (fixed) costs—taxes and maintenance, principally—amount to $1500 per year. His direct (variable) costs—utilities, firewood, and linen service—come to $20 per week for each week that a cabin is occupied. Alfy reports income from his modest enterprise as follows:

Alfy's rental proceeds (30 weeks @ $100 for each cabin)		$9000
Less: Direct costs	$1800	
Less: Overhead costs	1500	
Less: Depreciation	1200	4500
Net proceeds before income taxes		$4500

Benjy is Alfy's neighbor and friend. In 1974, he decided that cabins like Alfy's are a good source of income. He bought a lot adjoining Alfy's property, and built as many cabins as he could afford—only one, because construction and land costs had risen to a total of $25000 in the intervening years. Benjy rents at the same rate and with the same overhead and direct costs as Alfy, and has the same thirty-week occupancy in an average year. His income statement looks like this:

Benjy's rental proceeds		$3000
Less: Direct costs	$ 600	
Less: Overhead costs	1500	
Less: Depreciation	1250	3350
Loss before income taxes		($ 350)

Obviously, the two businesses are identical, except that Alfy's is a threefold magnification of Benjy's. Either businessman could sell any one of the cabins to be used as a private vacation home, for a current market price of $25000: by remaining in the rental business both men are foregoing an opportunity to sell out and invest the proceeds in government securities. With an 8 percent interest rate, an economist would calculate the costs per cabin as

Direct costs	$ 600	
Overhead costs	1500	
Opportunity cost (Interest foregone)	2000	$4100.

By the economist's reckoning, both men would do well financially to sell out and buy government bonds.

The difference between the economist's calculation and the accounting calculations of Alfy and Benjy hinge on the way that the value of the property is charged against the proceeds from rental. The *depreciation* that they each charge is a simple conventional representation: it is assumed that a cabin has a lifetime of twenty years, and that it "contributes" an amount equal to its original purchase price uniformly over its lifetime to the value of output. Thus, each of Alfy's cabins is "costed" at $8000/20 = $400 per year, while Benjy's is costed at $1250.

What is the lesson here? There are four points.

1. Accounting cost, especially depreciation, may have little correspondence to the relevant opportunity cost concept.
2. New firms, with new plant and equipment, typically enter an industry at smaller-than-average size. In a time of inflation, new plant and equipment will cost more than old equipment. These two factors, taken together, imply that smaller firms will report higher depreciation costs per unit of output, even on essentially the same kind of physical capital as is used by larger firms.
3. If Benjy were to grow to Alfy's size, he could not report the same low costs reported by Alfy.
4. There is some evidence, given the superior opportunity confronting both Alfy and Benjy to sell out and invest in government bonds, that *neither* firm is in equilibrium; hence neither can properly be said to lie on his long-run cost curve.

This parable oversimplifies in some degree, but the points as stated can be extended to a variety of sophisticated industrial contexts.

*APPENDIX III
MARGINAL COST EQUALS PRICE WITH OPTIMAL INPUT USE

A competitive firm (for simplicity) makes one output and uses two inputs. Its production function is

$$y = \phi(x_1, x_2)$$

where y is the rate of output and the x's are input utilization rates. The profit function is

$$\pi = Py - w_1 x_1 - w_2 x_2$$

where P, w_1, and w_2 are respectively the prices of output and the two inputs.

To optimize input use, we differentiate with respect to x_1 and x_2:

$$\pi_1 = \partial\pi/\partial x_1 = P\phi_1 - w_1 = 0$$
$$\pi_2 = \qquad\qquad P\phi_2 - w_2 = 0$$

where ϕ_1 and ϕ_2 are the first partial derivatives of ϕ with respect to x_1 and x_2. Thus, necessary conditions for optimum input usage are

$$P\phi_1 = w_1; P\phi_2 = w_2. \qquad\qquad (\text{A-1})$$

If we denote $\partial_2\phi/\partial_1^2$ by ϕ_{11}, and $\partial_2\phi/\partial x_1\partial x_2$ by ϕ_{12}, then sufficient conditions for a maximum are

$$\phi_{11}\phi_{22} - \phi_{12}^2 > 0 \text{ and } \phi_{11} < 0.$$

See a calculus book for details. We will assume that the production function ϕ has convex differentiable isoquants, which will mean that the sufficient conditions are fulfilled at any point, so the necessary conditions (A-1) locate the optimum.

Suppose the conditions (A-1) are satisfied when x_1^* and x_2^* are the input utilization rates. The firm's total revenue is

$$P\phi(x_1^*, x_2^*)$$

and its total cost is

$$w_1 x_1^* = w_2 x_2^*.$$

With that input combination, marginal cost dTC/dy is obtained from the differentials

$$dTC = w_1 dx_1 \Big|_{x_1 = x_1^*} + w_2 dx_2 \Big|_{x_2 = x_2^*}.$$

$$dy = \phi_1 dx_1 \Big|_{x_1 = x_1^*} + \phi_2 dx_2 \Big|_{x_2 = x_2^*}.$$

From (A-1) we have that

$$dTC = P\phi_1 dx_1 \Big|_{x_1 = x_1^*} + P\phi_2 dx_2 \Big|_{x_2 = x_2^*}.$$

Thus, with the input combination x_1^* and x_2^*, we have

$$\frac{dTC}{dy} = P\frac{[\phi_1 dx_1 + \phi_2 dx_2]}{\phi_1 dx_1 + \phi_2 dx_2}$$

or

$$MC = P,$$

as was to be shown.

APPLICATIONS AND EXTENSIONS

1. Given the definition of short run and long run that we have used in this chapter, it is possible for the short run to be as long or longer than the long run. How?

2. A firm's long-run cost curve, as illustrated in Figure 8.7, can be thought of as a set of points, each one chosen from an individual short-run curve. Explain why any point on the long-run curve must also be on some short-run curve. If a producer is operat-

ing at a point on one particular short-run curve where it intersects the long-run curve, and he moves to a different point on that same short-run curve, can he possibly stay on the long-run curve?

3. Illustrate this proposition, called the *principle of substitution,* with either a geometric or a calculus argument:

    In a two-input production process, a producer will substitute input x_1 for input x_2 when the price of x_1 declines relative to the price of x_2.

4. It is sometimes contended that large producers can avoid increasing long-run average cost by obtaining much more favorable price deals from suppliers of inputs than would normally be observed in the markets for inputs. If that is indeed the case, is it an argument for or against the "social desirability" of very large firms?

5. Figure 8.15 depicts two different short-run average cost curves. Under what circumstances would a producer prefer to own Plant A rather than Plant B, given that his current optimum output rate is y^0?

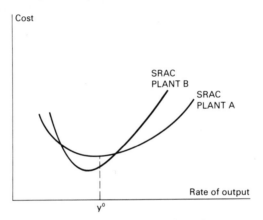

FIGURE 8.15.   Illustration for Question 5.

BIBLIOGRAPHICAL NOTE

The ideas presented in this chapter in important part come from J. Viner, "Cost Curves and Supply Curves," reprinted in G. J. Stigler and K. Boulding, eds, *AEA Readings in Price Theory* (Homewood, Ill.: Irwin, 1952). Viner's paper cleared up a number of loose ends in Alfred Marshall's *Principles of Economics,* 8th ed. (New York: Macmillan, 1925).

The Samuelson and Hicks books, cited in the Bibliographical Note to Chapter 6, further refined and standardized the analysis. For a full rigorous mathematical treatment, try the K. G. Kogiku book, cited in the Bibliographical Note to Chapter 5.

CHAPTER NINE

Interest, Capital, and Resource Allocation Through Time

A wonderful bird is the pelican,
His bill will hold more than his belican.
He can take in his beak,
food enough for a week,
But I'm damned if I see how the helican.

DIXON LANIER MERRITT (1910)

9.1. ALLOCATION DECISIONS WHEN CONDITIONS CHANGE RAPIDLY

The main purpose of this chapter is to modify the analysis of the market system in such a way that *time* plays an explicit role. Thus far, time has been in the analysis, but in a trivial way. The important variables of the supply and demand analysis that was developed in the foregoing chapters are *flows:* the firm's *output* is the quantity produced (and sold) per unit of time; its *cost* is the rate of return on the opportunities that must be foregone in order to achieve its chosen output; the consumer's *optimal consumption bundle* contains the amounts of the various goods purchased per unit of time, and his *income* is the increase in his personal holdings (wealth) during a period of time. However, supply and demand analysis assumes that those choices are made by firms and individuals on the basis of information that does not change through time; and, hence, time played no essential part in the analysis. The patterns of choice that are best today will also be best tomorrow (so most of our analysis has thus far assumed) because the situation affecting choice will not change in any important way between today and tomorrow. Because there are no important changes to reckon with, time's role is trivial. That *static analysis,* as developed in Chapters 4 to 8, is useful to our understanding of *equilibrium,* the patterns of behavior that emerge when the choices of individual consumers and producers have fully adjusted to the existing and unvarying tastes of consumers and unchanging techniques of production.

We also saw that static analysis can readily and usefully be extended to analyze the changes in patterns of choice that occur in response to a one-shot, or once-and-for-all, change, such as a change in taste, change in the availability of some important resource, or change in technology of production. The imposition of a tax on a commodity is a typical example of a one-shot change that is handled well by the analysis (see Chapter 4, Section 4.4). The study of the effects that one-shot changes have on equilibrium and patterns of choice is called *comparative static analysis.*

It happens that neither static analysis nor comparative static analysis can be applied usefully to some very important questions. For example, suppose a business firm is confronted by three alternatives: it can continue operating as it has done in the past, which will result in an expected flow of returns through time as shown by the curve (1) in Figure 9.1; or it can phase slowly into a new product

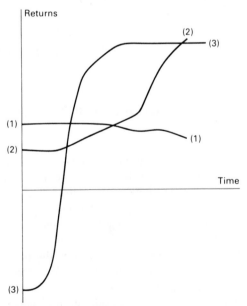

FIGURE 9.1. Hypothetical alternative payout rates for different production and marketing choices.

line, with no big attempt to make an immediate splash and without immediately abandoning its current product line, with returns indicated in curve (2); or it can jump into a new product line, with extensive conversion of its present equipment and extensive promotional expenditure, with the flow of returns shown as curve (3). Which of the three choices is best?

This chapter will show how our analysis can be extended so that it is capable of analyzing economic choices that are made in the presence of significant changes through time: questions that are exemplified by the hypothetical choice among the three different profits streams shown in Figure 9.1.

9.2. THE RATE OF INTEREST

9.2.1. Time Preference and Interest

Almost any individual, if pressed with careful questioning, will declare that he would prefer to receive a dollar today, rather than tomorrow. After all, receipt today permits all the alternatives that receipt tomorrow does—it is only necessary to put the dollar in a safe place and withdraw it tomorrow; and other alternatives are opened up by the choice to take the dollar today—a part or all of it can be spent today, and the recipient may be impatient to make a purchase that he regards as important. The dollar today increases the array of choices open to the individual. Finally, the recipient may recognize the possibility of death or disability, which would eliminate or reduce his pleasure from obtaining the money at the later time.

This generalized preference for current use over deferred use of (storable) money means that nobody will enter an impersonal transaction to exchange a dollar today for the promise of a dollar a year from now; even an iron-clad, absolutely guaranteed promise of repayment will fail to evoke a favorable response to the proposal of such an exchange. It generally will be necessary, then, to promise to pay *more* than a dollar later if you want to borrow a dollar today. The premium that you pay to fulfill a wish to borrow is called *interest*.

The allocation of society's holding of money (or *liquid capital*) among *borrowers* (those who are willing to promise to pay interest in order to obtain the use of money today) and *lenders* (those who are willing to accept interest and wait until some time in the future to use their money) is accomplished through the workings of a market that we call the *financial market*. The *current use of money*, then, is exactly like any other good in the way it is allocated. Its price, as determined by supply and demand on the financial market, is the rate of interest.

It is, perhaps, confusing to speak of "the" rate of interest, for as almost everyone knows, there are many different rates of interest that hold for different types of borrowing transactions. A bank may lend at 7 percent to a borrower who will use the money to buy a house (and promise to turn the house over to the bank to be sold for recovery of the loan if the borrower cannot meet his repayment obligations); the same bank may lend at around 16 percent to the same borrower if he wishes to purchase an automobile instead of a home. The bank's chance of being able to recover is greater when a house is explicitly offered as *collateral* than when a car is offered. Different promises to pay, which vary with respect to the length of time until repayment, the strength and reliability of the borrower, and the quality of the collateral, all call for different rates of interest. It is usually the case that the longer the time until repayment, and the greater the risk of loss due to the defection of the borrower, the higher will be the premium, or interest rate, that will be required to achieve an acceptable transaction. The usual way of viewing the world of many interest rates is to assert that there is a basic rate of interest that would be charged on a completely riskless, one-period loan. Then, any deviations from that basic rate can be attributed in part to risk and in part to different length of the term during which the loan is in effect. By viewing the problem in that way, formal economic analysis can proceed as if there were only one rate of interest, with additional explicit charges made to the borrower for riskiness and length of term of loan.

It is conventional to quote interest rates on any borrowing-lending transaction as if the term of the loan were one year and as if a year were 360 days long. Thus, a loan of $100, which must be repaid in 60 days in the amount of $101, is quoted as a 6 percent loan: 60 days is one-sixth of a year; the premium for using the $100 for 60 days is $1 (1 percent); and 1 percent for 60 days is viewed as the equivalent of 6 percent for 360 days (one year).

9.2.2. Present Value

The preference of individuals for a dollar today over a year from now means that at this moment, a dollar one year from now can be bought for less than a dollar. How much less? That depends on borrowing and lending desires as reflected in the rate of interest. Suppose the financial market is in equilibrium when the rate of interest is 10 percent. If an individual borrows $90.91 at 10 percent for one year, at the end of the year he will repay the amount he borrowed ($90.91) plus interest ($9.09), a total of $100. Each dollar the lender obtains a year from now costs him .9091 dollars (roughly 91 cents) today. Thus, at 10 percent interest, the present value of one dollar a year from now is .9091 dollars.

What about the present value of $1 *two* years from now? If a borrower obtains a loan of $82.65 at 10 percent interest, repayable in two years, the picture looks like this:

Amount borrowed	$ 82.65
Interest, first year	8.26
Amount owed after one year	90.91
Interest, second year	9.09
Amount owed after two years	$100.00

Thus, the *present value* of $1 two years from now, at a rate of interest of 10 percent, is .8265 dollars.

If the rate of interest is r, payable annually, then $1 today is worth $1 + r$ dollars a year from now. If that $1 + r$ dollars is held a second year, it will be worth $(1 + r)(1 + r) = (1 + r)^2$ dollars at the end of two years. In general, a dollar today, if the rate of interest is r, will be worth $(1 + r)^N$ dollars at the end of N years.

Conversely, we may calculate that if a dollar today is worth $1 + r$ dollars a year from now, then a dollar a year from now is worth $\dfrac{1}{1 + r}$ dollars today; a dollar two years from now is worth $\dfrac{1}{(1 + r)^2}$ dollars today, and so on. In general, then, if the rate of interest is r, the *present value* of $1 to be received at the end of N years is $\dfrac{1}{(1 + r)^N}$ dollars. (By this calculation, if $r = .10$ or 10 percent, a dollar one year from now is worth $\dfrac{1}{1.10}$, or .9091, as asserted in the numerical example that was given at the beginning of this section.) The expression $\dfrac{1}{(1 + r)}$ is called the *discount factor,* and the procedure whereby present values of sums to be received in the future are calculated is called *discounting.* Calculating present values enables us to answer questions like the one involving a firm's optimal choice of production and investment plans, which was raised in Section 9.1.

Suppose that in the time periods 1, 2, 3, 4, . . . the firm's returns from the first alternative are $\Pi_1^1, \Pi_2^1, \Pi_3^1, \Pi_4^1, \ldots$, from the second alternative the returns are $\Pi_1^2, \Pi_2^2, \Pi_3^2, \Pi_4^2, \ldots$, and so on. (In this notation, Π_j^i is the return from the ith alternative in the jth period.) The values of returns in each period, associated with each alternative, are written out in Table 9.1. These are the Π_j^i values for the specific example, illustrated in Figure 9.1, which we are working with.

The criterion by which the firm will choose among the three alternatives is: which of the available choices leads to maximum *present value* of the entire stream of returns through year 10 (which we assume to be the most distant future year that the firm considers in making its current plans)?

The calculation of the present value of the different alternative returns streams is quite easy if we know the rate of interest at which the firm can readily borrow large sums of money in order to finance major projects like the new product line discussed in our example. To calculate the present value of returns from the first alternative (which is not to develop the new product), we first calculate the present values of the returns in each year which result from that alter-

TABLE 9.1.

YEAR	1	2	3	4	5	6	7	8	9	10
Alternative										
(1)	100	100	100	100	100	95	90	90	85	80
(2)	60	65	70	75	90	100	120	160	200	220
(3)	−150	−100	100	180	200	220	220	220	220	220
				at 15% discount rate						
(1)	100	86.96	75.61	65.75	57.18	47.23	36.96	28.93	21.38	14.87
(2)	60	52.17	45.37	46.02	45.74	44.75	49.72	60.15	65.38	62.54
(3)	−150	−86.96	75.61	118.35	114.35	109.38	95.11	82.71	71.92	62.54
				at 8% discount rate						
(1)	100	92.59	85.73	79.38	73.50	64.66	56.72	52.51	45.92	40.02
(2)	60	55.56	51.44	55.57	58.80	61.25	72.47	93.36	108.05	110.05
(3)	−150	−92.59	85.73	142.89	147.01	149.73	138.64	128.37	118.86	110.05

native and then add up those present values. If the firm's borrowing rate of interest is 15 percent, then the returns streams from the three alternatives shown in Table 9.1 have present values in each period as shown in the first column of Table 9.2; the calculation shows that the first alternative (making no change) is the most profitable. On the other hand, if the firm's borrowing rate of interest were lower—only 8 percent, say—the third alternative (which is to enter with heavy promotion) conveys the highest returns (as seen in the second column of Table 9.2).

TABLE 9.2.

Alternative	PRESENT VALUE AT	
	15 Percent	8 Percent
(1)	534.87	691.03
(2)	479.67	726.55
(3)	493.01	728.69

9.2.3. A General Formulation of Present Value

In general, with a rate of interest r, the present values in each year from a stream of returns $\Pi_1, \Pi_2, \ldots, \Pi_N$ are

$$v_1 = \Pi_1/(1 + r)$$
$$v_2 = \Pi_2/(1 + r)^2$$

and so forth, until

$$v_N = \Pi_N/(1 + r)_N.$$

The total present value of the stream of returns is

$$V = v_1 + v_2 + \ldots + v_N,$$

or in more compact notation

$$V = \sum_{j=1}^{N} v_i = \sum_{j=1}^{N} \Pi_j/(1 + r)_j^i.$$

Our present-value formulas and numerical example show an important fact: *an increase in the rate of interest will cause anyone who is making an allocation decision to weigh present returns more heavily than before. A fall in the rate of interest will lead to more careful consideration of future period returns.* We turn now to a more systematic investigation of the way that interest enters into the decisions of individuals who are involved in allocation through time.

9.3. ALLOCATION THROUGH TIME

9.3.1. Allocation without Production

Simple geometrical analyses of individual choice were presented in Chapters 5 and 6, and in this section they will be extended to the problem of allocation through time. As usual, geometrical analysis has its limitations; and in this case, those limitations are visible in the restriction of analysis to only one good and two time periods called "present" and "future."

In Figure 9.2, an individual's rate of consumption of the good in the present period is represented by distances along the horizontal axis, and his rate of consumption of the good in the future period by distances along the vertical axis. His *wealth,* or ability to consume as he enters the present period, is indicated by the point W: were he to sacrifice all future consumption in order to maximize present consumption, he could consume W in the present period. A standard "indifference map," with convex and continuous indifference curves, is drawn, which reflects the individual's subjective evaluation and ranking of the various possible bundles of present goods and future goods.

Now suppose the individual can lend out a part of his wealth in the current period to be repaid in the future period. If r is the rate of interest, he will receive $1 + r$ units of the good in the future period for every unit that he lends out in the present period. The individual's budget line in Figure 9.2 passes through the point W and has a slope of $-(1 + r)$. He can have any bundle of present and future goods that lies on or below the budget line. If the individual were to consume his entire wealth in the future period (assuming he could somehow survive with zero present consumption), his future consumption would be $'X = (1 + r)W$. Actually, as is clear from Figure 9.2, the individual's best choice is to consume P units in the present and F units in the future, for at that

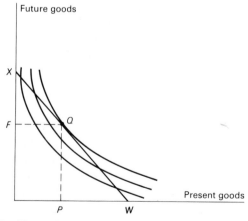

FIGURE 9.2. The optimal lending decision from wealth endowment W

point the highest achievable level of satisfaction is attained, as indicated by the tangency between the budget line and an indifference curve at the point Q.

That simple analysis can be made more "realistic" if we assume that the individual receives income in the amount I_P (present period) and I_F (future period) and that he borrows at a higher rate of interest than he can obtain if he lends. He can use all of his future income in the future period, or he can borrow against that future income to obtain present consumption at the rate of interest r_B. The opportunities from borrowing are traced out by the negatively sloped line connecting the points E and B (Figure 9.3); that line has the slope $-(1 + r_B)$. Similarly, the individual can consume his entire present income I_P in the present period or he can lend a part or all of it at his lending rate r_L, with resulting opportunities shown by the line connecting the points E and L with slope $-(1 + r_L)$.

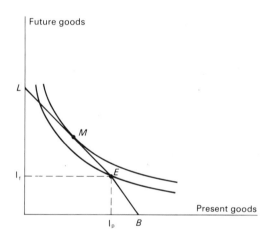

FIGURE 9.3.   The optimum disposition of endowment with borrowing and lending at different rates.

The borrowing and lending opportunity lines together reflect the opportunities open to the individual for the allocation of his income in each period as shown in Figure 9.3. The individual's optimal choice will be to stay at E (if E lies on the highest attainable indifference curve); otherwise the optimal choice will be defined by a tangency between the borrowing line or the lending line and an indifference curve (as at the point M of Figure 9.3). The intercept of the borrowing line on the horizontal axis is the present value of the individual's income in the two periods. That present value is exactly equivalent to his wealth. Because *wealth* and the *present value of an income stream* are precisely the same thing, the two analyses of Figures 9.2 and 9.3 are formally identical (except for a minor modification: the latter assumes that the individual borrows and lends at different rates of interest).

9.3.2. Allocation through Time with Production

The foregoing analysis can be made more general if we recognize that in addition to consuming or lending his wealth, an individual may be able to use it in production. For concreteness, suppose that corn or wheat is the single good that is dealt with in the analysis. A farmer can eat part of his crop and lend some of it in exchange for a promise of future repayment. But he can also use a part of his crop for seed; and if he does, he increases the amount of grain that will be available for consumption in the future period. In Figure 9.4, D is the individual's grain holding as of the beginning of the present period. A curve, called the *production transformation curve,* is drawn connecting D to D^1. Each point on that curve represents a combination of current-period consumption and future-period consumption. These are the *efficient* combinations of current and future consumption that the individual can obtain by *producing*—that is, by using grain withheld from current-period consumption to grow more grain for future-period consumption. At every point along the transformation curve DD^1, the individual's wealth is allocated between current consumption and the production of goods for future consumption. Future goods can also be obtained by lending in the current period, with opportunities shown by the line DE; but as Figure 9.4 shows, lending *instead of* producing is unattractive, because DD^1 reaches higher indifference curves than DE does.

When confronted by production opportunities, as in Figure 9.4, the individual apparently reaches the highest attainable level of satisfaction by moving to the point A, where he consumes P^* units of his endowment and plants $D - P^*$ units, from which he obtains a yield of F^* units in the future period. No other combination of present and future goods anywhere along the transformation curve DD^1 is preferred to the combination at A.

But suppose that *in addition* to producing, the individual can also borrow or

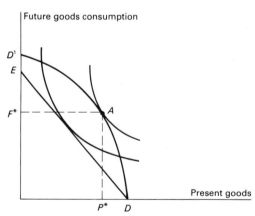

FIGURE 9.4.   Production opens better prospects than lending for this individual.

lend. He will be able, by borrowing or lending as well as producing, to move to a combination that is preferred to A.

Suppose he produces the combination B instead of A (Figure 9.5). At B, the transformation curve DD^1 has a slope equal to $-(1 + r)$, where r is the rate of interest at which borrowing *or* lending takes place. From B, the individual can borrow against his output of future goods along the line bl, and he can move to a point like C where he has more of both present and future consumption than he would have had at A. The combination B gives the best production choice; at B, the highest attainable borrowing and lending line is reached. If he were to go above and to the left of B along DD^1 (say, to point X), he would obtain fewer future goods in production in exchange for his reduced current consumption than he could get by producing at B and lending to the point Y; conversely, if he stopped short of B (say, at the point A), he would keep more for present consumption at the cost of less future consumption. But the same reduction in future consumption would yield a greater increase in current consumption if he produced at B and borrowed to the point C.

After choosing to produce to the point B, the individual's borrowing and lending activities lie along the line bl, which passes through B, and has the slope $-(1 + r)$. The optimal combination is found where bl is tangent to an indifference curve; that point is marked Q^* in Figure 9.6.

9.4. EQUILIBRIUM IN THE FINANCIAL MARKET

How is an equilibrium rate of interest determined? Individual choices of production, borrowing, lending, and consumption affect the relative availability of

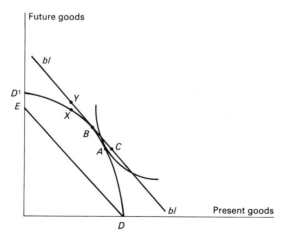

FIGURE 9.5.   Borrowing or lending, *and* producing, is a "better" strategy than simply producing.

future-period and present-period goods. In Figure 9.6 the response of one individual to a particular rate of interest r is shown. The borrowing decision of that individual is represented by a move from the point B to the point Q^*. If r is an equilibrium rate of interest, the total volume of such borrowings by all individuals must be precisely equal to the total quantity of loans made available by other individuals who elect to lend when the interest rate is r. If loans are like any other commodity, there will be an equilibrium rate of interest in the financial market; equilibrium, of course, holds when the total borrowing demand is equal to the total supply of lending (or, stated differently, when the excess demand for loans is zero). The rate of interest also affects the volume of consumption foregone in the current period and the volume of production that takes place for future-period consumption. With a concave production possibility frontier, like the one drawn in Figure 9.6, a reduction in the rate of interest means an increase in production for future consumption. This effect is shown in Figure 9.7: when the rate of interest is r, production of present goods is P and of future goods is F. At the lower rate of interest r', the production of present goods falls to P', and future goods output increases to F'.

To summarize, then: our very simple analysis of individual choice behavior in borrowing, lending, and producing reveals that

1. The rate of interest affects every individual's production and consumption: the higher the rate, the more will be consumed now and the less will be used for production to be consumed in the future (Figure 9.7).
2. The rate of interest affects every individual's borrowing and lending decisions. The higher the rate, the more likely any given individual is to be a lender and not a borrower. (Explain why to yourself with the help of Figure 9.6.)
3. Through adjustments in production, borrowing, or lending, all individuals together determine the rate of interest. As the rate of interest increases, the quantity

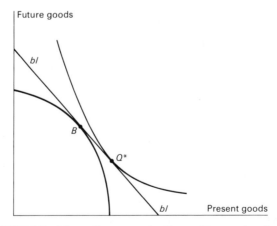

FIGURE 9.6.   The optimum production and borrowing decision.

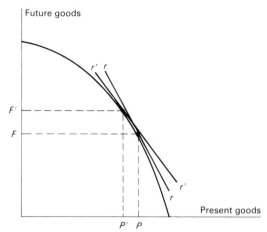

FIGURE 9.7.   When the interest rate falls, more current consumption is foregone for the sake of production (future consumption).

of future goods production declines; and with the decline in production, the scarcity of future goods is increased relative to current goods. The reduced supply of future goods reduces the desire to borrow (to give up future goods in order to get more current goods), and the reduced desire to borrow tends to inhibit further increases in the interest rate.

This model, though quite simple, points out several important facts about the allocation of resources through time.

First, the more we consume today, the less *capital* we will have with which to produce goods for future consumption, and hence the smaller our future consumption will be. If we refrain from consuming today and instead *invest* (add to capital), we will be able to consume more in the future.

Second, *individual preferences* and *available production opportunities* determine the balance between current consumption and production for future consumption.

Third, the mechanism that determines the balance between investment and consumption is not guided by any single plan or intelligence; it is a decentralized mechanism that responds to and itself influences the actions of profit-motivated individuals.

9.5. THE NATURE OF CAPITAL

9.5.1. What is Capital?

A leading character in the economic drama has been lurking in the wings, waiting to enter on cue. That character is *capital*, and he is sometimes a difficult character to figure out. Some who study his role say he is ''plant, equipment, and physical things." Others say he is "money saved by individuals." In this brief section, we will build upon the simple foregoing analysis to clarify what capital is. In the process of defining capital, we will find it useful to classify several related topics, namely, *income, wealth, saving,* and *investment.*

In the context of the simplest one-good, two-period analysis, an individual's endowment E consists of two incomes, I_P and I_F (Figure 9.3, p. 181). An individual's *income* is defined as the addition to his command over consumption goods. It is defined with respect to a specified period of time. Thus, in the two-period analysis, I_P is the amount of consumable good that the individual gains in the present period.

The *wealth* of an individual is simply the present value of his stream of income. In a two-period world, wealth is

$$W = I_P + I_F/(1 + r)$$

where r is his borrowing rate of interest.

The individual's *saving* in any period is simply the difference between his income and his consumption in that period. If he borrows and consumes, to the extent that consumption exceeds income, then saving is negative.

In the simple world of one good, the tie between saving and investment is particularly easy to see. Saving is done for one purpose, to increase the individual's claim against the output of future goods in the society. Investment is the process whereby saving today is transformed into the production of future goods. In a one-good world, the same physical objects that are saved are used directly to produce future goods (in the transparent case in which the good is grain, saving is the withholding of grain from consumption, and investment is the act of using that seed grain in the production of next period's crop). In our one-good model, we did not require that the individual who did the saving make the investment decision. The saver could loan his savings to another individual, who would use the saved good productively. Whether he produces directly or lends, the saver's claim against future goods is increased by the act of saving.

Saving decisions and investment decisions are coordinated through the interest rate, as determined on the capital market (Section 9.4); and our simple model pretty well describes essential features of how the job gets done in the real world. The amount that an individual invests will depend on the interest rate and on his production possibilities; the amount that he saves will depend on the interest rate, and his preference ordering of present and future goods.

Investment, finally, brings us to *capital.* Capital is the remnant of all past investment activity that is still usable for production. When we look at the real world, the capital that we see is the accumulated plant, equipment, and improvements to land and human skill that has not yet been worn out or used up. Capital is not valued because it can be consumed directly, but rather because it can be used to produce things that yield satisfaction in consumption. When discussing capital in this plant-and-equipment sense, it is advisable to use the term *capital goods:* that term reflects the physical nature of the objects in question. In our one-good model, the only capital goods that appear are the goods that are invested in the first period. Because the model limits itself to two periods, there is no accumulation of capital that is carried through more than one time period.

The word "capital" is used in other than the capital goods sense. We sometimes hear a sophisticated individual refer to the money that he has saved as his "capital." The unambiguous and proper term to use in that context is *liquid capital*. Liquid capital is what is saved, loaned, borrowed, and used to purchase capital goods. Investment is the act of buying capital goods with saved or borrowed liquid capital.

Finally, the word is used in a sense that reflects the desire to measure the effect that additional capital goods can have on future income. The present value of the increment in future consumption that an individual gets by installing a capital good is referred to as the *capital value* of that good.

Capital goods of the type that we have been discussing here can be increased in number or accumulated more rapidly through time. As that occurs, the potential rate of future consumption within the economy also increases. But some types of capital, such as mineral resources of the earth, apparently cannot be accumulated in greater quantity through time; and other types, such as redwood trees, seem to be declining in quantity, even though there is no reason in principle why they cannot be increased. Natural resource problems vex some people quite deeply; these people express the fear that private ownership and market allocation of such resources must turn out badly. In Chapter 14 we will investigate whether such forms of capital can be allocated sensibly to production at different points in time by a market system.

9.5.2. Natural Resources: "Capital" or "Land"?

In the past, it was traditional to classify natural resources as "land" rather than capital. The distinction was drawn partly because land exists in a state of nature, but capital requires effort to accumulate. That particular distinction does not stand up under scrutiny, however. Land must be cleared to be productive (and other natural resources must be extracted, removed, or transformed). To refer to a natural resource, such as a pool of crude petroleum, as "capital" is to acknowledge its important role in increasing potential future consumption. The decision as to how such a resource should be used through time is formally quite similar to the decision as to how grain should be used through time.

APPLICATIONS AND EXTENSIONS

1. What reason is there to suppose that the production curve *DD'* of Figure 9.7 is concave? Suppose it were shaped as shown by the curve *A* in Figure 9.8, would that have any effect on the analysis? What about the curve *B*?

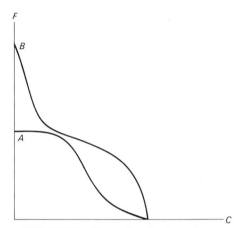

FIGURE 9.8.   Illustration for Question 1.

2. Consider a case in which an individual borrows first, *then* produces. If his initial endowment point is on the horizontal axis as in Figure 9.6, borrowing will carry him into a region of negative future good holdings; to get his future goods positive, he will have to produce. Will reversing the sequence of the borrowing and production operations have any effect on the final optimum, or will it remain at $Q*$ (Figure 9.6)?

3. What particular aspect of the production problem discussed in Section 9.3.2 makes that problem different from one of simply finding an optimum consumption rate for period 1, and then finding an optimum consumption rate for period 2?

4. In earlier discussions of production, capital was treated as a productive input in the same way that labor was: x_1 and x_2 represented the rates of use of these inputs, w_1 and w_2 represented their prices, and their marginal productivities were calculated in precisely the same way. But capital is something that a producer purchases and pays for ''now'' but uses up slowly over many time periods, while labor is something that the producer hires in each period; and he uses only the amount that he pays for in each period.

    Try to think of some ways to get around, or out of, this conceptual difficulty. It can be done.

5. Which, if any, of the following are *not* capital accumulation activities?
    (a) Taking a cram course for the state bar (law) exam.
    (b) Tinting the west windows of an office to reduce afternoon glare.
    (c) Tearing down an office building to make room for a private tennis club.
    (d) Buying a new typewriter for a male stenographer.
    (e) Burning down a neighborhood to punish and discourage its unloved occupants.

6. If capital formation is principally and substantially the activity of private individuals, and if it is voluntarily undertaken, what basis is there for an assertion like Proudhon's, quoted in Chapter 1, Section 1.2.2?

7. ''In a one-good, two-period world, the slope of the production transformation curve is the negative of capital value.'' Explain why this statement is true (or untrue).

BIBLIOGRAPHICAL   NOTE

The seminal genius of Irving Fisher, the greatest economic theorist (and one of the worst investment portfolio managers) in the history of the United States, is here acknowledged. His *Theory of Interest* (New York, Macmillan, 1930), develops these ideas fully and presents them in accessible form. Fisher's theory is updated and extended by Jack Hirshleifer, *Investment, Interest and Capital* (Englewood Cliffs, N.J., Prentice-Hall Inc., 1970).

CHAPTER TEN

Individual Welfare
in the
Idealized Market System

The best is the enemy of the good.

VOLTAIRE (1764)

10.1. WELFARE ECONOMICS

The first economists were moral philosophers, and ethical concerns are the old-est motives that underlie economic enquiry. Ethical concerns remain in focus, despite the growing regard for economics as a theoretical and empirical science. They are manifested in interpretations of the existing order and prescriptions of policies to control, modify, or replace parts of that order. To study economics *only* as a positive science, ignoring the ethical implications of the subject, is a bit like reading the Old Testament as a historical novel: it can be done, but much of the consequential impact is lost.

Roughly speaking, there are three approaches to the question of how the economic welfare of society's individuals can best be assured and protected. First, there is the view that market systems have many desirable properties. A number of shortcomings are acknowledged to exist, but these are viewed as chal-lenges to politicians, educators, and social designers. Second, there is the view that the market system is hopeless as a social institution, and should be greatly curtailed in scope. Third, there is the view that the market system, while admit-tedly deficient in comparison to a demanding and probably unattainable theoreti-cal ideal, is superior to any alternative that human intelligence can come up with on the spot. Those who hold this third view can point to numerous attempts at reform or social betterment which have turned out badly. There is, they say, usually little benefit and/or great cost attached to well-meaning attempts to reform or improve market allocation, and their prescription is to extend, rather than circumscribe, the scope of market allocation.

This chapter gives a brief summary of the welfare implications of allocation through an idealized market system. In the remainder of the book, attention is devoted to a number of important forces that upset or impede the workings of existing market systems, and create a gap between the ideal and the actual. We want to develop a sufficient understanding of market systems, their workings, and their problems, so that "remedies" and policies can be intelligently evaluated.

The first approach to *welfare economics* (the evaluation of the economic order from an ethical perspective) takes the view that a competitive market system offers a benchmark against which existing economies can be compared. That approach will not be advocated strongly in this book, but there are interesting reasons why it is taken by some economists, and those reasons will be explored now.

10.2. THE MARKET SYSTEM AND WELFARE

10.2.1. An Individualist Social Welfare Function

A social welfare function is an explicit expression of "society's" ranking of outcomes. In that regard, it may be very much like an individual's preference ordering: the social welfare function can tell us whether outcome A is preferred or not preferred to outcome B, and society's goal can be viewed as that of finding the most preferred attainable outcome.

The analogy between individual preferences and social goals is in every respect a troublesome one. The first and most obvious difficulty is: who speaks for "society"? Who *defines* social goals? To some ardent souls, this question is red herring. Their clarity of vision makes the correct direction for society so obvious, and social needs so evident, that any delay in moving in the right direction or answering those needs is criminally negligent. In effect, those visionaries would use their own perceptions to serve as society's. And it does seem to happen, with remarkable frequency, that such willing servants turn up among the ranks of politicians, union leaders, and university faculties, to name but three common sources.

There is, of course, no reason why any one individual's preferences should be taken as a guide to social choice. A superior alternative, in the view of most people, is a comprehensive mechanism, one that takes into account the preferences of all individuals in the society. The difficulty with such a notion is that it is impossible to find a (complete and transitive) ordering which takes the preferences of affected individuals into account in a nonarbitrary fashion, unless comparisons are made between the preference orderings of different individuals, of the type "Mr. A prefers 1 over 2 by more than Mr. B prefers 2 over 1."[1]

The search for a social ordering that operates like an individual preference ordering, then, is doomed to failure *unless* some means can be found whereby the *strength* of individual preferences can not only be measured, but compared between individuals. Most observers regard such comparisons as a hopeless undertaking. Thus, in discourse on economic science, it is usually held that an individualist social welfare function—one that takes individual preferences into account—is an unrealistic goal.

10.2.2. The Pareto Condition

There is one ranking of outcomes in a society that does not make comparisons between individual preferences. The Pareto Condition ranks outcomes 1 and 2 on this basis: outcome 1 is better than outcome 2 if some individual is better off given 1, and no individual is worse off given 1. Thus, the Pareto Condition avoids comparisons between the strengths of individual preferences. The main drawback of the Pareto Condition is that it does not provide a complete ordering of outcomes. To see this, consider the familiar Edgeworth Box diagram for a two-person, two-good society (Figure 10.1). We know that any allocation in the shaded region is preferred to the point O; but we also know that there are many allocations outside the shaded region to which O cannot be compared; and we further know that inside the shaded region, many allocations cannot be ranked vis-à-vis each other (α and β cannot be compared, for example).

Despite its incompleteness, the Pareto Condition remains attractive as a rank-

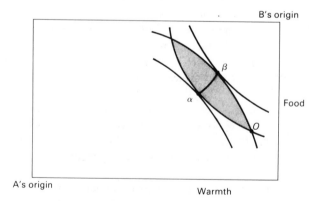

FIGURE 10.1.   Two-person, two-good exchange again. α and β are superior to O by the Pareto Condition, but cannot be directly compared to each other.

[1]The work of Kenneth Arrow on this problem is cited in the bibliographical note to this chapter.

ing scheme, not only because it does not require interpersonal comparisons but also because its fulfillment implies the efficient use of resources consonant with individual tastes and preferences. On the balance, however, many people regard the Pareto Condition as an inadequate criterion for ranking alternative outcomes.

10.2.3. The Marginal Conditions: Interpretation

In Chapters 5 through 8 a number of conditions were displayed concerning the outcomes of choice behavior of households and firms. Consider first the condition (from Chapter 8, Section 8.2.1)

$$P_j = MC_j, \qquad j = 1,\ldots, n,$$

which must hold for the output of any good by any firm. The price P_j is a measure of the amount that society's individuals, as consumers, would be willing to pay for an additional unit of the good j. The MC_j is the *opportunity cost* of producing one more unit of good j. That is, MC_j is the value of the goods that could be produced by other firms if they used the resources that the good j producers would need to increase their own outputs of good j by one unit. Thus the $P_j = MC_j$ condition implies that the society's consumers value an additional unit of good j by neither more nor less than they value the other goods that must be given up to increase any firm's output of good j by an additional unit. *No transfer of resources into or out of any firm will yield a higher-valued output when $P_j = MC_j$ for all goods.* In that sense, the output is "optimal." The reason for the quote marks around the word optimal will be clarified in the next few pages.

The second condition to note (from Chapter 8, Section 8.1) is

$$VMP_{ij} = w_i; \qquad \begin{array}{l} j = 1,\ldots, n \\ i = 1,\ldots, m; \end{array}$$

the value of the marginal product of every resource in every firm is equal to the compensation paid to the resource. Firms adjust their usage rates of resources so that the value resulting from using one more unit of any resource in production equals the cost of hiring it.

Insofar as the resource "labor" is concerned, the second condition also implies that no individual will supply more labor at the prevailing wage, if the hourly wage is lower than the value he places on an additional hour of leisure.

Finally, the third condition (from Chapter 6, Section 6.2)

$$\frac{MU_j^{(l)}}{P_j} = \frac{MU_k^{(l)}}{P_k} \qquad \begin{array}{l} j,k = 1,\ldots, n \\ l = 1,\ldots, r \end{array}$$

holds across all pairs of goods j and k, and all consumers l. The "marginal utility" per added dollar of expenditure is the same across all goods. Thus there are no possibilities of additional benefit to any consumer either from reallocating his income among goods, or from exchange with other consumers.

Competitive production and exchange, in short, takes the resource allocation processes of the society to a point at which the Pareto Condition is satisfied.

10.2.4. Conditions for Success

In order to attain the full benefit implied by the three marginal equalities that were discussed in the preceding section, several important conditions must hold.

First, no producer, consumer, or resource supplier can be sufficiently large so that his decisions or choices by themselves affect any price. This condition is very important, as we will see in the next few chapters. Second, every consumer and every producer has information regarding all currently prevailing prices in all markets. Without that information, some decisions might be made which violate the $P = MC$ condition; or profitable opportunities for exchange between individuals might be overlooked. Third, goods must be *divisible*. Restriction of choice in the consumption of some goods to either large quantities or to nothing impairs the efficiency of market allocation. Fourth, there can be no restriction that prevents any individual or firm from producing or purchasing any good. Restrictions on production, such as patents or license laws, and restrictions on consumption, such as exclusive real estate covenants, are definitely a barrier to the attainment of the desired and desirable marginal conditions. Fifth, there can be no government activity that imposes nonvoluntary payment on an individual: taxes are okay as long as they are paid in exchange for services that the individual has agreed he wants, but any tax that is arbitrarily levied as an individual's share of payment for government activity will distort one or more of the three marginal conditions. Sixth, there can be no *externalities* in either consumption or production. An externality is a cost or benefit to a third party resulting from exchange between two individuals, or from the productive activity leading up to that exchange. Seventh, the distribution of income must be acceptable to all of the society's individuals. If there is strong judgment widely shared that some people enter the exchange process with far too much in the way of disposable income while others enter with far too little, then there will be dissatisfaction with the *justice* of the outcome of that process. And finally, even if all the foregoing conditions are satisfied, there are some who will complain that participation in a division-of-labor, business-firm-centered production system is an "alienating" or "dehumanizing" experience. All of these exceptions, and more, too, can be indicated as reasons why the theoretical ability of exchange processes to satisfy the Pareto Condition should not be taken as evidence of the "innate superiority" of such processes. In fact, the discrepancies between the conditions that assure the beneficial working of exchange systems on the one hand, and conditions that actually prevail on the other, are so large that they cause despair that the ideal can ever be achieved.

The major conditions that qualify the optimality of exchange, that were enumerated in the preceding paragraph, will be examined in detail in Part Three of this book. The major political responses to those conditions, socialism and programmatic interventionism, are evaluated in Part Four.

We turn now to a topic that clearly illustrates the inherent limitations of general market equilibrium analysis as a source of "norms" or guidelines in evaluating social well-being. What happens if a society contains a government, as well as a market system? Some interesting questions arise; the one we will examine in detail is posed by taxation and its role in resource allocation.

10.3. TAXATION AND EFFICIENCY

The efficiency of competitive market allocation, as reflected in the three marginal conditions that were discussed earlier, has long held considerable appeal for many economists. In the real world, of course, the system cannot possibly work exactly as the idealized model describes; for one thing, in the real world we have governments, and governments collect taxes and spend money. Economists have considered whether government taxation and expenditure can be designed in such a way that the appealing marginal efficiency conditions continue to hold.

Income taxation, in particular, has offered an interesting problem. The effect of an income tax in the theoretical market system is to "drive a wedge" between the worker's wage and the value of his marginal product: the employer pays the worker the value of his marginal product, but the worker must pay a tax on that payment, and so the money he can keep for himself—the incentive to which he responds—is less than his *VMP*. The theoretical result is that *too little* labor is used. A similar outcome is seen to hold when sales taxes or excise taxes are charged against the selling prices of some or all goods. Suppose every candlemaker must pay a flat tax rate of 10 cents per pound on the candles he produces. The effect is to raise average and marginal cost as shown in Figure 10.2; and that, in turn, immediately shifts the supply curve as shown in Figure 10.3.

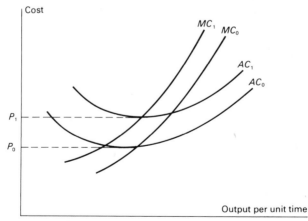

FIGURE 10.2. **An excise tax shifts *AC* and *MC* upward (from C_0 to C_1). P_0 and P_1 are the long-run equilibrium prices before and after the tax.**

At the price of P_0 and the output Q_0, the price of candles is equal to the opportunity cost of the resources used in candle production. At the after-tax price P_1 and output Q_1, the price-marginal cost equality no longer holds, and the allocation of resources no longer satisfies the Pareto Condition.

For a time it was believed that a different kind of tax structure could be imposed, without the problem of inefficiency ever arising. It was suggested that *lump-sum* taxes charged against producers or individual consumers would preserve efficient operation. When charged against a producer, the effect of a lump-sum tax is to increase his average cost without affecting his marginal cost. The tax, as its name implies, is simply a charge that is imposed on the firm regardless of the amount produced by the firm. In Figure 10.4 we see that a lump-

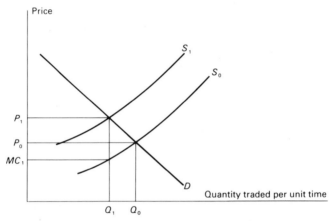

FIGURE 10.3.   Market supply response to an excise tax. Note that the marginal production cost after the tax MC_1 is less than the equilibrium price by the amount of the tax.

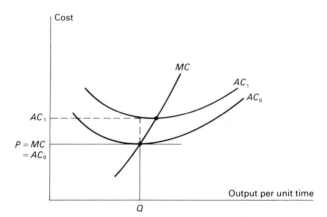

FIGURE 10.4.   A lump-sum tax shifts *AC* but not *MC*.

sum tax causes no change in the firm's marginal cost curve. It therefore will cause no shift in market supply, and hence will leave market price unchanged. Moreover, it preserves the $P = MC$ efficiency condition, *all in the short run.* In the long run, it appears that firms will leave the taxed industry because profits are negative after the tax is imposed; but if a cleverly structured group of lump-sum taxes are imposed on *all* firms, then opportunity costs of resource use elsewhere will decline, and in fact the tax need not make the profit rate negative. Long-run equilibrium in our firm can, if lump-sum taxes are imposed omnisciently on all firms, be made to remain precisely where it would be in the absence of taxation. Thus, it appears, lump-sum taxes do not ''distort'' resource allocation. The marginal conditions of allocation continue to hold as before.

However, it is not true that lump-sum taxes convey no distortionary effects; where they are used, they affect the *supply of productive effort* (the willingness of individuals to work). This is most easily seen by assuming that the lump-sum taxes are collected directly from individuals, rather than from firms. In the ideal market system, a worker will weigh the ''utility'' to be obtained by spending the wage for another hour of work, against the ''utility'' sacrificed by giving up an hour of leisure: the marginal utility of leisure is equated to the marginal utility from expenditure of wages, as shown in Figure 10.5. The line PP' shows how leisure can be transformed into goods by a representative worker. He can devote all his time to leisure, thereby operating at the point P', or he can sacrifice all his leisure, operating at the extreme P. The indifference curves are from his preference ordering on goods and leisure. His optimum point is A, where he enjoys L hours of leisure, and devotes his remaining time to work.

When a lump-sum tax is imposed (Figure 10.6), the line PP' is shifted downward by the amount of the tax, to pp'. Along pp', the optimum point is a,

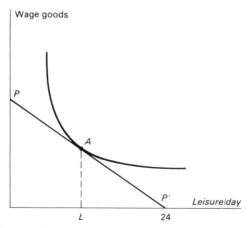

FIGURE 10.5. Equilibrium of the individual worker who allocates his day, at the equilibrium A, between L leisure hours and $(24 - L)$ work hours.

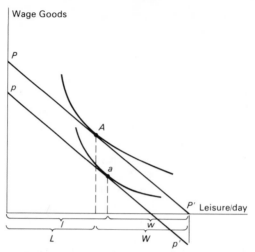

FIGURE 10.6.   **Effect of a lump-sum tax on the work-leisure choice. The worker here increases his leisure from L to l, after a tax in the amount equivalent to $w_0 - w_1$ units of wage goods per day has been imposed.**

with l hours of leisure. As Figure 10.6 is drawn, the effect of the lump-sum tax is to increase the demand for leisure, and hence the ratio of leisure to work. Unless preferences are so structured that a and A in the figure involve the same amount of leisure, there will be a shift in work effort in response to the lump-sum tax. It appears that the likelihood of nondistorting taxation by government is extremely small. That analysis tells us that competitive market equilibrium is an unrealistic sort of "ideal" or benchmark by which to judge allocation in the society; it does not tell us that there should be no government, or no taxation.

We turn now to the analysis of two problems, one essentially economic in nature, the other essentially political-philosophical. They are examined in the two remaining sections of this chapter.

10.4. GOODS INDIVISIBILITY, PRODUCTION ECONOMIES, AND MARKET SIZE

Goods indivisibility can pose a problem in both production and consumption. The technical development of some production processes may make it very uneconomical to produce some goods at very low production rates. It is far cheaper (on a per-unit-of-output basis) to make hundreds of thousands of auto bodies per year than to make dozens; the former rate will be obtained with the assistance of large and expensive hydraulic pressing equipment, while the latter will almost surely be done by hand. There are no small, cheap, or convertible hydraulic presses suitable for a very small car manufacturer.

Similarly, any person who wishes to obtain the convenience of having a private automobile at his service is confronted by indivisibility problems of sorts, not only because one auto is the smallest number he can own, but because he must have a driver's license and accident insurance, inputs whose prices do not steadily diminish as the amount of driving that is planned goes to zero.

The problem of indivisibilities in consumption can be illustrated (Figure 10.7.) If an individual's consumption possibilities are limited as shown by indivisibilities in the purchase of good x_2, then the marginal condition

$$\frac{MU_1}{P_1} = \frac{MU_2}{P_2}$$

will not hold. That condition would hold at the point A; but in the presence of indivisibility of good x_2, the consumer cannot reach A; he can do no better than the point B. The failure of the marginal condition at B indicates the superiority of A over B.

Indivisibilities are to some degree mitigated by market processes. Substitutes exist that can be used economically on a smaller scale than the indivisible good—bicycles, motorcycles, or public transit are substituted for an automobile; more frequent trips to the grocery store are substituted for a refrigerator or freezer; brooms are substituted for vacuum cleaners. And rental markets permit part-time and less expensive use of autos, color TV sets, carpet cleaners, pianos, and power tools in applications where the use of such items is not sufficiently frequent to warrant their purchase. Rental is a way whereby several users can share the use and cost of expensive capital goods.

A similar situation is encountered when a good that does not seem to be indivisible is economically produced on a large scale. It would be costly for any in-

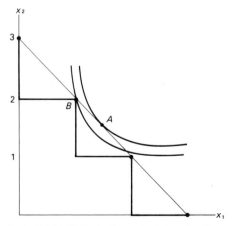

FIGURE 10.7. An individual's budget constraint and optimum choice when the good x_2 is indivisible.

dividual building contractor to make all the plumbing fixtures that he uses in the structures that he builds. For that reason, a few plumbing suppliers make those fixtures in large quantity to sell to the tens of thousands of contractors. In effect, one phase of the construction industry, the manufacture of plumbing fixtures, has been separated out for operation in a large-scale way. Similarly, a few can manufacturers make the cans and buckets for the hundreds of brands of paint that are sold in the U.S. Such arrangements are very similar to rental markets, in that they involve sharing the use of a capital good that cannot economically be made to yield output flows as small as some users would like.

For a rental market to operate effectively it is necessary that there be a sufficient number of renters. For a manufacturer of building supplies or paint cans to prosper, it is necessary that their goods be demanded by a sufficient number of contractors or paint makers.

The size (or extent) of the market, then, will in large measure determine the extent to which indivisibilities or large-scale production economies cause problems. Symphony concerts are few and far between in Shell, Wyoming, and a resident of that community will find such entertainment expensive (in time and money: She must travel to Denver or Minneapolis to find a season of concerts). Her problem arises because it costs as much to perform for one listener as for many: concerts are indivisible in production.

The problem of market size, however, is not exclusively a problem of sparsely populated regions. A person who wishes to work from 4:00 P.M. to noon, two days a week, finds his choice of occupation somewhat constrained. Perhaps he can drive a taxi or win a Nobel Prize in a physics lab; but not enough others share his taste to permit him to function in any interactive capacity; and even such noninteractive tasks as night watchman cannot be considered.

The tastes of one's fellows, then, constrain the range of economic choice to a much greater extent than the theory of general production and exchange equilibrium suggests. In the next section we will see how this simple fact can be inflated into an important political dogma.

10.5. ALIENATION AND THE DIVISION OF LABOR

In Chapter 7, the efficiency-increasing qualities of production through division of labor were discussed. But what, if any, are the drawbacks of division-of-labor production? Adam Smith, in a famous passage, expressed concern regarding the impact of specialization on the moral and intellectual capacity of the populace:

> In the progress of the division of labour, the employment of the far greater part of those who live by labour, that is, of the great body of the people, comes to be confixed to a few very simple operations, frequently to one or two. But the understandings of the greater part of men are necessarily formed by their ordinary employments. The man whose life is spent performing in a few very simple operations . . . has no occa-

sion to exert his understanding, or to exercise his invention in finding out expedients for removing difficulties which never occur. He naturally loses, therefore, the habit of such exertion, and generally becomes as stupid and ignorant as it is possible for a human creature to become. The torpor of his mind renders him, not only incapable of relishing or bearing a part in any rational conversation, but of conceiving any gener-ous, noble, or tender sentiment, and consequently of forming any just judgment con-cerning . . . many . . . of the ordinary duties of private life. . . . His dexterity at his own particular trade seems, in this manner, to be acquired at the expence of his intel-lectual, social, and martial virtues. But in every improved and civilized society this is the state into which the labouring poor, that is, the great body of the people, must nec-essarily fall, unless government takes some pains to prevent it.[2]

This view has been repeatedly echoed by writers of the Marxist and socialist traditions; and concern over the ''dehumanizing'' or ''alienating'' aspects of the division of labor has led to experiments in contemporary China, in which specialists are encouraged or even forced to partake in occupations that are re-mote from their specialities: scientists into steel manufacture, and steel-workers into agriculture, for example.

Concern for the ''whole man'' is all to the good, but we cannot overlook the important consequences of high productivity for the general condition of the population. The very survival of a large part of the world's population is threatened by shortages of such mundane goods as food and fiber, and we may well question the wisdom of a priority system that places well-roundedness ahead of survival.

There seem to be three further points to be made concerning the problems of monotony and lack of intellectual challenge that are adjuncts of division-of-labor production. First, it should be noted that because the division of labor increases productivity, it makes possible more leisure. The standard forty-hour work week of today is a far cry from the schedule that was required of rural citizens of the nineteenth century. Those people certainly practiced countless diverse trades—baking, blacksmithing, weaving, and midwifery, for example—but even so it is to be doubted that their intellectual horizons were as broad as those of their coun-terparts of today who work at monotonous specialized assembly-line labor for a wage. Today's worker cannot find much creative satisfaction on the job, but he can typically enjoy considerable freedom off the job, and choose from among an extraordinary variety of hobbies and avocations ''to keep the mind alive.'' If he does not do so, but rather prefers to fill his off-work hours with the stereotyped beer-and-TV existence, we can wonder at the wisdom of a social order in which leisure occupation reinforces the idleness of mind fostered on the job; but if the only alternative is to withdraw free choice by a forced pattern of interoccupa-tional transfer, Chinese style, then the cure may be worse than the disease.

As a second point, we should note that if individual workers prefer variety in

[2]*An Inquiry Into the Nature and Causes of the Wealth of Nations,* Book IV, Chapter I, Article II, 1776.

their occupation, then variety may be had at the price of lower wages. A worker who performs on a furniture assembly line is more productive than a similar worker who is employed in a cabinet shop. The former may spend his life in managing a single machine that dowels and glues table legs, the latter may create and even design beautiful furniture, from raw lumber to finished product. Typically, the assembly-line worker will earn a higher income than the hand craftsman. Yet hand craftsmen do exist and do practice their craft, presumably because they value the variety and sense of accomplishment that their craft gives to them more than they value the higher wages they could receive as assembly-line workers. If this feeling were widespread among workers, living standards in general would be lower, as we measure them: there would be far fewer goods produced to be used within the society. Workers can bring about that change on their own volition: they have simply to indicate the willingness to accept a much lower wage in order to get the much pleasanter work that they desire. A search for a pleasanter, lower-paying job is a meaningful indication of that willingness, and thus far, only a few workers have given that indication.

Finally, we must ask: does the division of labor create the "torpor of mind" that Adam Smith notes and deplores, or is a division-of-labor productive organization simply a good way of using workers who tend toward intellectual inertness anyway? The question is an important one. If, as some critics conceive, the natural state of man is one of intellectual liveliness and creativity, then division-of-labor production does destroy valuable intellectual, moral, or spiritual resources: assembly-line workers are forced to suppress that intellectual liveliness and creativity. If, on the other hand, no form of occupational organization can bring forth a significant indication of intellectual growth among most people, then division-of-labor production provides goods more abundantly, without destroying significant resources.

This topic can be closed on an optimistic note. Since the Industrial Revolution of the nineteenth century, mankind has progressed enormously in industrial societies. Today's worker is better educated, fed, housed, clothed, and medicated than was the middle class of a century ago, while working about half the number of hours per week. The productivity gains from division of labor have gone in part to provide those improvements. There is no reason to suppose that those gains cannot or will not continue; and future gains may be used to provide work that is organized in a more challenging way, instead of, as in the past, providing more leisure to the workers. That choice will rest to a large degree with the workers themselves.

That last point—the presence of a significant degree of choice in regard to productive activity as well as consumption—may be the strongest single argument in favor of a market system when the welfare of society's individuals is considered. The system functions imperfectly compared to the ideal of theoretically perfect competition; but then, it may be true that *every* operable system will look bad by that standard.

APPLICATIONS AND EXTENSIONS

1. One of the amusing aspects of welfare economics is that in its formal analyses of allocative systems, it usually proceeds as if there were no government. Yet if "the man in the street" were asked what the term "welfare economics" means, he would almost surely say that it deals with such government programs as unemployment compensation, public housing, poor relief, and so forth. In fact, such programs are enormously significant, both in terms of the resources they allocate, and the resources they consume. The following questions are intended to focus attention on the potential importance of these issues.

   (a) Welfare benefits are part of the currency of political office. How is it that a politician can win votes by promising higher benefits to some voter groups, and not lose votes when a very large voter group, the taxpayers, realizes that they must foot the bill?

   (b) Much light can be shed on political activity by analysis in terms of conflict and compromise among political interest groups. What are the interests of the government employees (bureaucrats) that are charged with administration of various welfare programs? On this question, you may want to consult Anthony Downs, *Inside Bureaucracy* (New York, Little Brown, 1967).

   (c) To what extent, in your opinion, is the Pareto Condition employed as a guideline in the construction of government welfare programs, i.e., to what extent do they reflect a concern to make somebody "better off" without loss to others?

   (d) In your considered opinion, is private charity more likely or less likely to conform to the Pareto Condition than government welfare programs do?

2. A *Bergson* social welfare function in a two-person society is of the form

$$W = W(U_1, U_2) \qquad \delta W/\delta U_j > 0 \quad , \quad j = 1, 2$$

where U_1 and U_2 are the "utility levels" of the two individuals. (Remember that a "utility function" is simply a numerical representation of an individual's preference ordering over the set of possible consumption alternatives.) If there are two goods in the society, the individual j's utility function is

$$U_j = U_j \ (x_1^j, x_2^j) \qquad\qquad j = 1, 2$$

where x_1^j, x_2^j are the amounts of the two goods consumed by j.

   Using an Edgeworth box diagram, show that (a) if the utility of individual 2 is made as large as possible, without diminishing 1's utility below some specified level, then the allocation of the two goods between the two individuals must lie on the contract curve; (b) if the Pareto Condition is not satisfied, a higher level of Bergson social welfare can readily be achieved by reallocation between individuals 1 and 2.

BIBLIOGRAPHICAL NOTE

F. M. Bator, "The Simple Analytics of Welfare Maximization," *American Economic Review* (March 1957) provides a neat graphical treatment of this chapter's topic. J. de V. Graaff's *Theoretical Welfare Economics* (New York: Cambridge University Press, 1967), offers good perspective on theoretical perfect competition as an ideal, and deals with an important idea that we barely touch here, the "social welfare function." For a deeper discussion of taxation, J. Buchanan, *The Public Finances,* 2nd ed. (Homewood Ill.: Irwin, 1965) is a useful source.

A related topic of importance that is mentioned but not explored here stems from the work of K. J. Arrow, *Social Choice and Individual Values,* 2nd ed. (New York: Wiley, 1966). Arrow asks: is it possible to devise a ranking of possible outcomes within a society which satisfies some plausible consistency conditions, and which is neither arbitrarily chosen, nor dictated by one individual? The answer, he finds, is no. The most immediate implication for welfare economics is that it will not be possible to decide upon a social preference ordering by democratic means, if that preference ordering is to have the desirable completeness and transitivity properties of the individual orderings that we worked with in Chapter 5.

MARKET "FAILURE"

The idealized market economy of Part Two has been criticized on the ground that it is prone to malfunction. The most serious criticisms will be reviewed and evaluated here in Part Three. Chapters 11, 12, and 13 are concerned with the problem of monopoly. Monopoly power causes resources to be misallocated; the reason it happens and the potential seriousness of the problem are discussed in Chapters 11 and 12. Advertising, which some observers regard as both a source of monopoly power and a social abuse, is discussed in Chapter 13. Chapter 14 examines the frequent complaint that market allocation is myopic—it pays too little attention to future needs and too much attention to current profits. Chapter 15 turns to the issue of third-party effects, or externalities, and the related topic of public goods. Externalities and public goods are also frequently discussed as sources of "market failure." Chapters 16 and 17 are concerned with the problem of income distribution. What forces determine how much an individual earns in a market economy? What does the structure of individual compensations look like in the American economy? Is it true that "the rich get richer, and the poor get poorer"? What should be done about poverty, or about the existence of great wealth? These issues—monopoly, external effects, impatience, or myopia, and maldistribution—are three of the main sources of interesting and theoretically viable criticism of a capitalist order. The goal of this section is to understand the content of such criticisms and evaluate their strength. We also want to see what policy actions have been recommended and what may be appropriate as a response in the presence of those issues.

CHAPTER ELEVEN

Competition
and Monopoly

We have always known that heedless self-interest was bad
morals; we know now that it is bad economics.

FRANKLIN D. ROOSEVELT (1937)

11.1. COMPETITION

11.1.1. Sufficient Conditions for Competition

One extremely important consideration underlies the analysis of production and
allocation by supply and demand as it was developed in the preceding chapters.
That condition, simply stated, is that *both buyers and sellers must view price as
"given"*: that is, every participant in the market process must behave as if price
were unaffected by his own decisions regarding how much he should purchase
or produce. If an individual buyer or seller behaves according to that condition,
his behavior is said to be "competitive." There is considerable concern that in
fact many important sellers do not behave in accord with that condition. The
growth in importance of large business firms leads some economists to believe
that competition (as defined here) is no longer a characteristic of market supply.

Because there is more concern about the behavior of sellers than of buyers,
we will focus in this chapter on the question of what happens when competition
breaks down in the *supply* of a good. The analysis when competition fails in the
demand for a good is quite similar in both procedure and results, as will be seen
in Section 11.5.

Usually, four conditions are stipulated as sufficient to assure that firms will behave as "price takers," or competitors. If these conditions hold, we confidently assert that there will be competition; but we may have competition even if one or more of the conditions should fail to hold.

First: no supplying firm can have a dominant share of the market. Two patterns of behavior that are attributed to dominantly large firms are inconsistent with competition, and will be analyzed later in this chapter. These behavior patterns are *price leadership* and *dominant firm pricing.* Nobody has succeeded yet in identifying when a firm has grown "too big" relative to the rest of its industry: the only condition that indicates excessive size is noncompetitive pricing behavior.

Second: there must be a significant degree of uniformity (in the view of buyers in the market) among the products of the supplying firms. Should any firm produce a product that is unique in the eyes of customers, that firm will learn that the price it receives is sensitive to the quantity of output that it offers for sale. If its product is unique, in the view of consumers, then a firm is not well-advised to behave as a "price taker."

Third: the number of firms engaged in supplying the market (or potentially capable of supplying the market) must be large enough so that "conspiracies in restraint of trade" among the several suppliers cannot survive. It will always be in the interest of suppliers to attempt to restrict the total quantity supplied to the market, because by restricting supply, they can secure a higher price and higher returns than can be earned under conditions of competition. As we will see, agreements to restrict output by imposing quotas for each supplier will tend to break down. Such an agreement may be reached; but, curiously, once the agreement is established, it is in the interest of every supplier to "cheat" by increasing his own output above his quota if that cheating can be done in secret. As the number of supplying firms increases, it becomes easier and more attractive to cheat, and hence, harder to maintain and enforce agreements to restrict output.

Fourth: no substantial legal or financial barriers must stand in the way of any firm that wishes to "enter the industry" (that is, any firm that may decide to begin producing the good must be permitted to do so). Legal barriers, such as patents or trademarks, can prevent competition. So can financial barriers: if very large outputs and sales are necessary in order for a firm to earn normal returns, the costs of achieving a sufficiently large rate of operation for success may discourage potential entrants.

If these four conditions are fulfilled, then competition should characterize the market. However, the conditions are stated in such qualitative, comparative, and subjective terms that there is much room for controversy as to whether they all hold in a particular case. Are toothpastes significantly nonuniform? Will four major U.S. automobile suppliers be a large enough number so that collusion in pricing behavior cannot succeed? These are difficult questions.

There is, in fact, little in the way of concrete and satisfactory characterization of competition to be found anywhere in the literature of economics. Despite the lack of any widely accepted standards that can be used to decide whether or not the four conditions hold, it is worth examining in detail why each one is potentially important in assuring the presence of competition. But before doing so, we investigate why the basic condition of competition—that each supplier regards market price as unaffected by his output and sales decision—is important. To help in understanding that important condition, we next describe the behavior of a competitive firm when it is in equilibrium.

11.1.2. The Equilibrium of the Competitive Firm

This section traces the response in a competitive firm and industry to a change in market demand.

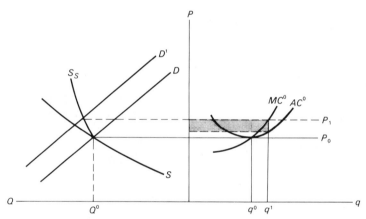

FIGURE 11.1. **Short-run equilibrium adjustments in the market and in a typical firm that supplies the market.**

In Figure 11.1, market demand and supply determine the price P^o. (Market supply increases as we move from right to left in Figure 11.1.) The typical firm serving the market is in equilibrium: there are no forces tending to produce any change in behavior. The firm's output q^o is a small fraction of the market equilibrium output Q^o. At q^o, two conditions hold in the firm:

$$P^o = MC^o(q^o)$$
$$P^o = AC^o(q^o).$$

The first condition implies that output is at its returns-maximizing rate. The second condition implies that the firm is just exactly covering its opportunity costs of production.

Now, suppose demand shifts to D^1 from D^o. The shift in market price will induce an increase in output from the firm; maintaining the condition $P = MC$, the firm moves to the output q^1. The firm is in short-run equilibrium; the conditions

$$P^1 = MC^o(q^1)$$
$$P^1 > AC^o(q^1)$$

hold. The second condition implies that the firm is *more than* covering its opportunity costs of production; it is in fact earning *profits* in the amount shown in the shaded rectangle:

$$q^1 \cdot [P^1 - AC^o(q^1)].$$

Long-run equilibrium is brought about by increasing the amount of capital that is applied in the industry. The simplest way to show that increase is to assume that it comes about as new firms enter the industry. Entry is induced by the presence of extraordinary returns at a price of P^1. The effect of entry is to increase market supply from S_S to S_L (Figure 11.2). The process of entry stops only when price has fallen from P^1 to P^*. At P^*, the conditions

$$P^* = MC^*(Q^*)$$
$$P^* = AC^*(q^*)$$

again hold for suppliers, and the process of adjustment is complete.

The costs faced by the firm may rise in the manner illustrated in Figure 11.2. MC^o and AC^o are the firm's costs when the industry output is Q^o; MC^* and AC^*, when it is Q^*. The cost difference, if any, will be the result of higher resource prices that the firm must pay at higher rates of resource use by the whole industry.

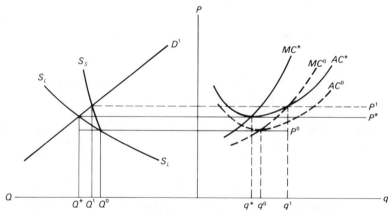

**FIGURE 11.2. Long-run equilibrium adjustment in the firm when
production cost increases as new firms enter to increase
market supply.**

Subtle but important differences in the firm's equilibrium are seen to exist if the firm has monopoly power; that is, if it behaves as though its output decisions significantly affect the price it receives.

11.2. MONOPOLY

11.2.1. Price, Marginal Revenue, and Output Decisions

Suppose, as in Figure 11.3, a market is in equilibrium when price is $1, and output is 10,000 units. If output is increased by 110 units, price falls to 99 cents. The change in revenue accompanying that output increase can be viewed as consisting of two parts. First, there is the originally prevailing price times the change in output, or $1 × 110 = $110. Second, there is the induced change in price which results from the output increase, times the total rate of output after the increase, or (−$.01) × 10,110 = −$101.

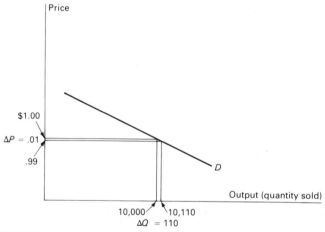

FIGURE 11.3. A monopolist's demand curve, illustrating the way that price falls when the output rate is increased.

If a single firm supplies that market, it will learn that an increase in output will induce a reduction in price, and it will calculate the effect of both the greater output and the lower price on the revenues that it obtains. The first component of the revenue change, written $P\Delta Q$, is the initial price times the output change. This component always tends to increase revenue; but the second component $(Q + \Delta Q)\Delta P$, the revenue effect of the induced price change, always moves in a direction opposite to the first component, because ΔQ and ΔP are negatively related (price drops when output increases). The *net* of these two effects on revenue is called *marginal revenue*. Marginal revenue can be positive or negative, depending on whether $P\Delta Q$ is greater or less than $(Q + \Delta Q)\Delta P$. But positive or negative, marginal revenue is always less than price, as long as the demand curve is negatively sloped. This is seen by setting ΔQ equal to 1: then the expression for marginal revenue is $P + (Q + 1)\Delta P$, and ΔP is negative.[1] *If the single firm that supplies the market is operating at an output rate where marginal revenue is larger than the cost of increasing output (marginal cost), it will be profitable for the firm to increase its output.*

The output decision of a monopolist can be displayed as in Figure 11.4. At any output Q, the market price is found from the demand curve D. The marginal revenue at any Q will be less than price. The curve MR indicates the value of marginal revenue for all outputs Q. The monopolist's output rule is: set output at the rate at which marginal cost equals marginal revenue (Q_M in Figure 11.4); at Q_M his price will be P_M.

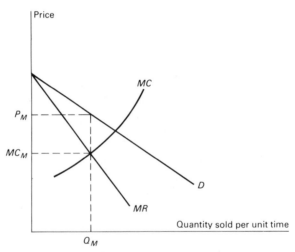

FIGURE 11.4. The monopolist is in equilibrium at output Q_M, where price (P_M) exceeds marginal cost (MC_M).

Now, suppose that instead of only one firm supplying the market there are many. The firms may not perceive the effect of their own output decisions on price. Returning to Figure 11.3, suppose the largest output increase that any one firm might consider making is 10 units. Firms will be justified in ignoring the effects of induced price changes in making their output decisions; after all, it would require eleven such output increases by supplying firms to bring about a price change of one penny (a 1 percent change). Suppose that the manager of a firm in which price exceeds marginal cost, is considering a ten-unit increase in output. He knows that his additional ten units aren't going to affect market price very much, and so his decision to expand will be based on whether price exceeds

---

[1]More rigorously, marginal revenue is dTR/dQ where $TR = P \cdot Q$ = total revenue. We have $MR = dTR/dQ = QdP/dQ + P$ and since $dP/dQ < 1$, $MR < P$.

marginal cost. But even if he knows that other firms will probably be expanding their outputs, and that market price will probably drop, there is not much reason for him not to increase his own output, since the change in price will depend on what everybody else does—he can't prevent the price drop by abstaining from an output increase; and he stands to lose money by holding output unchanged, because at the time of his decision, price exceeds marginal cost.

In a market supplied by a large number of small firms, then, whenever market price exceeds any firm's marginal cost of production, that firm will increase its output. *Whether or not suppliers respond by increasing output when price exceeds marginal cost is very important in evaluating the way that markets allocate resources.* We saw why that response is important in Chapter 10; but the idea bears review. Recall that *cost* is measured by alternative opportunities foregone. The marginal cost of a lawnmower, for example, is the highest return that could be obtained by producing something else, like bicycles, with the resources needed to produce an additional lawnmower. Those returns from the alternative use of resources will depend on the market-determined values that members of society attach to the alternative goods, and on the productivity of resources when applied in producing the alternative goods. Suppose, for example, that two bicycles can be produced with the resources necessary to obtain three additional lawnmowers. Then, if a bicycle sells for less than half again as much as a lawnmower, it will pay to divert the resources out of bicycle production and into mower production. The price of a lawnmower measures the market-determined value that society attaches to another lawnmower. *When price is greater than marginal cost in the lawnmower industry, the members of society are, in effect, voting that they value another lawnmower more highly than they value the next best thing that could be produced instead of a lawnmower.* Hence, by adjusting output to eliminate the difference between price and marginal cost, lawnmower producers are using resources to produce goods that conform most to the tastes of society's individuals, as those tastes are revealed by the processes of market action.

A single supplier, who systematically holds his output to the rate at which marginal revenue equals marginal cost, fails to allocate resources in the beneficial way that competitive suppliers do, since his chosen output will always be less than the one at which price equals marginal cost.

11.2.2. The Theoretical Effects of Monopoly Power

An "industry" is a group of firms serving the same market, producing a single common product. The essential feature of competition is the way that suppliers respond in the presence of higher-than-normal returns. Under competition, suppliers expand output in an attempt to cash in on such opportunities. Competition reaches its highest and most refined form when suppliers respond to profit incentives as if their own output decisions have no effect on market price.

The antithesis of competition is monopoly. The term "monopoly" has suffered from poor use; in some polemics, any large business is referred to as a monopoly. Etymologically, the term means "single seller," but we use the word to characterize some markets with more than one seller, for reasons to be discussed presently. Markets may be "monopolized" to different degrees as a result of the failure of any of the four conditions of competition listed earlier in the chapter.

What are the characteristics of monopoly power and monopoly behavior that make monopoly an important contrast to competition? First, as we have pointed out, monopolists may tend to restrict their outputs because they are conscious of the fact that the price they receive is affected by their own choice of output rate. Second, monopolists may obtain high returns, and be able to prevent other firms from cutting into those returns by bringing close substitute goods to the market. Both characteristics of monopoly have unfortunate consequences for the efficient allocation of productive resources in society.

Consciousness of the revenue effects of output decisions. A seller with some monopoly power is aware that the price he receives will respond to changes in his rate of output, and so the comparison between price and marginal cost is abandoned (rationally and correctly, given his objectives); instead he makes a comparison between marginal revenue and marginal cost. Because the demand curve is negatively sloped, price at any output Q will be greater than marginal revenue, as demonstrated in Section 11.2 and plotted in Figure 11.4. The monopolist's output will always be at a rate such that $P > MC$; he always produces at a rate at which consumers, by their market choice behavior, reveal that they would rather have more of the monopolized good and less of the goods that would have to be relinquished to achieve higher output of the monopolized good. This *misallocation* occurs because the monopoly is sensitive to the effect of its output rate on its price; and because entry into the production of close substitutes for its product is blocked to other firms.

Monopoly returns. Monopoly returns also affect resource allocation, but the effect is more subtle and harder to explain than is the effect of the $MR = MC$ output decision rule. Monopoly "profits," of course, are a favorite target of the polemicist, and it is probably true that many firms with a measure of monopoly control do earn higher-than-average returns. But the relation between monopoly control and high rate of return is not as obvious as might *a priori* appear (as we shall see in Chapter 12).

Higher-than-normal returns due to monopoly can be criticized on grounds of both ethical and economic concern. First, monopoly returns represent a reward that is in no way connected with performance in the satisfaction of wants. Second, because monopoly returns can be perpetuated over time, they can lead to maldistribution of wealth; founders of firms that hold monopoly positions become rich faster than other people. Third, monopoly returns may in part be allocated toward activities of doubtful social benefit; crime syndicates expend a part of their monopoly returns on terrorism, and more respectable enterprises spend a part of their returns on advertising or on the development of gimmicky product changes (like automobile model changes). Both terrorism and the other activities have the objective of protecting a monopoly position, and in the eyes of some people, both are equally damaging to society.

None of these three contentions about monopoly returns is securely demonstrated, of course; where and how any one of them may fail is not hard to discover. All three contentions, to be forceful, require that monopoly returns be stable over time and susceptible to protection by the actions of the monopolist himself. The issues of how well monopoly holds up in a changing economy, and how well advertising and product changes can serve to protect a monopoly position, are questions that have been and are being examined, and on which there remains a divergence of opinion. What we do know is that if there are returns above normal that persist over long periods of time, then resources surely are not responding to earning opportunities, and misallocation exists.

Some possible offsetting results. Every cloud has a silver lining, we are told, and the presence of a monopoly may carry benefits as well as costs to society. First, because of its large scale of operation, a monopoly may produce more cheaply than can enterprises that operate under conditions of competition. This permits the monopoly to increase its output more cheaply than can be achieved under competitive organization; and as a result, the monopoly does not operate as far short of the competitive output as Figure 11.4 suggests. In fact, if its cost advantage were large enough, the monopoly might continue producing up to, or even beyond, the competitive output.

In addition, some economists have suggested that under conditions of monopoly, the society will experience a more rapid rate of genuine economic progress, because there are greater incentives for individual firms to devote resources to the discovery and development of new products. In an industry with free entry, rival firms can copy significant new products and thereby bid away part of the returns to be made from those products. This reduces the incentive to engage in the costly and risky processes of product research and development. (In recognition of the desirability of preserving incentives for research and development, the government has passed various laws which provide for patents, oil depletion allowances, and the like.) This particular apology for monopoly is not entirely convincing, either. There is, after all, no reason why a firm should engage in research if it has a solid and well-protected monopoly position. Who needs to pursue the search for new products vigorously if the present ones are guaranteed to be profitable for a long time to come?

Monopoly, equilibrium, and supply. Several striking differences emerge from the analysis of industry equilibrium in the presence of monopoly. We have already noted two: namely, that the competitive outcome of equality between price and marginal cost will not hold, and that higher-than-normal returns may persist over time. A third important difference emerges under conditions of monopoly—there is no such thing as a supply curve in a monopolized market. Price is not sufficient information for a monopolist to make his supply decision; he also must know how sensitive demand will be to an output change before he can choose his most advantageous output.[2] Hence, if a market is monopolized, there is no way to construct a supply schedule in the absence of knowledge about demand. By contrast, under competition, demand and supply can be analyzed independently of each other.

The monopolist is not malevolent—he does not necessarily wish ill on society. Like the firms that supply a competitive industry, he only seeks the highest possible returns available to him. But whereas in the competitive industry the search for highest return leads to an equalization of returns among industries and an output mixture that is preferred by individuals, the effect under conditions of monopoly is unequal returns and an inferior output mix.

11.3. A CLOSER EXAMINATION OF CONDITIONS FOR COMPETITION

We turn now to a closer examination of the four conditions that contribute to competitive behavior in an industry. These are (1) product homogeneity among suppliers; (2) a large number of firms supplying the industry's market; (3) the "insignificance" of the industry's largest firm compared to all its other firms, and (4) freedom of entry into the industry.

11.3.1. Homogeneous Product

If the products of Firm A and Firm B are perfect substitutes for each other, then no customer will buy any of B's output as long as it is higher in price than A's. The products of two wheat farmers will likely meet this condition of perfect substitutability (if customers know that both farmers exist); while the product of two auto manufacturers almost certainly do not. A measure of the extent to which two goods are substitutes is

$$\frac{\Delta Q_B}{\Delta P_A} \cdot \frac{P_A}{Q_B},$$

called the *cross-elasticity of demand* for B's output with respect to A's price. In the formula, Δ as usual signifies "change in": ΔQ_B is the change in the output of Firm B. When the cross-elasticity is zero, the change in A's price has no effect on B's sales; at the opposite extreme, a cross-elasticity of infinity implies

---

[2]Knowledge of price and demand elasticity is a sufficient basis for an optimal decision by the monopolist.

that any miniscule decrease in P_A can send Q_B to zero, implying a very strong dependency—in effect, the outputs of the two firms are the same good.

Why, then, do we not define an arbitrary value of cross-elasticity to be a cutoff point that separates competition from monopoly? If the cross-elasticity is higher than the selected value, the product is "sufficiently homogeneous" for competition; if lower, the product is "insufficiently homogeneous." Difficulties would predictably arise out of such a construction: for example, the cross-elasticity between coffee and tea may be very high. Suppose the supply of coffee is monopolized, and price rises above marginal cost. Tea-growers can do little or nothing about adjusting the supply of coffee; they only increase the supply of tea in response to higher tea prices, which result from the effect of higher coffee prices on the demand for tea. Their response may not force coffee prices down sufficiently to eliminate all of the difference between price and marginal cost in the coffee market.

Thus, the cross-elasticity measure is too crude as a definition of product homogeneity: technical capability in supply must be considered, as well as close connection in demand, in determining whether two producers supply the same good. There is obvious need, in studying a specific industry, to consider whether the outputs of different suppliers are substitutes. A producer whose output has extremely weak substitutes (a monopoly) will *always* look at the effect of his output adjustments on the price he obtains, and the $P = MC$ condition will never be satisfied.

11.3.2. No Dominant Seller

If one firm supplying a market is very large relative to rival firms, then competition is threatened. A pattern of pricing, called *dominant firm pricing,* is virtually indistinguishable from outright monopoly behavior. The essential feature of dominant firm pricing is that smaller firms are permitted to sell any amount they wish to offer, *at a price determined by the dominant firm.* The dominant firm simply responds as a monopolist to unfilled demand. In Figure 11.5, D is the market demand curve, and Σmc is the sum of marginal cost schedules of smaller producers. Each of the smaller firms will supply up to the point at which market price is equal to its marginal cost, because they all perceive the effect of their own output on price to be negligible. The difference between D and Σmc is plotted as the curve d in Figure 11.5. The dominant firm acts as if it were a monopolist, and d were the demand curve in the monopolized market. The dominant firm sets its output in accord with the rule $MC = MR$, where it is understood that the marginal revenue curve is calculated from d, not D. In Figure 11.5, MC is the dominant firm's marginal cost, MR the curve marginal to the residual demand curve d, Q is the output of the dominant firm, P is the market price determined by the dominant firm, and q is the total output of the smaller

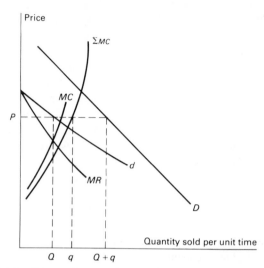

FIGURE 11.5. Price and output in a market with a dominant firm.

firms. The competitive efficiency condition $P = MC$ is satisfied among smaller producers, but not by the dominant firm, nor in the market as a whole.

A second pattern of behavior supposed to occur in industries dominated by large firms is *price leadership*. Price leadership is a pattern of collusive behavior. In numerous industries, the list prices charged by firms show a striking degree of uniformity, and price changes are usually initiated by one of the suppliers, called the price leader. There are advantages to suppliers in maintaining uniformly high prices, close to the level that would be charged if the industry were monopolized, and it may help to maintain market discipline if one firm initiates all price changes. Price changes reflect either a response to changed conditions of demand or cost, or an attempt by some renegade to undercut the rest of the group. With a price leader, it is easy to tell authorized changes that benefit the group from unauthorized ones that do not.

Price leadership does not require a dominant firm, and in some industries in which price leadership has been pretty clearly observed, the price leaders have not been the largest firms. Thus, the absence of a dominantly large firm is not sufficient to avoid anti-competitive behavior. To escape all manifestations of collusive behavior, large numbers of suppliers may be necessary.

11.3.3. A "Sufficient" Number of Sellers

What can be asserted about the need for "a large enough number of firms" supplying the market? Not very much; except that the prospects for success among four or five suppliers in collusion to restrict output are probably more limited than most people realize. It is asserted, in connection with a famous case of conspiracy in restraint of trade during the 1950s, that *three* manufacturers of heavy electrical generating equipment found it difficult to maintain the discipline of a secret joint agreement to maintain artificially high prices. We may well wonder: if three suppliers, who bid for contracts to produce according to the specification of customers, found it difficult to maintain discipline, can we expect larger groups of suppliers to collude successfully, especially if their output is made for sale on the open market?

Once again, we have only conjectures and impressions to go on, but the difficulties that attend price-fixing agreements in industries with as many as seven or eight suppliers may well be so great that the problem of collusion with that number of suppliers is not worth much worry. Later in this chapter we will investigate some of the difficulties of establishing and maintaining collusive price-fixing agreements among a "small" number of firms.

11.3.4. "Free" Entry

This is an exceedingly important condition, for it implies the ability of new firms to enter markets wherever the lure of prospective return is sufficient. Free entry need not imply costless entry; freedom in the sense of this discussion implies the absence of barriers to entry. Entry is *free* whenever a new supplier can expand the quantity available on the market about as cheaply and effectively as could an established existing supplier. When the costs to new suppliers compared to the costs to established suppliers are sufficiently higher so that new suppliers are discouraged from entering, we say that entry is *barred* or *blocked*. There may well be "start-up" costs entailed in getting a new product established, as is often the case when the most economical operating rates are extremely high ones, or when brand names are important to customers in a particular market. In these cases, an extremely high initial capital outlay may be necessary to get the new producer's line launched successfully. The riskier the prospects of return appear to be, and the higher the capital outlays that are required to start a firm off, the less likely it is that new competition will appear in the attempt to bid away high returns from existing suppliers. Such conditions are called *financial barriers to entry*.

Financial barriers to entry can take the form of excessively large outlays on advertising and promotion that are necessary to obtain a sustaining share of the market (a share large enough to enable an entrant to operate at an economically large scale). When such costs are present, the future stream of returns may be insufficient to compensate for the initial outlays, even if a sustaining market share is obtained. Clearly, the "financial barriers" phenomenon depends on the condition that a small scale of operation is uneconomical. If entering firms can begin small and cover their costs, then there is no significant issue of financial barriers.

There may be other entry barriers of a legal nature. A patent prevented firms other than duPont from producing nylon for several years after it was invented;

before patent rights elapsed, duPont sold production rights to other firms, but controlled terms of sale. The purpose of the patent law is to encourage invention. An inventor is given exclusive rights to his idea for seventeen years, during which time he can earn enough on it to compensate him for time and effort. The patent law does have the effect of creating monopolies, at least on a temporary basis.

Licensing is another important legal barrier to entry. The state controls entry into certain professions and occupations by requiring a license—realtors, morticians, beauticians, and doctors are important examples—and the prices of services provided by these occupational groups are undoubtedly higher as a result of licensure.

11.3.5. The Importance of Information

In some descriptions of competition, it is insisted that a fifth condition must prevail if competition is to exist: all buyers and sellers must have full information about the willingness of all other buyers and sellers to engage in market transactions at different prices. Full information, then, would involve everyone in the market knowing every buyer's demand curve and every supplier's marginal cost curve for the good being traded.

That condition is, of course, impossible of fulfillment. The best approximation that can be hoped for is that accurate information on the willingness of *some* potential trading partners to transact is available cheaply to *all* potential buyers and sellers in the market.

Actually, a separate requirement on the availability of information is redundant. If there are many buyers and sellers of a good, and no buyer or seller is "dominantly" large; and if the output of one seller is highly substitutable for the output of numerous other sellers, then information about good availability will be made available at low cost by sellers. It simply is not in anyone's interest to conceal terms of exchange under those circumstances; on the contrary, it is in everyone's interest to announce widely one's willingness and ability to engage in sale or purchase.

11.3.6. Variety versus Efficiency

In our discussion of product homogeneity, we noted that a finite positive cross-elasticity of demand between two goods (the percentage change in quantity of one with respect to a small change in the price of the other) implies that the two good are substitutes, but not perfect substitutes. When the two goods in question are different "brands" of the same "commodity," there may be less-than-perfect substitutability. This fact disturbs some commentators greatly. They feel that because Ford and Plymouth automobiles are not perfect substitutes in the eyes of consumers, the theory of competitive markets can tell us little or nothing about the market for automobiles. On the other hand, monopoly may also be a poor description of the automobile market: no producer can ignore the decisions of other producers. Because economists have never been one hundred percent successful in the attempt to analyze and predict behavior in markets that are not literally monopolized at one extreme, or served by numerous producers of indistinguishable goods on the other, and because those polar extremes are seldom if ever observed, economic theory is judged by some pessimists to be useless.

That is an excessively severe judgment. In the case of Plymouth versus Ford, the two goods in question differ in some attributes, such as trim and upholstery pattern, which to social critics are useless differences. On the other hand, they also differ in wheelbase, knee, head, and hip room, rear axle ratio, and frequency-of-repair record; and concern over those attributes is certainly reasonable. The fact that Ford and Plymouth are not perfect substitutes means that if the price of one exceeds its marginal cost, the other may not be induced to expand output and correct the revealed misuse of resources. The small amount of diversity between the two products may prevent the condition $P = MC$ from holding, as it would if the two producers were competing in the supply of perfect substitutes. Some judgment is then necessary as to whether this state of affairs is bad or not. If we believe, as some extreme social critics do, that product differences all are superficial and meaningless and exist only to trick the consumer into buying and paying more than is strictly necessary, then any failure of price to equal marginal cost must be viewed as a net loss to society. On the other hand, if we view product differences as a means of providing a wider base of meaningful choice to consumers, then we must look upon the difference between the market price of a good and its marginal cost as the "price of diversity." If diversity is desired by and beneficial to the buying public, and if resources must be used to provide it, then it is unreasonable to suppose that it can or should be available at no cost.

One apologetic view of the market system holds that as long as there are no barriers to entry into the production of a good, the only discrepancies that we will find between price and marginal cost are due to the cost of providing diversity and variety of choice to consumers. The failure of the $P = MC$ efficiency condition is then less disturbing. If costs could be measured accurately, the apologetic view would be susceptible to direct test. In some industries the misallocation $P = MC$ may be larger than necessary to cover the costs of providing the observed degree of variety that is found in the industry's products.

11.3.7. The Role of Competition: A Summary

Competition is the process of switching resources in response to the presence of attractive profits. When Ford gambled in 1965 on the belief that personal, "sporty" automobiles would be desired by the public, they built Mustang, and won. Through most of the year, they were able to sell Mustangs at the "window-sticker" (factory list) price; on other makes of automobiles, and other Ford models, discounts below list price were standard. The reward to Ford for gambling successfully was the high return on a model that had very little market competition. But competition was attracted by Ford's experience—and subsequent model years saw Barracudas, Camaros, Chargers, Cougars, and Javelins—to name a few of the entries into the market. Today a careful shopper can choose among those alternatives, and it is no more likely that he will have to pay full list price on any of them than on a station wagon or a four-door sedan. In a system where competition works, the efficiency condition $P = MC$ will hold at equilibrium: resources will be allocated in response to the dollar "votes" of individual consumers in such a way that there is no opportunity to transfer resources from the production of one good to another, with resulting higher returns.

11.4. MARKETS WITH SEVERAL SELLERS: MONOPOLY OR COMPETITION?

We have defined *monopoly behavior* as consciousness on the part of the firm of the effects of its own pricing decisions. *Monopoly misallocation* is the failure of the important $P = MC$ condition in markets where monopoly exists. *Monopoly profits* are the returns in excess of the normal rate that can accompany monopoly behavior.

The main purpose of this section is to consider whether monopoly behavior is likely in industries like automobile and electrical appliance production, which absorb a substantial share of the incomes of private individuals, and which are characterized by a small number of sellers. Monopoly behavior is certainly a precondition of monopoly returns and monopoly misallocation. We now want to see whether monopoly pricing behavior can be expected to emerge from industries characterized by a few large sellers—*oligopoly* industries, as they are called.

We preface our discussion with a warning—there is a large literature on the behavior of small numbers of sellers, called oligopoly theory; and that literature is one of the least well developed and least satisfying of any in economics. The reason, in part, is because individual sellers who are confronted by a small number of rivals are highly interdependent and are aware that they are interdependent. Firm A must take Firm B's response into account as A plans its own actions, and the difficulty of analysis is magnified enormously. The consequence is that our analysis can only point out crucial considerations and suggest plausible relations; it cannot yield predictions that justify a high degree of confidence.

Consider an industry in which three firms—two large and one small—are serving a market. Let market demand and market marginal revenue, and the marginal cost curves of the three firms, be as shown in Figure 11.6. If the firms can agree on how returns should be divided, it is in their clear interest to operate at the industry output Q^*, where MC is equal to MR, for Q^* is the output that

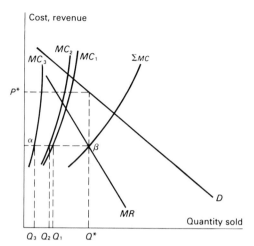

FIGURE 11.6.   The joint profit maximum in a market with three suppliers is at output Q*.

maximizes the total returns available for division among the three. Suppose they agree to divide the market in proportion to the outputs Q_1, Q_2, and Q_3 $(Q_1 + Q_2 + Q_3 = Q^*)$. This arrangement seems equitable and just; it con-forms to the slogan "from each according to his ability, to each according to his deed." But it does present Firm 3 with a strong inducement to "cheat" on the agreement by expanding its output.

In Figure 11.7, we examine the consequence of expanded output by Firm 3. The curve IMC_3 is the marginal cost of expanding *industry* output above the rate Q^*, when the entire expansion takes place in Firm 3. It is constructed by shifting the curve MC_3 in Figure 11.6 to the right in such a way that the point α coin-cides with the point β. Return to Figure 11.7. Firm 3 can expand its output so that industry output moves to the level Q^{**}. Price drops to P^{**}. Firm 3 loses re-turns in the amount $Q_3(P^* - P^{**})$, from its share of the joint profit maximum, as a result of expanded output. But it gains returns in an amount equal to the shaded area of Figure 11.7, the sum of price minus marginal cost over all units of the increase in output. Once Firm 3 has increased its output in the manner in-dicated, Firms 1 and/or 2 have incentive to expand their own outputs: first, in an attempt to recapture the lost returns resulting from the drop in price that ac-companied Firm 3's action; second, in an attempt to beat the other large supplier to the punch (the first large firm to expand output enjoys a temporary returns ad-vantage over the other); and third, to "punish" the malefactor, Firm 3, for having reneged on the market sharing agreement. The process of output adjust-ment (or price-cutting) can proceed to the benefit of one party or another until the output Q^c (the "competitive" output) is reached.

The point of the foregoing exercise is that price-fixing or market-sharing

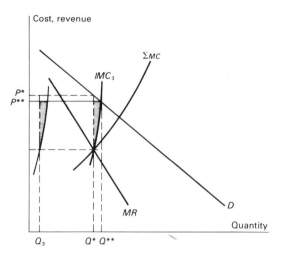

FIGURE 11.7.   The short term gains realized by Firm 3 when it "cheats" on its market-sharing output quota.

agreements are inherently unstable. Economic incentives exist to induce the violation of those agreements. (Firm 3 would not make the first output increase if it knew that 1 or 2 would follow immediately; 3 must weigh the present value of the short-term gains realized before 1 and 2 discover that 3's output has been increased, against the present value of the long-term losses that result because the market-sharing agreement breaks down after that discovery.)

The foregoing analysis of the market behavior of small groups of firms may be a good rough description of the way that small groups of suppliers usually operate; and it may require only some mechanism for predicting when and in what sequence changes occur, and something about the behavior of such important variables as advertising and quality differences among products, to be a predictively reliable theory of oligopoly pricing. If the story has widespread validity, then concern that the $P = MC$ condition will fail should not be the principal concern of those who criticize oligopoly industries out of fear of monopoly power. Instead, the primary concern should be the implications of excessive monopoly returns, which still can accrue even with $P = MC$, if entry into the industry is blocked.

11.5. THE ABUSE OF MONOPOLY POWER

Thus far, we have seen that monopolists have the power to withhold goods from the market, and to assure themselves of receiving a higher price in so doing. This behavior, because it leads to misallocation, is not in the best interest of society. It is also pretty tame stuff compared to the behavior that some social critics impute to large corporations. It has been suggested that (a) monopolists can shape or create demand for their output through advertising; (b) that monopolists influence legislative processes in their own self-interest, to the detriment of the public interest; (c) that monopolists exploit their workers; (d) that monopolists ruthlessly exploit the raw-materials-producing areas of the "third world." Suggestion (a) will be examined analytically later in this book (Chapter 13). Suggestion (b) can, it seems, be dismissed as a straw man, on the ground that any monopoly by itself constitutes a recognizable interest group, and it can be predicted that *any* interest group will attempt to influence legislative processes: monopolies are far from unique in adhering to this pattern of behavior. Hardly anyone has suggested that agriculture is monopolized, and few industries have benefited from governmental largesse in the degree that agriculture has. Other nonmonopolized industries, such as the textile industry, have benefited from favoring legislation on tariffs and import quotas. Thus, the issues of monopoly, and legislation to favor special interests, appear to be separable and separate issues.

The last two suggestions are both interesting and important. We turn to the first of these: that monopoly leads to a lower wage. This accusation needs to be refined; if it is, it can be shown to have a measure of validity. The problem of depressed wages is not one that arises in connection with large firms that dominate the market for the goods they produce—monopolies—but rather, it arises in connection with firms that are large relative to local labor markets. If a firm is the sole employer in a community, or the sole employer of some particular type of worker such as unskilled workers or stenographers, then it has a kind of "monopoly position" on the buying side of the market for labor. Etymologically, recall, monopoly means "single seller." If a firm is a "single buyer," it is technically called a *monopsony*. It is not necessary for a firm to be large to be a monopsony. For example, in Lake Township, Benzie County, Michigan, one of the world's great golf courses employs eight greenskeepers. That golf course is a "large" employer of unskilled labor in a sparsely populated area. It may well have a monopsony position, reflected in the fact that if it wished to employ ten or twelve greenskeepers, it might find it necessary to pay a higher wage to attract the extra men.

The essential feature of monopsony, then, is that the monopsonist is conscious of the fact that he must pay a higher wage to attract more workers. This is entirely symmetric with the monopolist's concern; if the monopolist wishes to sell more output, he must lower his price. By contrast, if a firm is a *competitive* user of labor services, it can increase or reduce its employment without affecting the prevailing wage rate.

In Figure 11.8, let S be the relation between the number of man-hours of labor available to the firm and the wage rate. S, then, is a standard sort of supply curve. The firm notices that in increasing its use of labor services, the cost of an additional man-hour is not simply the wage rate, for the wage rate must rise to

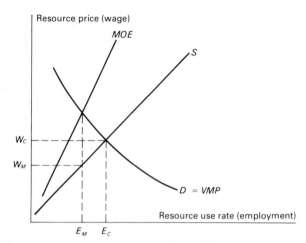

**FIGURE 11.8. Input resource use by a firm with monopsony power: The
value of the resource's marginal product exceeds the
payment by the firm to the resource owners.**

attract the additional man-hour into the firm's service. The cost of an additional
man-hour is the marginal outlay on employment *(MOE)*. We have

$$MOE = (W + \Delta W)(E + \Delta E) - WE = \Delta W(E + \Delta E) + W\Delta E,$$

where W is the wage rate when employment is E, and $W + \Delta W$ is the wage rate
when employment is $E + \Delta E$. This *MOE* relationship is plotted as a function of
E in Figure 11.8. *MOE* lies above S, if S is positively sloped. This is because the
increase in wages that is necessary to bring forth a larger labor supply is paid to
all workers, not just to *newly hired workers*. S tells us how much must be paid
per man-hour to sustain a given level of employment; *MOE* tells us how much it
costs the firm to increase that level of employment by one man-hour.[3]

The wage rate that results from the monopsonist's employment decision is
below the rate that would prevail if there were competition on the demand side
of labor markets. Suppose, in Figure 11.8, that D is the market demand for labor,
where we now are dealing with a market in which there are many employers. The
wage would be W_C and the employment rate E_C. If all employers were merged
into a single firm, that firm would behave as a monopsonist. The wage would fall
to W_M and the employment rate to E_M. Thus, monopsony can lead to a depression
in the status of workers.

---

[3]The point is easier with calculus. Let $S(E)$ be the wage associated with the employment rate E.
Then

$$MOE = dE \cdot S(E)/dE = S(E) + E\,\frac{dS}{dE} > S(E).$$

What of the problem of monopolies exploiting the third world's people by securing rights to develop mineral resources in those countries under favorable terms? The question is an emotional one. Critics of American corporate practices abroad point to the facts that some mineral resources are available more cheaply abroad because of abundant supply and cheap labor, and that corporations enjoy extraordinary returns on these foreign operations. According to critics, American firms should exhibit greater concern that the value of resources removed from places like Chile and Zaire be used for the benefit of the people of those countries. Too often, it is contended, favorable deals have been worked out with corrupt politicians or despotic Sheikhs, and little or nothing of value has been passed on to the people of such lands as a result of resource extraction by American businesses.

Virtually all of this indictment is true. As far as the prices paid to the foreign governments is concerned, if American firms involved are operating as monopsonists (single buyers for the resources in question), they are paying lower prices for the resources than they would with competition. On the other hand, if numerous American firms, or numerous firms of different national origin, are bidding for the rights to resource development, it is less likely that the poor countries are being underpaid for their resources.

Those who criticize our corporations' international relations, however, are usually less dismayed over the simple issue of price than over the other issues: lack of concern for the welfare of the common people and patronage to totalitarian governments. These criticisms are not in the realm of economics, but an economist can observe, first, that if there is international competition among the developed countries for the resources of the less developed countries, then the existing regime in a less developed country can choose its trading partners, and is almost sure to find some developed nation that will overlook the social arrangement in the underdeveloped country, no matter how oppressive. The idea, simply put, is if we don't, then someone else will; the people of the country in question would be no better off, and we would be worse off if American corporations refused to deal with unsavory foreign regimes.

Second, it may be contended that business firms are not social welfare agencies. The role of the corporation is to earn returns; interference in political processes will likely be inimical to that end. (But that contention has looked very thin on those occasions when firms have been engaged in active political intrigue abroad in order to obtain advantage, as apparently happens.)

Thus, in regard to corporate capitalism's relations with the underdeveloped world, competition among buyers is a mixed blessing to the inhabitants of the selling nations. It leads to higher prices for the resources that they sell; but if it were not for competition, the tolerance by purchasers of any political *status quo* in those countries, no matter how oppressive, might be more difficult to rationalize.

11.6. THE PRICE POLICY OF A DISCRIMINATING MONOPOLIST

Earlier in the chapter, we examined the operating decision of a monopolist, and concluded that he would regulate his output in such a way that the quantity Q^* would be sold at the price P^* (Figure 11.9). If the monopolist could market his output one unit at a time, selling each successive unit to the highest bidder instead of selling every unit at the price P^*, the revenue he would obtain from each successive unit sold could be found by reading down the demand curve. The demand curve would in effect be a marginal revenue curve.

If the monopolist does sell his output "one unit at a time," with each unit sold going to the highest bidder, instead of selling all units of output at the same market price, then at the output Q^*, revenue will be greater by an amount equal to the area of the triangle with vertices marked a, P^*, c (Figure 11.9). In addition, he will want to produce Q^{**} instead of Q^*, for by operating at that higher rate of output, he can increase his returns by an additional amount equal to the area of the triangle with vertices marked c, d, e. The output Q^{**}, of course, is the competitive output.

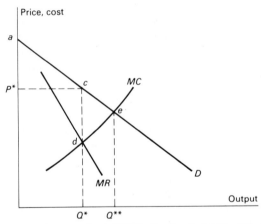

FIGURE 11.9.   If a monopolist is "Perfectly discriminating" he will operate at Q**, where price and marginal cost are equal.

In order to capture the maximum possible revenue on every unit sold, the monopolist must keep his customers "isolated" from one another, to prevent customers who purchase at very high prices from finding out about better deals for other customers, and to prevent customers who can buy at low prices from reselling the good to customers who would otherwise be forced to pay high prices. To prevent any interchange of information or flow of goods among consumers is an unrealistic goal. It can occasionally be partially accomplished by creating several outlets and blocking the access of some customers of some of the outlets. An example would be a manufacturer who produces a good that is restricted in trade between the U.S. and Canada. He could segregate his U.S. customers from his Canadian customers, if it were illegal to transport the good across the border; he then could "exploit" different demand elasticities in the two countries by charging a higher price in the country with less elastic demand. If a seller charges different prices to different customers on the basis of differences in demand (and not on the basis of differences in cost), then the seller is practicing *price discrimination*.

Another way to maintain a discriminatory advantage is by restricting the flow of information about transactions. For example, many universities act as discriminating monopsonists. In those places, it is viewed as bad protocol for faculty members to exchange salary information. That genteel rule of behavior works to the advantage of the university budget; it is possible for Professor A to go on believing that he is well-treated, if he does not know that his junior colleague Professor B is earning a salary several thousand dollars higher than his own. Another example of the same behavioral pattern is found in the automobile price sticker. Those stickers were originally legislated into existence to prevent automobile dealers from "milking" eager or naive buyers. However, those "suggested delivered prices" on the stickers are significantly higher than the market prices in most areas. Consequently, the stickers probably do lead some gullible buyers to pay more than the market price. Yet a third example can be found in urban supermarket prices. Stores in minority neighborhoods typically offer higher-priced merchandise than those in middle-class white neighborhoods. Those price differentials would break down, of course, in the presence of a free flow of commerce throughout the city; that is, if minority housewives were sufficiently mobile and felt sufficiently welcome so that they shopped around, the price differentials would disappear. (For this last example to be a valid one, it is necessary that costs of doing business not differ among different parts of the city.)

Such pricing practices as are discussed in our examples will strike some readers as dishonest or unscrupulous. It is the traditional view that in market exchange, anyone who lays out $x for a bundle of goods reveals that in his own subjective view the bundle he obtains will be worth $x or more to him. That he could have obtained the same bundle for less elsewhere does not mean that he was cheated, unless he was prevented from trading elsewhere. It does mean that he was careless, or not sufficiently diligent in collecting information, or simply very anxious to buy. This, of course, is a view that is constantly under attack by the benevolent, as in the current wave of "consumer protection" legislation. The common law has always protected consumers against fraud and deception, but the law is a costly instrument to use after an injury has been done. In the traditional view of the problem, competition, bolstered by the common law, offers adequate protection to buyers. The growing number and complexity of available goods calls that view into question; it remains to be seen whether the new wave of paternalistic protection will leave individuals better off or worse off than the traditional alternative.

*APPENDIX I
THE FIRM UNDER COMPETITION AND MONOPOLY

A monopoly firm's objective is to find the output which maximizes his returns; the returns
function is

$$\Pi = Q \cdot P(Q) - C(Q)$$

where $p(Q)$ is the demand function (a mapping of output into price), and $C(Q)$ is the
cost-of-production function. The first-order maximum conditions are given by

$$\frac{d\Pi}{dQ} = 0 = P + Q\frac{dP}{dQ} - \frac{dC}{dQ}$$

or

$$P + Q\frac{dP}{dQ} = \frac{dC}{dQ}$$

The expression $P + Q\frac{dP}{dQ}$ is marginal revenue; since dP/dQ is negative (the law of demand), marginal revenue is less than price. The term $\frac{dC}{dQ}$ is marginal cost.

   The competitive firm, by contrast, takes market price as determined independent of
its own actions. Thus, it views its problem as the maximization of

$$\Pi = PQ - C(Q)$$

which, by the same reasoning as was used in solving the monopolist's problem, leads to

the prescription: set output so that $P - \frac{dC}{dQ} = 0$ (Price = Marginal Cost). There are, of

course, a set of consistency conditions that must hold in the competitive market: the
profit-maximizing outputs of all firms must result in a market price equal to the one
that entered the output decision calculations of the various firms; and the simple objective function fails to capture the entry-inducing effects of higher-than-normal returns,
if any are present in the industry.

*APPENDIX II
RENTS

In the discussion of equilibrium in the competitive market (Section 11.1.2) an issue
was glossed over which sometimes puzzles the careful reader. How can we be sure
that *all* supplying firms will be at zero profit when the industry is at equilibrium? For
example, some firms may have better locations or more astute managers than others, and

*The material in this section may be too advanced for some introductory coverage.

their costs of operation may be reduced as a result. Thus, in Figure 11.10 at a price *P*, no new entrants may be induced to appear in the industry; but Firm A appears to be earning a rate of return higher than normal, while Firm B earns the normal return. This could happen because A has the advantage of a superior location, manager, or other input resource. The economist deftly sidesteps this issue by *imputing* the returns (measured by the area of the rectangle with corners *abcd* in Figure 11.10) to the *superior resource,* rather than to the firm. Once the source of the higher-than-normal returns has been identified, it should by careful bargaining be possible to "rent" the superior resource to some other producer for an amount that would just absorb the greater value of the product that the renter would obtain by using the superior resource. By not engaging in such a rental agreement, the owner of the resource is passing up an opportunity, and hence incurring a cost. When rents he could be obtaining from superior resources are included in his cost curves (as they properly should be), then average cost shifts to *AC* from the $AC - R/Q$ (average cost minus rent per unit of output) level, at which higher-than-normal returns appeared to be present (Figure 11.11).

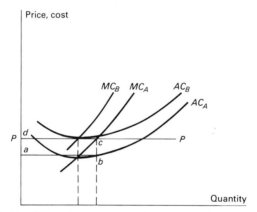

FIGURE 11.10. **If Firm A owns a superior resource, its costs of operation appear to be lower than those of Firm B.**

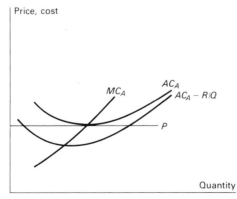

FIGURE 11.11. **The costs of Firm A, taking the rent of the superior resource into account.**

How can we be sure that MC intersects both AC and $AC - R/Q$ at their bottom points, as shown in Figure 11.11?

$$TC = Q \cdot AC + R \qquad\qquad (TC = \text{total cost})$$

$$TC - R = Q \cdot AC$$

$$MC = dTC/dQ = d[TC - R]/dQ \quad (\text{since } R \text{ is independent of } Q).$$

and we want to show that $MC = AC$ when dAC/dQ is zero; also $MC = AC + R/Q$ when $d[AC + R/Q]dQ$ is zero.

Taking the first case, $dAC/dQ = d[\dfrac{TC - R}{Q}]/dQ$

$$= \frac{Q\dfrac{dTC}{dQ} - TC + R}{Q^2} = \frac{1}{Q}[\frac{dTC}{dQ} - AC] = 0$$

which implies that

$$AC = dTC/dQ,$$

as was to be shown. Also,

$$d[AC + R/Q]/dQ = d[\frac{TC - R}{Q} + \frac{R}{Q}]/dQ = d(\frac{TC}{Q})/dQ$$

and when

$$0 = d(\frac{TC}{Q})/dQ = \frac{Q\dfrac{dTC}{dQ} - TC}{Q^2}$$

$$Q\frac{dTC}{dQ} = TC = Q[AC + R/Q];$$

thus

$$MC = \frac{dTC}{dQ} = AC + R/Q,$$

as was to be shown.

*APPENDIX III
LIGHT BULB AND STORAGE BATTERY MONOPOLISTS[4]

A persistent element in American folklore is the story of the firm that suppresses inventions that are capable of yielding better service at lower cost. Two commonly encountered examples involve light bulbs and automobile storage batteries. Such tales, which have

---

[4]This issue was treated by Jack Hirshleifer in *The Journal of Political Economy*, 79 (March–April 1971).

been around for a long time, differ in specification; the central theme, however, doesn't vary. An inventor perfects a superior battery; he obtains a patent on it, and tries to sell it to a producer. Major manufacturers are willing to pay a high price for the battery, but only to suppress it. Once a major manufacturer owns patent rights, the idea is destroyed, to keep the longer-lived battery out of the hands of the public, where it would ''spoil the market'' for batteries.

As for light bulbs, the story is that mazda bulbs originally lasted upward of a thousand hours, but manufacturers invested heavily to develop a shorter-lived bulb for which replacement demand would be more brisk, and on which higher returns would be gained. The result is the 500-hour bulb that we buy today.

These stories confirm our deep-seated prejudices about how businesses operate, and that makes them credible. However, a little economic analysis casts doubt on their truth. For we see that if the stories were true, the guilty manufacturers who suppress the superior product would be acting in a way that leads to lower returns. Because their motive in suppressing the invention is higher returns, the story is internally self-contradictory.

To see why suppression of lower-cost, superior appliances leads to lower returns, first consider a case in which the appliance is marketed under conditions of competition. If a manufacturer is approached with a superior invention, he can gain greatly relative to his competitors if he markets the invention. If he buys the invention and fails to market it, he is out the purchase price of the patent rights; and in addition he runs the risk that a competitor will obtain a similar appliance (sufficiently different to be patentable in its own right), and the competitor will obtain the more favorable market position that can be earned with a significantly improved good.

Suppose, though, that the market is monopolized: the purchaser of the patent has no competitors. Will he then suppress the invention if it is longer-lived than the existing product? Consider the battery example.

A monopolistic producer of storage batteries is not selling heavy ugly black boxes; he is selling the services that a battery gives—principally, starts of an auto engine. The demand for starts is illustrated in Figure 11.12. The marginal cost of the conventional battery is labeled *MC,* and of the invention, *mc.* That is, because a given number of starts

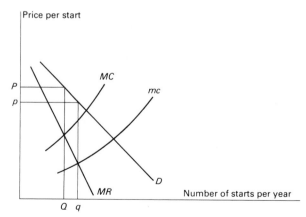

FIGURE 11.12.   Equilibrium in the storage battery market with a superior battery *(mc)* and a conventional battery *(MC).*

can be provided with a much smaller number of the more durable batteries, the marginal cost of providing the desired service is much lower when the invention is marketed.

Lower marginal cost is not sufficient to assure higher returns, because the lower marginal cost alternative may have heavy fixed costs associated with it. These fixed costs might be caused by new equipment needed to make the more durable new battery. Thus, lower marginal cost of providing the desired service does not automatically mean that the monopolist will benefit from immediate conversion. However, as existing equipment wears out, it will pay the monopolist to install equipment to produce the new product, instead of replacing existing equipment to produce the less durable batteries.

Thus, we would expect a returns-conscious monopolist to market the new battery, albeit, perhaps, only after considerable delay. The delay since rumors of these batteries began to spread is now more than considerable—I first heard of their existence at the time when my parents bought our first new postwar car, in 1946.

The case of light bulbs involves similar analysis. People purchase foot-candles of illumination, not glass bubbles (how many people do you know who keep light bulbs after they are burned out?) Hence a light bulb monopolist would seek the highest return in a market where the demand for light, and the marginal costs of providing light by alternative methods, are the important data schedules. He, too, will sell the longer-lived bulbs if they lead to higher returns than can be realized from the shorter-lived bulbs.

It may be that shorter-lived bulbs were developed in the 1920s, as the story says. But an economist would guess that these shorter-lived bulbs are sufficiently cheaper to produce so that the monopolist is not losing returns by making them. It follows from a diagram identical to Figure 11.12 that customers are not injured by a monopolist's choice of the cheaper process: if MC is the cost of illumination from the longer-lived expensive bulb and mc is that cost from the shorter-lived cheaper bulb, then the customers get more light at a lower price by replacing their bulbs more often.

APPLICATIONS AND EXTENSIONS

1. Does monopoly power provide a guarantee of profitability? Analyze either diagrammatically or with the help of the calculus.

2. *Limit pricing* is an alleged method of market protection by monopolists. The monopolist keeps his price low enough so that competition from entering firms is not attracted into the monopolist's market. Under what circumstances will a limit price coincide with the competitive price? Again, devise a formal analytical answer.

3. "If a monopolist's demand curve were infinitely elastic (horizontal), the monopolized industry would perform just like a competitive industry because price and marginal revenue would be equal at all rates of output." Why is this statement seriously incomplete?

4. List four examples of price discrimination that you personally have encountered. Do you think that you as a consumer are made better off or worse off by such pricing behavior?

5. Name a different firm that you think has monopoly power for each of the following reasons: (a) government protection, (b) economies of large operating size, (c) patents, (d) trademarks.

BIBLIOGRAPHICAL NOTE

Many of the numerous works on the subject of market power and pricing behavior are both accessible and worthwhile. A compendious theoretical treatment is F. Machlup, *The Political Economy of Monopoly* (Baltimore: Johns Hopkins University Press, 1952). W. Fellner, *Competition Among the Few* (New York: Alfred A. Knopf, 1949), gives detailed treatment to the oligopoly theories ignored here. M. Shubik, *Strategy and Market Structure* (New York: Wiley, 1959) uses the theory of games to analyze problems involving small numbers of sellers. G. Stigler, *The Theory of Price,* 3rd ed. (New York: Macmillan, 1966) contains a fine treatment of monopoly; and his paper "Perfect Competition, Historically Contemplated" in his *Essays in the History of Economics* (Chicago: University of Chicago Press, 1965) is an absorbing view of how the idea of competition has evolved.

The current state of Marxist theorizing on market behavior is well-represented in P. Baran and P. Sweezy, *Monopoly Capital* (New York: Monthly Review Press, 1966).

CHAPTER TWELVE

Industry Concentration, the Extent of Monopoly, and Anti-Monopoly Policy

What's good for the country is good for General Motors, and what is good for General Motors is good for the country.

CHARLES E. WILSON (1952)

12.1. MEASURING THE EXTENT OF MONOPOLY

12.1.1. Price-Cost Margins and the Monopoly Problem

A matter of concern is: to what extent does actual economic performance resemble the competitive model? Our analysis of competition showed that prices act as signals which direct resources into the production of goods that individuals want. We see that those signals may work poorly unless the competitive model has some correspondence to actual economic conditions. This chapter examines statistical evidence on the structure of the American economy, and discusses a ''radical'' proposal which would improve economic performance by restructuring the federal laws governing the taxation of the income earned by corporations.

In Chapter 11, the theoretical effects of monopoly power were examined. In this chapter, we turn to the questions of how monopoly power is to be measured, and what responses can be conceived for dealing with it if and when it is found.

Laws governing financial disclosure by corporations have served to make available a certain amount of useful data on corporation activity. In economic theory, the important effects of monopoly power are manifested in two discrepancies: more importantly, between price and marginal cost, a discrepancy which means that resources are being improperly utilized; and less importantly, between price and average cost, a discrepancy which means that returns above normal exist. As was mentioned in Chapter 8, Appendix II, financial report data give only an extremely imperfect means of estimating those discrepancies, for several reasons. First, accountants are concerned with measurement of actual cash outlays when they measure costs, while the relevant cost concept in economic analysis is opportunity cost. If a resource user has significant monopsony buying power, cash outlays on resources will not accurately reflect the opportunity value of alternative uses of resources; and to the extent that a resource user purchases from a monopolistic seller, prices will not correspond to the values of foregone opportunities. Second, it is difficult to estimate the value of the services of capital used in production. Accountants and economists both are concerned with estimating the value that the services of a machine or some other capital good adds to the firm's marketable output. Economists, as always, are concerned about the value of alternative output foregone in a particular pattern of machine use, whereas accountants are concerned with the problem of "depreciating" the value of productive assets to reflect the fact that the assets are slowly "used up" in the process of production. Depreciation as an accountant measures it only remotely resembles what the economist has in mind; and the problem of finding a correspondence between the two concepts of capital's contribution to the production process is further confused by tax laws which limit the options open to the accountant. Third, the accountant measures events over a period of one year; the economist is concerned about the behavior of prices and costs in an equilibrium situation, and events during a year may reflect numerous and significant departures from equilibrium. For all of these reasons, financial report data are not directly useful in deciding whether individual firms show monopolistic or competitive price-cost relationships.

Because it is so difficult to determine whether a firm or industry is monopolistic or competitive by examining published cost and profit data, an indirect approach to the problem has been taken: economists measure something known as *industrial concentration* for purposes of keeping track of changes in the importance of monopoly power over time, instead of looking at accounting reports of price-cost relations.

The procedure for measuring concentration involves five steps: First, industries must be defined. Second, firms must be assigned to industries on the basis of their activity. Third, an indicator of size must be selected. (Frequently used indicators are employment, sales, returns, value added, or value of assets.) Fourth, the sizes of the firms that participate in each industry must be measured. Fifth, the size of the four largest firms in each industry must be tabulated and compared to the total size of all firms operating in the industry.

The result of all that calculation is what is called the *four-firm concentration ratio*. At each step, important guesses and judgmental decisions are made, which potentially affect the measured outcome.

12.1.2. Industry Classification

The U.S. Census Bureau has devised a classification system for the purpose of organizing statistical information on manufacturing industry. The classification system involves several graduated levels of descriptive refinement. Suppose, for example, we are concerned with classifying the companies that sell canned asparagus. These companies, at successively more refined levels of description, are located by industry and product according to the following scheme:

Classification Code	"Digit Level"	Category and Specific Name
20	2	*Major industry group:* Food and Kindred Products
203	3	*Industry group:* Canning and Preserving
2033	4	*Industry:* Canned Fruits and Vegetables
20332	5	*Product class:* Canned Seasonal Vegetables
2033211	7	*Product:* Canned Asparagus

The activity of individual firms must be allocated among the different products, product classes, and so on. Rarely, the entire activity of a single firm will be in a single product. Frequently, a firm is involved in several industry groups, and it is not uncommon for firms to be involved in several of the twenty major industry groups. As a result, the value of the firm's output, its number of employees, the value of its assets, or whatever indicator of size is used, must be apportioned among the various 2-, 3-, 4-, 5-, and 7-digit categories in which the firm participates.

Once the allocation of firms' activity among industries has been completed, a digit level is selected for examination. (Usually, the four-digit "industry" level is examined.) Firms are ranked by the size of their outputs within the industry, or their employment devoted to producing the industry's product; and then the *concentration ratio* (the four largest firms compared to the whole industry) can be calculated.

A concentration ratio close to 100 implies that nearly all the activity in a particular industry is accounted for by the four largest firms. (The four largest firms are chosen because the Census Bureau and the Internal Revenue Service protect sensitive privileged information by reporting on data by four-firm groups, and not by individual firms.) Important industries with extremely high ratios (in 1958) were Motor Vehicles (four-firm asset concentration ratio 75), Tires and Inner Tubes (74), Blast Furnaces and Steel Mills (53), Aluminum Rolling and Drawing (78), Tin Cans (80), Steam Turbines (87), Cigarettes (79), and Aircraft (59).

Concentration ratios, as reported in the preceding paragraph, convey very little information. Too many considerations are overlooked by the measure for it to be taken as a reliable or conclusive guide to the presence of monopoly. For example, an industry with four important firms and a concentration ratio of 80 may be more "competitive" (in terms of proximity of price to marginal cost, and in terms of absence of returns above normal) than is an industry with only one dominantly large firm and a concentration ratio of 50. Moreover, concentration ratios overlook the importance of competition from foreign-produced goods in some industries—imports do not enter into the classification. There is the further issue of whether the industrial classification itself is well-structured— how well are the categories at the various digit levels chosen to reflect the potential extent of competition?

12.1.3. Manufacturing versus Other Activities

Concern over the possibility of monopolization has focused almost entirely on the manufacturing sector of the economy. Other important sectors, notably agriculture; wholesale trade; retail trade; the service industries such as undertaking, beautifying, medical care, and advertising; and the construction trades display virtually no measurable four-firm or eight-firm concentration, even when concentration is measured within some reasonably defined local market area.

This important point should be kept in mind while reading the following, and similar investigations of the problem of monopoly. Monopoly is almost wholly a problem of manufacturing industry, except in such isolated and relatively trivial instances as the one-undertaker town, or in such governmentally sanctioned (and regulated) industries as the railroads and public utilities, or in cases in which occupational licensing is used to control entry (most notoriously, in the case of medical care). And manufacturing industry is far from the whole story in the economy, as Table 12.1 shows.

TABLE 12.1.

Year	Manufacturing Employment	As a Percent of Total Labor Force	Value Added in Manufacture	As a Percent of GNP
1963	16.958 million	22.4%	$192.083 billion	36.9%
1971	18.363 million	21.1%	$314.138 billion	29.9%

Source: U.S. Census Bureau, *Statistical Abstract of the United States* (Washington, D.C.: Government Printing Office, 1973).

In most discussions of the extent of monopoly, then, focus is almost exclusively on a sector of the economy in which a third or less of the nation's output is generated and about a fifth of the labor force is employed. These are by no means trivial categories, but they are far from the whole show.

12.2. CONCENTRATION THROUGH TIME

12.2.1. Industry Concentration

The chief value of the various available indexes of concentration comes from the opportunity to make comparisons over time. If a sharp change over time is observed in an individual industry, it may be worthwhile to find out why the change has occurred. However, the most important issue is the weighted performance of all the industry groups: is there a sharp tendency for *most* industry groups to become more heavily concentrated? If in fact such a tendency does exist, there may be genuine cause for alarm—a tendency for a concentration index to increase over time strongly suggests the possibility of a tendency toward monopoly in its industry. It is interesting to observe concentration indexes through time, among other reasons because Marxists have been telling us for nearly a century that an inexorable tendency toward monopoly exists in capitalist society. We turn to a quick summary of the evidence on this question.

Rough data are available which have enabled the calculation of concentration in numerous industries for the years 1901 and 1947 (Table 12.2). In both years, four-digit *industries* are examined within the context of their two-digit *major industry groups*. In each major industry group, some industries will show concentration ratios of more than 50, while other industries will have concentration ratios of less than 50. "Value added" in industries with four-firm asset concentration ratios of over 50 is compared to the total "value added" in the major industry group. (Value added is the firm's sales, less purchases from other firms.) The ratio

$$\frac{\text{value added by industries with concentration} > 50}{\text{total value added in major industry group}}$$

is an index that has been compiled for the twenty major industry groups in the two years, 1901 and 1947. The indexes are displayed in Table 12.2. There is an obvious general *decline* in concentration reflected in this measure between 1901 and 1947.

Beginning in the 1930s, our data base is much better, owing to a sharpening of financial disclosure laws that corporations must adhere to. For the years 1947 to 1958, a more refined compilation is possible. Instead of weighting each *major industry group* by the industries with concentration ratios of greater than 50, each *industry concentration ratio* is weighted by its individual share of value added within the major industry group. Thus, the index displayed in Table 12.3 is

$$\frac{(\text{value added, industry}) \cdot (\text{concentration ratio, industry})}{\text{value added, major industry group}}$$

TABLE 12.2.   Concentration Indexes, 1901 and 1947

Code	Major Industry Group	Concentration 1901	Concentration 1947
20	Food and Kindred Prod.	39.1	18.8
21	Tobacco Manufacturers	49.9	77.7
22	Textile Mill Products	20.3	9.0
23	Apparel and Related Prod.	—	2.2
24	Lumber and Wood Prod.	0.5	2.0
25	Furniture and Fixtures	—	8.1
26	Pulp, Paper, Paper Products	71.0	1.6
27	Printing and Publishing	1.0	0.0
28	Chemicals and Related Prod.	24.3	33.7
29	Petroleum and Coal Prod.	46.8	13.6
30	Rubber Prod.	100.0	59.9
31	Leather and Leather Prod.	26.3	0.0
32	Stone, Clay and Glass Prod.	13.3	43.9
33	Primary Metal Prod.	45.7	21.0
34	Fabricated Metal Prod.	—	8.4
35	Machinery except Electrical	41.4	18.5
36	Electrical Machinery	—	53.2
37	Transportation Equipt.	57.3	84.2
38	Instruments and Related Prod.	—	45.0
39	Miscellaneous Manufactures	2.7	21.2
	Total, all Industries	32.9	24.0

Source: M. A. Adelman, "Monopoly and Concentration: Comparisons in Time and Space," in U.S. Senate, Committee on the Judiciary, Subcommittee on Antitrust and Monopoly, Hearings, *Economic Concentration* (Washington, D.C.: Government Printing Office, 1964).

Interpretation: In 1901 26.3 percent of the value added in the Leather and Leather Products major industry group was added in those industries of the group which had four-firm concentration ratios of more than .5.

summed over all industries in the major industry group. Note the rather large discrepancy between 1947 concentration reported in this more refined manner and 1947 concentration reported in the cruder way (Table 12.2). From these indicators, and from other sources, we are drawn to the conclusion: concentration ratios tended to *decline* between 1901 and 1947. Since 1958, concentration has increased slightly; the summary concentration figure of 37.0 in 1958 (Table 12.3) had by 1966 risen slightly to 39.0.[1] No post-1966 information is readily available; but the pace of change has almost surely remained slow and its direction unpredictable. Certainly, over long periods of time, no evidence of widespread ''trends toward monopoly'' can be detected from the concentration data. (By monopoly, in this context, we do not mean literally ''single seller''; rather, we mean to designate patterns of behavior among the firms in an industry which result in important departures from the competitive ideal of price-taking behav-

[1]Reported by F. M. Scherer, *Industrial Market Structure and Economic Performance* (Chicago: Rand McNally, 1971), p. 63.

TABLE 12.3. Concentration Indexes, 1947, 1954, 1958

Code	1947	1954	1958
20	34.9	33.8	32.6
21	76.2	73.4	74.1
22	24.3	26.5	29.2
23	12.6	13.0	13.4
24	11.2	10.8	12.8
25	21.9	20.3	19.0
26	21.2	24.8	25.9
27	19.7	17.7	17.6
28	51.0	48.6	45.7
29	39.5	36.6	31.6
30	58.6	54.1	51.3
31	26.2	26.4	25.0
32	43.4	46.4	40.3
33	43.8	49.5	46.8
34	25.3	26.1	25.5
35	38.0	33.2	35.5
36	54.1	48.2	46.9
37	54.4	58.7	61.3
38	45.3	47.4	47.8
39	34.9	16.1	22.6
Total, all industries	35.3	36.9	37.0

Source: M. A. Adelman, "Monopoly and Concentration: Comparisons in Time and Space," in U.S. Senate, Committee on the Judiciary, Subcommittee on Antitrust and Monopoly, Hearings, *Economic Concentration* (Washington, D.C.: Government Printing Office, 1964).

TABLE 12.4. Supplement to Information Contained in Table 12.3.
Percent of Manufacturing Employment
Classified by Four-Firm Asset Concentration Ratios

% Concentration	1947		1954		1958	
80–100	3.0		3.9		2.7	
70–79	4.3	(7.3)	7.4	(11.3)	7.1	(9.8)
60–69	4.2	(11.5)	4.9	(16.2)	3.2	(13.0)
50–59	14.5	(26.0)	10.3	(26.5)	11.9	(24.9)
40–49	8.4	(34.4)	6.0	(32.5)	6.9	(31.8)
30–39	11.5	(45.9)	13.5	(46.0)	11.7	(43.5)
20–29	22.7	(68.6)	21.1	(67.1)	24.5	(68.0)
10–19	21.0	(89.6)	23.5	(90.6)	22.3	(90.3)
0–9	10.4	(100.0)	9.4	(100.0)	9.7	(100.0)

Shares of largest 8 and largest 20 firms are even more stable over time.

Source: William G. Shepherd, "Trends of Concentration in American Manufacturing Industries, 1947–58," *Review of Economics and Statistics,* XLVI, (1964).

Interpretation: Four-digit industries with asset concentration ratios between 50 and 59 accounted for 14.5 percent of employment in 1947, 10.3 percent in 1954, 11.9 percent in 1958. Figures in parentheses are cumulative totals.

ior. Such behavior patterns as price leadership, dominant firm pricing, or collusive pricing may result in large and prolonged discrepancies between price and marginal cost, or price and average cost.) Some industries have undoubtedly become more concentrated since 1900; others have, for one reason or another, grown less concentrated.

Experience in Britain and Canada is similar—no visible trend toward greater concentration on an industry-by-industry basis, and hence, no objective basis for concern over "monopolization" of industry.

12.2.2. Economy-Wide Concentration

Historically, the first major study that publicized the concentration issue compared the sizes of large firms to the whole economy,[2] rather than just to the industries in which they operate. What share of total assets in manufacturing is owned by the 200 largest firms? What fraction of the labor force is employed by the 100 largest corporations? What changes in these indicators can be perceived over time? Questions of this type pertain to the issue of *conglomerate* business concentration.

During the past two decades the rate of growth of large corporations has been greater than the rate of growth of the whole economy. This growth has occurred unaccompanied by any systematic increase in industry-by-industry concentration. There are two ways that large firms can grow even larger without causing an increase in industry concentration. First, certain whole industries, composed mainly of large firms, can be growing in importance; the automobile, petroleum refining, and airframe industries in the U.S. typify this possibility. The large firms in these industries can be growing more rapidly than the economy, without growing more rapidly than rival firms in the same industry; consequently, concentration within the industry does not change rapidly. Second, large firms can be growing by a process of entering different industries or industry groups. A firm can enter a new industry by founding an entirely new subsidiary to compete among existing firms; or (more commonly) it can acquire or merge with another firm already established in the industry. During the years 1967 to 1969, an unprecedented number of mergers took place among large firms operating in different industry groups. These are called "conglomerate" mergers.

This process of diversifying and growing through conglomerate merger is hard to evaluate. In terms of the conventional theory of industry structure, we would predict that if General Electric or IBM chose to enter the auto industry by building new factories and producing new makes of car, it would probably be a good thing—competition would almost certainly not suffer. On the other hand, if General Electric or IBM were to enter by merging with Chrysler, the results would be less easy to foresee.

A great deal has been said and written on both sides of the question of

[2] Adolph Berle and Gardiner Means, *The Modern Corporation and Private Property* (New York: Macmillan, 1932).

whether an increase in economy-wide concentration is bad. From that debate, we will attempt to winnow out a few facts and supportable arguments in answer to these questions: (1) How has economy-wide concentration changed over time in recent years? (2) How important have mergers been in producing the observed changes in economy-wide concentration? (3) What underlies the growth in mergers, particularly in conglomerate mergers? (4) What are the effects of conglomerate concentration? (5) What responses should be made by those who control government policy regarding the structure of industry?

The U.S. Senate Committee on the Judiciary, Subcommittee on Antitrust and Monopoly, in a series of hearings that began in 1964, has compiled a large volume of evidence and testimony on these questions. Our discussion is based in large part on information from the Subcommittee's hearings.

12.2.3. The Behavior of Economy-Wide Concentration

Table 12.5 presents the *share* of total manufacturing assets held by the 100 and the 200 largest firms, in selected years since 1925. This index is tabulated by

TABLE 12.5.

Year	SHARE HELD BY 100 LARGEST		SHARE HELD BY 200 LARGEST	
	Total Assets	Corporation Assets	Total Assets	Corporation Assets
1925	34.5	36.1	not available	
1929	38.2	45.8	45.8	47.7
1933	42.5	44.2	49.5	51.4
1937	42.1	43.7	49.1	50.9
1941	38.2	39.6	45.1	46.7
1948	38.6	40.3	46.3	48.3
1952	39.3	40.6	47.7	49.2
1956	43.9	45.0	52.8	54.1
1960	45.5	46.4	55.2	56.3
1964	45.8	46.5	55.8	56.6
1968	48.8	49.3	60.4	60.9

looking at the value of asset holdings in the accounting reports of large firms, and comparing those numbers to estimates of the total value of manufacturing assets in the economy. Most of the change since 1925 has occurred since the Korean War armistice (1952). Two important considerations should be weighed in examining the data of Table 12.5. First, are the evident increases in concentration dependent on the use of assets as a size measure? There is no point in getting excited over such figures if other indicators (profits, employment, value added, etc.) give contradictory evidence. In Table 12.6 we see that two other indicators, profits and value added, confirm the indication that our largest firms *are* growing in importance relative to the whole economy. The second question is: to what

TABLE 12.6.

Year	Share of Corporate Assets	200 LARGEST Share of Corporate Profits	Share of Value Added by Manufacturers
1947	47.2	41.7	30
1954	52.1	63.3	37
1958	56.6	64.1	38
1963	56.3	65.1	41
1966	56.7	58.6	42
1968	60.9	62.9	not available

extent is there a significant *turnover* in the membership of largest firms? If it is easy for a firm to insulate itself from the effects of competition by virtue of large size, we would expect to find that as economy-wide concentration increases, the membership of the large-firm population should stabilize. This question of turnover in the membership of the largest firms is less easy to answer in a summary fashion, in part because the question is not addressed directly in the hearings of the Senate Subcommittee. Table 12.7 is an index of turnover, decade by decade

TABLE 12.7.

Year	Turnover*	Largest 4 / Largest 100
1909	-	32.2
1919	40	23.9
1929	31	21.0
1935	16	23.5
1948	20	21.4
1958	16	22.7
1967	23	not available

Sources: 1909–58: Norman Collins and Lee Preston, "The Size Structure of the Largest Industrial Firms: 1909–58," *American Economic Review* (1961). 1967: *Fortune* Magazine.

*Measured by number of firms from the last year listed that no longer are listed among 100 largest. 1968 turnover is on *sales,* not assets, ranking of top 100.

since 1900, among the *100* largest firms. The evidence of Table 12.7 raises a few questions. In the decades between successive measurements, what caused the firms that were removed from the "100 largest" category to vanish? Did they "die" with a declining industry? Were they surpassed because of a merger between two firms that in the preceding tally had both been smaller? Were they merged out of existence themselves, to become part of a supergiant? Or were they merely outgrown by firms that performed more vigorously and better? Depending on how these questions are answered, we may be encouraged or discouraged by the record underlying the changes in the population of the 100 largest firms; unfortunately, answers to these questions seem to be unavailable without some major research effort into the chronicles of American industrial history. We can report that between 1958 and 1967, six firms that grew mainly by merger[3] were newly listed among the top 100; none of these were among the top 500 in 1958. A number of other firms showed sufficiently remarkable jumps in sales to enter the 100 largest list between 1958 and 1967 owing to conglomerate merger activity.[4] Indeed, the largest number of the new entrants into the ''100 largest'' list of 1967 got there by merger, often with firms primarily engaged in entirely different major industry groups.

12.2.4. The Role of Mergers

The last column, which shows the asset holdings of the four largest firms relative to the asset holdings of the 100 largest firms, suggests that until the 1960s, firms did not depart from the 100 largest by being merged into other firms within the 100 largest. If such mergers between giants were common, we would expect the asset share of the very largest firms to grow over time. We can feel mildly encouraged that the ratio has not shown a historical tendency to increase.

Nonetheless, there is evidence presented in Table 12.8 that in recent years merger activity among the 100 largest firms has been on the increase. The increase in merger activity of 1967–68 shows up clearly in these figures: there were 19 acquisitions of other large firms by the 100 largest in 1966, 36 in 1967, and 45 in 1968. It does appear that the 100 largest firms were systematically looking for partners for merger, to a degree in 1966–68 that did not hold in 1948–50 or 1957–59. In 1948–50 the average large firm acquired by anyone in a merger had assets of $23 million; the average large firm acquired through merger with a member of the largest 100 firms had assets of $13 million. In 1957–59, the average large firm acquired had assets of $29 million; the average large firm acquired by a member of the top 100 had assets of $21 million. In 1966–68, the average large firm acquired had assets of $56 million; the average large firm acquired by a member of the top 100 had assets of $121 million.

To summarize this evidence: the first conclusion, that economy-wide concentration has increased markedly during the past couple of decades, is firmly based; the second conclusion, that mergers have been an important factor in the increases that are perceived, is tentative.

We next ask: what are the effects of concentration? First, the issue of industry concentration is examined. Then we return to the effects of economy-wide concentration.

[3]General Telephone and Electronics, Ling-Temco-Vought, Tenneco, Litton Industries, Getty Oil, and Genesco.

[4]Including Avco, TRW, Honeywell, U.S. Plywood-Champion Paper, Atlantic-Richfield, FMC, Signal Oil, and Textron.

TABLE 12.8.   Acquisitions of Large Manufacturing and Mining Firms by Companies Ranked Among the 100 Largest and the 200 Largest Manufacturers of 1968 During the Period 1948–1968

	TOTAL		ACQUIRED BY 100 LARGEST MANUFACTURERS	
	No.	Assets ($millions)	No.	Assets ($millions)
1948	6	$ 101	4	$ 65
1949	5	67	4	45
1950	4	173	1	20
1954	35	1,426	7	490
1957	51	1,442	13	548
1958	37	1,077	15	563
1959	64	1,959	19	872
1962	72	2,174	20	889
1966	99	4,167	19	1,911
1967	167	9,062	36	4,025
1968	201	12,800	45	6,168

Source: Bureau of Economics, Federal Trade Commission. Presented in *Economic Concentration, Part I: Overall and Conglomerate Aspects,* Hearings before the Senate Committee on the Judiciary, Subcommittee on Antitrust and Monopoly, 88 Congress, 2 Session (Washington, D.C.: Government Printing Office, 1969).

Note: Large acquired companies are those that had $10 million or more in total assets at the time they were acquired.

12.3. INDUSTRY CONCENTRATION AND PROFITABILITY

As a simple working hypothesis, the higher concentration is in an industry, the more likely the industry should be to approach a pattern of monopoly performance. If we accept that hypothesis, we expect to find that the higher concentration is in an industry, the more profitable on the average the firms in the industry are.

That simple idea has been tested and retested. As we will see, the process of testing such an idea is far from straightforward; and each of the successive commentators on the question has had something to add to the discussion, in terms of new issues confronted or new problems solved. However, the question of concentration and profitability is still an open one to most observers. The kinds of results that have emerged from the numerous investigations will now be described.

The study that we will review[5] uses income data from the period 1936–40 for 42 industries defined at the four-digit level. The 42 industries represent a careful winnowing of the 340 four-digit Census of Manufactures industries. Most

[5]J. S. Bain, "Relation of Profit Rate to Industry Concentration: American Manufacturing, 1936–1940," *Quarterly Journal of Economics,* 65 (August 1951).

of the 340 were eliminated because profit data were not available; others were eliminated because they serve local rather than national markets owing to transportation costs; still others were not included because of evidence of misclassification. The remaining 42 were then subjected to a comparison of eight-firm concentration ratios and rate of profit. The following three conclusions can be drawn from a statistical analysis of profitability and concentration in the 42 industries.

1. The "best-fitting" simple linear relation of the form

    $$\text{profit rate} = P + p \cdot (\text{concentration})$$

    can be calculated. The coefficient of concentration in explaining the profit rate in the data, p, is .0563. Thus, according to the estimated relation, if industry concentration rises by one percentage point, then the average rate of profit of firms in the industry will rise by a little over one-twentieth of a percentage point.
2. The linear relation so calculated is a rather poor fit to the data: the points that are being fitted lie broadly scattered around the line. In fact, only about *10 percent* of the variation in the profit rate data can be explained by variation in concentration.
3. Finally, while a linear relationship fitted to the data does display a rather weak tie between concentration and profitability, it is also true that the same data could have been obtained with high probability by sampling a population in which it is known that there is *no* relation between profitability and concentration. Thus, the observed weak tie might be due entirely to the particular sample that was used.

When the data are displayed differently, however, an association between profitability and concentration is seen to emerge. Industries with eight-firm concentration ratios of more than .7 show an average profit rate of 12.1 percent; firms below the .7 concentration figure returned an average of 6.9 percent in profit. Thus the tentative conclusion: there is tendency toward the appearance of monopoly performance in industries with an eight-firm concentration ratio of more than .7.

Broadly similar results have emerged from numerous other broadly similar studies. In every case, procedural and interpretive choices must be made that cast doubt on the validity of the results. The more important of these involve the following problems: (1) Do the industry definitions at the three- or four-digit levels represent sufficiently homogeneous categories, or do the firms that are classified to fall within those industries produce widely divergent and non-overlapping arrays of goods? (2) In small firms, those with assets of less than a million dollars, say, it is frequently the case that the large-share owners of the firm are also employed as the managers. These people can reduce the taxes on their incomes by taking income in the form of salary instead of in the form of profit. (If they take it as salary, they pay the ordinary personal income tax. If they take it as profit, the firm first pays corporation income tax on it and the owner-managers then pay personal income tax on the dividends.) In firms that are closely controlled by owner-managers, then, we expect to find inflated salary payments, and diminished profits. This effect must be taken into account in measuring profitability; if it is not, industries with low concentration (which typically include a larger proportion of such small firms) will show measured profit rates that are below the true profit rates. (3) The valuation of assets, the basis on which profitability rates are calculated, poses treacherous problems (as can be seen in Chapter 8, Appendix II).

There are other lesser difficulties which confront the use of financial report data in empirical research, but the major problems, which have never been handled to everyone's satisfaction, are the ones listed.

12.4. MERGERS AND "CONGLOMERATE" CORPORATIONS

12.4.1. Why Did the Rate of Merger Activity Rise?

The critics of economic theory think it absurd to assume that business firms maximize profits. Yet the wave of mergers in the late 1960s lends indirect support to that traditional assumption. Numerous strong incentives to merge were presented, all leading to higher profits, and in fact firms seemed to respond to those incentives.

A profit-maximizing hypothesis cannot be tested by observing the behavior of firms unless a time horizon is specified. That is, we cannot simply assert that "as a rule of behavior, firms maximize profits" unless we further stipulate the time period they take into account in making the decisions that lead to outcomes of greater or lesser profitability. At one extreme, the profit-maximization hypothesis does not imply that firms are willing to destroy themselves at the end of the current year in order to enjoy a super rate of return during the current year. At the other extreme, the hypothesis does not mean that the firm will give all its product away this year in order to build good will toward some "long-run" profitability. What the hypothesis does assert is that the highest attainable present value of the firm's net earnings stream is the meaningful target or goal. Most of the sophisticated recent analyses of the behavior of firms hold that management decisions are guided by a desire to maximize the *market value* of firms—the value that stockholders and potential stockholders determine by their daily decisions to buy and sell shares of ownership in the firm. Market value is seen to be closely related to the assessment that owners make of the firm's future earnings stream. The higher the estimated present value of that stream, the more owners and prospective owners are willing to pay for ownership shares in the firm.

If in fact corporate managers do observe the impact of their decisions on the market value of the firm's stock, then various laws governing the reporting and taxation of assets and income will provide a series of incentives to merge: merger increases the market value of the firm's stock, because of those laws. By merging, then, managers are responding in a predictable way to economic incentives, and as long as such incentives exist, we should expect mergers to continue.

The major incentives to merger are furnished by ambiguities in the laws governing the reporting of earnings in corporations, which permit gains to be realized from merging by *both* parties involved in the merger. With no considerations of tax advantage, the gain of the buyer (or seller) would be approximately equal to the loss of the seller (or buyer). The only basis on which a net gain could be realized is when the buyer has greater skill in managing the acquired firm's assets than the seller had.

Accounting practices (governing the valuation of inventories, depreciation, the charging of research costs, the treatment of pension funds, the use of stock options instead of bonuses for management, and the treatment of capital gains within the firm) affect the net profit that the firm reports. A firm that has taken a consistently "conservative" approach on these issues may find that its reported earnings are less than half what they could have been had a more flamboyant set of reporting rules been employed. By the same token, a firm that has operated conservatively on an independent basis may find itself a prime candidate for takeover by another firm that seeks a quick route to high reported earnings. Mergers between firms in unrelated industries "have an enormous potential for seeming to improve the performance of the firms. . . . If [a company] were acquired, its earnings could be doubled in a single year through accounting changes. What might seem to be an . . . [amazingly advantageous combination] is, from an economic standpoint, only a mirage created by accounting."[6]

12.4.2. Tax Laws and the Profitability of Merger

The "something for nothing" effect that comes with the ability to manipulate the reporting of income is further enhanced by a similar ability to manipulate the tax laws after a merger. First, if the acquiring firm issues bonds to finance the acquisition, interest payments on those bonds can be treated as an ordinary business expense, and charged off against taxable income. Hence, a firm that is taken over need only convey returns greater than the *after-tax* cost to the acquiring firm. For example, suppose a firm issues a $100 bond at a 7½ percent interest charge, to exchange for one share of stock in a firm that reports $5 per share in earnings after taxes. The $7.50 interest cost is a business expense, and with taxable income reduced by $7.50, the tax saving will be about $3.75. That amount, plus the $5 earnings of the acquired firm, total to $8.75, or considerably more than the $7.50 in interest expenses associated with the bond issue.

Second, former owners of the acquired firm sometimes can defer taxation of the proceeds from the sale for several years, resulting in considerable saving to them. For example, suppose that one share of American Airlines stock (market value $10) is exchanged for every share of Nevada Nightflight Freightways (market value, before merger discussion, $5). Then NNF owners come in for a $5 per-share capital gain, which is not taxed until they sell their holdings in

---

[6]This quote appeared on p. 129, part 8a of the Congressional hearings cited in Table 12.5.

American Airlines. Meantime, the NNF owners can borrow against their new higher-valued holdings, and they may realize a higher dividend from AA than NNF paid. "Of the 706 large mergers that occurred between 1963 and 1968, information is available for 411—about 85 percent of these received tax-free treatment."[7]

Third, there are "tax loss carryovers" that make the big losers of previous years desirable targets for merger. Douglas Aircraft and Studebaker-Packard are but two examples of firms that, paradoxically, were valued for past records of dismal performance. A prosperous acquiring firm can deduct past losses of newly acquired subsidiaries from current taxable income, thus greatly lowering the burden of taxes.

These are but the most important incentives that the tax laws give to merger.

12.4.3. Alleged Abuses by Conglomerates

What potential difficulties, if any, can be seen to arise out of conglomerate mergers? Some analysts see no bad economic effects; but others point to two particular abuses: *reciprocity* and *cross-subsidization*.

Reciprocity.   This term describes the behavior of buying from one's customers. Mergers that cross industry lines may very well increase the scope of and opportunity for such dealing. One such example involves General Dynamics, The Prophet Company, Liquid Carbonic (an acquisition of General Dynamics), and the Borden Company. Prophet was the caterer in the G-D lunch facilities. Prophet was asked to, and did, put pressure on Borden to purchase carbon dioxide from Liquid Carbonic. The buying relationships between G-D and Prophet, and Prophet and Borden, were exploited to induce (or coerce) Borden into buying from Liquid Carbonic.

While such "you scratch my back, and I'll scratch yours" dealings are out of keeping with the usual picture of impersonal market forces in operation, we may well wonder whether there is any abuse of the public interest inherent in them. The reciprocal agreements must imply an advantage to both parties, for in a world of uncertain sales volumes, any agreement that enables a firm to forecast its future sales more accurately works in the direction of greater efficiency in resource use; and a firm like Borden may be willing to give up an occasional slight cost advantage in the purchase of carbon dioxide in order to assure itself of a stable sales outlet for some small part of its final output. Certainly, there is no reason why any firm should tolerate reciprocal arrangements that act against its own best interest.

Cross-Subsidization.   One of the most persistent unsubstantiated elements in the literature of economics is the notion that a diversified firm will routinely decide to carry out "predatory pricing" actions against its undiversified rivals.

[7]Ibid., p. 143.

To gain a monopoly position in refrigerators and dishwashers, General Motors could cut the price of Frigidare appliances below cost, subsidizing the deficits out of returns from automobile production. Or General Electric could subsidize computer sales below cost out of returns on its numerous other products (appliances, jet engines, lighting equipment). Such behavior has been often alleged as a means of gaining a monopoly position, but such allegations have never been satisfactorily documented. Several questions crop up time and again: (1) Instead of paying money to diversify so that it can then subsidize predatory pricing activities, why does a firm not subsidize those activities without first diversifying? (2) Why is predatory pricing a more likely way to influence a rival firm's behavior than the alternative of bribing the rival? (3) When a diversified firm carries out a "price war" in good A, why do rivals in the production of goods B, C, D . . . not take advantage of the temporarily weaker position in those other goods to attack the first firm's market position in those goods? (This last question asks: how can a firm systematically embark on a program of loss-taking without attracting hungry rivals?) (4) If a monopoly position is obtained by predatory pricing, why does the later attempt to exploit that monopoly position not attract competitors back into production?

A strategy of ruining a rival firm is not to be embarked on lightly. First, it is almost inevitably more costly than buying the rival out.[8] Second, unless the ruined rival's capital assets are acquired, the monopoly position that is attained by predatory pricing probably cannot be satisfactorily exploited—re-entry is too easy. Finally, the connection between predatory pricing and diversification is tenuous if it pays a firm to attempt to ruin or otherwise punish a rival, it surely pays whether or not the firm has other product lines. It would appear, in fact, that diversification and rival-ruining work at cross-purposes: capital tied up in a program of diversification is not available to fund the predatory activity.

Two potential abuses of conglomerate bigness—reciprocity and cross-subsidization—have been examined. One contention is that prices will be inadequately responsive to cost conditions; cronyism will replace opportunity foregone as a guide to pricing within the firm, according to those who fear reciprocity. At the other extreme, it is alleged that diversified firms may pursue flexible-price policies to the detriment of competition. Neither concern is wholly convincing. It is clear that reciprocity exists in dealings among firms, and it would seem that diversification greatly enlarges the scope of opportunity for reciprocal action. It is less clear that reciprocity is detrimental to efficient operation. It also is true that price warfare and other "predatory" behavior is sometimes manifested. It is less clear that this is done for the purpose of monopolizing; price wars are often associated with excessive supplies that need to be

---

[8]See Lester Telser, "Cutthroat Competition and The Long Purse," *Journal of Law and Economics,* 8 (October 1966).

unloaded. Nor is the association between diversification and predatory price behavior a meaningful one in theory; one wonders whether it is meaningful in practice, or whether undiversified firms aren't as often as not the aggressive cutters of price.

Conglomerate bigness does not lead to power in single markets, and hence, offers little cause for the type of concern that is usually engendered by monopoly. Commentators who have sought to foster concern have been able to come up with reciprocity and cross-subsidization, but little else. Surely conglomerate bigness deserves a low ranking on a thoughtful person's list of "pressing socioeconomic problems."

12.5. TAXES AND MERGERS

As an exercise in the application of rudimentary economic theory, we will discuss the effect of taxation on mergers, and see how a change in tax laws can effectively remove incentives for business firms to merge. The policies discussed here were proposed a long time ago by Henry Simons, an authority on taxation at the University of Chicago and a gifted analyst of the large problems of economic and social organization.[9]

The measures Simons proposed, and discussed here, include the following:

1. Eliminate the corporation income tax.
2. Tax dividends and capital-gains income of individuals at the same rate as ordinary wage or salary income.
3. Tax individual stockholders on their share of earnings retained within a firm.
4. Reform the laws governing business disclosure on the sources and uses of income.
5. Reform the range of acceptable practices that can be followed by firms in reporting income.

This is a "right radical" program: "right" (politically) because it is directed at the efficient satisfaction of individual preferences, with reliance on market mechanisms; "radical" because it involves a substantial departure from current practice. Steps 4 and 5 are directed at a better and more reliable flow of information about investment opportunities; if effected, these changes would eliminate some of the incentive for conglomerate merger (see Section 12.4.2). Steps 1 to 3 require some further discussion.

In the structure of the present law, the reason for taxing capital gains less heavily than ordinary personal income is to encourage long-term investment of private capital, and to recognize that ordinary taxes imposed on capital gains, plus corporate income taxes, would constitute a double tax liability on corporate

---

[9]Reported in H. Simons, *Economic Policy for a Free Society* (Chicago: University of Chicago Press, 1948).

earnings. Elimination of the corporate tax would remove the problem of double taxation, and would also serve to channel funds into investment. A corporation that returns 8 percent after paying half its income in taxes can return 16 percent without taxes; elimination of the corporate tax would increase the return on private investment in the corporate sector, and hence it would stimulate investment.

Moreover, the effect of the corporate income tax, accompanied by a lower rate of taxation on capital gains than is imposed on ordinary income, has strong distorting effects on resource allocation. The lower capital gains rate creates an incentive *against* the payment of dividends, which are a form of ordinary income. Instead, firms have an incentive to retain their earnings and reinvest them to make the owners' stock-holdings appreciate in value. If capital gains and dividends were taxed at the same rate, stock owners would prefer to obtain their returns more quickly, and hence would prefer dividends to capital gains; corporations in turn would respond with heavier dividend payments and less earnings retention in the firm. Reduction in earnings retention would operate against acquisition and merger. The third provision would enforce that response: owners would pay income tax on income that is held in the firm. Hence, only in instances where the firm can promise (and deliver) above-normal returns on new capital would the owners prefer to leave their earnings in the firm, instead of taking them out in dividends and then reinvesting or lending them back to the firm.

The fact is that laws and government taxation policies provide a large measure of the incentive that exists for the growth of firms by merger. With elimination of the corporate income tax, and removal of the incentive for retained earnings, conglomerate concentration would predictably diminish. With the proposed changes, the necessity for revisions of *anti-trust laws* to combat conglomerate merger waves like the one of 1967 to 1969 will be made unnecessary.

A program of the type discussed here has virtually no chance of adoption. It treads too heavily on entrenched financial interests to be politically feasible. Instead of reform, we must rely on legal mechanisms and government agencies that monitor and combat monopoly.

12.6. REGULATION AND ANTI-TRUST

12.6.1. Good Laws and Bad in Anti-Trust

One can predict numerous reasons why tax reform, along the lines outlined in the preceding section, will never have any substantial chance of being implemented. There is considerable antipathy to profits in our society, and few politicians, even if they grasp the advantages of reform, will have the audacity to openly advocate a course that is sure to be unpopular with most of the electorate. A second obstacle may lie in the fact that a part of the government bureaucracy may see such a program as inimical to its members' self-interest. There has been a persistent tendency of government to respond to the emergence of problems not by eliminating potential causes and simplifying its own structure, but rather by creating study commissions, funding new programs, and enlarging the bureaucracy. Any attempt to break the pattern of increased administrative complexity will predictably be viewed by the bureaucracy as threatening; and lobbyists for the interests of the bureaucracy, such as government employee unions, will doubtless offer resistance.

Again, in these remarks, we are predicting the dominant sway of self-interest. Politicians want to be re-elected, and so they play up to the anti-profit prejudices of the electorate in order to win favor. Bureaucrats want more power, responsibility, and income, so they view with alarm any threat to the growth of their sphere of responsibility. And both groups, of course, act in the unshakable conviction that their actions are in "the public interest."

It is further instructive regarding the pervasive power of self-interest to see how we have in fact responded to the monopoly problem in America.

Our earliest political response came in 1891, with the passage of the Sherman Anti-Trust Act. That law quite simply made it illegal to contract, combine, or conspire to restrain trade or commerce if the affected activity had significant interstate or international scope. It further provided that any person who did so conspire was guilty of a misdemeanor.

The Sherman Act is a model of simplicity and clarity, and it has been used from time to time with good effect. Major trusts were broken up in tobacco (1911), petroleum (1911), and steel (1920); and numerous lesser cases served further to constrain the scope of unacceptable behavior by business. There can be little doubt that the Sherman Act served to dampen the conspiratorial ardor of business rivals in America.

In 1914, the Clayton Act specifically prohibited mergers or acquisitions that might serve to create a monopoly or to lessen competition substantially. The anti-merger force of the Clayton Act was further strengthened by amendment in 1950.

There have, however, been movements away from the protection of competition in the legislative actions of the U.S. Congress. In 1918, the Webb-Pomerene Act made possible the formation of export trade associations; market-sharing and price-fixing, the goals of conspiratorial businesses, were legalized insofar as *export* trade is concerned. The Millard-Tydings amendment of the Sherman Act (1937) made it legal for manufacturers to set the minimum price at which retailers can sell their output. This provision, known as "fair trade," inhibits competition at the retail level, and makes it easier for collusive manufacturers to divide a market and maintain stable market shares. Finally, the Robinson-Patman amendment of the Clayton Act (1936) makes it illegal for any supplier to charge one customer a lower price than the supplier receives from another customer. Robinson-Patman is an attempt to curb the buying power of large chain retailers by making it illegal to supply them at a lower price than is charged to their single-store competitors.

Thus, in the annals of law governing business behavior, we see a mixture of restraint on monopoly on the one hand, and restraint on competition on the other.

12.6.2. Regulation: With Friends Like That, Who Needs Enemies?

There are numerous industries that are widely believed to be subject to diminishing long-run average costs. Railways, some public utilities, and other firms characterized by a high component of fixed cost all at one time or another have been considered to be ''natural monopolies.'' By virtue of the technical conditions under which they produce, it is argued, the natural form of organization of their markets is the monopoly form—duplication of suppliers is simply too costly.

Because of the possibility of monopoly, there was concern that such industries might evolve into ''antisocial'' patterns of behavior. Thus it was decided that such industries should be regulated by government, federal or state; and so we have numerous state public utility commissions, to regulate the prices charged by electricity and gas suppliers, the tolls on intrastate telephone calls, and the fares of intrastate airlines; and in Washington we have the Interstate Commerce Commission, the Federal Communications Commission, and numerous others, each charged with overseeing the affairs of one or more subject industries.

It has become increasingly clear through time that the various regulatory agencies on the balance do more to destroy or inhibit competition than to protect it. In various but not all cases, they regulate entry, set minimum prices, and grant exclusive service franchises. Many of the regulated industries have become extremely inefficient and unresponsive to customer preferences. Yet, with the support of a governmentally enforced monopoly, and by virtue of governmentally approved high prices, such firms manage to survive indefinitely.

Why has regulatory action worked out in such a perverse way? Why are regulators subject to the charge of being enemies of competition? The answers, unsurprisingly, hinge on the self-interest of affected parties. First, in order to find experts who are intimately acquainted with the problems of the industry that is being regulated, it has been customary to go to the industry to hire staff for the commission. It is not uncommon for a commissioner to be chosen from the managerial ranks of a regulated firm, and then to leave ''the public service'' after a few years to assume a high-paying job in the industry he has been regulating. Second, we must inquire into the criteria by which the performance of the commissions is judged within government. A commission that enforced competitive practice in industries like railroading, motor freight transportation, or public utilities would undoubtedly create a monumental chaos in the short run; and that chaos would be taken to be evidence of bad performance.

Thus, on the balance, the results of government efforts in fostering and protecting competition have been mixed, to say the least. In many cases, the threat of monopoly has evoked the formation of a regulatory bureaucracy, which often has perversely protected a pattern of monopoly behavior by the regulated firms, long after such behavior would have ceased to be possible in an unregulated market. And the laws regulating trade-restraining behavior have been to a degree subverted by exceptions, and have furthermore been somewhat erratically enforced. Add to these activities the fostering of governmentally operated monopolies, such as the post office and the public schools (which in some communities are *de facto* monopolies), and the whole picture is more convincingly explained in terms of the enhancement of politicians' and bureaucrats' power than in terms of "the public interest."

APPLICATIONS AND EXTENSIONS

1. The Miller-Tydings Act of 1937 provides that manufacturers of branded merchandise can prevent retailers from selling the good below a list price that the manufacturer sets. The manufacturer can punish a retailer who cuts the price on a such a "fair traded" item, by refusing to let the retailer sell the item in the future; in so doing, the manufacturer is explicitly ruled *not* to be in violation of the anti-trust laws.

    It is easy to see why *retailers* want to have "fair trade" laws. But why should manufacturers want to have such laws enforced? The lower the price charged by the retailer, the larger the manufacturers' sales, and any price cut comes out of the retailer's profit margin. [See Lester Telser, "Why Should Manufacturers Want Fair Trade?" *Journal of Law and Economics,* 3 (October 1960).]

2. Producers of movies engage in an activity called "block booking." A theatre owner who wishes to show a hit film may be required to rent not only that film but another one of lesser appeal as well. Again we have a practice that seems to make little sense: why should a theatre owner be willing to pay more for two films together than he would pay for each separately?

    It turns out that the explanation of this practice hinges on the fact that production companies are not permitted to price-discriminate among theatre owners. Consider the following setup:

	Film 1	Film 2
Theatre A	60	15
Theatre B	40	27

The entries in the table constitute the maximum rentals that a theatre is willing to pay for a film. What are the producer's revenue-maximizing rental rates if Film 1 and Film 2 are priced separately? And what is the revenue-maximizing rate if the two films are rented as a package (assuming that requiring both to be taken does not change the maximum rental information in the table)?

BIBLIOGRAPHICAL NOTE

Consult the reference librarian in the government documents section of your library for help in finding the anti-trust subcommittee hearings cited in this chapter.

F. M. Scherer, *Industrial Market Structure and Economic Performance* (Chicago: Rand McNally, 1971) is a virtual encyclopedia on the specialized topics of this chapter. It is the logical starting place for any systematic study of industry organization. G. J. Stigler, *Capital and Rates of Return in Manufacturing Industry* (Princeton, N.J.: Princeton University Press for the National Bureau of Economic Research, 1963) contains an excellent summary in Chapter 4 of the difficulty of relating profitability to concentration, and presents estimates different from Bain's which we displayed (pages 247–49). Two other books are interesting for both the material they present, and the strong but contrasting points of view regarding intervention that they imply. These are J. S. McGee, *In Defense of Industrial Concentration* (New York: Praeger Books, 1971); and W. G. Shepherd, *Market Power and Economic Welfare* (New York: Random House, 1970).

CHAPTER THIRTEEN

Advertising, Information, and Consumer Sovereignty

You can tell the ideals of a nation by its advertisements.

NORMAN DOUGLAS (1917)

13.1. SCOPE OF ADVERTISING

Advertising may be the most controversial legal activity in the contemporary capitalist economy. A broad range of criticism is leveled against advertising by a variety of social critics, including economists. As usual, such criticism ranges from the interesting and thought-provoking to the useless and puerile. Before analyzing the criticism, we should get some idea of who does how much advertising and where the advertising is done.

In 1966, according to *Printer's Ink,* roughly $16.6 billion was spent on advertising. That amount was about 2.23 percent of the total value of output in the society (called gross national product, or GNP) for that year. By contrast, in 1929 (a year of vigorous business activity) advertising totaled about $2.6 billion when GNP was $103.1 billion; and in 1933 (during the depth of the Great Depression) advertising was $1.4 billion on a GNP of $55.6 billion. The percentages of GNP in both 1929 and 1933 was (coincidentally) 2.52 percent. Thus, there may well have been a *decline* in advertising, measured as a fraction of total goods and services produced in the economy, during the past forty-five years.

In Table 13.1 a breakdown by medium is presented, with estimates of the extent to which efforts are directed at local markets and at national markets. Table 13.2 shows the industry class that does the advertising. Both tables may contain surprises for you.[1]

Two potentially important tentative conclusions emerge from this data: first, the already mentioned possibility that advertising is *declining* in relation to national product; second, the possibility that a significant part of advertising outlay

TABLE 13.1.　*Printer's Ink* **1966 Advertising Estimates**

Newspapers		4895.0
National	975.0	
Local	3920.0	
General Magazine		1264.4
Farm Magazines		70.1
National	36.6	
Regional	33.5	
Business Papers		711.5
Television		2784.0
Network	1385.0	
National Spot	931.0	
Local	642.0	
Radio		1001.0
Network	64.8	
National Spot	294.2	
Local	642.0	
Direct Mail		2454.0
Outdoor		177.7
National	117.7	
Local	60.0	
Transit		33.6
National	16.6	
Local	17.0	
Miscellaneous Media		3219.7
National	1875.2	
Local	1344.5	
Total		16601.0
National	10116.0	
Local	6485.0	

Source: *Printer's Ink,* August 25, 1967. Prepared by the McCann-Erickson Agency.
All figures in millions of dollars.

[1] I personally was surprised at the small fraction of advertising resources devoted to TV and outdoor advertising (Table 13.1); my prior feeling was that these two categories are extremely important, and one of them, as we see, is quite unimportant. However, I was not surprised to find in Table 13.2 that manufacturing and retail trade establishments dominate the advertising outlays by category of business—together, these two categories account for over two-thirds of advertising outlays.

TABLE 13.2. *Advertising Age* 1966 Advertising Estimates

Agriculture, Forestry, and Fisheries	170
Mining	32
Construction	240
Manufacturing	7,490
Transportation, Communication, Other Public Utilities	515
Wholesale Trade	1,280
Retail Trade	4,100
Trade Not Allocable	95
Finance, Insurance, Real Estate	1,270
Services	1,610
Business Not Allocable	8
Total	16,810

Source: *Advertising Age,* January 2, 1967.
All figures in millions of dollars.

is devoted to *informing* customers of such potentially crucial facts as availability, price, and technical characteristics of products, which would imply that the usual impatient view of advertising as exclusively a *persuasive* activity may well be false. This second possibility is perceived in the significant share of advertising outlays in newspapers and trade media. These advertising outlets are normally not thought to be effective vehicles for "hidden persuasion." Of course, any judgment of whether a particular advertising item is persuasive or informative in content and intent, is necessarily subjective. Seldom do we encounter a chronicle of pure fact devoid of implicit praise, and perhaps equally seldom do we encounter complete fantasy unadulterated by objective fact. Thus, any attempt to classify advertising activity will necessarily involve significant subjective evaluation. We will have occasion to return to these conclusions later on in this chapter, in commenting on some of the criticisms that have been leveled against advertising.

13.2. CRITICISMS OF ADVERTISING: DISCUSSIONS

Much of the remainder of this chapter is devoted to a statement and economic analysis of five criticisms of advertising: (1) Advertising is offensive to good taste and intelligence. (2) To the extent that advertising conveys a real service to consumers, that service is badly (inefficiently) provided. (3) Advertising represents a waste; the advertising outlays of one oligopolist do nothing but offset the effects of rival oligopolists. (4) Advertising causes people to want and to purchase "useless" or "unnecessary" goods. (5) Advertising inhibits competition and fosters monopoly by restricting entry of new firms into the supply of the advertised goods.

We turn to comment on the criticisms, in the order of their presentation.

13.2.1. Criticism 1: Advertising is in Bad Taste

Anything can be accorded hostile criticism on ground of taste, and taste is a shifting thing. Films that in 1960 would have been widely regarded as bits of pornographic trash are at this writing routinely being designated as the "best films of the year." If the aesthetic standards of the arts are applied to advertising, then much advertising looks offensive. If a separate aesthetic were defined for advertising, there would still be controversy over the merits of individual advertisements, including controversy as to whether or not they were in good taste. In addition, the taste evident in advertising is a relative of the society. British and Canadian TV and magazine advertising is remarkably less shrill and cute than advertising in those media in the U.S. Cross-cultural comparisons make it appear that there is nothing inherently offensive in advertising: if it works, it is used, and in some societies "vulgarity" apparently has wide appeal. Finally, attitude studies reveal that certain types of advertising are more bothersome than others. Soap, liquor, tobacco, and personal hygiene advertising is found distasteful by a wide variety of respondents; automobiles are less offensively advertised, and sporting goods advertising causes no complaints at all.

At a somewhat deeper level, we hear criticisms of the organization of contemporary society on the ground that it is so heavily oriented toward the crass activity of profitable exchange. In response to that type of criticism, we ask: if 2.23 percent of GNP represents an excessive amount of resources to devote to inviting and arranging exchanges, what level *is* appropriate? To suggest a zero level would make no sense. To know what level is appropriate, we need some reliable new theory of the way that exchange should be arranged and how information should be transmitted. And that brings us to the second criticism.

13.2.2. Criticism 2: Advertising Transmits Information Poorly

There are several questions to be looked at here. Is too much advertising being done? Why does a firm give away the service of announcing the terms of transactions that it will enter into?—or more accurately, why is that information sold jointly with the firm's output? In the next major section we turn to a related important question: Can a more rational system be conceived for conveying information and arranging transactions, and if so, what measures will be necessary to enforce the use of that system?

The first question—is too much advertising being done—is a hard one to answer because we don't know how to determine what is a large or a small amount of advertising. The fact that advertising is noticeable everywhere we go may only mean that it is done in an extremely effective way. What direction can a theory of socially optimal advertising take, and what are the steps in setting up such a theory? First, objectives must be defined. Because we are concerned with the social aspects of advertising in discussing criticism 2, let's examine a possible objective, not from the standpoint of a firm that seeks to increase its demand, but rather from the standpoint of a society that seeks (a) to provide sufficient information to individual consumers to enable them to spend their incomes in ways that yield as much satisfaction as possible; and (b) to serve some reasonable standards of aesthetics and truth.

In principle it is possible to measure how well our current advertising arrangements convey information, and how well they conform to some operational aesthetic standard. There exists a theory of information transmission. A unit of information is defined, and technological costs of transmitting information are known. Misinformation (lies or deceptive claims) can be viewed as negative units of information. The amount of information required for intelligent allocation of income under different circumstances—age, income level, family status, etc.—could be estimated. With this framework, alternative systems of information transmission, including the existing one, could be evaluated. Such a task, while by no means a small one, might be within the grasp of economic science, given our current capability in sampling, in processing data, in judging statistical reliability, and in measuring information. Needless to say, such a study has not yet been undertaken: critics and defenders of advertising both find it easier to rap off the tops of their heads than to get involved in so arduous a program of research.

The second question raised in this section—if information about products is a useful good, why isn't it sold separately from the products, instead of being included as part of a package with the products—is easier to answer. Before answering that question, we must be certain that the terms of the question are clear.

Two goods are sold jointly if one is always sold with the other. Examples are shoes and shoelaces; shirts and collars; left and right socks; beer and a container for beer; and any product and its advertising. Just as you cannot buy a left sock for less than the price of a pair of socks, so you cannot buy an Oldsmobile without paying for some part of the advertising done by General Motors.

Why is this? In part it may be because firms perceive that an attempt to sell information as a separate good might diminish total sales (of the final product plus the information). Customers would be attracted to any firm that provided the good and information about it in one package, so to speak; the joint provision contributes to customer convenience. Alternatively, the joint provision can be viewed as a way that the firm can attain lower cost. In some instances, conspicuously those involving expensive mail-order catalogs, the provision of information and the provision of goods are priced separately, on the ground that separate pricing leads to lower cost of operation with reductions in sales that are less than offsetting. But mail order may be atypical; for most circumstances, joint pricing is probably economical.

In measuring the cost of advertising, we must keep in mind the vast subsidies to nonadvertising activities that are included in the expenditure data of Table 13.1. The nearly $10 billion of newspaper, TV, magazine, and radio advertising

in 1966 was in substantial measure devoted to the provision of news and entertainment at much lower direct cost to readers, viewers, and listeners than would
otherwise have been possible. The buyer of a good actually pays for three things:
the good, advertisement of the good, and some subsidy on the consumption of
media content; and so to count the entire amount shown in Tables 13.1 and 13.2
as devoted to advertising alone is to overlook the important third good.

In this discussion of the second criticism of advertising, we have made very
little progress on an important issue: how efficient is the current arrangement for
providing information about goods and arranging transactions? A second and related question—what changes can be envisioned that will lead to clear-cut social improvement in the way that information transmission is organized?—will
be taken up shortly. The difficulty of these questions is clear, and the best response for individuals who are turned off by the current system may well be (1)
actively to support measures that decouple the joint provision of goods, information, and medium content (pay TV is such a measure) and (2) to assist actively in
the enforcement of standards of truth and taste in advertising, by avoiding offensively or inaccurately advertised goods. Direct controls and restrictions on advertising are at best a partial answer, as billboard control legislation and the performance of certain regulated industries like pharmaceuticals will attest. Flows
of information about available choices would seem to be necessary for any society in which choice exists; whether the present system best provides that information can be doubted; but whether better ways can easily be found is also
doubtful.

13.2.3. Criticism 3: Advertising is Wasteful

Advertising is supposed to work in a very simple way. Figure 13.1 shows the
"ideal" impact of advertising, viewed from the standpoint of the firm. As a result of a particular fixed outlay on advertising, average cost shifts from C to C'.
Demand shifts and tilts from D to D'. The "tilt" in demand reflects less sensitiv-
ity of quantity sold to price (lower price elasticity), which will result if advertising brings greater "brand loyalty."

In studying Figure 13.1, note that the fixed advertising outlay affects D and
average cost, but not *marginal* cost. $MR(D')$ is a segment of the marginal revenue schedule associated with the new demand curve D'. After advertising is
begun, price rises from p^* to α, and output falls from Q^* to Q. The effect, which
in Figure 13.1 is illustrated in terms of a firm that had originally been competitive, is to generate profits (returns above normal) in amount equal to the area of
the rectangle $\alpha\beta\gamma\delta$. If demand is less responsive to advertising than is shown in
the figure, then average cost after advertising may exceed price. In such cases,
advertising does not pay.

Some critics of advertising contend that the story does not end here. They
hold that if advertising yields profits, then other firms will also advertise, with

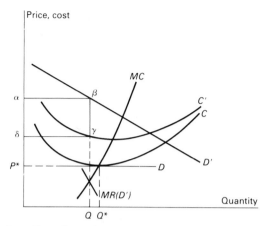

FIGURE 13.1. The effect of advertising upon demand, cost, and profit, without advertising by rival firms.

the result that the demand curve will shift to the left from D', until the "returns rectangle" $\alpha\beta\gamma\delta$ disappears. The net effect of advertising is higher cost *(C'* instead of *C)*, no greater output, and reduced efficiency. Yet the firm cannot afford to stop advertising, for to do so would be to lose out to rival firms that continue advertising. The final outcome, the critics contend, then looks like Figure 13.2. The elimination of excess returns is assured by the ability of new firms to enter the industry and to start advertising *their* products, if excess returns should persist. Any activity that leads *only* to higher costs is *per se* wasteful. By this criterion, advertising is wasteful.

Note the change in tone and emphasis that can be perceived in this criticism, compared to the second criticism. There, in line with the goals of the society, it was assumed that the objective of advertising is to convey information; here the

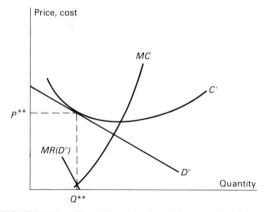

FIGURE 13.2. The effect of advertising by rival firms.

underlying view reflects the perspective of the firm and it is suggested that advertising should serve to alter preferences and create permanent differences among alternative products in the mind of the consumer.

We may accept that advertising fails at altering demand, but is hard to surpass at conveying information; hence, advertising is useful. Or we may hold that advertising can be surpassed easily by other means of conveying information, and it does a good job of differentiating products in the eyes of consumers, in which case we probably will be disposed to regard advertising as bad. Unfortunately, there is very little in the way of genuine evidence on either of these points.

13.2.4. Criticism 4: Advertisers are "Hidden Persuaders"

This criticism, which I have headnoted with the title of a muckraking best-seller (1957) by Vance Packard, is potentially the most profound criticism of advertising. The view that advertisers hypnotize customers for the purpose of creating a market and sustaining the consumption-oriented society, if correct, challenges consumer sovereignty as a foundation of the market economy. Capitalism has been advocated on the ground that it does an unsurpassed job of delivering goods to people who want them. If people "don't *really* want" those goods—if people instead are mere puppets whose strings are being pulled and twisted by the advertisers—then the ability of a capitalist order to deliver goods can be made to look like an anti-human conspiracy for the enrichment of villains. A condition stipulated by the Individualist Precept is that no human being should be used as a mere instrument for the convenience, enrichment, or gratification of another. If this compelling rule is violated by the way that advertisers manipulate consumers, then advertising is antisocial activity. If the market exchange system must have advertising to survive, then the system itself may be bad.

Numerous writers have attempted by this argument to paint capitalism's alleged virtue as an important vice—Packard, Baran and Sweezy, Galbraith, Marcuse, and others[2] have seen the power of advertising, and have rushed forward to save society from the evil. It is very important, then, to see whether the charges that advertisers manipulate customers can be sustained on intellectual and scientific grounds; it is not intelligent social policy to act on charges that are established only on emotional grounds.

Viewed from the perspective of economic theory, the interesting question concerning the effects of advertising on consumers is: do people respond to the *information content* of advertising as they choose in accordance with their established preferences? Or does advertising intrude to cause frequent changes in the preference ordering itself, so that people passively select advertised goods *because* they are advertised? The difficulty in answering that question directly

[2] Vance Packard, *The Hidden Persuaders* (New York: McKay, 1957); Paul Baran and Paul Sweezy, *Monopoly Capital* (New York: Monthly Review Press, 1966); John K. Galbraith, *The New Industrial State* (Boston: Houghton Mifflin, 1971); Herbert Marcuse, *One Dimensional Man* (Boston: Beacon Press, 1964).

should be perfectly clear to everyone: after all, we cannot observe anybody's preference ordering directly. We can, however, infer two patterns of behavior that might be observed if advertising had a significant controlling effect on consumers.

First, we might find that in order to sell more goods in the economy at large, more intensive advertising effort is necessary. Careful studies reveal that *total* consumer purchases in the economy are unaffected by the level of advertising. In fact, a good case apparently can be made that increases in consumer purchases cause businesses to advertise more, which is just opposite to the postulated effect of advertising causing consumption.

Second, we might find that "persuasive" advertising cements consumers into habitual patterns of consumption, and causes buyers to resist changing their consumption patterns in ways that would lead to higher levels of satisfaction. In regard to that inferred pattern of behavior, we know that high levels of advertising are not typically associated with a high degree of brand loyalty or a stable share of market. Advertising is heavier in soaps and toiletries than in certain packaged food lines, but consumer surveys and market studies have shown that market shares of leading brands have been less stable and secure in soaps and toiletries. Turnover among the sales leaders has been *greater* in the heavily advertised product line. Thus, advertising apparently is not associated with a stable share of market. If market shares are not stabilized by advertising, then advertising is probably wasteful from the standpoint of advertisers, as discussed under criticism 3. However, that issue has little bearing on the question of whether advertising is persuasive or informative.

The evidence that exists against the "hidden persuaders" theory is not very impressive. But it does exist, which is more than can be said concerning evidence *for* the theory. If advertising causes or sustains the materialist orientation of contemporary American society, then perhaps we need an advertising campaign against materialism.

13.2.5. Criticism 5: Advertising Creates Monopoly

It has been suggested that advertising contributes to conditions of monopoly—price in excess of marginal cost and returns above the normal rate. This argument depends on the view that advertising by established enterprises can deter other firms from entering into an industry. The steps of the argument are (1) to fare successfully in an industry where established firms advertise, entering firms also must advertise. (2) There is a "threshold" effect—too little advertising has no impact, and the amount of advertising necessary for impact is fairly substantial. (3) The threshold rises as established firms step up their advertising activity. Hence, the capital required to carry out the necessary advertising is a part of the cost of entering the industry, and that cost can be raised by established firms—they simply adjust their advertising outlays higher if they wish to thwart entry.

As a test of this criticism, economists have searched for relations between advertising and profitability. If industries with heavy advertising show high rates of return, it is argued, advertising does tend to foster monopoly and the associated higher profits of monopoly. Conversely, if there is no relation between advertising and rate of return, the criticism that advertising fosters monopoly is held to be weakened.

There is a difficulty with conclusions drawn from simple relationships between two variables like advertising and returns. Recall that earlier we discussed the difficulty of estimating demand curves from simple price and quantity observations (Chapter 6). The problem with such measures, we noted, is that they assume that conditions of demand are unchanged—they neglect the influence of shifts in demand on the sequence of prices that is observed. In much the same manner, studies that relate advertising and profit neglect the possibility that firms may advertise because they are profitable—if a relationship between advertising and profit is discovered, it does not follow that firms are profitable because they advertise. Theoretical studies of advertising policy suggest that we should expect more profitable firms to advertise more intensively—that is, to devote a larger ratio of their total sales revenues to advertising. To grasp this important point, you may want to work through the mathematical example that is provided in the Appendix to this chapter. That exercise reveals clearly that if a firm has a high ratio of price to marginal cost, it will want to devote a higher proportion of its revenues to advertising than it would with a lower ratio of price to marginal cost. This finding makes good sense. The greater the return per unit sold, the more the firm should be willing to spend on advertising to try to sell additional units. There is no implication anywhere in the model that the profitability of the firm is affected by advertising: the model depends only on the condition that the firm already posesses a measure of monopoly power.

Two types of indirect evidence exist on the question of whether or not advertising strengthens monopoly. The first type compares advertising outlays to the average profitability of firms within an industry. The finding usually is that profitability and advertising are related statistically: the greater the ratio of advertising expenditures to sales, the greater the profitability. The difficulty with such studies, we have noted, is that the profitability may be ''causing'' the advertising, instead of vice versa (see the Appendix to this chapter).

The second type of study relates advertising outlays to industrial concentration, at the four-digit (industry) level. There are mixed findings from this type of study. First, it appears that there is a very weak relationship between advertising and concentration: firms in more highly concentrated industries tend to advertise slightly more than firms in less highly concentrated industries. On the other hand, when changes over time are observed, we find an association between *reductions* in advertising and *increases* in concentration—but again, a very weak one. Because of the well-known difficulties (discussed in Chapter 12) in establishing relationships between monopoly power and degree of concentration, these studies are most inconclusive. All that the studies do suggest is that the case against advertising on the ground that it fosters monopoly has not been supported by fact.

In concluding our evaluation of these five important criticisms of advertising, we should note that criticism 3 is a contradiction of criticisms 4 and 5. Criticism 3 holds that advertising is effective only in keeping the name of a product fixed in the consciousness of the public, and would in large part be unnecessary if rival products were not advertised. By contrast, the fourth and fifth criticisms hold that consumers are actively responsive to advertising. If the fourth criticism were valid, we would expect demand for a product that is produced by several firms, such as razor blades, to be increased and stabilized by advertising. The advertising activity of rival producers would have the effect of increasing the total demand for razor blades of all brands, if consumers are persuaded by advertising. In addition, if criticism 5 were true, a firm's advertising would help it to maintain a market share in the face of advertising activity by rivals and potential rivals.

There seems to be clear evidence that advertising does *not* stimulate *total* demand for a product. When American Tobacco held a cigarette monopoly in 1910, advertising of cigarettes was about $13 million. In 1913, after the monopoly was broken up into four major independent firms, advertising outlays were $25 million, but cigarette sales per capita were about the same. This suggests that much of the advertising effort in 1913 worked only to defend the market shares of the rival firms. Much the same situation holds true today: in 1971, cigarette advertising was banned from television, an action that the cigarette firms welcomed, because it enabled them to cut down significantly on their advertising outlays, and they predicted that total sales would not be much affected. That indeed seems to be the way things have worked out for the cigarette companies: less money spent in offsetting the ad campaigns of rival producers, and no fewer sales. Similar experience is shown in numerous other markets. Thus there appears to be strong support for the view that advertising is a wasteful by-product of many industries. That same evidence offers some mild support for the view that criticisms 2 and 3 are poorly conceived: advertising does not reshape people's preferences to an extent that shows up in the *total* sales of soap, cigarettes, razor blades, etc.; nor does more advertising by a firm assure a greater or more stable market share for the firm's brands of soap or cigarettes or razor blades.

13.3. TAX-FINANCED SUPPORT FOR TRANSMITTING INFORMATION

Goods provided by different firms may appear to be the same, but actually differ widely in important characteristics. One dramatic example involves life insurance. Suppose a man of age 35 wants a $1000 "straight life" insurance policy.

The basic arrangement of such a policy is that he pays a specified amount, called the *premium,* to the insurance company every year until his death. When he dies, his beneficiary receives $1000 from the insurance company. A bewildering variety of additional conditions can be found to accompany that basic pricing arrangement. Some insurance companies pay dividends to their policy-holders; these have the effect of reducing the cost of coverage. Some policies provide "double indemnity"—$2000 instead of $1000 in the event of accidental death. Other policies provide for "waiver of premium" in the event of a disabling illness or injury. The net result of all these possibilities is that the insurance buyer knows very little about the actuarial value of the protection he is buying.[3]

An insurance expert calculated the range of costs per $1000 in actuarial value of protection for "straight life" policies that were widely available from well-established insurance companies in 1962. The range of costs on such policies was $4 to $13 per year for a twenty-one year old. Here, then, is a threefold range in price on a good that is supplied under conditions that are at least potentially competitive. The reason underlying the wide variations in price may simply be lack of easy access to the relevant information on the part of insurance buyers.

If poor information is the explanation of those price discrepancies, and if such discrepancies are found in the markets for many goods, then an important problem of poor consumer information can be identified in the society. Without that information, markets will not function competitively, and the benefits of market exchange will be lost.

How can information be provided? Two avenues suggest themselves immediately. First, there are consumer information services, such as Consumers' Union. This organization operates on funds collected from buyers, and provides information on "quality" of different makes, models, etc. of the goods that it tests. The service has three drawbacks: first, there are scale problems—the present organization is too small. Selective, rather than general testing of available makes or brands is the rule, and exclusion puts the untested and unreported brands at a disadvantage. Moreover, the sample size on tested items is absurdly small from the standpoint of statistical reliability, usually being one item. The second drawback is that information becomes obsolete very quickly, and to keep such a service up to date would be an undertaking of major importance. Third, the organization as it is currently constituted attempts to rank or rate the alternative items tested, and the partially subjective basis of that ranking will make the service less useful to some consumers than to others.

A second means of providing information is much less ambitious. Directory

---

[3]The actuarial value of the policy is the sum of the values of all the payoffs of the policy, with each payoff weighted by the probability of the event that would cause the payoff to occur. The value of an indemnity clause, for example, is the extra $1000, multiplied by the probability that death is accidental and not "natural," and discounted by the different possible durations until death, each duration having a probability of occurrence.

services, not unlike the yellow pages, could be kept up to date by regular or occasional supplements that would provide current price and availability information. Under this directory arrangement, information about "quality" would be nonexistent or unreliable; but that, after all, is hardly different from the present situation in which quality judgments are based on word of mouth, the sellers' own assertions in advertising, or other impressions of dubious authenticity.

Whether either or a combination of the suggested alternatives would provide more reliable and comprehensive information at lower cost to the consumer compared to the present arrangement of seller-supplied information is a matter for conjecture. The opportunities for corruption in a service administered by the government or by a consumer organization are not to be overlooked. Moreover, it is doubtful that sellers would willingly change over to a revised arrangement, and relinquish the prerogative of providing information about their own products. Thus, we might find that if either alternative arrangement is to replace the existing policy of providing information through advertising, some (coercive) legal restriction on the direct advertising activity of sellers will be necessary to enforce the change. Because it is by no means proved that either arrangement would fare as well as the existing one from the standpoint of individuals' welfare (although the suggestion that either would be an improvement is certainly plausible), and because issues of freedom of speech would surely be raised if advertising were restricted, it is improbable that a move will be made in that direction. This means, then, that the supplementary provision of consumer information would coexist with advertising.

At the present time, the budget of Consumers' Union (CU) is under $12 million per year, or less than a tenth of Procter & Gamble's advertising expenditure. CU's proceeds are entirely from the sale of a magazine, called *Consumer Reports,* and the magazine is the means whereby information on product availability and product quality is transmitted to CU's members. *If in fact the information obtained and transmitted by CU is accurate and complete, there is an argument for subsidizing the activity of that organization, or of similar organizations.*

Consumer information is a *public good* (Chapter 15); your use of the information does not diminish the amount that is available for me to use. It is in the nature of public goods that unless their supply is subsidized, they will be made available in less than the optimal quantity: if I can freeload by using information that you pay for, and vice versa, then neither of us will purchase information up to the point at which the value we realize from additional information equals the cost of obtaining and transmitting it. Thus, it is in our mutual interest to take steps to assure that a sufficient amount of information is provided. In the society at large, private associations (clubs), and public associations (government subsidy) are workable ways of providing an adequate flow of consumer information.

Suppose agreement has been reached on the desirability of governmentally subsidizing the flow of consumer information. There remain the questions: who should generate the information? What sources of revenue should be tapped to pay for it?

The problem of structuring a service, whether private or governmental, for the provision of reliable, complete, current, and unbiased information is an enormously difficult one. Power on occasion breeds arrogance, arbitrariness, and susceptibility to corruption, and clearly, any single agency charged with evaluating goods would be very powerful. It is also true that power may breed extreme caution against making bad mistakes; and the result could be the withholding of information on potentially beneficial but "insufficiently proven" products, such as pharmaceuticals, with the end result that those products are underutilized to an extremely costly degree. The answer might be to fund numerous agencies, each independently operated.

The question of where the revenues are to come from does not ask what type of taxes should be raised to pay for the information service; rather, the question asks whether the tax-paying populace will realize sufficient benefit from the information to offset the costs incurred in making it available. In regard to this question, an interesting possibility exists. We have argued that firms will very likely want to continue advertising, even if independent and highly reliable sources of information arise. If information made available by those sources leads to a reduction in the returns that businesses realize from their advertising and selling expenditures, then the expenditures will diminish, perhaps greatly. The lower prices made possible by reductions in expenditure on sales effort would compensate consumers for the taxes they paid to provide information.

However, if firms raise prices in order to step up their sales efforts, in an attempt to offset or drown out the "truth" made available by the information agencies, then the impulse might be to impose a tax on newspaper, magazine, billboard, and TV advertising and to eliminate the postal rate subsidy on direct-mail advertising. Such a system would not be readily accepted. However, without reduction in advertising and resulting lower product prices, the benefits from better consumer information would come entirely from better allocation by consumers: the greater satisfaction obtained from income spent well would be the payoff realized from the program of subsidized information. Whether or not that gain would compensate for the cost of providing the information would have to be seen.

13.4. CONCLUSIONS

In a market economy, the surest way to obtain the removal of billboards, to promote low-key TV ads featuring splendid scenery and classical music, and to encourage establishments marked by discreet brass nameplates instead of Giant Signs That Go 'Round in the Sky is not to patronize those who offend. Advertising does pollute the environment, in the view of many observers. Those people can, by selective patronage, encourage cleanup.

As far as more serious issues are concerned: there may be more efficient ways of conveying information than the one we employ—advertising—but nobody has spelled them out in detail as yet; the previous section points to one possibility. Any scheme that uses coercion to eliminate advertising should be viewed with extreme caution, because there is no good evidence that advertising is itself coercive: nobody has shown that it creates or sustains monopoly power, or that it changes the preferences of consumers to make them want things they "don't need." That leaves us with the criticism that much advertising effort is unproductive, which is a close relative of the criticism that the organization for providing product information is inefficient. The two issues that emerge, then, are (1) Is there a less wasteful way of providing information and arranging transactions? What is required to establish that way, if it exists? The suggestions in the previous section are intended as a beginning point from which to approach that issue. (2) If we are stuck with advertising as the primary means for providing information, what, short of legislating an economy of monotonously homogeneous and extremely scarce products into existence, can be done to improve the situation that now exists? The answer to the first question is a hard one; for the second, try consuming selectively, to penalize those who offend you. The market system looks to consumer sovereignty as an important ideological underpinning: but if the benefits of market allocation are to be realized, that sovereignty must be exercised by consumers. The freedom of choice in consumption is made less meaningful unless it is exercised to say "no" to goods of low quality, excessive price, unknown purpose, or offensive advertising.

*APPENDIX I
DOES PROFITABILITY "CAUSE" ADVERTISING
AND NOT *VICE VERSA?*

Consider a firm whose sales quantity (Q) depends on two variables: the number of advertising messages purchased (A) and the selling price of the good produced (P). The firm possesses a measure of monopoly power—its price varies with the firm's own output decision. The firm's total revenues (sales receipts) are

$$\$P \cdot Q(P, A)$$

and its cost of production is

$$\$C(Q).$$

The advertising messages are assumed to be purchased at a fixed outlay of $\$T$ per message; advertising outlays then are $\$TA$.

The decision problem of the firm, then, is to choose a P and A so that net returns

$$\pi = P \cdot Q(P, A) - C\big[Q(P, A)\big] - TA$$

are maximized.

*The material in this section may be too advanced for some introductory coverage.

The first-order conditions for a maximum are

$$\frac{\partial \pi}{\partial P} = 0, \frac{\partial \pi}{\partial A} = 0$$

or

$$Q + P\frac{\partial Q}{\partial P} - \frac{\partial C}{\partial Q} \cdot \frac{\partial Q}{\partial P} = 0$$

and

$$P\frac{\partial Q}{\partial A} - \frac{\partial C}{\partial Q} \cdot \frac{\partial Q}{\partial A} - T = 0.$$

From this last equation, we can, by rearrangement of terms, and multiplication by A/PQ, obtain

$$\frac{TA}{PQ} = \frac{(\partial Q/\partial A)A(P - \partial C/\partial Q)}{PQ}.$$

Now, $(\partial Q/\partial A) \cdot A/Q$ is the elasticity of sales with respect to advertising messages. Denote this elasticity by α. The left side of the equation, TA/PQ, is the ratio of advertising outlays to sales revenues. We then have that

$$\frac{TA}{PQ} = \alpha \frac{(P - \partial C/\partial Q)}{P}:$$

the fraction of sales revenues spent on advertising are directly proportional to the "profit margin," which is price minus marginal cost, divided by price. The more profitable a good is at the margin of production (the greater the value of $(P - MC)/P$, the more the firm will advertise. Notice that the profit margin need not depend on advertising outlays for the stated conclusion to hold: all that is required is that there be an incentive to seek expanded sales, and advertising will be expanded.

APPLICATIONS AND EXTENSIONS

1. This will require that you collaborate with a friend or classmate. Without comparing notes, each person compile a list of answers to each of the following questions. In considering your answer, do not take price into account. Don't be overly sophisticated: try to write down a single name or brand in response to each question.

    1. What is the best U.S. university?
    2. What is the best brand of passenger car tire?
    3. What is the best brand of camera?
    4. What is the best brand of men's knit underwear?
    5. What is the best brand of women's hosiery?
    6. What is the best national chain of motels and restaurants?
    7. Who makes the world's best passenger automobile?
    8. What is the name of the best U.S.-made passenger automobile?

9. Who makes the best film for color slides or color movies?

10. What is the best ginger ale?

11. What is the best U.S. brand of beer?

12. What is the best color TV set?

13. What is the best newspaper in the United States?

(a) Next to each answer, make a check mark if you have had sufficient personal experience with the category in question to judge intelligently.

(b) Compare your list with your collaborator's. If each of you is playing the game seriously, using the best information at your disposal to come up with an answer, you should agree in about half the answers.

(c) In how many of the thirteen instances would you be able to formulate any answer at all in the absence of advertising? Do you think you would be likely to agree with a classmate or friend as often as you did? With me (a perfect stranger, and senile curmudgeon) in *any* instances?

The purpose of the exercise is to dramatize a point made by Philip Nelson, in "Advertising as Information," *Journal of Political Economy* Vol. 82, (July–August 1964). Nelson contends that some of the most significant information contained in an advertisement is that a good *is* advertised. When confronted with a choice that must be made on the basis of little or no experience, people tend to respond to the fact that advertising of a brand has occurred, and hence, the producer thinks the good is worth advertising. (This effect is particularly strong in such "repeat purchase" categories as soaps, breakfast cereals, etc.)

A purchaser faced with a choice among unknown brands on a shelf is in a similar (but by no means identical) situation to yours when you are asked to rank items that lie outside your experience—and you, and the purchaser, are likely to respond to a remembered name.

2. Attempt to make plausible the proposition: "Advertising is not Pareto-optimal, because ways can be found to provide *more reliable* information to *more* consumers at *lower* cost (even ignoring the media subsidy) than advertising does." (Sketch out some system or other which in fact might fulfill those claims.)

BIBLIOGRAPHICAL NOTE

In preparing this chapter, I have relied heavily on R. L. Schmalensee, *The Economics of Advertising* (Amsterdam: North-Holland Publishing Co., 1972). Another valuable source is Lester G. Telser, "Advertising and Competition," *Journal of Political Economy* Vol. 72, (December 1964).

Much useful information is presented in a paper which unfortunately is flawed by the view that profitability is caused by advertising and cannot cause it: W. S. Comanor and T. A. Wilson, "Advertising, Market Structure and Performance," *Review of Economics and Statistics* Vol. 49, (November 1967).

All three sources contain some arguments that will be difficult for a newcomer to economics, but all also contain much that is interesting and intelligible.

CHAPTER FOURTEEN

Running Out of Gas: Myopia in Resource Use

To waste, to destroy, our natural resources, to skin and exhaust
the land instead of using it so as to increase its usefulness, will
result in undermining in the days of our children the very pros-
perity which we ought by right to hand down to them. . . .

THEODORE ROOSEVELT (1907)

14.1. PRICING A SCARCE NATURAL RESOURCE

Quite often it is contended that the production, borrowing, and lending
mechanism whereby resources are allocated through time, which was described
in Chapter 9, leads people to make wasteful choices. For example, historians
have bemoaned the way that the forests and lands of eastern North America were
treated during colonial times.

> The early settlers showed a callous disregard for the resource heritage of the colonies.
> A homesteader would claim forty acres of forest land. He would girdle the trees to kill
> them, and a season later cut them down and burn them. The ashes of trees worth mil-
> lions of dollars on today's market served only to fertilize the crops that were grown
> among the stumps. After a few years of ignorant agricultural practice, the land became
> depleted, crop yields diminished, and the homesteader and his family moved on to
> another tract which they ravished in much the same way. . . .[1]

[1] E. von Weissmilch, *A Critical History of Colonial America* (unpublished, 1930).

If we accept the view that the goal of the farmer is to obtain a returns stream with the highest attainable present value, and if we further accept that a desirable outcome for society is to obtain the stream of agricultural produce that has the highest present value,[2] then we cannot immediately find fault with the practices described in the above quotation. In the seventeenth and eighteenth centuries, natural resources like land and timber were extraordinarily abundant in the United States. Human labor and transportation resources were very scarce. No settler in the Ohio territory could economically harvest the trees from his homestead tract, turn them into lumber, transport them to urban markets on the east coast, and show a profit. The trees were a nuisance; the land had to be made to yield food and fiber, and the trees were in the way. Similarly, when land wore out, new land could be obtained for the cost of clearing it; the old land would have required comparatively sophisticated and expensive fertilization to be made productive once again.

It is unlikely that America would be as wealthy a nation as she is today if "frugal" European agricultural practices, appropriate to a world of scarce land and abundant labor, had been used in the New World. The labor resources that would have been required to practice European-style agriculture would not have been available for use in other nonagricultural occupations; the nation would have accumulated capital in the form of more productive farm land and a greater stock of timber and wood products, instead of the forms in which capital actually was accumulated. The consequence almost surely would have been far lower standards of living than actually were experienced had a "conservationist" approach been imposed on the nation's development.[3]

Criticisms of resource exploitation under market capitalism persist to this day. We read of the necessity to regulate timber cutting in order to assure an adequate supply of pulpwood for future generations; concern is expressed that oil must be conserved for future use; and at one time in the late 1930s there was some widespread concern that coal supplies would be exhausted during the twentieth century; the year 2001 would find us all shivering, or living on the Gulf Coast.

Such concerns as those have in the past usually turned out to be groundless. Two kinds of activity have solved depletion problems before they have arisen:

---

[2]What do we mean by "the present value of a stream of agricultural produce"? Suppose the rate of interest in the society is r and all agricultural commodities are subject to the same degree of time preference. Then one unit of any commodity today will exchange in production (in the manner indicated in Figure 9.6) for $1 + r$ units of that same commodity—be it bushels of wheat, pounds of beef, pecks of turnips or potatoes, etc.—one year from now. If different commodities are subject to different degrees of time preference (as could happen if tastes or production techniques are foreseen to change through time), the present value of the output stream of each commodity is calculated according to its own rate of interest.

[3]What is it that is being conserved? Conservationism, as a popular movement, seeks to conserve natural resources. But in order to conserve natural resources, labor must be used more intensively. Colonial America was "conservationist"; but it conserved labor at the expense of natural resources.

exploration uncovers new supplies of a useful natural resource; and *technical change* indicates more efficient methods of extracting or using the resource, or leads to the resource being supplanted in use by some cheaper resource. (Anthracite coal is an example of a resource that once was a high-quality energy source and now is almost entirely out of use.) But even if future exploration and technical change do not increase the known supplies of mineral resources and the efficiency with which they are used, the market mechanism will not ignore future demands. We turn now to a formal analysis of how the price system allocates the fixed and unchanging supply of a resource through time. We begin with the simplest case of a monopoly supplier.

14.2. RATIONING BY A MONOPOLIST

Suppose a monopolist knows the demand in all future periods of time for a resource that he extracts and sells. Further, suppose he knows the costs of extraction in all future periods. To simplify the discussion of his planning decision, we will assume that he faces only two periods of equal length.[4]

The demand, marginal revenue, and marginal cost curves drawn in Figure 14.1 are the known relationships that the monopolist faces in periods 1 and 2. The curves of cost and revenue that are drawn for period 2 are *discounted*. That is, the dollar value of cost and revenue that are drawn for period 2 are the *present values* of future receipts and payments, as calculated in Chapter 9, Section

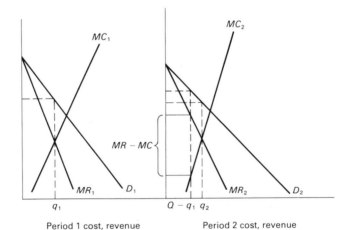

**FIGURE 14.1.   Nonoptimal (myopic) allocation of a scarce resource through
time.**

[4]In actuality, the question of how far a planner looks into the future is affected by profit considerations. Planners who are either excessively farsighted or myopic suffer losses. With the aid of some mathematics, our simple two-period analysis can be extended farther into the future; but the main points will remain unchanged.

9.2.2. If the interest rate is r, $(1 + r)p$ is the price actually received in period 2. The present value of that price is p; and hence, the present value of total revenue associated with the output q in period 2 is pq.

If there were no limit on the total available supply of the resource that the monopolist is selling, the optimum quantities for him to plan now to sell in each of the two periods would be, respectively, q_1 and q_2 (Figure 14.1). But suppose the total known available supply Q is less than $q_1 + q_2$. It is necessary that the monopolist *ration* the available supply in some intelligent way between the two periods. Suppose he does so by selling q_1 in the first period and the remaining quantity $Q - q_1$, which is less than q_2, in the second period. Would that be an intelligent way to handle the problem?

It appears that it would not. Notice that if one unit less were sold in period 1, and one unit more in period 2, the monopolist would be giving up a unit of sale from which the revenue is just equal to the cost of supply ($MR = MC$ in period 1 at the sales rate q_1); and the revenue from the added unit sold in period 2 would exceed the cost of supplying that additional unit in period 2 by a considerable amount. Thus, if outputs in the two periods were q_1 and $Q - q_1$, it would pay to reduce period 1 output and increase period 2 output.

Suppose, then, that the monopolist goes on transferring the total available supply Q between the two time periods until the *difference* between marginal revenue and the marginal cost of production is equal in both periods. This condition is illustrated in Figure 14.2. There will no longer be any opportunity to gain by changing the output rates of the two periods: the allocation of Q is accomplished in the most profitable way.

The fact that price is higher in the first period than it would be if there were no limit on the availability of the resource suggests that the market process rations the resource through time with due regard for future period needs. The pattern is

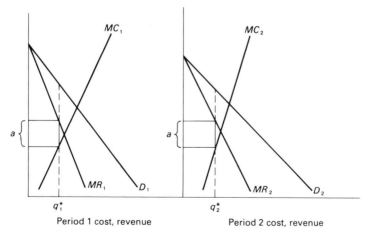

FIGURE 14.2. **Optimal allocation of a scarce resource through time.**

not one in which a normal sort of price is charged until the resource suddenly turns out to be all gone. A higher price is charged in the current period to cut down on current-period use of the resource and to make more available for use in the future period. It turns out that *it is in the firm's own interest to provide this rationing service;* no planner or central agent is required to direct firms to do so, because the firm's profits are higher if it does ration in the indicated manner.

14.3. INTERPERIOD ALLOCATION OF A RENEWABLE RESOURCE UNDER COMPETITION

The monopoly solution just treated has an important feature that is missing from situations with many suppliers. The monopolist is aware of demand levels in the two periods, and he is aware that his supply decisions will affect his prices and profits in the two periods. But in a competitive market, this type of price consciousness is explicitly ruled out by assumption. How is allocation through time accomplished under conditions of competition?

The answer is provided by an activity that is widely misunderstood and much maligned: *speculation.* To see how speculation works, we will look at a problem involving a renewable resource, food.

Suppose food harvests in a normal year are represented by the supply curve S_1 in Figure 14.3. Due to the outbreak of a war, or the invasion of an insect pest at a time when the use of effective pesticides is declared illegal, it is foreseen that the supply curve will shift to S_2 in the following year. If market action were completely myopic, the result would be price p_1 and p_2 in the two years and quantities consumed of q_1 and q_2. To lend drama to the story, we can suppose that q_2 is sufficiently small so that it imposes significant hardship on the society.

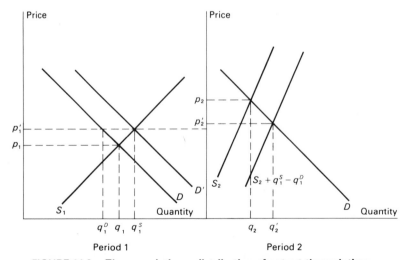

FIGURE 14.3.   The speculative redistribution of output through time.

But because the drop in period 2 supply is foreseen, and because there are individuals who are motivated by gain, the price increase from p_1 to p_2 depicted in Figure 14.3 will not in fact occur.

Speculators will enter the market. In period 1, they will buy goods with the express intent of selling them at a higher price at some later date. The speculative demand for food shifts the demand curve in period 1 from D to D'. Price rises from p_1 to p_1', and the quantity consumed in period 1 falls from q_1 to q_1^D, while the quantity produced rises from q_1 to q_1^S. The difference $q_1^S - q_1^D$ is bought up and stored by the speculators.

In period 2, that quantity $q_1^S - q_1^D$ is added to the available supply. As a result, price in period 2 is p_2' instead of p_2; and the quantity consumed is q_2' instead of q_2.

It will profit speculators to transfer the good from period 1 to period 2, as long as the price obtained in period 2 exceeds the period 1 price plus costs of storage. (Figure 14.3 shows that p_2' is slightly higher than p_1'; the difference between the two is the cost of storage.)

In any circumstance in which a significant change in supply conditions is widely foreseen, individual consumers will act as speculators on their own behalf. Persons will buy canned foodstuffs, soap, clothing—anything that can be stored in anticipation of a price rise. In circumstances that are less easy to foresee, specialists will emerge who watch market conditions closely and study past patterns of behavior; these persons will be the principal agents who undertake to smooth out the pattern of price and consumption through time.

The degree of price uniformity through time that is assumed in Figures 14.2 and 14.3 will, of course, not regularly be observed in the real world because the perfect foresight regarding demand and supply that went into those figures doesn't exist in the world. Intertemporal allocation becomes a sort of high-powered guessing game in which self-interested individuals match wits. Trader A feels that Trader B has underestimated the extent of the coming price rise, and B feels that A has overestimated it. So B sells his holdings to A. If B is right, he gains and A loses. But in either case, everyone else gains as a result of their dealings with each other if we believe that greater uniformity of price and consumption through time is better than lesser uniformity. Only if speculators *as a class* misread the direction of a coming price change does their activity work to the detriment of the rest of society. And if they do misread the direction of a coming price change, and they stock up on a good whose price is going to drop, then they take a pretty good pounding themselves. *They cannot injure the rest of society and profit by it.*

14.4. DISCOUNTING AND RATIONAL ALLOCATION

The present value of a dollar of returns is less to a firm the farther in the future that the dollar of returns is received. An unusually profitable event, foreseen to occur fifteen years in the future, has less impact on both the value and the actions of a firm than would the same profitable event foreseen to occur one year hence.

There are good reasons why we should be pleased that business decisions are more sensitive to immediate events than they are to remote future events. These reasons all center around the kinds of change in the economy that result from new discoveries, technical change, or changes in taste. If a petroleum supplier bases his forecast of the demand for oil on a forecast of energy requirements, he will likely do better in predicting demand for his product in the near future compared to the distant future. Over longer time periods, it is likely that cheaper and more efficient alternative energy sources will be discovered and developed. In addition, there may be changes in the lifestyle (and hence in the tastes) of the whole population over longer periods of time. Suppose, for instance, that the ecology movement convinces people to get rid of automobiles, air conditioners, and television sets within twenty years. That change would have profound effects on society's energy demand, and unless it were foreseen, it would have profound effects on society's demand for oil. Such a change is less likely to occur in an important way over a shorter period: within the time span of one year it is highly improbable that such a change will occur.

In light of the possibility of important changes in taste and technology, it would be a strategic blunder (and a waste of society's resources) for firms to count as heavily on, or prepare as carefully for, events in the distant future as they do for more immediate events. In allocating a resource that is in scarce supply, the effect of discounting is to weigh demands and costs according to how far in the future they are expected to occur; this is a practice which makes excellent sense in light of the changes of taste and of technique that regularly occur to disrupt predicted demands and predicted costs.

14.5. PROPERTY RIGHTS AND CONSERVATION

The foregoing analysis indicates the possibility that rational allocation and a market system are not incompatible *per se*. We have already suggested that resource use in the American colonies during the seventeenth and eighteenth centuries was not as irrational as some commentators suggest: it may have been both smart and good to clear forests and "destroy" land as it was done. However, we see examples of the same kind of behavior in the world today; and we well may question whether things have not changed sufficiently since the American Revolution so that different patterns of behavior are in order.

For example:

1. The Great Lakes, perhaps the world's largest single source of high-quality fresh water in 1900, have been severely polluted in places; only the northerly reaches of Lakes Michigan and Huron, and most of Lake Superior, can

still be said to have high-quality water. Moreover, at the present time when future water needs can be perceived as vast, the rate of pollution is increasing. How can we be sanguine about the ability of a market system to accommodate future needs in the face of this situation?

2.   The populations of certain pellagic (migratory) fish, which are highly valued as food, are being systematically depleted. Salmon, cod, and tuna are probably being overfished. Herring catches have diminished. The same story is true of certain species of whale: they now face extinction due to the predation of man. How can these facts be rationalized with a belief in the sanity of market action?

3.   Frequent examples have occurred in the past in which competing oil drillers, both of whom had drilled into the same underground deposit, extracted oil at such a rate that only a small part of the reserve could be recovered—by squandering the pressure of natural gas instead of using and controlling it, by failing to cap wasteful "gushers," by drilling more wells than a deposit could economically supply—all of these actions led to waste.

These three examples point to apparent failures of the market system. The three instances have a significant element in common: *property rights in the scarce resource are not* (or in the case of oil, were not) *adequately defined so that the market process could do its job.*

Consider the Great Lakes. They are the common property of the people of Canada and the U.S. However, they have long been treated like the high seas—as a fit dumping ground for refuse. The people of Canada and the U.S. have not taken adequate steps to protect their property rights in the lake system. A private individual who owns a lake will not tolerate its use as a dumping ground if he sees that dumping is harmful to his personal interest. If the citizens of the two countries could perceive that their collective interest is being abused by misuse of the lakes, then actions could be taken to protect their interest. The failure to take such action bespeaks the difficulty of mobilizing public opinion on issues in which the extent of private interest is neither very large for most individuals nor very immediate.

Similarly, in the case of the fisheries, nobody owns that resource; and hence, nobody feels a strong interest in controlling its use so that it yields a maximum revenue stream over time. Indeed, quite the opposite is true. Because the resource is available in recognizably limited supply, there is a scramble among fishermen, each to get his own share of the resource before the other fishermen completely deplete the resource.

The case of oil exploitation is essentially the same as the case of the fisheries. The excessive and wasteful pace of pumping is employed because more than one driller is tapping a single reservoir of oil. This gives each driller an incentive to pump faster in an effort to get the oil out before it is taken out by his rival. In an effort to control this impulse, the oil-producing states have instituted regulations to govern the pace of pumping. Ideally, such regulations would give each producer exclusive rights to a single reservoir. If the reservoirs were approximately identical in capacity, ease of drilling access, and proximity to pipelines, all drillers would operate efficiently, restrained only by the rule that no firm may tap another's reservoir. The result would be a competitive solution: each firm would produce up to the output at which price equals marginal cost, and no firm would perceive an effect of its output decision on market price. The state regulatory commissions (most notoriously, the curiously named Texas Railroad Commission) have not instituted a competitive solution, however. Instead, they typically have restricted output in such a way that a price near the monopoly price prevails on the market. By their regulatory action, the social abuse of excessively fast resource use is overcome; but the social abuse of monopoly profit is instituted in its stead. A much better solution would follow from the suggested system of property rights, which would permit markets to allocate in a competitive manner.

APPLICATIONS AND EXTENSIONS

1. Work out and draw graphs for the theory of exhaustible resource allocation under conditions of competition. Show the equilibrium conditions that will hold in the market and in the individual supplying firms.

2. On what ground does it make sense to judge that uniform prices and usage rates through time are preferable to irregular prices and usage rates? Can you think of any reasonable general circumstances under which irregularity would be preferred?

3. There is an exception to the statement that speculators cannot profit if their activity injures the rest of society. If they *corner a market* (obtain control of the entire stock of a good or commodity), they can do harm. How does this fact relate to the topic of Chapter 11?

4. What elasticity conditions on demand must hold in order for a market corner to be profitable?

BIBLIOGRAPHICAL NOTE

The literature on resource allocation through time and on speculation is largely pretty abstract technical stuff. The classical paper on intertemporal allocation is Harold Hotelling, "The Economics of Exhaustible Resources," *Journal of Political Economy,* 47 (April 1939). Hotelling's paper can be understood by patient readers of this book. There is a very nice, very elementary, treatment of speculation in Abba Lerner, *Everybody's Business* (New York: Harper Torchbooks, 1968).

CHAPTER FIFTEEN

Externalities and Public Goods

Every man holds his property subject to the general right of the community to regulate its use to whatever degree the public welfare may require it.

THEODORE ROOSEVELT (1910)

The theoretical analysis conducted in Chapters 4 to 10 led us to conclude that competitive market allocation can have highly favorable implications for the welfare of society if several important conditions hold. Among these conditions is the requirement that market transactions between two individuals must not have effects on other individuals. If third-party effects are present, the marginal conditions interpreted in Chapter 10 can still be made to hold, by charging the transactors an amount that reflects the unhappiness that each additional unit traded causes to third parties. (If the third-party effects are *positive,* then the appropriate response is to subsidize the transactors in a way that reflects the additional benefits that their activity engenders.) This process of compensating or penalizing the transactors we will call *rationalization* of third-party effects.

If *unrationalized* third-party effects can be shown to exist, then even if the economy is in competitive equilibrium, it cannot be asserted that the Pareto Condition holds. Market allocation may still be working pretty well compared to alternative possible systems, but it is working less well than competitive equilibrium theory predicts. This deficiency compared to a theoretical ideal has led economists to look for ways by which third-party effects can be rationalized. It appears that rationalization in general requires that the transacting parties be given incentives to expand or reduce the scope of their actions, whichever is appropriate.

Third-party effects are increasingly an element in the reckonings of economic policy-makers who are concerned with the problem of finding rules which assign appropriate restrictions, penalties, or compensations as a matter of law. Certain federal bureaus and agencies, with the Environmental Protection Agency as a conspicuous example, are concerned with little else.

Our discussion of third-party effects will for convenience be divided into two main categories: *externalities* and *public goods*. The categories are not exclusive: we will see that a public good type of third-party effect always has externality aspects. Nonetheless, the indicated pair of topics does serve to clarify and focus the discussion; and the division is further made reasonable because government policies that constitute an appropriate response to externalities will usually differ from policies that will be considered when a public goods problem arises.

15.1. EXTERNALITIES

15.1.1. Examples

The topic of externalities is most easily approached through examples, and we will proceed from particular illustration to general definition.

1.   The first example involves two neighbors. Henry is a gardening enthusiast. The grounds surrounding his home are alive with carefully groomed blooms virtually all year round. George is a slacker on yardwork, but he enjoys the display furnished by Henry next door. Thus, George derives positive pleasure from Henry's leisure habit. In addition, the market value of George's home is enhanced because it is next to Henry's attractive garden. If Henry sells his house, and the new owner does not maintain the property to the former high standard, then George's property declines in value. Henry's home sale transaction affects George's sense of well-being, and the value of his property; but neither effect is recognized in the transaction, and it doesn't influence the terms of the transaction. Henry's transaction has *external effects,* which take the form of a *diseconomy* (loss of wealth) to George; and George is not a participant in the transaction.

2.   Isaac owns an orchard, and John, his neighbor, keeps bees. John calculates in a standard way the number of hives that he wishes to maintain: he compares the cost of an additional hive (the value he could obtain somewhere else from the extra work and other resources that another hive would require) to the benefit yielded by an additional hive (the proceeds from the sale of the honey that it would produce). Now, Isaac's fruit is pollinated by John's bees, which conveys substantial value to Isaac—his fruit harvest is greater than it would be without John's bees. The value conveyed to Isaac by the bees is not recognized by John and does not influence John's decision as to how many hives he should keep. Isaac's pollinated orchard is an *external economy* from John's production of honey.

3. A slaughterhouse located on a major river dumps its wastes into the water. A municipality downstream takes it water supply from the river and is forced to install special filtration and purification equipment to offset the filth dumped into the water upstream. The slaughterhouse uses the river as the cheapest way to dispose of its wastes: it uses fewer of *its own* resources by this method than any other method available to it. By transacting in that "economical" way, the slaughterhouse imposes costs on the community downstream. These costs do not affect the amount of waste the slaughterhouse dumps in the river, since they aren't borne by the slaughterhouse. They constitute an *external diseconomy* from meat production in the slaughterhouse, and the diseconomy is borne by the downstream taxpayers. (This illustration has wide applicability: most polution problems involve external diseconomies.)

15.1.2. The Crucial Analytic Property of External Effects

These and similar illustrations have been known to economists for years, and an attempt has been made to identify the elements or characteristics they have in common. The crucial property, it seems, is that in each case the welfare or the income of an individual is affected by a transaction, but in a way that operates *outside* the price system.

To appreciate what is meant by operating outside the price system, we first should notice that all transactions that take place within an economy can influence the welfare or income of any individual *through* the price system. For example, if nobody else wants to buy an electric typewriter and I do, it will be very costly to produce such a typewriter for me; whereas if many people can be persuaded to buy one, the economies of large-scale production will make it less costly to produce the one I buy. There is an effect on my welfare of transactions in the typewriter market, but that effect is felt through the price of the typewriter that I buy. In a similar way, if many people set out to buy vacation and recreation land on one of the choice clear-water lakes in Michigan, then the price of that land will be higher; and my welfare will be lower if I too wish to purchase such a parcel of land. Again my welfare is affected by the crucial variable, market-determined price.

Those effects, operating as they do through the prices that face individuals, differ from the effects that are present in situations involving externalities. The dumping of wastes by the slaughterhouse negatively affected the welfare of citizens in the downstream community *directly* (as well as positively through a lower price of meat) in our third illustration of external effects.

*APPENDIX I
EXTERNAL EFFECTS: FORMAL DEFINITION

In response to the important need to distinguish external effects (those which are not transmitted through the mechanism of market action and the price system) from market

*The material in this section may be too advanced for some introductory coverage.

effects, we introduce the *definition:* a transaction has *external effects* (or *externalities*) if the rate of consumption (or production) by one party to the transaction directly affects the welfare of another person who is not a participant in the transaction.

Mathematically, let the preference ordering of individual α be written

$$U^\alpha = U^\alpha(p_1, p_2, \ldots, p_n).$$

Then α's welfare depends only on the prices of the n goods within the economy, and there are no external effects which impinge on person α. By contrast, suppose

$$U^\alpha = U^\alpha(p_1, p_2, \ldots, p_n; q_i^\beta)$$

where q_i^β is person β's consumption of good i. Or let

$$U^\alpha = U^\alpha(p_1, p_2, \ldots, p_n; Q_j^A)$$

where Q_j^A is firm A's production of good j. In either of these last two cases, a change in a quantity consumed or produced affects α's utility directly, and hence the two cases involve *externalities*.

15.1.3. "Social" versus "Private" Costs: More Terminology

The total of all the costs borne by the individual members of society, which result from a particular consumption or production activity, are called the *social costs* of that activity. The costs borne by transactors who are engaged directly in the activity are called the *private costs* of the activity. Thus, any third-party effects (externalities) which arise out of a production or consumption activity are the difference between private and social costs.

15.1.4. Externalities and the Pareto Condition

If externalities result from any of the transactions within a competitive market system, then market allocation may not fulfill the Pareto Condition. *Within the society,* costs and benefits may be unequal at the margin, if the amount to be consumed and produced is decided upon with regard only for the private costs and benefits of the transacting parties. If by some means or another external effects could be rationalized in market transactions so that social costs and benefits were compared at the margin for each transaction, then externalities would not prevent market allocation from satisfying the Pareto Condition. But to achieve the rationalization of third-party effects by market action, it is necessary that the affected third parties make known the true value that they attach to one unit more (or one unit less) of the good exchanged between the transacting parties; and it is further necessary that the announced value be taken into consideration by the transacting parties, who in response must increase or reduce the amount of the good exchanged. We turn now to the problems of rationalizing external effects.

15.2. EXTERNALITIES AND THE NORMATIVE VIEW OF MARKET ACTION

Our definition of externality poses definite problems for the economic analyst and policy-maker. Quite simply, it is virtually impossible to visualize a market transaction that is completely free of external effects. Certainly, our example of river pollution can reasonably be called a consequential externality. But also consider that when some people exercise their tastes in clothing or hairstyle or house color or mode of entertainment or transport, they may offend others. The choice of occupation (or refusal to be occupied) that some individuals make is a source of concern to others. My cigar offends your nose, your unwashed shirt offends mine. The candy manufacturer contributes to the tooth decay of my neighbor's children, causing me dismay when they smile. (It also causes my dental bills to rise because of the greater resulting demand for dental services. But that effect is not an externality, because the higher price of dental service is felt through market action.) The list of externalities, both consequential and trivial, can be extended almost indefinitely.

Because externalities are so prevalent, two important questions must be faced. What policies can be adopted to prevent consequential externalities from causing unfortunate misallocations of society's resources? By what means can consequential externalities be distinguished from nonconsequential ones? (This second question is taken up in Section 15.4.)

In response to the first question, we will consider four major methods for the control of externalities. They are (1) extension of private contract, (2) reliance on property-protecting provisions of the common law, (3) direct government control, and (4) government-enforced extensions of the price system.

15.2.1. Private Contractual Action and the Common Law

Private contract can be extended by methods that are straightforward and traditional. In the example of the bee keeper and the fruit grower, it is quite likely that the two will join forces, by merger or by a formal or informal contract. If either or both activities are pursued at too small a scale when the mutual external benefits are ignored, then the problem can be rectified through merger or some other form of private contract. The bee-keeping activity then will be carried out at a scale that reflects the gains resulting from pollination, as well as the gains resulting from the sale of honey.[1]

Cattle and Grain: Example. More elaborate cases involving the extension of private contract can be hypothesized. One farmer keeps cattle, a second grows

---

[1]In fact, contractual arrangements between bee keepers and orchard owners always have been the standard practice in the Western United States. See Steven Cheung, "The Fable of the Bees: An Economic Investigation," *Journal of Law and Economics,* 16 (April 1973).

grain. It is not possible to keep the cattle out of the grain at all times: fences are broken down by falling trees, gates are left open by trespassers, and so on. The common law provides that the cattle raiser shall compensate the grain grower for any damage done by the cattle. The incentive effect of this arrangement is only in part the correct one: the cattle raiser is given an incentive to cut down on the scope of his activity: fewer cattle, doubly fenced away from the growing grain, will cause less damage and hence mean lower cost. Thus, the cattle raiser is given a correct kind of incentive. On the other hand, the arrangement provided under the common law may lead the grain grower to grow *too much* grain. He will be compensated for any and all damage caused by cattle, and hence he will plant grain densely, right up to the edge of the field adjoining the cattle raiser's land, where it is extremely likely to be destroyed or where it inhibits the activity of the cattle raiser to an excessive degree. The correct arrangement is one that encourages the two farmers to produce the maximum *combined* value of grain and livestock on their two plots of land. This may mean that *both* farms should be devoted to production of the same good; in more interesting cases, it will mean that the two farms will be split between the two goods, in a way different from the one that prevails under separate private ownership. An arrangement in which the two farms are jointly owned will produce this desired *socially optimal* result. As an alternative to joint ownership, if the cattle raiser could be made to pay damages only *up to* an amount equal to the difference between the socially optimal amount of grain and the amount harvested after cattle damage, then there will be no incentive to plant too much grain—or to raise too few cattle. Finally, the same desirable result could be obtained if the grain grower *bribed* the cattle raiser to cut his herd down to the socially optimal size, and recovered *no* compensation for any damages done by that optimum-sized herd.

Let's pause for a moment to unravel the threads of analysis that run through this example. First, if the number of cattle raised affects the returns realized by the grain grower, then there are externalities in the activity of cattle-raising. However, if the cattle raiser is made liable for *all* damage to grain done by his herd, then there will be externalities from the activity of grain-growing which impinge on the cattle raiser: the returns realized by the cattle raiser then are very much affected by the level of grain-growing activity. For this reason, the common-law solution to the problem is flawed. If the two farms are most profitably devoted to a mixed output of grain and cattle, and if there are no other external effects on parties not previously mentioned, then the socially optimal output from the two farms is the one that yields the highest combined market value of the two crops. Merger provides an easy way to achieve this highest market value, because then the interests of the two growers will not be in conflict. With merger, resources will be used in grain-growing, cattle-raising, and fencing. Fencing will be provided up to the point at which an additional dollar spent will reduce the expected present and future damages to grain by just a dollar, given that an optimal quantity of grain is planted and an optimal number of cattle are raised. The cattle herd will be set at a size at which the selling price of an additional steer just equals the total cost of raising the beast, including the expected cost of damage done to grain. Finally, grain output will satisfy a condition that price received per bushel just equals marginal cost of production, including the cost of foregone opportunity to use the unharvested grain as cattle fodder.

When joint ownership is not possible, then the correct output can be realized by making the stockman pay a penalty for damages equal to the reduction in the value of grain output below the socially optimal amount; or by having the grain grower make a side payment to the stockman sufficient to induce him to cut his herd to the socially optimal size. Either of the two alternative payment arrangements will serve to induce the correct output of both grain and cattle.

A distinguishing feature of this example is that the appropriate outputs and use of resources can be achieved by private contract, as well as through a system of carefully designed and governmentally enforced legal penalties. We next turn to a problem in which no purely private solution is presently possible, partly because no rights of property ownership are defined for some of the resources that enter crucially into the problem. The alternatives that lead to a solution to this next problem all require government action, either in the form of direct controls or in the form of carefully designed financial penalties.

Air Pollution: Example.   Consider the origins of air pollution: almost always it is combustion, in stationary furnaces and boilers, or in mobile boilers or engines. Fuels may be natural gas, petroleum products, coal, or some waste material like garbage or discarded automobile tires. Waste gases such as carbon monoxide, sulfur dioxide and nitrous oxide, and waste particles, are always a product of combustion. Air pollution, then, is simply the dumping of waste into the atmosphere. Like highway littering, air pollution is certainly aesthetically displeasing (and in many parts of the world, it is a hazard to public health at present levels). Also like highway littering, air pollution occurs because it is seen to be such a very cheap means of waste disposal by the man with waste to dispose of: he uses little of his own resources when he gets rid of his waste by polluting the air. There is no economic incentive for him to consider the wishes, tastes, or preferences of others as he decides whether or not to pollute. Indeed, if there are many different sources of pollution, as where much of it is caused by automobile exhaust, a single individual polluter could take a public-spirited stance, and reduce his own polluting activity, without having any measurable effect on the total pollution level.

At present there are no property rights in the air. Hence, there is no possibility of a solution to the pollution problem that involves merger, as there would be if an "air owner" could merge with the many waste owners to decide on how much of the waste should be dumped into the air, how much should be disposed of by other means, and how much should not be created in the first place. (Such a decision would not be easy to calculate even if there *were* property rights in air;

however, in the absence of those rights such a decision is not merely difficult, it is impossible.) The lack of property rights in air also is an obstacle to the kind of common-law solution that emerges when cattle destroy grain. At the present time there is no individual or group with an interest, clearly recognized by law, that is adversely affected by polluting, as there would be if some person or group "owned" the air. It may come to be recognized that individual citizens have a legal and moral right to clean air; and it may even be recognized that some people have an economic interest in clean air as well. However, that view is not yet sufficiently codified; presently it is rare that an interested group can be put together to institute legal action on behalf of clean air. This may be because there is significant uncertainty regarding the benefits to be obtained by taking part in such a legal action; or because it is rare that a single polluter can be identified against whom legal action can be directed; or because it is more convenient to keep on waiting until some other interested party takes the action from which all will benefit. Whatever the reason, it appears at present that private action offers little hope of progress on the problem of air pollution.[2]

There remains the possibility of *direct public* action taken on the basis of specific legislation, rather than on the basis of general property-protecting traditions in the common law. Government, if it has sufficient jurisdiction, can act effectively against pollution, but as has often been seen in practice, the question of jurisdiction is definitely important. Los Angeles County has had laws against rubbish burning for years, but those laws have not protected Angelinos from the stench of burning automobile tires, taken to a neighboring county for disposal. (Even in the absence of adequate jurisdiction, local authorities can help to reduce pollution, but adequate jurisdiction always offers the promise of greater gain, accomplished at less expense.)

15.2.2. Direct Government Controls

A government seeking to reduce atmospheric or water pollution normally proceeds by passing laws against engaging in certain activities (such as burning bituminous coal), or requiring other activities (such as driving only vehicles having specific pollution-control devices attached to the engine). This direct control approach has its drawbacks. First, it is inflexible, and is based on a false implicit premise that everyone should behave in the same way for the sake of the public welfare. The inflexibility of direct legal control may actually cause a reduction in

---

[2]For a brief time beginning in the 1960s, it appeared that progress would be made on problems like air pollution through "class action" lawsuits. An attorney, for example, could bring suit against General Motors or Chrysler on the ground that the exhausts from auto engines endangered the health of a class of people—such as residents of Orange County, for example. In 1974, however, the Supreme Court declared that class action suits could be brought only in instances where all individual members of the injured class could show a clear and substantial loss as a result of the defendant's activity. The Court was concerned that class action suits were a potential instrument of harassment and persecution, and so took steps to constrain their use.

public welfare, as would happen if bituminous coal were the only feasible fuel in the manufacture of some particular important good, and a law were passed against burning it. Society would have to do without the good, and workers employed in manufacture of the good would be deprived of livelihood if the law were stringently enforced. Under those conditions it would be enlightened to exercise a degree of flexible good judgment by granting "exceptions" in enforcement of the law; but such exceptions tend to undermine the law. Hence the hypothetical dilemma: either do away with the important good by doing away with soft-coal burning; or grant an exception to preserve the good, thereby undermining the law and opening the gates for numerous petitions from others who want to be relieved from obeying the law.

Under perfectly realistic circumstances, a direct-control type of law injures some people greatly without producing much benefit for society. Suppose, for example, that a truly effective smog-control device could be added to an automobile engine for $125. A traveling salesman who drives 50,000 miles per year can add such a device to his car, and the device will cost him a quarter of a cent per mile over one year's driving. A little old lady who drives her car 1,250 miles per year, to the hospital for therapy, to the grocery store, and to church, say, would see her costs escalated by ten cents per mile for a year's driving if the law required her to install such a device on her car. The device spares society four hundred times as much pollution from the traveling salesman as from the old lady, yet both are forced to make the same outlay; it is much as if an anti-litter law specified the same penalty for discarding a chewing gum wrapper as for emptying a truckload of garbage.

Moreover, direct controls may at times give the wrong economic incentives. If there is a law requiring a particular kind of smog-control device, then there may be little incentive for auto manufacturers to engage in the search for better devices—they would be gambling that the law would be changed to require the better devices that they find, as well as gambling on being successful. And if they find a device that is much cheaper to produce, but very slightly less effective than the one required by law, then they stand very little chance of obtaining authorization to market their discovery. Conversely, if they find a much more expensive and much more effective device, they may decide to hide the discovery on the ground that the law might require the device; its requirement would force up the price of cars and reduce automobile sales.

15.2.3. Government-Enforced Extensions of the Price System

As an alternative to systems of direct control, the government can adopt financial incentive schemes that are similar in their working to the price system. Suppose, to continue with examples already in use, the law were to set financial penalties in direct proportion, or nearly in direct proportion, to the amount of polluting actually done. For a factory or home, pollution output could be measured in much the same way as water or gas consumption is now measured—by meters. For an automobile the problem is more difficult: the bulk and weight of a metering system might prove to be excessive. However, the amount of pollution caused can be measured more simply, if less accurately, by measuring the amount of fuel used, and by examining the design and condition of the engine in which it is burned. Thus, a tax on fuel could serve as a basis for a system of financial penalties levied against polluting activity. Car types with "cleaner" engines could be charged a lower basic tax rate per gallon than those with "dirtier" engines; similarly, owners of home furnaces that burn coal with low outputs of gaseous and particulate residue would pay a lower rate per ton of coal than would owners of "dirty" heating plants.

Such a procedure brings clean air into the price system, much as if an owner of clean air were charging others for the privilege of dumping into it. The higher the charge, the lower the volume dumped; and the public authority would be authorized to find a price, or a system of prices, that would equilibrate the system at the point where the benefits of less dirt in the atmosphere are just balanced off against the costs. (The costs of less pollution take the form of higher prices for goods which can be produced more cheaply when pollution is not controlled.)

This type of "pollution pricing" scheme has significant advantages, once it is in effect. First, it takes care of the inequities problem that is embodied in the example of the traveling salesman and the little old lady. If the system is structured properly, the salesman will almost surely find it economical to install a pollution control device, while the old lady may find it cheaper to pay the penalty of higher-priced fuel, given the short distance she travels (and given the small amount of polluting she does, that decision may be perfectly acceptable to society).

On the ground of equity, then, the arrangement of "granting a license to pollute" (as some critics of the fee-fine arrangement call it) seems to have advantages over the approach that relies on absolute controls: to achieve the kind of flexibility that fees and fines permit, myriad exceptions would be necessary in a system of direct controls; and the direct-control approach would be very difficult to administer.

Similarly, "pollution pricing" offers efficiency advantages. Large costs are not imposed on individuals in order to obtain small social benefits; the pricing approach permits the same kind of private decision about costs and benefits to the decision-maker that characterizes all market action. It may not be a straightforward matter to set the proper prices on different types and amounts of pollution; but the alternative, of simply outlawing pollution, faces the problem that if it is technically impossible or extremely costly to get rid of the pollution, then avoidance of the law, or loss of valued output, must be the consequence. Avoidance of the law or loss of output may both have more severe consequences for society than would the mix of pollution and valued output that would result from establishing the wrong set of pollution penalties. Almost certainly, in every line of economic activity that results in pollution, the socially most advantageous solution will involve some reduction in pollution levels, obtained at the cost of some reductions in the output of desired goods. The direct-control approach can lead to a solution with no change in the status quo (exceptions granted), or no output (shutdown to meet restrictions). More enlightened direct-control systems would assign pollution quotas to producers in order to avoid shutting them down completely, but that approach does not offer the prospect of fewer administrative problems or errors in rule-making compared to the pricing approach.

In general terms, the problem of pollution control is to measure the benefits of different amounts of pollution reduction, to measure the costs (in terms of goods output lost) of obtaining those reductions, and to specify the pollution quotas or to set the pollution prices that will cause producers to cut back their activity to a point where the gain from less pollution just equals the loss of desired output. Any scheme will prove difficult to establish and to administer, but the pricing approach seems to offer efficiency and flexibility advantages over primitive systems of direct controls, and it appears more feasible to administer than enlightened systems of pollution quotas.

15.2.4. The Problem of Measuring Costs and Benefits

By establishing systems of prices to be charged for engaging in activities that pollute, society's production mix can be made more satisfactory. However, there will inevitably be controversy as to how prices should be set, as exemplified in the Black Mesa problem.

Power demands in the Southwestern United States are steadily increasing, coastal nuclear stations are resisted by environment-conscious activists, and coal-powered or oil-powered generating stations are not favored in urban areas because of the air pollution problem. A solution proposed by the power industry is to locate the power stations in remote and sparsely populated corners of the desert states, where deposits of low-grade coal can be used as fuel. A power station at Black Mesa (near Farmington, New Mexico and Cortez, Colorado) is the first such installation.

Because the smoke from this station is noticeable and incongruous in a previously clean area, the furor that has accompanied its operation has been tremendous. Some angry observers argue that the station would be better located in Los Angeles, where the air is already so dirty that the added smoke would be inconspicuous!

The dilemma, then, is this: is it better to pollute in an area of clean air where few can observe and fewer can feel direct effects, or in an area where many feel the effects, and are spared observing only by the fact that the air is already overpoweringly foul? Are the sensibilities of dozens of sheep-herders and thousands of tourists to be weighed more heavily than the health and comfort of millions of urban dwellers? A difficult question. One good solution, perhaps, would be to raise the price of electrical current, and to use some of the resulting revenues to put smoke-control devices on the desert smokestacks. (The price of electricity could be made high enough to assure that repair of the damage done by the strip-mining of coal can be paid for after the coal supplies are exhausted, as well.) However, consumers of electricity are not strong advocates of high rates, and the power companies also dislike the prospect of a lower quantity demanded, and join in resisting any move toward significant rate increases. Moreover, the currently available techniques of smoke abatement fail to trap sulfur dioxide gas; and that gas accumulates in the atmosphere, sometimes to the extent that when it rains, it rains sulfurous acid. (The sulfur dioxide tends to precipitate out of the atmosphere with particle waste if the smoke discharges aren't "scrubbed.")

The point of this example is that the measurement of external costs isn't straightforward at all, especially when an attempt is made to take aesthetic values into account. The argument as to whether added pollution is more harmful in northeast Arizona or in Los Angeles is easily settled if only economic costs are considered; but when aesthetic criteria are allowed to predominate, the issue becomes imponderable. If the conflict is not resolved on the basis of economic cost and benefit, then it will be resolved by the exercise of political power; instead of gains and losses in dollar terms, the calculation will be of gains and losses in votes. Vote trading does not always lead to better outcomes than dollar trading, even if the criteria are aesthetic. The almost infuriating complexity of this example does serve to explain the appeal of various romantic proposals to reduce population, to reduce living standards, and to reduce resource use. With few (or no) people, such problems would simply go away.

15.3. EXTERNAL EFFECTS IN GOVERNMENT ALLOCATION

The literature on the subject of externalities has always treated the problem as being exclusively associated with private market allocation. This focus is understandable: concern over externalities has always been in large part associated with the question of how well a private market economy can be expected to work, from the standpoint of approaching or fulfilling the Pareto efficiency criterion.

It is worth pointing out, in light of this historical concern, that allocative transactions involving the government are susceptible to the same problems of external effect as are market transactions between private persons. And like private market externalities, governmentally induced external effects may stem from the neglect of property rights, or a too-narrow apportionment of property rights.

A conspicuous example of the kind of problem that can arise is afforded by the way in which inland waterways are maintained in the Chicago area. Until 1960 or so, Lake Michigan was a very clean lake; the growth of algae was remarkably slow, and sewage pollution problems were confined to the coastal area near Milwaukee and one or two other communities which steadfastly refused to treat sewage adequately before dumping it into the lake.

In the middle 1960s, concern over the deteriorating condition of Lake Michigan began to spread. Levels of all major pollutants were increasing rapidly, in part owing to changes in agricultural techniques (more fertilizers and pesticides were being washed into the lake), in part because of the increase of population around the lake, and in part owing to the much heavier shipping traffic that resulted when the St. Lawrence Seaway opened the Great Lakes to ocean-going vessels.

Ship and barge canals move much cargo into and out of Chicago; these canals are the principal link between the Mississippi waterway system and the Great Lakes. These canals also are the route by which Chicago channels its sewage *away from* Lake Michigan. The canals are maintained by the U.S. Army Corps of Engineers. Maintenance involves dredging, as well as repair of banks, locks, docking facilities, etc. The Army engineers, in the interest of "economy," routinely dumped the dredgings from the canal system into Lake Michigan—at some distance from shore, so that the effects were not directly observable, but in such a way that water quality was definitely affected. Considerable time was required to stop this dumping in the lake. Why? Because the cost of other methods of disposing of dredgings from the canals was much higher, and that cost was an item in the Corps of Engineers' budget. Like any person or organization, the Corps was responsive to an economic incentive; it wanted to do as much within its budget as possible. The fact that the Corps was held responsible for keeping the canals open, but not for keeping the lake clean, led to the dumping of waste in the lake: the Corps perceived no organizational "property right" in clean lake water, and no person or organization with such a right was watching out to protect the water.

The example suggests, and the suggestion can be confirmed from many other examples, that government agencies are little different from private individuals or business firms: they must be given the proper economic incentives, or they must have imposed on them the proper restraints, or else they will overlook the third-party effects of their actions.

15.4. CONSEQUENTIAL EXTERNALITIES AND THE NEED FOR INTERVENTION

As is true of so many problems, consciousness of externalities has undoubtedly grown more rapidly than has the problem itself. To suggest that externality problems are probably greatly overdramatized is not to suggest that they are unimportant; there is a large middle ground between the prophecy of doom today at the one extreme and the refusal to acknowledge any problem at all at the other; and somewhere in that middle ground the truth is to be found. We are, in fact, *not* dying like flies because of air or water pollution, or because of the use of chemical pesticides, or because of the careless disposal of radioactive or heavy metal poisons, or because of the mishandling of crude petroleum and its refined products. The occasional incidents when numbers of people are severely physically harmed by those externality-inducing activities are dramatic: we still remember, and Nader's Raiders like to describe, the killer smog that snuffed out dozens of lives in Donora, Pennsylvania in 1948. But the fact that Donora is so memorable illustrates the point—there haven't been any subsequent incidents of remotely comparable impact.

And yet, problems undoubtedly exist which call for responsive action. The world is not at the brink of unresolvable ecological crisis, but we have succeeded in befouling large parts of it and making it less fit or unfit to support human life. Our befouling actions are not all of a potentially lethal character, either. Some people sincerely look upon blaring transistor radios in Chicago parks or thundering snowmobiles in Michigan meadows as a greater danger and menace to human health than nuclear power stations (and they may be correct).

The purpose of this section is twofold: first, to review the important but vague and subjective distinction between consequential and inconsequential externalities; and second, to describe important circumstances under which even consequential externalities do not imply the need to intervene.

15.4.1. Consequentiality

We have already seen that very few social activities fail to have external effects. Human beings are capable of being meddlesome, querulous, and tyrannical in petty ways, and an unrestrained society frequently persecutes the individual who chooses to go his own way in matters of lifestyle. This fact was most vividly recognized and discussed more than a century ago by John Stuart Mill in his classic tract, *On Liberty*. Mill's message, in part, is this: in a pluralistic society, all kinds of external diseconomies will be perpetually emerging from patterns of individual behavior. The society that squelches pluralism to avoid these externalities is acting in a short-sighted and anti-progressive way. For "offbeat" lifestyles sometimes yield enriching new ideas.

There is, then, a need to recognize that social organization implies interaction and contact. Every individual reaps incalculably great gains from social organization; without it there are no hospitals, no symphony orchestras (or rock groups), no libraries, no division-of-labor production with the vast increase in material well-being that it implies, no ceremonial activity of any kind. The price paid by each individual for these and other benefits is by comparison small: (1) he must try to find a useful and satisfying role for himself; (2) he must maintain a degree of respect for the sensibilities and aspirations of other individuals; and (3) he must maintain a degree of good humor and understanding when other individuals thoughtlessly encroach on his own sensibilities and aspirations. The condition (3) is necessary if pluralism is to survive. The alternative seems to be a social order in which rigid rules governing behavior are laid down and enforced by majority action. Even rigid rules cannot eliminate the friction of social interaction; they can only reduce that friction and provide the satisfaction of reprisal if friction becomes excessive.

It is unrealistic, then, to look for ways in which *all* costs and benefits are balanced at the margin of every transaction, which must be done if the Pareto Condition is to hold. For every transaction can be seen to have myriad third-party effects, most of which stem from differences in taste and preference. A system of penalties and compensations that could rationalize the effects of every transaction on every individual in the society is unthinkably unwieldy. *The goal, instead, must be a system in which almost everybody feels reasonably well-treated by the workings of the exchange process in its entirety.* Instead of pursuing the ideal of balancing out the effects of *every transaction* (which we must do to fulfill the Pareto Condition), our rules, penalties, and compensations must be structured with the ideal of leaving *no individual* feeling systematically injured by production and exchange activity throughout the society.

There remains a class of third-party effects that merit consideration for intervention on a case-by-case basis. These are the ones that involve significant *financial* or *physical* (and not merely psychic) costs or benefits to third parties. In any such case where it can be determined that significant overproduction or underproduction of some good results from purely private action, and where private solutions seem to be ruled out by the deficiencies of our legal institutions or technical capabilities, then government intervention may be highly desirable.

15.4.2. When is Intervention Unnecessary?

The first point to emphasize is that there may be significant third-party benefits from some activity, but the full range of those benefits can be realized at a scale of operation that is smaller than the one decided upon by market decision-making. If in the orchard-bees example of Section 15.1.1, Isaac's orchard would receive the full benefit of adequate pollination even if John cut the size of his apiary by half, then no action is necessary, even though external benefits from bee-keeping exist. (In this example, a purely private arrangement could have solved the problem in any case; no intervention would have been necessary, even if Isaac would have benefited from more bees, as was seen.) The amount of bee-keeping and fruit-growing that is decided upon under a private market arrangement need not be too small; the returns from producing honey may be sufficient to induce John to keep the number of bees required to pollinate Isaac's orchard properly. This example shows us: *externalities do not automatically mean that intervention by government, or other remedial action, is necessary to get proper resource allocation.*

An individual who bears costs that arise out of transactions in which he does not participate directly can ask himself: how much would I be willing to pay to obtain complete relief from this burden? How much would I pay for x percent relief? Based on answers to questions of this type, the subjective cost to the individual of the offending activity can be discovered. In fact, calculations of that type are worked out by the market process with regard to a variety of externalities. Real estate located near airports, beneath the flight paths of departing and arriving aircraft, typically has a lower market value than similar real estate in quieter areas of the same city. The home buyer then has a choice: a lower-priced home in a noisy area, or a higher price for "the same" home without the noise. Such an arrangement can approximately equate the marginal costs and marginal benefits for all affected parties as long as the level of noise does not increase in an unforeseen way. The "market solution" to the airport noise problem departs from the ideal in two important respects, though. First, the individuals who owned the property *before* the airport was built all experience a change of property value as soon as the airport flight patterns are established. Those changes cannot be recovered through market action. Second, instead of the ideal pattern in which the transactors who make the noise interact with the third parties in deciding on noise levels, the affected third parties are compensated by all members of the society who pay higher prices for housing away from the noise (higher than the prices would be if there were no airport that affects some housing by noise). Because the society at large compensates the injured third parties and not the makers of noise themselves, there is no incentive for reduction of noise, as there would be under an arrangement in which air passengers paid. However, even though purely private action cannot bring about the Pareto ideal, it does enable homeowners near airports to escape some of the inequity and unpleasantness that would otherwise be their fate.

By much the same kind of arrangement, individuals are compensated for some of the burden imposed by smog. In Los Angeles, whose smog is the most famous, if not the worst, in the world, the density and severity of smog varies in different parts of town. Near the ocean, prevailing breezes reduce the problem. Inland it is much worse. Real estate values reflect the differences in degree of smog—and it doesn't work out that low-income people tend to be driven into the smoggy areas while high-income people reserve the clean air for themselves. For example, San Marino, one of the highest-income communities in America, suffers some of the worst smog. Real estate values there are much lower than in Pacific Palisades, another plush area on the ocean, with comparatively low smog levels. A hundred-thousand-dollar house in San Marino might sell for three times as much in the Palisades, but that amount isn't in your typical poor man's price range. High-income Los Angelinos can choose: lots of house and lots of smog per dollar expended on housing, or appreciably less of both. At a price, they can relieve themselves of smog. The same possibilities are open to lower-income groups as well. People choose their residential location and outlays on housing according in part to how heavy the burden of smog is for them to bear.

15.4.3. Paternalism, or Abatement of Externalities?

Adjustment by choice among differently priced residential locations will probably not strike many readers as an ideal solution to the problem of smog. Yet it is the pattern that must be evaluated and compared to the best that can be accomplished by intervention, when the decision is being made whether to intervene. If successful, intervention enables members of a population to improve their individual situations more markedly than they can accomplish on their own through private action. In the examples of this chapter, we have given detailed consideration to ways that society can adjust or respond to two types of situation involving external effects. These are (1) commercial activities, government or private, that convey significant economic benefits or losses to individuals who are themselves not directly involved in those activities; and (2) activities that convey a substantial loss in environmental amenity. A third class of activity will be discussed now—namely, activities that result in significant hazards to the health and safety of third parties. Certain occupations are very hazardous to health, coal-mining being an example. The greater the risks to health, the higher the wage that is necessary to attract men out of other low-skilled occupations into mining. In effect, a risk premium (or bad-health premium) is paid to miners. Is society then justified, through the mechanism of government, in passing laws to regulate working conditions that affect the health and safety of miners? Many people will defend the enactment of such laws, and nobody can say they are incorrect in doing so. Yet it must be recognized that such laws can be based only in the most tenuous way on an externality argument: we all dislike suffering, and therefore we intervene to prevent it (despite the fact that the sufferers, given a genuine choice in the matter, might prefer suffering at a higher wage to deliverance at a lower one, a choice that is taken away from them if regulatory laws are enforced).

On the other hand, there are genuine and significant externalities that can arise out of mining activity. Mining practices may affect the safety and property of persons living in buildings above the mine tunnels, in which case there is a clear and unambiguous externality argument on which to base government intervention: laws that prescribe timbering and roofing of tunnels to prevent cave-ins and surface subsidence will serve the goal of efficiency in resource use.

Similarly, laws compelling inoculation against disease can be justified on the ground that they protect third parties against unwanted illness: an inoculated person does not carry polio, diphtheria, or smallpox, and hence he is less of a hazard to his community than an uninoculated person. On the other hand, if an individual can transmit a disease despite inoculation, then the externality argument for compulsory inoculation is much weaker. In that case, if we force inoculation, it is because we dislike suffering and seek to prevent it. There is a *paternalistic* impulse underlying the removal of choice from an individual who is required to enter into a transaction he might, whether rationally or not, prefer to avoid. Paternalism is simply the view that individuals are incapable of making choices of certain types on their own behalf. Paternalistic legislation can take various forms: compulsory church attendance (as in seventeenth-century New England); the licensing of physicians (to protect us from the evil of abundant but imperfect medical care); restrictions on the sale of such varied substances as marijuana and chemical sugar substitutes (to protect us from dangers, sometimes remote, of inflicting injury upon ourselves); and many others.

We turn now to the important topic of public goods.

15.5. PUBLIC GOODS

15.5.1. Attributes of Public Goods

First, suppose I transact for a good which I value, and my purchase of the good conveys significant external benefits to you. Second, suppose that when I use the good, the benefit that you receive from it is in no way diminished. Third, suppose I cannot obtain any recompense from you in return for the benefit that my purchase of the good brings to you. If all three of those conditions hold, the good that we are discussing is a *pure public good*.

Two properties, in addition to conveying external benefits, define a public good. These properties, called *nonexhaustibility in consumption* and *nonexclusivity,* need to be explored, with the help of examples.

Nonexhaustability in consumption. If I arrange to have a television broadcast signal beamed to my home, I can receive that broadcast and thereby use it; but the broadcast will be there for you to receive and use, also. My use of it in no way diminishes or interferes with the benefit that you can obtain from it. In fact, everyone within range of the broadcast signal can tune in and use it, also. The cost of providing the broadcast is the same whether only I receive it or everybody within its range uses it: the marginal cost of providing the broadcast service to additional users within its range is *zero.*

No good is literally nonexhaustible in consumption. A highway can accommodate additional users at no cost when the number of users is small, but highways become congested. An anti-missile defense system diminishes the threat of attack by a hostile foreign power, and thus protects my home in San Diego and your home in Tallahassee to the same degree; but in the event of an attack, one of us may suffer if the marginal defense emplacement has been assigned to the other's home area.

Nonexclusivity. Consider the problem of providing personal security in a society with no governmentally funded police. If my neighbor should hire a watchman or buy a barking dog, my property would be made more secure by his transaction. I need not compensate him for the benefits he would thereby render to me: I get a "free ride" from his purchase. Symmetrically, should I transact, he would stand to benefit. Under those circumstances we might find ourselves playing a kind of game, each waiting for the other to provide the desired service, and the possibility faces us that the desired good will be obtained in less than the optimum amount unless we can get together to arrange how much each of us shall provide.

Consider, too, parks in urban areas. The city of London is dotted with many lovely privately owned parks, gardens, and crescents. Each is fenced off against public use, but homes facing on the parks enjoy a higher value as a result of their location; and passersby enjoy the opportunity for a stroll in streets adjoining the parks. The value realized by a park's owner stems from his enjoyment in his own use and any proceeds he can obtain by renting privileges of use to others. However, those who pay no rent also can in some degree enjoy benefits from the park's presence, and there is no means whereby the owner can collect from those who are unwilling to pay and who nevertheless enjoy limited benefits from the parks. Were it possible to collect compensation for all benefits they render, such parks would be larger and more numerous: it would be economically worthwhile to devote a larger part of the city's land resources to the provision of parks, if "free riders" could be eliminated and all who benefit from the parks could be made to pay in proportion to benefits received. The institution of public ownership of urban park properties and the provision of park amenities at public expense can be justified on the ground that such parks are a public good.

Finally, we look at education. A literate population conveys enormous benefits to nearly everyone: the possession of reading and writing skills by one's fellow citizens makes commerce and communication easier, the society wealthier, and life pleasanter. An educated person cannot prevent his fellow citizens from deriving benefits from his own education. Education is a good that has the characteristic of nonexclusivity. The provision of education at public expense, at least up to the level at which a working level of literacy has been transmitted, and sometimes far beyond that level, is advocated on the ground that education is a public good.

15.5.2. Governmental Provision of Public Goods

Education embodies both properties of a public good in large degree. It is nonexhaustible in use, and the user cannot exclude third parties from benefit. Does it follow that it is necessary to provide education at public expense because education is a public good? Some type of intervention is justified if *too little* education would be undertaken under purely private arrangements, but there are less drastic ways to intervene than by the outright provision of the good. The State could, as one possibility, simply require that all capable citizens attain some specified level of literacy through any private arrangement that suits them. The economic rewards to an individual from education are substantial and widely publicized and understood; and it may well be that these rewards are sufficient to assure that people will voluntarily obtain enough education so that the desired state of universal literacy is realized. The question of what amount of education is "enough" or "too little" from a social standpoint, of course, must be settled by social consensus. If the attainment of a newspaper-reading level of literacy is a satisfactory minimum, then it may not be true that external benefits would be lost without subsidy. On the other hand, if it is the view that society benefits when every individual absorbs all the education he is intellectually equipped to handle, and anything less is not enough, then some degree of subsidy will surely be required. For people will need to be paid to go on learning in the face of opportunities to work, which are increasingly available as the level of education already absorbed increases. The view that everyone should be educated to the limit of his ability to absorb knowledge is a tempting one, at least superficially, and it no doubt underlies much of the popular support for public funding of education that can be observed almost everywhere. Yet the possibility exists that much of the large volume of resources used in education, which is provided at government expense, are being wasted. The phenomenon of the shoestore salesman who holds an MA in international relations from someplace like CCNY or UCLA is increasingly frequently encountered. Is the economic system "bad" because a man capable of earning such a degree is selling shoes for a living? Or is it that the act of intervening to provide an unused and perhaps unusable education to such a man was misguided and wasteful?

Some readers will be quick to point out, in response to those questions, that the educated shoestore clerk leads a more satisfying and rewarding life as a result of having been highly educated. We can grant that this is indeed a possibility; unused education then is viewed as a form of consumption good, like symphony concerts or fireworks displays. The argument that third parties are benefited has been abandoned, and with it any pretense that unused education is a public good.

Finally, there is the view that highly educated shoestore clerks make "better citizens" than less educated shoestore clerks, and hence their education should be subsidized. That argument is simply an expression of the view, thinly disguised, that the ideology and values of the educated class is superior to the ideology and values of the working class. That view, of course, is more sympathetically held among assistant professors on the local university campus than among apprentice steam-fitters at the local power plant.

Turn, now, to television broadcasting. There seem to be three ways to provide this public good: "public television," or governmentally financed and governmentally controlled broadcasts; "commercial television," the prevalent system in the U.S.; and "pay television," an arrangement whereby viewers would be charged for television broadcasts that they actually receive. Much interest has centered on the discussion of which arrangement is "best."

Suppose the *content* of broadcasting would be the same regardless of the arrangement that is chosen: the same number of hours of the same material would be broadcast, regardless of mode of payment. Then public TV is a clear best choice: commercial TV has the defect of unnecessarily making people pay for TV broadcasts not because they view them but because they buy the advertisers' products; and pay TV has the two defects of making viewers pay for a good that can be supplied to them at zero marginal cost, and using resources to measure the amount of TV viewed in each household.

It is likely, however, that the content of TV broadcasting would vary markedly among the three alternative arrangements. The commercial arrangement that we now have is heavily weighted toward securing the largest possible audience, because it is assumed that the more widely advertising messages are viewed, the more of the advertised good will be sold. This leads to a broadcast schedule of six bogus dramas on the same night, all of which fantasize on such professions as spying or detective work. Instead of consumer sovereignty, the present system is a modified form of majority tyranny, with the modifications due to the grace of some advertisers, the presence of one publicly supported network, and the arbitrary rules in program content laid down by the Federal Communications Commission, a government agency which regulates television broadcasting.

Public TV might attempt to achieve the ideal of consumer sovereignty: a public broadcasting authority might be willing to broadcast all legally permissible material that can find an audience willing to cover the costs of its transmission. But as is true of all allocative activities by government, it is hard for the agency to see how much value the public attaches to a little more of one type of activity, compared to a little more of another: there is no direct feedback from the consumer to the producer. And it is also true that funds for TV broadcasting may be obtained from the same logrolling-porkbarreling legislative activities that finance all other government projects. (Although this need not happen. In Britain and other Western European nations, broadcasting is paid for largely by an annual tax levied against TV sets.) Nonetheless, it must be noted that if broadcast funding becomes a matter of politics, then broadcast content may also become a matter of politics.

Pay TV would undoubtedly be most expensive to the chronic television viewer. All viewers would have to underwrite the added costs of measuring their viewing activity; and individual programs would be priced to the viewer not according to how much it costs to include him in the viewing audience, but instead according to how much he is willing to pay to watch. The main argument favoring pay TV is that it can best serve the diversity of tastes and interests that are found in the population at large. If one hundred thousand people nationally are willing to pay a dollar each to watch a Shakespeare drama, or an hour of information on how to grow better camellias, then it may pay to broadcast those programs. The vast majority will still have conventional programming available at fifteen cents an hour (a price, come to think of it, that might be high enough to turn away many of the viewers of numerous of today's shows).

We have looked at two goods, education and television broadcasting. Both embody the conditions that define public goods. It may be that society is well-served by the government provision of education at all levels, and would be better served if government provided TV broadcasts as well. However, neither proposition has been fully demonstrated; the fact that both goods are ''public goods'' doesn't automatically clinch the case for their provision at public expense. Finally, however, we should notice that if private producers of education and of TV broadcast signals could not exclude consumers from partaking of their output, then taxation might be the only mechanism whereby the costs of production could be covered.

15.5.3 The Demand for a Public Good

The third Nobel laureate in economics (and most successful textbook author), Paul A. Samuelson, has been influential in stimulating the thought of economists on the subject of public goods. Samuelson has shown that the demand for a public good can be analyzed formally in terms that are strikingly different from the analysis that pertains to ''ordinary'' goods—ones that do not have the nonexhaustibility property. Suppose that in a two-man society, the two single individual demands for a public good are as shown in Figure 15.1. Individual A's demand curve, D_A, shows the amounts he would consume at different prices of the good, or the amounts he would willingly pay for different quantities of the good; sim-

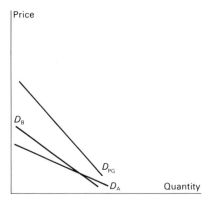

FIGURE 15.1.   The demand for a public good, calculated by *vertical* summation of individual demand curves.

ilarly, individual B's curve, D_B. But whereas the society's demand for ordinary, exhaustible goods is found by adding up all the quantities that each individual demands at every price, the society's demand for a public good is found by adding the *prices* that individuals would each be willing to pay for different quantities of the good. In Figure 15.1, D_{PG} is the demand in the two-person society for a public good, found by *vertical* summation of the individual demands (adding up of prices for different given quantities).

Thus, suppose the public good in question is *national defense*. If individual A is willing to pay $1000 to have "100 units of defense" provided, and if individual B will pay $1200 for that same amount, then the two-person society at large should willingly pay up to $2200 for that amount of defense. A's "consumption" of defense doesn't exhaust the good; the same 100 units that A consumes are available for B's protection as well.

The chief virtue of Samuelson's definition, based on nonexhaustibility, is that the foregoing difference between "ordinary" and public goods in the conditions of society's demand is made clear. The chief drawback of his definition, it would seem, is that there is no such thing as a "pure" public good. The cost of extending any service to an additional user, be it TV broadcasting, police protection, or defense, is never zero at all levels of production. The problem of providing the correct amount of a public good is best approached not by consulting a demand curve that is composed by vertical summation of individual demands, in the manner shown in the figure; rather, it is best approached by asking: if an additional unit of the good is provided, beyond the amount arranged for through private transactions, who benefits, and in what amount? Based on the answer to that question, a policy based on intervention by government can be designed for providing the good and for collecting the revenues to pay for it. Finally, we note that unless private transactors in the good have difficulty in excluding benefited third parties, purely private arrangements may lead to the provision of optimal quantities of the good .

*APPENDIX II
MORE ON CATTLE AND GRAIN

The purpose of this appendix is to provide an explicit analysis of the cattle-grain problem that was treated in Section 15.2.1 of this chapter.

Notation: let

C be the size of the cattle herd

G be the "amount of grain planted," that is, the yield at harvest that could be anticipated in the absence of cattle damage

F be the amount of fencing (efficiently) installed

P be the market price per unit for cattle

   p be the market price per unit for grain
$x(C)$ be the cost of raising a herd of size C for market: $x' = dx/dC > 0$
$y(G)$ be the cost of raising a grain crop of size G for market: $y' = dy/dG > 0$
$z(F)$ be the cost of installing and maintaining fencing in amount F: $z' > 0$
$g(C,F,G)$ be the amount of grain actually harvested, when G is planted, the neighbor's herd is of size C, and F units of fencing are in place.

The maximum social benefit is obtained from the two farms when the combined sales revenues, less the costs of production, are highest. Thus, the net social benefit function is

$$P \cdot C + p \cdot g(C,F,G) - x(C) - y(G) - z(F)$$

and the conditions that must be satisfied if net social benefits are to be at a maximum are (letting $\partial g/\partial C$ be denoted g_C)

$$0 = P + pg_C - x'$$
$$0 = pg_F - z'$$
$$0 = pg_G - y'.$$

Given some obvious and innocuous conditions on the function g (in particular, $1 > g_G > 0$; $g_F > 0$; $g_C > 0$), we will be able to find values G^*, C^*, and F^*, which simultaneously satisfy the necessary conditions.

The common law solution, whereby the herder pays for all damage done by his herd, will not yield the social optimum solution (G^*,C^*,F^*).

Under the common law, the grain grower's objective is

$$\underset{G}{\text{Max}} \ \{p \cdot G - y(G)\}.$$

He certainly has no incentive to install any fence to protect against his neighbor's cattle. His optimal choice of G will satisfy

$$0 = p - y';$$

and in light of the conditions $g_G < 1$ and $y' > 0$, his planting will exceed G^*.

The herder's objective is

$$\underset{C,F}{\text{Max}} \ \{P \cdot C - x(C) - z(F) - p[G - g(C,F,G)]\}.$$

His first order conditions will be formally the same as in the social optimum case; but with the grower planting more than G^*, and with the second partial derivatives

$$g_{CG} < 0, \qquad g_{FG} > 0$$

(another obvious pair of conditions), the herder's solution will have C smaller than C^*, and F larger than F^*. Too much grain will be grown, too much fencing installed, and too few cattle raised.

Suppose, instead of the common law solution, the herder is compelled to pay the grower in the amount

$$p[g(C^*,F^*,G) - g(C,F,G)].$$

The first term in the brackets is the grain harvest that would be obtained if the optimum herd size and fencing are used in conjunction with the grower's chosen amount of planted G. The second bracketed term is the actual harvest.

The grower's objective then is

$$\underset{G}{\text{Max}} \{p \cdot g(C^*,F^*,G) - y(G)\}:$$

the first order condition that G must satisfy is

$$pg_G \big|_{\substack{C^* = C \\ F^* = F}} - y' = 0;$$

but that is precisely the condition satisfied in the social optimum solution. Thus, the grower's choice will be G^*. With that choice, the herder's objective is

$$\underset{C,G}{\text{Max}} \{P \cdot C - x(C) - z(F) - p[g(C^*,F^*,G) - g(C,F,G^*)]\}.$$

His first-order conditions are

$$P - x' + pg_C = 0$$

$$pg_F - z' = 0$$

and with $G = G^*$, his solution will be (C^*,F^*). In effect, this penalty scheme modifies the common law approach to convey proper incentives to the grower; his response then in turn conveys proper incentives to the herder.

As a final alternative, suppose the law imposes *no* penalty whatever on the herder for any damage that his cattle might do. The herder's objective then is

$$\underset{C}{\text{Max}} \{P \cdot C - x(C)\}.$$

He has no incentive to install fencing. His optimal herd will be of size C^0.

Suppose the grower offers the herder a bribe of size B to cut the herd to size C^b. The grower will also install fencing. If the herd is not cut to size C^b (or smaller) no payment changes hands.

The herder's objective then is

$$\underset{C}{\text{Max}} \left\{ P \cdot C - x(C) + \begin{cases} B \text{ if } C \leqslant C^b \\ 0 \text{ if } C > C^b \end{cases} \right\}$$

Without the bribe, the herder's net revenue is

$$PC^0 - x(C^0).$$

Thus, to be compelling, the bribe must satisfy

$$B \geqslant P(C^0 - C^b) - x(C^0) + x(C^b).$$

With a bribe of that size paid, the grower can control the herd size, and C^b then in effect becomes a variable in the grower's objective function:

$$\underset{G,F,C^b}{\text{Max}} \{p \cdot g(C^b,F,G) - y(G) - z(F) - B(C^b)\}$$

where the last term in the objective is

$$B(C^b) = P(C^0 - C^b) - x(C^0) + x(C^b).$$

Thus, his objective is

$$\underset{G,F,C^b}{\text{Max}} \{PC^b + p \cdot g(C^b,F,G) - x(C^b) - y(G) - Z(F) - Q\}$$

where Q is the constant

$$Q = x(C^0) - PC^0.$$

The grower's objective differs from the net social benefit function only by a constant term: hence the optimal values will be $G = G^*$, $F = F^*$, $C^b = C^*$. With this bribe scheme, the outputs differ from the social optimum only by a transfer payment from the grower to the herder: outputs of goods and uses of resources are identical.

APPLICATIONS AND EXTENSIONS

1. Do you think that externalities are likely to be viewed as an important problem in a holistic society? Focus on the following (not always hypothetical) cases, and identify "externality" elements that impinge on the preferences and tastes of other individuals.

    (a) A Chinese physician prefers to continue treating patients, rather than go to work on a collective farm for a year. He tries to enlist his patients to plead on his behalf.

    (b) A Moscow student sells a typewritten copy of an outlawed Solzhenitzyn novel to a friend.

    (c) An American male, born in 1950, buys a bus ticket to Canada rather than report for basic training in the U.S. Army in 1969.

    (d) An elderly widow, living in rural British Columbia (a province in Canada), is arrested for giving milk from her cow to a neighbor, in exchange for a load of firewood. She has violated a law which requires that all persons in the dairy industry be licensed.

2. It is frequently asserted that the best example of a pure public good is a lighthouse: it embodies the properties of nonexhaustibility in consumption, and nonexclusivity, to a high degree.

    (a) Can you think of a better example of a public good?

    (b) Do you agree that the nature of the "lighthouse industry" is such that profit-motivated lighthouse builders and operators will not be able to provide service on a market basis, and that the state *must* provide this service? [If you do, read Ronald Coase, "The Lighthouse in Economics," *Journal of Law and Economics* 17(October 1974).]

3. Oil spills by offshore drillers, in California and Louisiana, have been a recurrent issue since 1970 or so. Describe

(a) a system of direct control that best protects "the public interest" against the two dangers of shoreline pollution on the one hand, and oil "shortages" on the other.

(b) Describe how these two problems might be reconciled by a governmentally enforced extension of the price system.

BIBLIOGRAPHICAL NOTE

Francis Bator, "The Anatomy of Market Failure," *Quarterly Journal of Economics,* (August 1958), reviews sources and types of externality, discusses an important part of the literature, and states the widely believed, but logically flawed, syllogism:

—If private activity leads to fulfilment of the Pareto Condition, there should be no intervention.
—Private activity does not do so, therefore
—There should be intervention.

Ronald Coase, "The Problem of Social Cost," *Journal of Law and Economics,* 3(October 1960), establishes two important propositions. First, under conditions of competition, transfers of property rights and legally imposed penalties and rewards can move society toward fulfillment of the Pareto Condition. Enforcement through the courts is frequently sufficient; it is not necessary for the government to take a direct role as producer or consumer in order to rationalize third-party effects. Second, the courts in England and the United States, in their findings on various property damage and nuisance cases tried under common law, returned verdicts that seemed to be guided by a concern to find the maximum general welfare rather than by any mechanistic rules.

L. E. Ruff, "The Economic Common Sense of Pollution," *The Public Interest,* 19(Spring 1970), contains a proposal for pricing institutions to control air pollution.

Paul A. Samuelson, "Diagrammatic Exposition of A Theory of Public Expenditure," *Review of Economics and Statistics,* 37(November 1955), presents a classic exposition of the importance of nonexhaustibility in consumption. All these papers are accessible to any persistent reader who has gotten this far through this book.

CHAPTER SIXTEEN

Wages
and Wage-Setting
Institutions

Creation's cry goes up on high
from age to cheated age:
"Send us the men who do the work
For which *they* draw the wage!"

RUDYARD KIPLING (1903)

16.1. MARGINAL PRODUCTIVITY

16.1.1. Payments for Productive Inputs

In the "idealized market economy" of Part Two, producers hire additional units of an input if the value of the input's marginal product is greater than the input price. In that idealized regime input resource owners are given price signals. The owners' responses to those signals—directing their resources to the highest bidders—result in the equalization of resource productivities across all possible uses.

The marginal productivity rule, then, is the basis on which *distribution* is accomplished in the idealized market economy. By distribution we do not mean the transportation of goods to markets, but rather the apportionment of the value of output among productive resources—the answer to the "for whom" question, in short.

The total value of output from any productive undertaking is equal, by definition, to the sum of wages, rents, interest payments, and profit. *Wages* are payments to labor. *Rents* are payments to resources in completely inelastic supply, such as land. *Interest* is payment to capital. And *profit* is residual value, positive or negative, that is kept by the organizer of productive activity after he has paid wages, interest, and rents.

Those traditional names for payments to productive inputs are clearcut in meaning as long as we remain within the theoretical framework of the idealized market system; but in the analysis of real-world problems there is some difficulty, frequently, in deciding the character of particular resources, and hence, in deciding what the returns to those resources should be called. For example, a human being's labor is paid a *wage;* but educated or specially skilled human beings are paid more highly. Some analysts have noticed that the process of acquiring skills is very much like the process of accumulating and assembling capital: both processes take time and involve a reduction in consumption "today" in order to generate a larger earnings stream "tomorrow." Hence, those analysts have suggested that the payments to skilled labor in part is an ordinary wage, in part an interest payment to "human capital," or capital embodied in a human being. Such issues should be recognized as purely terminological. The theory of market processes predicts that any resource, regardless of which category or categories it is fitted into, will be paid an amount equal to the value of its marginal product; and that prediction serves as a basis for the analysis of real-world systems. Theory tells us, for example, that when wages in a firm rise (as a result of union negotiations, say), the likely effect is a substitution of other inputs for labor.

In addition to such descriptive and analytical use of the marginal productivity theory, there has been a tendency to regard the theory as a *norm* or guide to what returns to productive inputs *should* be. That normative question is an explosively emotional one, and marginal productivity does not do much to defuse it. The emotional content of the theory is derived from the wide range of incomes in any society: very poor families may subsist on a tenth of the average income level, year in and year out, while very rich families enjoy incomes thousands of times above the average. Even if we agree to put these extreme cases aside, however, marginal productivity does not have much to say regarding how people *should* be compensated for the labor they expend or the productive resources they own. The theory merely predicts the outcome of a competitive market process.

16.1.2. The Firm's Demand for Labor Services

The question of resource demand can be approached formally. We begin by studying the demand of a single producer for a resource, and turn to market demand. For simplicity, we will assume that a producer uses two resources, labor and capital, in producing a single type of output.

Let

$$y = f(K, L)$$

be the producer's production function: the rate of output y depends on the rates of (efficient) use of capital K and labor L. The *marginal physical product* of labor is determined as follows. Let the rate of use of labor be increased by a small amount ΔL. Then output will change by some amount Δy:

$$y + \Delta y = f(K, L + \Delta L).$$

The *marginal physical product of labor* is the ratio of the change in the output rate to the change in the rate of input use:[1]

$$MPP_L = \Delta y/\Delta L.$$

If the producer's output good sells competitively at a price of P, then that price, multiplied by marginal physical product of labor, yields the *value of the marginal product of labor:*

$$VMP_L = P \cdot MPP_L$$

VMP_L measures the increase of the producer's sales revenue rate when he increases his rate of use of the labor input by a small amount.

If labor can be hired competitively at a wage rate w, it will pay the firm to choose the employment rate for which

$$w = VMP_L.$$

The outlay w on the marginal worker is just equal to VMP, the value realized by hiring him. Thus, if we know what the VMP of labor is at every employment rate, we know what the firm's employment rate will be once we are told what w is. In Figure 16.1, if we are told that the wage rate is w_1, we can immediately "read off" the firm's optimal employment rate L_1.

What will the VMP curve generally look like? The negative slope in Figure 16.1 is a consequence of the *law of diminishing returns.*

The "law of diminishing returns," which we met in Chapter 8 tells us that the marginal physical product of any resource will eventually decline: beyond some value L^*, as L increases, the ratio $\Delta y/\Delta L$ gets smaller. The law of diminishing returns, then, predicts that the higher the firm's employment rate rises, the lower the value of labor's marginal product will be. Thus, a lower wage is necessary to induce a higher desired level of employment. The value of labor's marginal product defines the firm's demand for labor as a function of the wage rate, so long as the price of the firm's output doesn't change with changes in the wage rate.

The market demand for labor is simply the horizontal sum of all the individual firm demand curves: at any wage rate, the quantities demanded by each employer are added to determine total quantity demanded at that wage rate.

---

[1]MPP_L is the partial derivative of f with respect to L:

$$MPP_L = \partial f/\partial L = f_L.$$

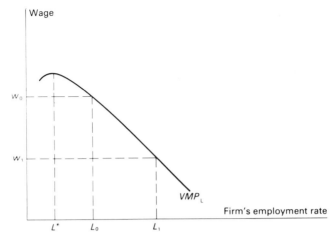

FIGURE 16.1. **The relation between wages and employment in the firm, determined by marginal productivity.**

16.1.3. Market Demand for Labor Services

The market demand for labor will *not* be simply the horizontal sum of all individual firm VMP_L curves. Suppose wages fall from w_0 to w_1 in Figure 16.1, for example. The value of labor's marginal product, computed by multiplying the marginal physical product of labor by the current price of the firm's output, indicates that employment should increase from L_0 to L_1 in the illustrated firm.

But if the wage decline brings about a similar employment increase in all firms, the total marketed output of the illustrated firm's product may be significantly higher; there will be a rightward shift in market supply, and hence a lower market price for the firm's output. That drop in price causes a downward shift in the VMP_L curve as shown in Figure 16.2.

Hence, the employment increase in response to lower wages will be smaller than indicated in Figure 16.1. The downward shift in VMP_L, caused by the drop in price of the firm's output, leads to a new employment rate of $L_1{}^*$, as shown in Figure 16.2. VMP_L^0 is the value of marginal product when the wage rate is w_0, VMP_L^1 when the wage rate is w^1; and D_L is the firm's component share of the market demand for labor. The market demand for labor is the sum of D_L curves across all firms.

16.1.4. Demand Elasticity for a Productive Resource

What affects the elasticity of demand for a productive resource like labor? It will depend on several things:

   1. *The elasticity of demand for labor (or any input) depends directly on the elasticity of demand for the good in which the input is used.* The more elastic the demand for

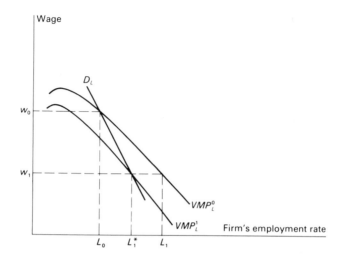

**FIGURE 16.2.   The firm's demand for labor, taking account of price
changes in output.**

the final good, the easier it will be for producers of the final good to pass input price increases along to customers, and the more willing the producers will be to go on using the input in the face of price rise. If final output demand has infinite elasticity, there is no VMP_L shift of the type shown in Figure 16.2.

2. *The elasticity of demand for labor (or any input) depends inversely on the elasticity of substitution with other resources in production.* If other resources can readily be substituted for labor, then a rise in wages will induce a large drop in labor demand.

3. *The elasticity of demand for labor (or any resource) depends inversely on the elasticity of* supply *of other productive inputs.* The less the price of another input rises when its usage rate is increased, the cheaper it will be to substitute that other input for labor. Hence, a highly elastic supply of capital tends to make the demand for labor more elastic: a given increase in wages will cause a larger substitution of capital for labor when the price of capital rises very little compared to when the price of capital rises a lot.

4. *The elasticity of demand for labor (or any resource) will increase, the larger the wage bill (or the total outlay for the resource) is, relative to total costs of production.* The smaller the outlay for a resource is relative to total production cost, the larger the increases in the price of the resource that can be tolerated without significantly affecting total cost.

16.2. LABOR SUPPLY

In an idealized competitive market system, an individual worker's decision regarding the amount of time he wants to work will not depend on the similar decisions of other workers. His decision will depend on the wage that he can command and on the value that he attaches to an additional hour of leisure. His marginal tradeoff will be based on the decision: is another hour of leisure worth more than the goods and pleasures that can be bought with the wage earned in another hour of work, or not?

Figure 16.3 illustrates his choice. The individual's preferences for different combinations of *leisure* (whose quantity is marked along the horizontal axis) and *money* (which can be used to buy goods and which is marked along the vertical axis) are graphed; indifference curves from that preference ordering are drawn.

The higher the wage rate, the larger the worker's choice set: the lines w^1, w^2, w^3... are the goods-leisure budget constraints at successively higher wage rates.

At different wage rates the optimal work-leisure choice will vary along the offer curve, labeled OC. Where OC is negatively sloped, the quantity of leisure diminishes as the wage rate rises: at the wage rate w^2, for example, l^2 hours of leisure and $(24 - l^2)$ hours of work are chosen each day. At the lower wage rate w^1 the consumption of leisure is greater than at w^2. The offer curve OC may also be positively sloped over some interval of wage rates.

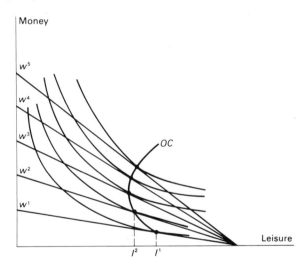

FIGURE 16.3. "Offer curve" illustrating the work-leisure choice at different wage rates.

A positively sloped OC curve has an interesting implication: it implies that as his wage rises, the quantity of labor that the individual supplies will fall. Thus, with an OC curve as drawn in Figure 16.3, the supply curve of labor will have the backward-bending form shown in Figure 16.4. An individual whose supply curve of labor is backward-bending is in effect saying that at high wage rates he prefers to take some of the additional income that a higher wage implies in the form of leisure.

The market supply of labor will be composed of the horizontal sum of all individual labor supply curves, just as the market supply of a good is the horizontal sum of marginal cost curves.

16.3. DIFFERENT "GRADES" OF LABOR

The equilibrium of the labor market determines the wage rate in the economy. As anyone will recognize, that statement is a bit of an oversimplification, as far as description of reality is concerned. There are many wage rates, because there are many different types of employment. If it were possible for any worker to hold down any job in the economy, and if the labor market were sufficiently fluid so that workers could bid for each other's jobs, then the differences that would be observed in wage rates would depend on differences in the degree to which jobs are risky or safe, exciting or dull, pleasant or disgusting, ennobling or demeaning. As it happens, however, not every worker has the capacity to hold down every job.Therefore, wage rates reflect not only working conditions but the supply of and demand for certain types of ability and skill as well. In the long run, the element of skill or training should disappear as an influence on the structure of prevailing wage rates—wage premiums paid for special skills will induce workers to acquire those skills; and the increase in supply of workers possessing the skills will make the wage premiums disappear. In the long run in a competitive labor market, then, differences in compensation among individuals would be due to differences in working conditions and differences in native ability. But we do not have competitive labor markets.

16.4. DEPARTURES FROM COMPETITION IN THE LABOR MARKET

16.4.1. Minimum Wage Laws Revisited

In Chapter 4, the minimum wage was presented as an example of applied supply and demand analysis. There it was demonstrated that in a labor market that is otherwise competitive, the effect of a minimum wage is to maintain a gap between labor supply and labor demand: the minimum wage, if it is high enough to affect existing job categories, practically assures unemployment. In returning to the topic now, there are two issues to be considered. We first want to consider the effect of a high minimum wage, compared to a low minimum wage in an economy with many different grades of labor. We then want to consider the effects of a minimum wage under the peculiar condition of a labor market with only one employer.

A high minimum wage will have precisely the effects depicted in Chapter 4, Section 4.3.4. It can be judged to be high if it affects a substantial portion of the labor force, not just a few scattered workers or job categories of extremely low

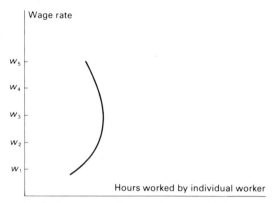

FIGURE 16.4.   Backward-bending supply curve of labor: as wages rise, consumption of leisure eventually increases.

skill. The United States has had a legal minimum wage since 1937. At no time has it been high enough to affect large numbers of workers.

What, then, are the effects of a low minimum wage? First, it must be noted that the effects, if any, will be felt by very low-wage workers. Persons of low skill, whose marginal productivities are below the minimum wage rate, will be laid off. Perhaps more important, persons of ability but deficient in training will find it more difficult to obtain on-the-job training as a result of minimum wage laws. Because the minimum-wage makes on-the-job training at a low wage more difficult to obtain, persons of higher skill face less competition and hence can look forward to higher wages. Thus, minimum wage laws may be a significant impediment to workers with the ability and desire to move out of low-skill categories. The law makes the lines between different "grades" of labor harder to cross.

The second topic is both more cheerful to relate and more difficult to follow. We will see that if we can locate a monopsony (single-buyer) labor market, we will have found an instance in which a minimum wage is unambiguously beneficial if it is set intelligently. A monopoly employer, or monopsonist, is conscious of the effect that his employment rate can have on the wage rate he pays. He will employ fewer workers than he would want to hire if he were just one of many employers. Moreover, the monopsonist pays a lower wage than would prevail under a competitive labor market regime.

In Figure 16.5 the demand curve D for labor services is the value of labor's marginal product in the employing firm. The supply curve S of labor services reflects the willingness of the labor force to give up leisure and furnish additional man-hours at different wage rates. If the employer wants to know how much his wage bill will be at some employment rate, he can read that information from S. For example, if L^* units of labor are used, the wage rate is w^* and the outlay on labor (the wage bill) is L^* multiplied by w^*.

Suppose an employer is operating at L^*, and he decides to increase his labor

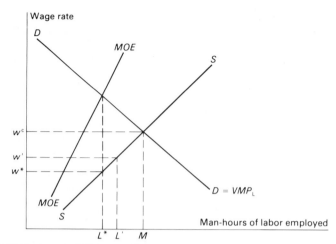

FIGURE 16.5. Employment and wages in a monopsonized labor market, compared to a competitive labor market.

force to L'. The new wage bill is $L' \times w'$, *where* w' *is higher than* w*. The wage bill rises more than in proportion to the increase in employment, because higher wage rates must be offered by the monopsonist to attract additional labor. The increase in wages necessary to sustain the desired higher employment rate is *(w' − w*)*. A curve, called the *marginal outlay on employment* curve, is labeled *MOE* in Figure 16.5. The *MOE* curve shows the addition to the wage bill that results if the work force is increased by one man-hour of employment. *MOE* will vary with the level of employment because the wage paid varies with the level of employment. And *MOE exceeds* the wage rate, because if employment is to increase, wages must be raised; and the rise in wages means that all workers already employed will be paid more too. The cost of expanding the workforce is not just the higher wages paid to *additional* workers; it is a higher wage level that applies to *all* workers.[2] Thus, the analytic role of the *MOE* curve in monopsony is symmetric with that of the marginal revenue curve in the analysis of monopoly sellers.

If the firm calculates the effect of its employment decision on the wage rate that it must pay, the rule it employs in hiring is to increase employment until *MOE* equals *D:* the additional outlay that accompanies increased use of labor is

[2]Note that if there is unemployment in the economy, the monopoly employer can obtain additional labor services with no increase in the wage rate. The effect of unemployment is to make S infinitely elastic (a horizontal line) and to make *MOE* coincide with S. Reason this out in terms of the definitions of *MOE* and S, or note that the *MOE* is

$$\frac{\partial L \cdot w}{\partial L} = w + L \frac{\partial w}{\partial L}$$

if the demand curve is horizontal at w, $\dfrac{\partial w}{\partial L} = 0$, and *MOE* $= w$ also.

equated to the total increase in the value of output that stems from increased labor use. By virtue of this rule, an employment rate of L^* and a wage rate of w^* prevail, compared with the employment rate of M and the wage rate of w^c that would obtain under conditions of competition (Figure 16.5).

A well-chosen minimum wage can remedy the effects of a monopoly employer. Suppose a minimum wage of w^0 is imposed by law. The supply curve of labor with a minimum wage is a horizontal line at the level w^0, up to the point of intersection with the market supply curve S; the market supply curve is effective for employment rates higher than L^0 (Figure 16.6). The marginal outlay on employment *(MOE)* also remains constant at the value w^0 up to the employment rate of L^0; *MOE* then jumps to the value b and follows the market *MOE* curve on employment rates higher than L^0. Because the monopoly employer chooses his employment rate in accord with the rule $MOE = D$, the effect of the minimum wage, in the presence of a monopoly employer, is to raise the wage from w^* to w^0 and to *increase* employment in the firm from L^* to L^0; the effect on employment is opposite that predicted by a competitive analysis.

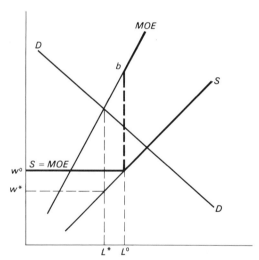

FIGURE 16.6. **The effect of a minimum wage in a monopsonized labor market.**

What is the effect of a minimum wage if there is unemployment in the economy? Reread footnote 2 before answering.

Critics of minimum wage legislation do not deny the potential benefits of the minimum wage in the presence of monopsony employers; they simply hold that the monopsony model seldom applies in the economy. They further point out that the minimum wage can make unemployment worse, even with monopsony employers, if unemployment already exists.

16.4.2. Labor Unions

For many years, beginning in the late nineteenth century and running through the 1950s, the American labor movement enjoyed good public relations and an unquestioned reputation as the beneficiary of the working man in particular and the nation in general. In recent years, however, a noticeable chill has developed; there is an occasional expression of resentment, much as though "big labor" were popularly viewed as being in the same class with "big business," as an undesirable presence in the American economy.

What, in fact, has been the role and impact of organized labor? In the nineteenth century, unions were viewed as criminal conspiracies, and strikers operated outside the law. By 1935, however, recognition was finally given to the fact that unions are here to stay; and the Wagner Act of that year required employers to recognize unions as bargaining agents for their employees, if a union was chosen by ballot of workers.

The movement hit a peak in the early 1950s when about a third of the U.S. non-agricultural labor force held membership in unions. That fraction has declined somewhat since; and were it not for the rapid spread of unionism among government employees, the decline would appear quite sharp. Industrial and trade unions definitely have waned, on the average, during the past twenty years. Table 16.1 gives data on trade union membership through time.

TABLE 16.1.   Labor Union Membership, as Percent of Labor Force, United States, 1930–1970

Year	Union Membership, United States	Percentage of Nonagricultural Labor Force
1930	3,401,000	11.7
1935	3,584,000	13.4
1940	8,717,000	26.9
1945	14,322,000	35.7
1950	14,267,000	31.5
1955	16,802,000	33.2
1960	17,049,000	31.4
1965	17,299,000	28.4
1970	19,381,000	27.4

Source: *Historical Statistics of the United States, Colonial Times to 1957,* Washington, D.C., Government Printing Office, 1960; U.S. Bureau of the Census, *Statistical Abstract of the United States, 1973,* Washington, D.C., Government Printing Office, 1973.

Four questions will be dealt with on the subject of unions. First, how do they operate and what are their methods? Second, what goals or objectives do they seem to be pursuing? Third, what is the effect of unions on the relative wage of unionized workers, compared to what their wages would be in the absence of unions? Fourth, what is their impact on the economy and society at large?

The methods employed by labor unions are precisely identical to the methods employed by a group of firms that attempt to collude to monopolize a market. The chief difference is that collusion by firms within a market is illegal, whereas collusion by workers within a firm is protected by law.

Once a union is recognized as the bargaining agent of the workforce within a firm, the goal is to obtain a higher price for labor services. That goal is pursued by the standard monopolistic practice of supply restriction. The supply of labor is restricted by a number of straightforward and subtle devices. Work conditions are set which "prevent the exploitation of the individual worker" and which reduce productivity. Entry into the unionized firm's workforce is restricted (or in the case of craft unions like plumbers or electricians, entry into the craft is restricted). And finally, the threat of halting the flow of labor services via a strike is the ultimate weapon against the employer.

The question of what the goals or objectives of unions are is one that hasn't been answered to anyone's satisfaction. They certainly do not seem to be easily classified or characterized in terms of any straightforward maximization hypothesis. Three overlapping objectives seem to underlie union behavior. These are: (1) the maintenance of a steady flow of increases in wages per member through time,[3] (2) growth in membership, and (3) maintenance of a parity in wage increases between the union's own membership and the members of other unions.

What effects have unions had on the wages enjoyed by their members compared to other workers? That question has been given considerable study. It has usually been asked in this form: how much higher are the wages of unionized workers compared to what we would expect those wages to be if there were no union?

The answer to that question is highly variable, depending on the industry and time period that is studied. Unionized workers appear to fare very well during periods of slack employment and especially well during the very rare periods of falling prices and wages, as in the 1930s. Unionization is naturally the most successful in industries in which the demand for labor is least elastic (see page 316). In some industries, the estimated wage gains from unionization range as high as 25 to 30 percent during periods of slack employment; in other industries (for example, the hotel workers), benefits have seldom or never been measurable.[4]

Finally, we want to know where the gains that unions derive for their members come from. There are three possibilities.

We know that total output in the society is equal to the sum of union members' wages, other wages, rents, interest, and profit. (This must be true, because profit is defined as the residual income net of the other payments.) We

---

[3]The term "wages" refers to worker compensation of all types, including "fringe benefits."

[4]For a summary of major results and references to the literature, see H. Gregg Lewis, "Labor Unions: Influence on Wages," in *The International Encyclopaedia of the Social Sciences* (Glencoe, Ill.: Free Press, 1968).

also know that the first component, union members' wages, is larger than the wages those workers would enjoy in the absence of a union. That gain must be due primarily to one or a combination of these three possible explanations:

   i.   An increase in total income in the society as a result of unionization, or

   ii.   A reduction in rents, interest, and profit, with total income unchanged, or

   iii.   A reduction in other (nonunion) wages with essentially no change in the other income categories.

The first possibility is the most attractive one to union enthusiasts but seems highly implausible to most economists. Unionization is the monopolization of a productive resource; and for the same reasons that monopolization of a good will lead to inefficient production, so monopolization of a resource will cause output to decline.

The second possibility also is an attractive one: the unions would be benefiting workers at the expense of the bosses and owners. Income from capital and property would be reduced and given to labor instead. That possibility, however, is contradicted by fact. Through time in America, total wage payments have accounted for a fairly constant percent of the nation's total income. That percent has been as high as 74 to 75 on occasion; in other years, as low as 68 to 70. But there has never been a time when "labor's share," the ratio of wages to the total value of output, has appeared to be related or sensitive to the level of union activity (number of wage settlements, strikes, etc.) or even to major changes in the level of union membership.

It appears, then, that the major source of the increases in wage payments to unionized workers is the earnings of nonunionized workers. That outcome is consistent with the restrictions that unions impose on job opportunities for nonunionized workers.

16.5. WAGES AND PRODUCTIVITY DURING A WORK LIFETIME

The value of a worker's marginal product will usually not be constant through time. A typical pattern throughout a working lifetime might look as shown in Figure 16.7. During the early period, the worker is untrained and unskilled. As his skills develop, his productivity rises. Productivity then peaks out at some middle age, depending on occupation (late twenties for an athlete or laborer, somewhat older for a scientist, older still for a business manager). Finally, in later years, productivity may decline, either gradually or precipitously, to the end of the working lifetime.

There are advantages to be derived by both a worker and his employer from a stable and enduring employment relationship. The worker avoids job search, household relocation, and other significant costs; and the employer avoids training expenses and the repeated necessity to appraise, evaluate, and assign new workers. Because stability in the employment relation is mutually beneficial, the equality between a worker's wage and the value of his marginal

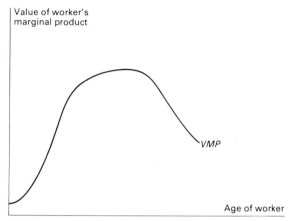

FIGURE 16.7. Typical age profile of worker productivity.

product will not hold at all times for all workers. It is simply too costly for a worker to relocate in order to avoid a small underpayment and too costly for firms to reclassify workers frequently to avoid overpayment.

Because job-switching is inconvenient for the worker, even if there were no restrictions or regulation of the labor market, the wage of an individual could not be expected to "track" the value of his marginal product perfectly. Discrepancies would be expected. Moreover, the restrictions that are imposed on labor markets may cause marked differences between an individual's wage and the value of his marginal product (VMP) at any point in time. Two of these restrictions—the minimum wage and union-imposed downward rigidity of wages—have significant impact on the employment relationship.

The minimum wage will for many workers be greater than their VMPs during the early years of their work lives. An employer who hires such workers at the minimum wage rate is in effect investing in them: he is paying out more than they are currently worth in the hope of a future gain. Figure 16.8 illustrates: up to the time t_1, the employer's outlays on the worker exceed the returns on hiring him.

As soon as the time t_1 is reached, the employment relationship becomes more delicate. If the firm immediately begins to raise the worker's wage to keep pace with his rising VMP, the firm can never capture any return on the investment made while the worker was drawing a minimum wage in excess of the value of his product. If the firm is too slow in raising the worker's wage, he may find a new employer; and again the investment is lost. The firm's goal is to find a way to capture a return on its investment: to keep the worker employed for a sufficiently long time after t_1 so that the investment is recaptured. In Figure 16.8, this goal is achieved when the area B is equal to the area A (or rather, enough larger to reflect the effects of time preference, which are felt because the investment A occurs early in time and the return B occurs late).

Why should the worker be prone to tolerate any discrepancy between wage

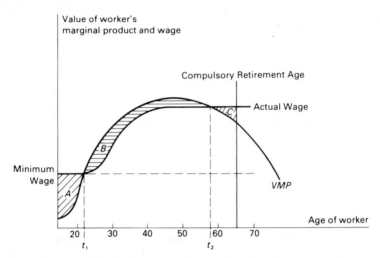

FIGURE 16.8. A hypothetical earnings-productivity history, showing the effects of minimum wage laws and downward rigidity of wages.

and marginal product after time t_1? There appear to be four main reasons. First, relocation is costly, as mentioned already. Second, firms may attempt to train the worker so that a part of his VMP is *specific* to the firm's own activity. At the extreme, the firm teaches him procedures and skills that are not used elsewhere and hence have no value elsewhere. Third, the firm may arrange it so that a part of the worker's past wage is tied to his remaining in the firm. A retirement plan that increases in value with seniority in service but is lost on resignation is typical of this third inducement to remain. And finally, many firms enlist labor unions as allies in the task of stabilizing the workforce. Unions such as the airline pilots heavily emphasize the importance of seniority: a pilot who leaves United and moves to TWA would have to start at something close to a beginner's wage, no matter how much he had earned at United. Such stipulations make it difficult for one employer to hire away the trained personnel of another by bidding up their wages.

By virtue of these devices, the firm is able to raise the worker's wage less rapidly than the rate of increase in his VMP after time t_1 in Figure 16.8.

At a later time t_2, declining VMP will necessitate either of two responses: termination of employment or a reduction in wage. In a setting where union pressure prevents the former, it is expected that either the wages of older workers will be flexible downward, or else wages in the time interval between t_1 and t_2 will be kept below the levels to which they otherwise would have risen: area B will have to offset C as well as A. In general, there is no way that the present value of wages can exceed the discounted values of marginal products through time for all or most of a firm's workers. Gains obtained early in the work life through minimum wages, or late in work life through a conventional compulsory age of retirement combined with downward wage rigidity, must be paid for out of wages below VMP in the middle years.

APPLICATIONS AND EXTENSIONS

1. Currently, the national minimum wage in the U.S. is just in excess of $2 per hour. (By the time you read this, it may be higher.) No union member anywhere (except in agriculture) earns as little as the minimum wage; yet labor unions are among the most enthusiastic supporters of the minimum wage. Can you think of a reason, other than benevolence, why that might be so?

2. Work out the effects of a minimum wage in a monopsonized labor market when there is significant unemployment in the market.

3. *Redistribution.* Suppose we number all income-earning units (households) in society according to income: richest number 1, next richest number 2, etc., until the poorest is ranked number 78 million and something. Next, divide the ranked households into ten groups, each containing the same number of households. (We will then have arranged the population in *decile* groups.) Next, suppose we devise methods whereby income is transferred from one group to another: for example, we might impose a tax on corporate security purchases and use the proceeds to pay for urban rat control. Because the first and second deciles do most of the securities purchasing, and the poorest decile does most of the suffering from rats in our cities, that would be a transfer from numbers 1 and 2 to number 10.

    Use your thoughtful judgment and guess which decile groups give up income, and which receive income, as a result of the following programs:

    (a) State support for public universities

    (b) Federal support for mortgages on single-family houses

    (c) Federal support of passenger-train service (AMTRAK)

    (d) State "closed shop" laws, which require union membership as a condition of employment in some firms

    (e) A federal tariff of 10% on foreign-produced automobiles

    (f) A state requirement that smog-control devices be installed on all automobiles over six years old.

4. *"Adding up."* Show that under conditions of full competitive equilibrium, if a firm pays every productive resource input at a rate per hour equal to the value of its marginal product to the firm, then the total payment to inputs must be equal to the total value of the firm's output.

BIBLIOGRAPHIC NOTE

Further readings on this topic are listed at the end of Chapter 17.

CHAPTER SEVENTEEN

The Distribution
of Personal Income

A Society without an aristocracy, without an elite minority, is
not a society.

JOSÉ ORTEGA Y GASSET (1922)

A decent provision for the poor is the true test of civilization.

SAMUEL JOHNSON (1770)

The question of how the output of a nation's economy is divided among its
citizens is a fascinating one, and one that immediately calls forth our ideas of
what is right or wrong, just or unjust. The plan of this chapter is to answer, to the
extent possible, these questions:

1. What do we know about the pattern of income distribution among persons in
    contemporary America?
2. How has that pattern changed through time?
3. How do economists explain the forces that determine income distribution among
    persons?
4. Who are the rich? What is their role in society? What, if anything, should be done
    about great wealth? Who are the poor? What steps can be taken to ease the burden
    of poverty?
5. What connections exist between race and income in America? Does poverty
    among minority-group members pose special or unusual problems?

These questions are of immediate concern to social science. The attitudes of individuals toward the society in which they live may depend, for a variety of reasons, not just upon how well individuals fare within the society on the average, but on how equitably they are treated. Income distribution is a subject central to the issue of economic equity; and on that issue opinions can be expected to differ. Unfortunately, the available data that are pertinent to income distribution are very imperfect, and further, there is little in the way of well-developed theory to offer guidance in interpreting the data that are available.

17.1. INCOME DISTRIBUTION IN THE UNITED STATES

17.1.1. Definitions, and a Quick Peek

Suppose it were possible to observe every household in America for a period of, say, one year, and to measure the total value of payments into each household from every possible source: wages or salaries of husband, wife, and working children; income from the rental of real property they own; dividends from ownership shares (stock) in corporations that they own; interest income from bonds, bank accounts, and accounts in savings and loan institutions; proceeds from the sale of goods that they directly produce (like eggs, tomatoes, paintings, or short stories); benefits received from insurance companies, pension plans, the Social Security system, unemployment compensation, or welfare payments; and the value of goods that they directly produce and consume themselves. Furthermore, we would like to add their share of profits retained by businesses that they partly own, as reflected in capital gains realized when their ownership shares are sold. Call that total value the household's *income,* and let incomes be arrayed by size, with the smallest first in line, the second smallest next, and so on, until at the end of the line households with the largest *incomes* are encountered. When so arrayed, the incomes can be described in a very compact way; we can say what percentage of the population has an income less than any specific amount; or, as a statistician would say, we can give information on the *empirical distribution* of income.

In examining this empirical distribution of income, we will find that a few of the smallest incomes are *negative,* if we look at so short a time period as one year: a businessman who owns his own store has a "bad year," and his expenses exceed his receipts. Or a household may be headed by a student who is forced to borrow money in order that he or she may finish up a degree program; if those borrowings cover expenses which exceed the household's total cash intake from other sources, the household's income is negative. Another household may have been beset by illness, and savings must be dipped into in order to make ends meet during the recovery period. At the other end of the scale, we may find the total income of some very high-income people is exaggerated or magnified by particularly fortunate happenings that contribute to a good year—sale of property is one important contributor to such effects. Because of these "good-year and bad-year effects," it would be desirable to have data on personal incomes which give average incomes over several years, or even a lifetime, for each individual or household in the society. Unfortunately, such *longitudinal* data are seldom reported.

Even if "good-year and bad-year effects" were removed from the data, we would find an enormous difference between the largest incomes in society and those that are approximately of average size; and we would find a further substantial (but nowhere nearly so significant) difference between average-sized and low incomes. Table 17.1 indicates the rough order of magnitude of the differences that are encountered throughout the income size range when the data are not corrected.

TABLE 17.1.   Representative Sizes of Annual Incomes at Different Points of the Personal Income Distribution, 1968

Largest incomes*	$25–150 million
Lowest income, top 20% of households	$13,000
Lowest income, second 20%	9,290
Mean household income, entire population	7,750
Lowest income, third 20%	6,300
Lowest income, fourth 20%	3,290
Smallest incomes	negative values

Source of remaining entries: U.S. Census Bureau, *Statistical Abstract of the U.S.,* Washington, D.C.: Government Printing Office, 1970.

*Incomes of wealthy individuals are not publicly known. The estimate in our table is made from other estimates of wealth, presented in F. Lundberg, *The Rich and the Super-Rich* (New York: Lyle Stuart, Inc. 1968), p. 45. A 5 to 10 percent rate of return on estimated wealth is the figure given as estimated income. There are probably fewer than fifty Americans with incomes in the indicated range.

Statistics like the ones displayed in Table 17.1 are obviously important. We must try to understand a social order in which fantastic riches can go to a very small minority of the population and dismal want can befall another somewhat larger minority. Equally or more important, we should try to understand the differences that are observed among larger groups: why does the top 20 percent of the population receive 45 percent of the income, while the bottom 20 percent receives less than 3½ percent? Our task is to find some explanation of the distribution as a whole; then to see what the position of the very rich and very poor looks like, and to discuss what (if anything) should be done with regard to the extremely rich and the extremely poor. Let's return to Table 17.1 for a careful examination, to make sure we know what information it contains.

First, the "top incomes" figure is an estimate of the incomes of a few of the very richest individuals in the U.S. Single-figure estimates would almost surely contain enormous enormous errors, because only a very few people are involved, and access to their financial records is not complete; thus the estimate is given as a range of values. Typically, the few families in this range obtain most of their income from business enterprises that they own outright, or control (by owning a large part of the stock). These people usually have important interests in more than one line of business; their holdings are diversified.

In the top quintile (the top 20 percent) of all income recipients, we find a wide range of incomes and attributes. Many are business tycoons, to be sure; but also most of our established professional men like doctors, lawyers, dentists, and holders of the Ph.D. degree (including most university professors and associate professors) fall in this range; as do many professional athletes; some actors; a fair proportion of white-collar salaried business employees and "executives"; and some nonprofessional self-employed people (successful owners of small businesses). More surprising, there are numerous skilled laborers: carpenters, plumbers, truck drivers, machine-tool operators, and others; and many salesmen are scattered throughout all but the very top reaches of this top quintile, as well. The range of incomes in this quintile is of course enormous: much greater than the range of incomes in the four remaining quintiles. (The range, in fact, of the top one quarter of one percent is greater than in the entire remaining 99.75 percent of the distribution!)

At the other extreme, in the lowest quintile of the income distribution, we have many types and categories. First, and most perplexing, are the people with little or no education or skill, and virtually no experience in work that anyone finds useful; they live on welfare, charity, and petty crime, and are a constant rebuke and problem to the rest of society. In addition, there are many other individuals in the lowest quintile whose problems can easily be overstressed. Retired people, living on pensions and savings, many of whom own their homes; students, with bright prospects for a lifetime of earnings ahead of them; owners of small businesses, in the costly throes of starting up, expanding, or changing over to a new line; one-person households; households benefiting from substantial unreported income; and perhaps others.

How trustworthy and significant are data like those presented in Table 17.1? The next section develops some perspective.

17.1.2. Our Sources of Information

The data summarized in Table 17.2 are far from ideal, for they give us a very inaccurate picture of the incomes of every household. Our chief sources for information on the incomes of households are the U.S. Bureau of Census and the Survey Research Center of the University of Michigan, both of which report data from a *sample* of households; and the Internal Revenue Service of the United States Treasury Department (our nation's official tax collector), which gives data on all income tax returns.

We must be careful not to attach too much weight to comparisons of income distribution statistics that are prepared by different sources. There will be surprisingly large variations in definitions of income, and very important variations in the income-earning units that are taken into account. For example: the Internal Revenue Service, in reporting incomes declared on individual income tax returns, lets each one of those tax returns define what is an income-earning unit. If a family with three working members files two income tax returns, its income will enter the statistics split two ways. If it files three returns, they are split three ways. The Census Bureau, by contrast, would record the family's total income as a single entry, provided all are sharing the same household. Some statistical indicators exclude benefits from social security and welfare from the income data; some record incomes only after taxes have been subtracted.[1]

Furthermore, it must be recognized that reported incomes are probably *biased* on the low side: that is, the reported figures are probably lower than actual incomes. This bias can be expected to occur in all income classes. The wealthy may occasionally fail to report dividends, interest earnings, or income from professional practice in full. Among the poor, many domestic workers (cleaning women, gardeners, handymen) fail to declare any earnings at all; people in lower-paid service trades, like waiters, barbers, and deliverymen probably fail to report some of their income from tipping; and illegally earned income is probably grossly underdeclared, by rich overlords of the crime syndicate and petty numbers-runners alike. There is, then, very likely a considerable downward bias in the reporting of incomes at all levels of the income range.

There is further bias in the fact that what we quaintly call "income in kind" is imperfectly estimated. This term refers to income received in the form of goods instead of money. The very rich are the beneficiaries of varied and sometimes lavish income in kind: corporations maintain private yachts and planes, season boxes for sports and music events alike, country club memberships, fleets of automobiles and a limousine or two, credit cards, and foreign offices in exotic spots around the world. It is usually the upper-echelon, higher-salaried employees who benefit most from these goodies. Taxation, incidentally, provides much of the reason why such luxuries are obtained by firms for the use of their top employees. A company yacht, used to entertain clients of the firm, can be declared a business expense, and the cost of owning and maintaining the yacht is deducted from the income on which the corporation pays tax. In effect, the yacht is in part paid for by money that would otherwise be taken away by the tax collector. More important, the "income"—the feeling of well-being—that the vice-president of sales gets from his use of the yacht is not taxable. As long

[1]For a survey of problems encountered in the interpretation of income statistics, see The U.S. Bureau of the Budget's *Family Income Distribution Statistics Reported by Federal Agencies*, Statistical Evaluation Report No. 5, December 1964. For a discussion of what "should" ideally be measured, compared to what is measured, see the Appendix on page 351. One remark: distribution statistics are often used in forming judgments about an issue on which they really have very little bearing. The U.S. Department of Commerce statistics, for example, are often cited in arguments about whether capitalism tends to make the poor worse off through time. But those statistics contain income transfer payments, and hence have more bearing on the question of how well the poor do after receiving the benefits of public welfare—quite a different question from how they are treated by the capitalist order.

as he is engaged in "business activity"—and that in fact may be no more than entertaining some friends who do business with his firm—his use of the yacht is not counted as a part of his income. At least some of the benefit he gains from his "business" yachting excursions should properly be counted as a part of his income, but it is not. Moreover, the tax incentive of the type just illustrated—to own property in the name of business—is even greater to owners of unincorporated businesses than it is to corporations; and the benefits of income in kind probably are greater (relative to total income) among proprietors of unincorporated businesses than to anyone else.

More modest forms of income in kind are received by the poor. We may list below-cost medical and dental care from public clinics; reduced rents to occupants of public housing; school lunch programs to children of the poor; "free" public education (or more accurately, public education that costs the school authority more to provide than the poor parent pays in the form of taxes); other similar public services (fire and police protection, libraries, sewers, roads). Also included are products of their own making that are consumed directly (such as farm produce, automobile repair services, or merchandise purchased at wholesale prices); and the value of services obtained from property (such as homes, automobiles, and appliances) that the individual owns outright. This last item is undoubtedly a more significant source of income in kind for the wealthier than the poorer members of society, however. Some of our income distribution statistical series include estimates of particular types of income in kind. Included, occasionally, is an allowance for food and fuel produced on farms; for "free" meals consumed by farm laborers and domestic workers on the job; and for the benefits obtained by homeowners from the houses that they own.

Because income is not reported consistently with respect to definition of recipient or what is counted as income, because the data lack full and desirable accuracy, and because only a small part of income in kind is included, the income levels shown in Table 17.1 may be quite dramatically misstated. We do not know—we can only guess—how extensive reporting errors are; and there is no good way to show that the errors are greater in the report of large incomes than of small incomes, or vice versa. Because we cannot judge whether the bias is greater for high- or low-income people, we have no way of knowing how the bias affects *income shares*, the data that are recorded in Table 17.2. Those share figures tell us the percentage of personal disposable income that goes to the richest 10 percent of the population, the second richest, and so on down to the poorest 10 percent.

Vague though they are, income-share figures are useful in two applications, if they are used with caution. The first application is in making comparisons through time within a particular society. Crude judgments may be formed as to whether the society is growing "more equal" or "less equal" over time. Other comparisons that may be useful can be made between nations.

Comparisons through time for the U.S. are given in Table 17.2. An interpretation of those data is the next order of business.

TABLE 17.2. Income Shares, Different Years, Reported by Decile

Year	Highest	(TENTHS OF THE POPULATION, RANKED BY INCOME SIZE)								Lowest
		2	3	4	5	6	7	8	9	
1910*	33.9	12.3	10.2	8.8	8.0	7.0	6.0	5.5	4.9	33.4
1921*	38.2	12.8	10.5	8.9	7.4	6.5	5.9	4.6	3.2	2.0
1929*	39.0	12.3	9.8	9.0	7.9	6.5	5.5	4.6	3.6	1.8
1937*	34.4	14.1	11.7	10.1	8.5	7.2	6.0	4.4	2.6	11.0
1945*	29.0	16.0	13.0	11.0	9.0	7.0	6.0	5.0	3.0	1.0
1945†	27.83	16.14	13.05	11.0	9.35	7.82	6.33	4.72	2.92	0.84
1950*	28.7	15.4	12.7	10.8	9.3	7.8	6.3	4.9	3.2	0.9
1950†	28.90	16.28	12.98	11.04	9.48	7.84	6.12	4.32	2.47	0.58
1954*	29.3	15.3	12.4	10.7	9.1	7.7	6.4	4.8	3.1	1.2
1954†	28.23	16.52	13.30	11.35	9.56	7.80	6.04	3.25	2.41	0.54
1958*	27.1	16.3	13.2	11.0	9.4	7.8	6.2	4.6	3.1	1.3
1958†	27.11	16.56	13.39	11.42	9.99	7.96	6.21	4.43	2.58	0.66
1964†	27.44	16.52	13.52	10.39	9.57	7.80	6.07	4.33	2.60	0.77
1968†	27.11	15.98	13.43	11.33	9.58	7.90	6.24	4.56	2.84	1.03

*Source: Gabriel Kolko, *Wealth and Power in America* (New York: Praeger Books, 1962). Primary sources are listed by Kolko (p. 14). Figures reported for 1910 and 1921 may be grossly inaccurate; they are estimates made in the early 1930s.

†Source: Edward C. Budd, "Postwar Changes in the Size Distribution of Income in the U.S.," *American Economic Review*, 9(May 1970), Table 4, p. 253. Budd used sample data from the U.S. Bureau of Census in preparing the figures reported above.

17.1.3. Progress Through Time?

There has been significant controversy as to whether income has in fact become more equally distributed in the United States. It has been conventional to point to the declining share of upper-income groups—the top 1, 5, 10, or 20 percent of income recipients—and to declare optimistically that distribution indeed is equalizing. Such a decline certainly is visible up to about 1945, when it leveled off. Historian Gabriel Kolko has offered a vigorous challenge to this optimistic point of view. He sees not a move toward equality but a move toward greater inequality. Kolko's arguments have been influential, and it is worthwhile evaluating them.

His view that inequality has increased is based on the following reasons: (1) the income share of the lowest and next-lowest deciles (tenths) of the population have declined dramatically since 1929; (2) while there is an apparent decline in the share of the top tenth, that decline is more apparent than real for three important reasons: (a) the rich are more prone than the poor to underdeclare their incomes; (b) the expense accounts, etc., which contribute enormously as income in kind to the rich, are not counted in the statistical tabulations; and (c) earnings retained within corporations owned by the rich (income earned by the firms but not paid out to shareholders) is not counted as a part of the income of the rich.

Kolko's first reason is flawed by the fact that he ignores changes in the *composition* of the poorest tenth of the population. America in 1968 was an *older* nation than in 1929; a larger portion of the population was past working age.[2] The elderly to a disproportionate degree have low incomes because they do not work regularly; it follows that an increase in the number of elderly means an increase in the number of very low-income persons. Moreover, in the years since 1929, the Social Security program—Federal Old Age and Survivors Insurance—came into being. This program has paid a pittance of income to large numbers of elderly since it was established; many of those recipients (who reported very low incomes) would under the conditions prevalent in 1929 have reported no income at all. The availability of that social security income, small though it is, has enabled numbers of elderly people to maintain their own households, whereas in earlier times they would have been dependent on their children (and counted in the children's household); or they would have been in an institution, and not counted as part of a household at all. It must also be remembered, in considering the economic situation of the elderly, that households headed by elderly persons are small (typically one or two members); many elderly who report low incomes are living in dwellings that they own outright; and some have accumulated savings to be used during retirement. For these reasons it is not safe to conclude that the decline in the income share of the

[2]The census of 1960 reported 19.9 million persons in a population of 203.2 million to be age 65 or above; in 1930, the figures were 6.7 million out of 123.1 million. The rise in the above-65 group is from 5.5 to 9.8 percent of total population.

poorest tenth of the population reflects a genuine loss of welfare to the people in that tenth. The poorest tenth in 1968, with their smaller share, may feel and be better off than individuals who occupied a similar role in society in 1929, when the income share reported for the lowest decile was larger.

The second part of Kolko's argument is that the rich are relatively better off now than in 1929 because of income in kind, under-reporting of income, and the increasing tendency for corporations' income to be retained within firms so that it does not appear in the statistics of personal income distribution. Two of those points are not spelled out with adequate clarity. It is undoubtedly true that upper-income groups receive large amounts of income in kind from such sources as expense accounts, and it is also true that such income is not measured in income distribution statistics. What is *not* shown is that this income in kind to the rich is a more important factor now than it was in the 1920s, a point that must be established in order to prove that the rich are better off now relative to the rest of society than they were in 1920. The same point can be made with regard to Kolko's assertion about under-reporting of income: do the rich under-report *relative to the rest of society* more now than they did in 1929?

The point that retained earnings now account for a larger share of corporate income than in 1929, and dividends for a smaller share, is a valid one. Because the owners of firms are made better off by retained earnings (the firm can use those funds to expand, and the price of the firm's shares will usually rise), and because retained earnings are not counted in the income distribution statistics, it would appear that Kolko has a strong point. However, if we look at data in which retained earnings are implicitly distributed as income to the owners of firms, we find that the same decline in upper-income shares is visible between 1929 and 1947, although it is slightly less pronounced.[3] Thus, Kolko has pointed to an effect that tends to support his argument, but the strength of that effect is not sufficiently great to validate his conclusion.

It appears from the record of Table 17.2 that a substantial reduction in income inequality occurred between 1929 and 1945. Since that time, the decile shares have changed very little.

17.2. INCOME INEQUALITY: SOURCES, PROBLEMS, POLICIES

17.2.1. Why Do We Have Inequality?

Through the mechanism of the market, society rewards individuals for performing services that are valued by other individuals. As the parable of the

[3]Two important older studies compare the effects of undistributed corporate income (retained earnings) on the distribution of personal income. These are Simon Kuznets, *Shares of Upper Income Groups in Income and Savings* (New York: National Bureau of Economic Research, 1953), and Selma Goldsmith et al., "Size Distribution of Income Since the Mid-Thirties," *Review of Economics and Statistics,* 36(February 1954).

island paradise in Chapter 2 illustrated, those services can be as diverse as bagging fertilizer and performing sonatas. Those two particular services nicely illustrate two points: the types of work into which individuals may enter are widely different in pleasantness and in the degree of skill that is required. Fertilizer bagging is a sweaty task that is not too pleasant, undemanding, and not very spiritually uplifting; music performance is the opposite on every count except possibly the first. Suppose every individual in every trade received precisely equal salary rewards: it is unlikely that many would elect to bag fertilizer if the option of playing golf or the piano, or teaching in a university, were open at the same pay, regardless of ability or skill. Obviously, some mechanism is required to direct individuals into activities in which their abilities will be of use to themselves and others; the mechanism of wages performs that role in a market system. It may be possible, by eliminating or radically curtailing choice of occupation, to direct people into useful occupations while maintaining absolutely equal wages for everyone. People could be assigned to jobs by a placement authority on the basis of achievement and aptitude tests, for example. The problem with such a scheme, beyond the extreme infringement on liberty that it involves, is that there is very little long-term incentive for anyone so placed to do a good job. A person may have the ability to be a good veterinarian, but if it is left to his conscience to regulate his performance, the welfare of his animal patients may suffer.

Moreover, under such a placement scheme, equality of incomes would not be preserved unless it were decreed that everyone should save the same amount out of his income. Savings in the society are nothing more than an excess of the value of current income over current consumption. Goods that are produced and not consumed become a part of capital, to be consumed or used for producing other goods in the future. Capital goods can be purchased with savings: the process of purchasing capital goods is called *investment*. If one individual wants to save a great deal, while another wants to consume everything he earns, the first will soon have made possible the purchase of a significant amount of capital; because that capital is useful in producing future goods, the first person is rewarded for making it available. He collects *interest* on his savings; and his interest income makes his total income higher than the second person's income. Thus enters income inequality: those who save make capital accumulation possible, and are rewarded. To avoid this source of income inequality, the mechanisms of saving, lending, and investing would have to be reshaped. The reshaping of those mechanisms would involve further loss of liberty and further inefficiency. Thus two important points emerge. First, in order to have income equality, it would be necessary to make significant sacrifice of liberty—free choice of occupation. Second, all decisions regarding not only occupation, but production as well, would be turned over to some authority: by assigning workers and capital to jobs, the authority would be determining what output rates of different goods and services are possible. It would be remarkable indeed if that authority could send the right kind of talent to every job as efficiently as the market mechanism does, or provide the performance incentives that the market mechanism provides. Income equality, then, would predictably carry a very large economic cost in the form of a less desirable and less abundant output mix: efficiency would suffer, as well as liberty.

The issue, then, that must be faced is not found in the question Why do we have income inequality? Rather, it is in the much more difficult complex of questions: Why is income unequally distributed to the degree that it is? How much of the existing inequality in incomes can be eliminated without loss of liberty or efficiency? How much inequality can be expected to arise under alternative ways of organizing the economy?

Income and ability.   Consider the population of working people in most societies. They are a very mixed lot, ranging from highly intelligent to pitifully slow-minded; physically powerful to very frail; dazzlingly attractive to repulsively ugly. Moreover, they range enormously with respect to specific aptitudes: some are mathematical geniuses while others are paralyzed by the task of compiling a bowling score; some can sing like thrushes, while others can only croak; some can strip down a complex fuel-injection Mercedes engine at first encounter and then put it back together correctly, while others cannot be trusted to wind an alarm clock properly.

Most measurements of physical and mental attributes are arbitrary. True, simple tests of strength can be made "objective." But other attributes—beauty, artistic talent, intelligence, mechanical skill, etc.—are either not measured at all or are measured only with reference to carefully designed but nevertheless arbitrarily scaled tests. Interestingly, however, in all tests of "native" human ability (whether "objective" like weight-lifting, or "arbitrary" like the Stanford-Binet test of IQ), the scores obtained in a large group of randomly chosen people are distributed symmetrically in the manner illustrated by Figure 17.1. Test scores cluster around a mean value M—that is, there are a small number of very low and very high scores, and the closer a score is to M, the larger is the number of individuals who are observed to receive it.

Incomes, on the other hand, are distributed roughly as shown in Figure 17.2: many people receive modest incomes, a few people receive fabulously large ones.

Some observers have noted that ability distributions like IQ scores tend to be symmetric and tightly clustered, while the income distribution has one enormously long tail (it is *skewed* to the right). They have taken these configurations as a sign that opportunity is not equal for all. Their judgment is insubstantial because there is no meaningful way to measure the equality or inequality of arbitrarily scaled ability distributions. The ratios of two persons' IQs is a meaningless number that depends entirely on the arbitrary assignment of a numerical value to a mean or average score. The ratio of two persons' incomes, by contrast, is a well-defined, unambiguous, and usable number.

It is worth exploring why the income distribution is skewed to the right.

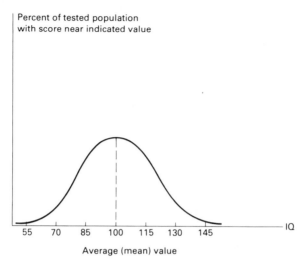

FIGURE 17.1. **Symmetric distribution of "talent" (as measured by IQ score).**

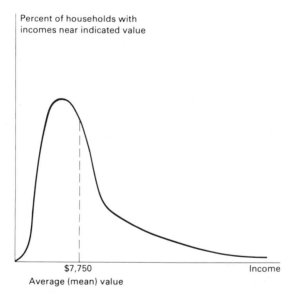

FIGURE 17.2. **Skewed distribution of income within American society, 1968 (compare to symmetric talent distribution).**

Explanations of skewness. First, and very important, income is a cumulative phenomenon. A person who earns a high salary can save a large part of it; and if he does, then after a few years we begin to observe that his income from the property that he owns begins to grow quite impressively. Table 17.3 illustrates: if an individual saves $1000 per year out of his salary, and he receives

TABLE 17.3.   The Growth of Income from Wealth at 5 Percent Compound Interest (Assuming $1000 Additions Annually from Wage Income)

Year	Amount of wealth	Income for year
1	$ 1,000.00	$ 50.00
2	2,050.00	102.50
3	3,152.50	157.63
5	5,525.63	276.28
10	12,577.89	628.89
15	21,578.56	1,578.93
20	33,065.95	1,653.30
25	47,727.10	2,386.35
30	66,438.85	3,321.94
35	90,320.31	4,516.01
40	120,799.77	6,039.99
50	209,348.00	10,467.40

a 5 percent return on the money he saves (a fairly modest rate of increase, even ignoring taxes), and if that income from savings also is saved, then his income from savings will be the amounts shown through time. Notice that after fifty years, the individual's income from savings is over $10,000 per year. Thus, even if wage incomes were equally or evenly distributed, very thrifty individuals with high wage incomes would tend to have very large property incomes toward the ends of their working lives. Also important, of course, is the fact that wage earnings tend to increase with age, further increasing income inequality in a group that contains individuals of all ages.

Second, it appears that the market process rewards many types of "super ability" very highly, while penalizing "sub abilities" in only a small amount. A golden voice, unusual athletic talent, or charismatic presence can be used in the building of a financial empire. At the other extreme, a person with subnormal gifts on all relevant dimensions is not plunged to the depths of great financial loss: at worst, he leads a menial and dreary existence on a few dollars a week; but his departure from the average on the low side is nowhere near as great as the departure from average of the fortunate on the high side. Thus, even earned incomes will spread over a much wider range of higher-than-average values, compared to lower-than-average values.

Third, two important choices—of occupation, and the way that property is put to work—are subject to *risk*. A young man often can choose between a first job with a safe, established institution like a bank or life insurance firm, or he can go to work for a land speculator in an area that may be on the verge of a development boom. The first choice will carry the promise of comfort and safety: a good salary, predictable working conditions, and little prospect of wealth. The second choice, if it pans out, can mean a rapid rise to the vice presidency of a fast-growing firm; or it can mean no job at all, with the outcome decided in a very few years.

Similarly, property can be put to work in a safe or a risky way. From Table 17.3, we find that at the end of about twenty-two years, our hypothetical individual has accumulated $40,000. He can continue the safe and sure process shown, so that after fifty years he will be worth over $200,000; or he can take his $40,000, buy an oil lease in some unexpected locale, and sink his money in a hole in the ground. If he strikes oil, he might own millions after fifty years; if he doesn't, he will own very little. Stories about super-rich individuals often involve oil exploration; there are a half-dozen or so very wealthy men who began as oil "wildcatters," staking everything on expensive holes in the Texas or Oklahoma prairie. The names missing from that very short list are the names of those who gambled and lost. Where in the income distribution do we find them and their heirs?

Finally, of course, different individuals with roughly the same talent will realize different incomes, because they choose to develop and apply their talents differently. Your economics teacher probably has the aptitude to be a competent corporation attorney. He probably would be earning more at this moment had he chosen to become one.

It would be desirable if economic theory could tell us whether income differences of the size that we observe are consistent with the marginal productivity theory of income shares (Chapter 16). That theory is the most important tool that economists have in explaining how the division of society's product is achieved. Unfortunately, neither the theory nor our observations of the economy are sufficiently refined to permit an estimate of whether observed differences are of a magnitude consistent with the theory's predictions.

We turn now to an examination of both tails of the income distribution, and we shall discuss "what should be done" about *both* the rich and the poor.

17.3. WEALTH

The top wealth-holders and income-earners in any society are very hard creatures to cope with in intellectual discourse. As recently as fifty years ago, the rich were much more of a "problem" than they are today: their consumption habits were far gaudier and more overtly "wasteful"; their outlook on life was far more self-serving; and their use of political and economic power was more direct and imperialistic. In the nineteenth century, the doctrines of "social Darwinism" were at their zenith; and numbers of sycophantic clergymen, journalists, intellectuals, and politicians made their careers by singing the praises of the God-blessed, fittest, and most deserving rich.

Today, the existence of great wealth is continually under attack. Various measures have been adopted which apparently aim to prevent the growth of a monied aristocracy; public attitudes toward great wealth are less tolerant; and in their substantial charitable efforts the very wealthy seek wide publicity in an attempt to offset some of the popular hostility toward wealth. We want to examine the political developments that have occurred, and to look into the implications of various possible treatments of and attitudes toward wealth.

17.3.1. The Politics of Envy

There is an undercurrent in American thought which seems to hold that wealth should not be tolerated at all. Numerous politicians have campaigned on proposals to "soak the rich,"[4] and because the vast majority of voters are far from rich, those campaigns have often had great popular appeal. Various tax laws have been adopted which apparently serve to take away the wealth of the wealthy; those measures, however, have invariably been accompanied by "loopholes" through which the wealthy can escape with little damage. Two types of taxation—the personal income tax and death duties on inheritances— have been the most important weapons used in attacking wealth.

Personal income taxes have varied tremendously over the past fifty years. In 1913, the U.S. Constitution was amended to provide explicitly that Congress could levy taxes on income from any source; since that time, the rates of taxation on personal incomes have fluctuated in the manner shown in Table 17.4. From 1954 to 1959, notice, an individual was subject to a tax of 91 cents on every dollar

TABLE 17.4.   Schedules of Personal Income Taxation
for Selected Years, 1913–1971

YEARS	EXEMPTIONS (NUMBER OF PERSONS IN HOUSEHOLD)			LOWEST BRACKET		TOP BRACKET	
					Taxable		Taxable
				Rate	income	Rate	income
	1	2	5	(%)	less than	(%)	over
1913–15	$3,000	$4,000	$4,000	1	$20,000	7	$ 500,000
1919–20	1,000	2,000	2,600	4	4,000	73	1,000,000
1929	1,500	3,500	4,700	3/8	4,000	24	100,000
1936–39	1,000	2,500	3,700	4	4,000	79	5,000,000
1944–45	500	1,000	2,500	23	2,000	86.5	200,000
1954–59	600	1,200	3,000	20	2,000	91	200,000
1965–67	600	1,200	3,000	24	1,200	70	500,000
1975	750	1,500	3,750	14	1,000	70	200,000

Source: U.S. Census Bureau, *Historical Statistics of the United States, Colonial Times to 1957*, Washington, D.C.: Government Printing Office, 1959; and *U.S. Census Bureau, Statistical Abstract of the United States* (various editions), Washington, D.C.: Government Printing Office.

[4]Huey Long, governor of Louisiana in the 1930s, the only state governor in the history of the U.S. to be assassinated, was a prominent redistribution advocate. According to Bronfenbrenner (see Bibliographical Note), Long advocated a minimum annual income of $5000, to be paid for out of taxes on high incomes and inheritances. Long overlooked the inconvenient fact that there was not enough income generated in the whole society in the 1930s to pay every family $5000; the proceeds of his taxation on high incomes and inheritances would have been negligible. Truly an artful practitioner of the politics of envy was Huey Long. (His assassin, by the way, was not a rich man out to save his fortune; he was "punishing" Long for using state funds illegally and rigging elections.)

of taxable income (income after deductions and exemptions) above $200,000. The effect of this steeply graduated tax rate, however, was in large measure offset by two considerations. First, earnings from the sale of certain types of property (transactions that result in long-term capital gains) are taxed at only half the rate of other income; and second, interest earned on certain types of government bonds (tax-free public authority bonds) are subject to no tax at all. Thus, wealthy individuals can protect large parts of their property income against erosion through taxation.

Taxation on inheritances and estates similarly appeared heavy. Table 17.5 indicates the tax rates on estates of different values. Since 1942, up to 60 percent of an inheritance of $10 million has been taken away in the form of federal taxes. Here the loopholes consist mainly of exemptions for trust funds and gifts. A wealthy father can establish trust funds for his heirs; the principal of those funds is tax-free as long as it is not spent, and the income (which is mainly capital gains and tax-free interest) is taxed like any other income. Moreover, that father can give each heir up to $5000 per year in gifts, tax-free, each year. If these are gifts of property, they can be valued at the price at which they were originally purchased—usually much less than the price for which they could be sold at the time they are given away.

TABLE 17.5. Estate Taxes in the United States Under 1941 Law

Size of estate	Tax on unmarried man	Tax on married man, half of estate left to wife
$ 100,000	$ 4,800	$ 0
120,000	9,500	0
150,000	17,900	1,050
200,000	32,700	4,800
500,000	126,000	47,700
750,000	212,200	86,500
1,000,000	303,500	126,500
2,000,000	726,200	303,500
5,000,000	2,430,400	968,800
10,000,000	6,042,600	2,430,400
20,000,000	13,742,000	6,042,600

The "politics of envy," then, appears to be taking large steps toward the elimination of great personal wealth; but those appearances are deceiving. True, it is no longer as easy to get rich or to stay rich without the help of competent lawyers and accountants; but it is far from impossible.

17.3.2. Policies toward Wealth

If we recognize the politics of envy for what it is, a scheme for obtaining voter support, we are not much attracted by it. It does not offer a serious answer to the question: what (if anything) should be done about the existence of large personal fortunes? In attempting an answer to that question, we will be guided by the considerations of liberty and efficiency that were outlined in Chapter 3, Section 3.3.

Who, we may ask, is "rich"? A family with three times the average income of the society? Five times? Fifteen times? Or one thousand times? With the mean family income of the U.S. currently around $10,000, we are looking for a definition that may be as low as $30,000 or as high as $10 million. The definition of "rich" is very much a matter of individual perspective: a man with an annual income of $200,000 probably would feel constrained and deprived at $50,000; anyone accustomed to an income of $10,000 would feel fabulously well off (for a while) at $50,000. Also, the operational definition must depend on the goals of a policy toward wealth. Do we want to obtain large sums to redistribute across the population, in order to make everyone more equal? Or do we simply want to prevent the emergence of an "income elite," people so much richer than everyone else that their financial power becomes a source of concern to the rest of society? If the first goal of making incomes equal guides policy, a relatively modest definition of wealth will be necessary—two or two and a half times the mean income, say—and taxation will have to fall very heavily on incomes above that rather modest cutoff. It is widely believed that poverty could be eliminated if we only would tax away most personal income of the ultra-rich and give it to the poor. Let everyone be taxed 95 percent of his income above half a million, say. But that idea is a delusion. The revenues so obtained would be a drop in the bucket, insufficient to assure a minimum income of 20 percent of the average. To get everyone up to half the average or above, taxation must fall very heavily on incomes in the $25 to 30,000 range and up.

The major economic drawback of such a massively redistributive taxation policy is the negative effect it can have on incentives. The promise of financial reward is an important inducement for persons of ingenuity and ability to exercise their talents. Remove that attraction, and the danger exists that talents may be used in less socially beneficial directions. Thus it appears that there are serious efficiency problems that confront any program that redistributes in an extreme way; and of course, liberty problems as well.

What, now, of the second goal, the prevention of wealth accumulation? Here the issues are more vague. It must be decided, first, whether the goal of policy should be to prevent the accumulation of wealth or to prevent the transmission of wealth to succeeding generations. The reasons behind such policies need not be simple envy; though it is no doubt the case that many people who advocate them are motivated either by envy or by totally naive views as to the morality of the way in which wealth is accumulated or used (a topic about which more will be said in a few pages). A large consensus of the society may hold the view that a classless society is desirable, and they may feel that the accumulation of wealth stands in the way of that goal. What can be done? The alternatives involve taxation. If prevention of the accumulation of wealth is desired, various measures to close tax ''loopholes'' and to increase the rate of taxation on high incomes can be considered. These two types of policy differ remarkably in their implications. Virtually anyone in the high-income brackets will prefer to have tax rates on ordinary income raised, rather than having loopholes closed. Because loopholes work more to the advantage of the very wealthy than the moderately well-off, they tend to make problems of inequality worse. In fact, a policy that closed up loopholes and *reduced* the rate of taxation on moderate to high incomes might work quite well in slowing down the rate of accumulation enjoyed by very wealthy individuals, while permitting a somewhat greater rate of accumulation among the less wealthy.

If the goal is to prevent the transmission of wealth to heirs, tax rates on inheritance can be increased, and existing laws to permit gifts and the establishment of trust funds can be tightened up. The taxation of inheritance is a widely popular policy; many people hold the view that a person should keep what he earns himself (''entitled to the fruits of his labor''), but the transmission of wealth to a son or daughter is less widely favored. Such attitudes lie outside the reach of economic analysis. One commentator, in defense of inheritance, has offered the view that inheritance is but one form of advantage that parents can pass along to children; beauty, brains, ambition, and health are other attributes that are in some measure hereditary.[5] Why, it is asked, should the parent who can give his children wealth be denied the opportunity to do so, when those other worthwhile attributes are passed along without any interference? Such an argument may fail to convince most observers. After all, the *regression effect* operates on biological attributes: Einstein's son, though an excellent mathematician, will never duplicate the intellectual feats of his father; and Henry Fonda's children, while not homely, are far from being reproductions of their handsome father. Wealth, on the other hand, does not seem to be subject to the same kind of intergenerational equalization.

A policy to reduce the importance of wealth transmission need not deprive a person of the right to leave his heirs comfortably well-off. A maximum size could be set on a trust fund or an inheritance which would assure the recipient of a secure life; the transmission of tens of millions of dollars is by no means necessary to attain such a goal, however.

Having pondered what can be done about wealth, we ask: what *should* be done? To get a better feel for the appropriateness of different possible policies, we ask: what function do the very wealthy perform in society? Does their presence have any beneficial or constructive effect?

[5]Milton Friedman, in *Capitalism and Freedom* (Chicago: University of Chicago Press, 1962) presents this argument.

17.3.3. What Are the Implications of Wealth?

The very wealthy live differently from most of the readers of this book, just as the very poor do. We read of magnificent homes, great art collections, private jet airplanes, lavish weddings and engagement parties, and expensive holidays in Acapulco, Corfu, or Hyannisport. But there has been a degree of social benefit in some of that lavish consumption. Many of the great art treasures from the past are the result of commissions to artists from wealthy patrons with good taste. For centuries, the wealthy were the custodians of the Western intellectual heritage: gentlemen-scholars did much to create and refine our store of scientific and humane knowledge. Certainly, much benefit is reaped by the present generation from the existence of past wealth; whether the existing degree of inequality is necessary to assure similar benefits to future generations is another matter, of course. However, it is not in consumption or the use of their leisure time that the wealthy exercise their most important roles within the society. Nor is it in their conspicuous and significant philanthropic effort.

The most significant role played by the wealthy individuals of society is that of steward or overseer of society's capital. The very wealthy hold the vast bulk of the ownership shares of our corporations. They seek to earn high returns on their financial capital. Firms that are embarked on promising projects attract funds to undertake those projects; firms whose activity no longer satisfies their customers have their capital funds withdrawn. Some of the very wealthy take an active part in running corporations; they sit on the policy-making councils that decide what their firms will do. Other major owners are apparently passive; but they hire investment counsellors and portfolio managers to direct their financial capital, and those counsellors and managers look for opportunities to back and for laggard firms to penalize. There are, of course, other ways stewardship can be handled, even without eliminating private property in capital. But it would be difficult to argue that this stewardship system, based on the concentration of wealth, has worked poorly.

But does a private stewardship system necessarily lead to a concentration of wealth as heavy as that which we observe in America today? Quite possibly, if steps were taken to enable more widespread ownership of wealth among medium-income individuals, more people with the requisite interest and aptitude might take their places among the important stewards of financial capital in society. Those steps would logically involve the closing of tax loopholes, and possibly also the reduction of tax rates on medium to high incomes.

Large-scale wealth, and policies to reduce its concentration, lead to questions of liberty. Heavy taxation of such wealth is a breach of the liberty of the wealthy; but the power that derives from great wealth may be a threat to the liberty of the less wealthy. In any case, there are important questions of efficiency to be considered. Can alternative hypothetical arrangements for the stewardship of society's capital do as well as the present arrangement? Radical departures, involving heavy redistribution or governmental control, don't offer much encouragement. The best bet may well be to stay with the present evolutionary process, involving a rather slow diffusion of wealth into the hands of medium-income individuals. That diffusion process would be speeded up by the tax law changes already suggested.

17.4. POVERTY

In the minds of some observers, the problems of wealth and poverty are a single problem, two sides of the same coin. Were it not for the rich, they feel, there would be no poor: it is exploitation that breeds both wealth and poverty. Such a view has never had the benefit of coherent supporting argument, and it need not detain us. Getting rid of the rich and the institutions that have enabled people to become rich doesn't really help the poor in any meaningful or lasting way. The problem of poverty demands consideration of two issues: what can be done to meliorate the evil of poverty for the current generation of poor, and what can be done to minimize its spread into the next generation?

The first of these goals, to help the current generation of poor, is conceptually easy but politically difficult. Gifts of money or goods help to relieve the more severe consequences of poverty, and the provision of those gifts on a reasonable scale through government programs is a straightforward response. There are, however, subtle aspects of the problem. Is it better to give money, or gifts of specific "necessities" like food, clothing, housing, and medical care? Which approach conveys the greatest good to the poor for a particular level of expenditure by the government? The gift of money can be defended on the ground that it is administratively simple, involves very little interference in the private lives of the recipients, and gives the recipients the greatest opportunity to function like all other members of society. Learning to exercise the important faculties of critical choice is an important step in taking a normal place in society. The gift of goods, on the other hand, is defended mainly on the ground that many poor would not use gifts of money to meet their needs, as a consensus of society perceives those needs. This may or may not be a realistic concern, but the fact remains that many people hold the view that popular support for relief of poverty would be greatly weakened if the poor were given relief funds that they can "drink up or gamble away."

Beyond direct relief, the best help for the contemporary poor lies in the assurance of a high and stable level of employment. When employment is high, even people of low skill find steady work.

Insofar as help for the future is concerned, enculturation and education of the poor youth is necessary. At the present time, there is some movement in the right direction. Steps have been taken to improve the quality of schooling provided to the poor in the past two decades. In higher education, special opportunity programs are being provided for minority groups and other poor by numerous public and private universities. In addition, numerous business firms and government agencies have undertaken special programs for the training of poor workers.

With regard to the development of skills and pride among the poorer classes, the existing programs of poor relief appear to be damaging. Numerous commentators have noticed the development of a "poverty subculture," in which a third generation is now being raised by welfare agencies. The welfare agencies have for the most part provided for the immediate physical needs of the poor, inadequately in some states, conspicuously well in others.[6] However, the phalanxes of social workers and welfare bureaucrats have not been successful in moving the poor out of their state of dependency. Whether it would help to change away from the present program of relief in the form of goods toward a program of direct money payments is an interesting question. A move in that direction is contemplated; the ill-fated Nixon Administration's "family assistance program," which was proposed in 1969 but never got through Congress, would have been such a move.

17.5. RACE AND INCOME IN AMERICA

The facts on this topic can be quickly summarized. Since World War Two, Negro family incomes have averaged about 40 percent of white family incomes in the rural South. In the urban North, the figure is about 70 percent. These figures move up and down slightly, depending on the rate of unemployment in the society: blacks are affected more adversely by unemployment than are whites. Incomes have been estimated for Negro households headed by both women and men. It is found that there has been an overall gain in black incomes relative to white since the 1930s (consistent with recovery from the Great Depression), but most of that gain has been concentrated in households headed by women.[7] More comprehensively, Table 17.6 records changes over time in the distribution of income of the white and nonwhite populations of the U.S.A.

These facts are disturbing, even though recent events may have produced movement toward remedy of the situation. The reasons for the income differences are visible and obvious. The complex of social and psychological forces that we call "racial prejudice" has led to inferior schooling for blacks; on the job, it has led to blacks being last hired, first fired, regardless of ability; it has created feelings of hopelessness and despair among blacks, and made them cynical toward such genuine opportunities as are occasionally offered to them.

---

[6]It is an anachronism of federalism that poverty relief is carried out on a state-by-state basis. In some states, like Mississippi and Arkansas, poor families obtain less than 10 percent of the benefits they would receive in wealthier states such as New York, Michigan, or Illinois.

[7]These facts are reported by Christopher Jencks and David Riesman, *The Academic Revolution* (Garden City, N.Y.: Doubleday, 1968) and cited by Bronfenbrenner (see Bibliographical Note).

TABLE 17.6. Percentages of the White and Nonwhite Populations in Different Income Classes

Year	Race	INCOME BRACKETS				
		Less than $1,000	$1,000–3,000	$3,000–6,000	$6,000–10,000	More than $10,000
1947	W	9.0	37.2	41.3	9.5	3.0
	N	28.8	52.3	15.9	3.0	0.1
1955	W	6.6	19.1	43.7	23.8	6.8
	N	19.0	38.3	34.1	7.9	0.6
1960	W	4.1	15.0	33.2	32.5	15.3
	N	13.4	33.1	33.1	15.4	4.9
1965	W	2.5	11.5	23.8	35.3	27.1
	N	7.1	28.2	35.1	20.5	9.0
1970	W	1.4	6.1	15.0	25.9	51.6
	N	3.4	16.7	26.0	25.6	28.2

Source: U.S. Bureau of the Census, *Statistical Abstract of the United States* (Washington, D.C.: Government Printing Office, 1972), Table 523.

What can be done? The answer is being acted out at present. A rapidly growing majority consensus now favors equal rights for minority citizens. Minority citizens themselves are growing in pride and self-awareness. Equal opportunity for minorities is far from a reality, but it is no longer a wildly impossible dream, as it appeared in the 1930s, when it was taken for granted by many whites that blacks were inferior and deserved inferior treatment as a part of the natural order of things.

The first step in the process of reversing that view was repeal of the "Jim Crow" laws which held in many Southern states until the middle 1950s. These laws provided for separation of the races in schooling; public transportation; entertainment like sports events and theaters; and public facilities like waiting rooms, restrooms, and drinking fountains. The impact of such laws on the racial consciousness of all citizens, black and white, cannot be overestimated.

The next steps taken, which affected voting rights and schooling, are instructive regarding the kinds of obstacle to progress that can arise. Grants of voting rights were resisted most strenuously in areas where Negroes were in or near a majority. In those areas, white political organizations could not face the threat of a large Negro vote, and obstacles of various types, including outright violence, were thrown up to prevent the registration of black voters. However, in less than a dozen years, the black franchise became a reality. Black mayors were elected in several major cities of the North; more important, black sheriffs and other officials were elected in numerous Southern counties.

The course of education for blacks has proceeded even less smoothly. A major obstacle to progress in education has been the attempt to combine the provision of adequate education with the racial integration of school groups. Integration may be a desirable goal in and of itself, but it is doubtful that a majority of whites supports that goal sufficiently strongly to make substantial personal sacrifices toward its attainment. Because integration involves the acceptance of one individual by a group of individuals, it would seem that its success hangs on the establishment of a common culture and the acceptance of and commitment to that culture by all affected parties. Education is an important step in the necessary enculturation; this includes education of the majority as well as the minority. Integration, to be fully successful, must be a spontaneous product of individual choice, people choosing their housing, schools, and personal associations without regard to race.[8]

At the present time, then, America has accomplished the abolition of all laws that call for unequal treatment of the races or denial of opportunity to minority races. A substantial majority of all citizens probably supports the ideas that all races should have equal opportunity and equal freedom. A smaller group, perhaps less than a majority, regards racial integration in schools and locale of residence as a desirable and necessary social goal. While progress has been made toward the goals of equal opportunity and equal treatment, there is much yet to be accomplished. Equal opportunity and equal treatment are the crucial goals to anyone who is concerned over this nation's inequality of income by race; when opportunity and treatment are equalized, incomes will equalize also (although more slowly; income from property will build up slowly, even after income from wages has equalized).

17.6. CONCLUSIONS

Information on the distribution of personal income, like that tabulated in this chapter, has always fascinated people who are interested in issues of social justice. The historic pattern of significant discrimination against blacks is visible in nonwhite earnings differences, and lately interest has focused on similar differences in male-female earnings patterns which offer evidence of discrimination by sex.

On a more cheerful note, the pattern through time seems to be one of increasing real incomes, with increases coming slightly faster to low income people than to high income people.

But optimists and pessimists alike should avoid attaching too much weight to the published data on the distribution of personal income. For reasons that were discussed extensively in this chapter, those data constitute a very shaky basis on which to rest conclusions, or construct policies, regarding such issues as justice, opportunity and progress.

---

[8]Even with complete freedom of choice, if individuals value the presence of similar and congenial individuals, highly segregated patterns of settlement will spontaneously emerge. A fascinating account of this point is given by Thomas C. Shelling in "The Ecology of Micromotives," *The Public Interest,* 25(Fall 1971).

*APPENDIX I
THE MEASUREMENT OF INDIVIDUAL INCOMES

17.A.1. The Measurement of Market Reward and Redistribution

Suppose it were possible to observe each and every household in America for a period of, say, one year, and to measure the total value of each household's *earned receipts* from every possible source. These would include

—Wages and salaries of working members of the household

—The value of other employee benefits obtained by working members of the household

—Proceeds from the rental of real property that is owned by the household

—Dividends from ownership shares (stock) of corporations owned by the household

—Interest income from bonds or savings accounts held by the household

—Proceeds from the sale of goods produced within the household (such as tomatoes grown, legal advice given, chickens raised, paintings or short stories created, textbooks written)

—The value of goods produced by the household, and consumed directly

—The value of services that the household obtains from the capital goods that it owns (the value of shelter from a house that it owns and lives in, for example)

When all these earned receipts are totaled, two adjustments are made:

—*Deduct* an allowance which reflects the cost of maintaining the household's income-yielding goods (the land, buildings, or equipment of a farmer; the building and equipment of a shopkeeper, the house of a homeowner)

—*Add* the household's share of earnings retained within corporations in which the household owns stock[9]

After making all those calculations, we would have a measure of every household's share of goods produced within the economy during the period of observation. For each household, that measure is called its *share of national income;* that measure can be used to answer the question: how well do individual households fare, relative to one another, as a result of the workings of the economic system?

Now, to measure a household's ability to purchase goods for consumption, the following changes are made in its share of national income:

—Subtract the household's share of earnings retained in corporations in which the household owns stock

—Add (or subtract) the net change in the market value of all goods and securities owned by the household

*The material in this section may be too detailed for some introductory coverage.

[9]This is conceptually a simple calculation. If the corporation has a million shares of stock outstanding, and it retains $2 million dollars of earnings during the year, then the household is credited with $2 for every share of the corporation's stock that it holds.

—Subtract the sum total of all taxes paid by the household (including the "tax" imposed by inflation)

—Add the market value of all public services consumed by the household, and paid for out of tax revenues by government

—Add the value of all income transfers received by the household (such as social security, unemployment compensation, welfare payments, and benefits from private life, health, employment, or retirement insurance plans)

—Subtract payments for employment and income insurance (such as payments to the social security system, to private pension and health plans)

The figure that is left after all those changes are made might be called *the household's share of personal disposable income*. By comparing that share for all households, we get a fairly good idea of how well society provides for individual households relative to one another. By comparing distributions of the two household shares, we observe the extent to which inequality is altered by government action and by private risk-sharing agreements (insurance).

17.A.2. The Measures Actually Compiled

The income distribution statistics actually compiled are a rather peculiar combination of the two possibilities described in the preceding section. The government series most frequently referred to, compiled from Bureau of Census survey data by the U.S. Department of Commerce, includes all types of earned income (wages and salaries, profits of privately owned firms, rental income, dividends, and interest); but it also includes transfer payments (social security benefits, etc.), an estimate of nonmoney wages (principally accruing to farm laborers and domestics), an estimate of the rental value of owner-occupied dwellings, food and fuel consumed by those who produce it, and a share of the property income retained by life insurance companies with which the household holds policies. From all this, the household's payments into the social security system are deducted. The resulting measure is not a good indicator of ability to consume— income from capital gains, private insurance, and tax-financed government service is not counted in, and taxes are not taken out. Nor is it a good measure of the rewards dispensed by the production system: government transfer payments are included and capital gains are not.

APPLICATIONS AND EXTENSIONS

1. Suppose you are instructed to evaluate the *justice* of the economic system in America. What evidence would you use in preparing that evaluation? What rules or conditions do you think an economic order must fulfill to be "just?"

2. What conditions would you like changed in the U.S. economic order as you look ahead to your years as an adult participant? Would your preferred alternative conditions make you more *secure*? More *free*? More *equal with regard to income*? What, in short, is your personal priority ordering among "social goods"?

3. Suppose that a society has found an income distribution that everyone agrees is perfectly just, and suppose that distribution in fact prevails. Now suppose a super-charismatic person appears, combining the athletic talent of Billie King, the voice of Joan Baez, the energy of Ethel Kennedy, and so forth—you complete the list of attributes and prototypes.

    This person is so multi-talented that her compatriots offer her extravagant sums, lying far outside the range of incomes in the ideal distribution, to perform certain tasks and roles. In fact, she not only becomes the leading income earner in the society, she accounts for ten percent of the total income of the society.

    (a) Does her great income and wealth constitute a social "problem?"

    (b) Should people be permitted to bid large sums for her services as professional quarterback, recording artist, astronaut, president, or what have you? If some upper bound is imposed on her earnings, does this constitute an infringement on the liberties of those who (say) would like to hear her recorded voice, but who cannot bid enough to induce her to take the time to make records?

    (c) In the absence of market signals, how should the effort and time of this phenomenal person be allocated?

4. What, if anything, is the difference between a *progressive income tax* and an income tax system which collects higher taxes from higher incomes?

5. "Money wages are not the only compensation for a job. In fact, it may not even be the most important compensation." List at least six other attributes of a job situation which contribute to its desirability (or lack of desirability).

BIBLIOGRAPHICAL NOTE

Martin Bronfenbrenner, *Income Distribution Theory* (Chicago: Aldine Press, 1971) is a wide-ranging treatise on the problem of how society's product is divided among groups and individuals. Much of this very worthwhile book is accessible to careful and persistent readers with small or no background in economics. Edward Budd, "Postwar Changes in the Size and Distribution of Income in the U.S.," *American Economic Review,* 60, May, 1970, is a useful source of information on comparatively recent developments in the United States. Gabriel Kolko, *Wealth and Power in America* (New York: Praeger Books, 1962) is a spirited, but not very carefully researched or tightly reasoned, statement of what has come to be regarded as the "radical" position on questions of income distribution.

Irving Kristol, "Poverty and Pecksniff," *The New Leader,* (March 30, 1964) contains a sharply critical attack on "the ideologues of poverty" whose peculiar views of the problem were important in bringing about the ill-fated "war on poverty" of the mid-1960s. Stanley Lebergott, "Income Distribution: Size," *International Encyclopedia of the Social Sciences* (Chicago: Free Press, 1968) is an excellent place to turn for more information; it contains a large collection of references, Lebergott's discussion of the reliability of simple inferences drawn from income distribution statistics is especially useful.

Ferdinand Lundberg, *The Rich and the Super-Rich* (New York: Lyle Stuart, Inc., 1968) is a gossipy and entertaining chronicle of who the wealthiest people are, how they got that way, and how they stay that way. The British edition has a useful introduction by Peter Wilsher on distribution in Great Britain. Lundberg may fancy himself a radical, but his book reads like a hymn to capitalism. Finally, Jan Pen, *Income Distribution* (New York: Praeger Books, 1971) is a verbose but useful chronicle of facts, theories, and policies aimed at the general reader.

Part Four

COLLECTIVIZE INTERVENE, OR . . . ?

The principal widely discussed modifications of the market system are *socialism* and piecemeal *programmatic intervention.* The former is a system of government ownership and control of productive resources. Socialism, as a theoretical system and as a working system, is discussed in Chapter 18. Programmatic intervention is pretty much the system under which we live in the U.S. today. It is a system that has known both success and failure in the task of "social betterment." Some of the more conspicuous examples of both success and failure are chronicled in Chapter 19 and an attempt is made to deduce some of the factors that contribute to the success of programs.

CHAPTER EIGHTEEN

The Alternative
of Socialism

After the revolution, man will become immeasurably stronger,
wiser and subtler; his body will become more harmonized,
his movements more rhythmic, his voice more musical. The
forms of life will become dynamically dramatic. The average
human type will rise to the heights of an Aristotle, a Goethe or a
Marx. And above this ridge, new peaks will rise.

LEON TROTSKY (1925)

Beware of false prophets, which come to you in sheep's
clothing, but inwardly they are ravening wolves.

MATTHEW 7:15

18.1. ALLOCATION DECISION BY THE STATE

18.1.1. Socialism Defined

The central issues of goods production and resource use in a society are well-summarized by the three questions *what, how,* and *for whom.* Throughout this book the emphasis has been on the answers given to these questions in a capitalist system. The prototype of ''ideal'' capitalism is a competitive market economy; the basic theory of competitive market processes is spelled out and interpreted in Chapters 4 through 10. Problems of monopoly, taste manipulation, externalities, and maldistribution of income, all of which at one time or another have been held to be serious drawbacks of the capitalist system, were explored in subsequent chapters. Our purpose in this chapter is to ask: How does *socialism* differ from capitalism in its structure and functioning? How are the three basic questions of resource allocation answered in a socialist economy? Is socialism superior to capitalism according to some explicit and reasonable meaning of "superior"?

Socialism has been defined in different ways by different authors. In its earliest form as a recognizable doctrine (c. 1835, as exemplified in the writings of Saint-Simon), two important departures from the capitalist system were clearly advocated: the "social" ownership of the means of production, and the administration of all economic activity under the direct guidance of experts and in the general interest of society. Thus (in less flowery language), socialism called for government ownership of productive resources and for government direction of productive activity. The private ownership of productive property and coordination of individual choices through market action were both to be replaced. Those two changes are still advocated by many socialists today; some socialists, however, no longer insist on the need for centralized control of resource use—they are content to define socialism in terms of the public ownership of productive resources.

Throughout its early years socialist theory developed slowly. Advocates of socialism tended to focus their energy on exposing the evils they perceived in the capitalist order, and in the process they tended to neglect practical questions regarding the workability and workings of a socialist system. A number of very important practical problems were not recognized by the nineteenth-century anti-capitalists. Their belief in the great wisdom of man and the perfectibility of society (as discussed in Chapter 3) led them to underestimate the importance and difficulty of the decisions capitalist societies make through market action.

Early in this century the question was raised whether in fact a central planner could devise a set of output instructions that are both *feasible* and *consistent*. Feasibility depends on the adequacy of available resources; if a plan requires more than the available amount of some resources, it is infeasible. The issue of consistency hinges on the fact that some goods must be used in the production of others. Steel must be used in the production of machinery, coal in the production of steel, and machinery in the production of coal. If the planner is to avoid wasteful overproduction of some goods and shortages of others, he must proceed in a very clever way in setting his production schedules so as to take into account the interdependency of goods in production. The early advocates of socialism who condemned the capitalist order apparently did not realize that feasibility and consistency are achieved automatically through market action within a capitalist market system. That system, with its profit motive, was heavily criticized; but the critics offered no alternative mechanism that would (probably) work in achieving feasibility and consistency.

18.1.2. The Problem of Socialist Calculation

It should be pointed out that feasibility and consistency are modest objectives for an economic system. A nation's output may be feasible and consistent without being either *efficient* or *desirable*. That is, there are many output programs that are feasible and consistent but that waste resources in an extravagant way (the problem of efficiency); and there are many other programs that combine resources efficiently in a technical sense but that lead to an output mix that simply isn't valued by the members of the society—a different output program, with a different mix of goods, would have been preferred.

Adopting the artifice of a one-person, two-good economy for purposes of illustration, the trick is to arrive at the point A (Figure 18.1) where the most highly preferred goods combination is produced. Any point in the diagram that lies on or below the production possibility frontier PP' is feasible and consistent; any point that lies on the frontier is efficient; but many points on the frontier are not highly valued by the society's consumer (point P, for example). In a capitalist economy the issues of feasibility and consistency do not arise; they are solved automatically in the process of interaction among individuals in markets. In a socialist economy, where a plan of some sort precedes action, the problems of feasibility and consistency are important.

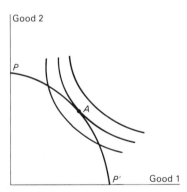

FIGURE 18.1.   **The efficient output is *A* for a two-good, one person economy.**

If feasibility and consistency are important difficulties in a planned economy, it would appear that efficiency and desirability must be even harder to assure under a system of planning; and that, indeed, seems to be the case. The difficulties of achieving a desired output efficiently were brought forcefully to the attention of socialism's advocates in the 1920s and 1930s by a group of pro-capitalist economists who, tired of seeing their own preferred economic order punched around by its socialist critics, decided to go on the intellectual counter-offensive. An Austrian, Ludwig von Mises, posed the problem in the form of an assertion: that "socialist calculation" is impossible; that is, central planning of economic performance cannot use resources systematically to satisfy human needs and wants. Somewhat earlier, an Italian, Enrico Barone, had demonstrated that by solving a system of equations that contained information on the demand for goods and technical conditions of production the central planner can attain not only feasibility and consistency, but efficiency as well. Barone's results were a proof of the *existence* of a workable centrally directed plan; but his results actually *supported* the views of the pro-capitalist critics, like von Mises, since Barone concluded that "The minister of production in a socialist state" would find it necessary to base his calculations on capitalist data and ideas like market-generated prices, profits, and interest rates, or else his task would be unapproachable. Because most of the early socialists scorned those artifacts of capitalism as meaningless, it is understandable that the problems of central economic control under socialism were viewed as unsolvable. Moreover, Barone pointed out that even if socialist resistance to allocation through prices and markets could be overcome, his own results don't quite touch the heart of the problem: it is one thing to assert that the solution of a system of equations yields a workable plan and quite another thing actually to obtain the necessary solution. Barone's results removed the problem of socialist calculation from the realm of *conceptual* impossibility, but they provided no answer to the criticism of *practical* impossibility.

At the time that von Mises was preparing his criticisms, the socialists were grappling with their first opportunity to put their ideas to work. The Russian Revolution of 1917 provided an occasion to design a socialist economy, with results to be sketched later on in this chapter. Perhaps the most important impact that the Soviet experience had on theorizing about socialist systems was that it focused attention squarely on the question of the *purposes* or *goals* of economic activity under Socialism (the political movement, spelled with a capital S).

18.1.3. Lessons From the Soviet Experience

Observation of the Soviet economy reinforced the view of von Mises and other critics that efficiency, as it is understood in a capitalist economy, must be scarce under socialism. Numerous examples of "failure" were rather gleefully seized upon and publicized. There were massive crop failures, which were mainly due to the "liquidation" of some private farmers and the removal of property rights in agricultural land from others; faulty production planning and coordination could also be blamed in part. There was a virtually complete breakdown in the production of goods for consumers and a high priority given to the accumulation of heavy industrial capacity—steel production, production of manufacturing machinery, hydroelectric generating plants, and similar undertakings. More subtle evidences of inefficiency could also be found. Modern plants and equipment were put together at enormous opportunity cost and used to produce goods that could have been obtained far more cheaply by labor-intensive, "primitive" methods. These modern plants were then held up to the world as showcases of Soviet efficiency and progress.

All of these shortcomings and inefficiencies were noted by critics who assumed that the purpose of Soviet economic activity is no different from the purpose of economic activity in Western society: to deliver goods that individual consumers want. In a society where individual preferences count, market action reveals the value of foregone alternatives in terms of the preferences of individual consumers. Efficiency in such a society is measured in terms of giving up as few alternative goods as possible in implementing any production plan. In Soviet Russian society, we now realize, the idea of catering to individual preferences simply was not entertained seriously. If modernization of the steel industry means that a given output of steel is obtained at the sacrifice of more consumer goods than would have been necessary without modernization, that fact was viewed as being of no consequence: modernization was itself the goal and not the efficient provision of consumer goods.

18.2. MARKET SOCIALISM

Advocates of socialism outside the Soviet Union, of course, could not take such a hard-nosed attitude regarding the unimportance of individual preferences and still hope to persuade people to their view of the desirability of socialism. It became necessary for them to find an answer to the charge that socialism either ignores the consumption preferences of individual citizens or does a poor job of meeting those preferences. The search for an answer was led in the 1930s by a Pole, Oskar Lange, and an Englishman, Abba Lerner. They proposed a way by which socialism could be made to serve individualist ends: the central planner must, by the use of prices and price adjustments, *simulate* the activity of competitive markets. Prices and wages would adjust, in response to the expressions of consumer preference, through the simulated market process. Producers, in turn, would choose their outputs in such a way that the profits on their operations would be maximized, given the prevailing prices and wages. In equilibrium, price and marginal social cost would be equal for all goods; and transfers of resources in production from one good to another could yield no greater satisfaction for consumers, just as under perfect competition in a market economy.

A number of practical problems are posed by the Lange-Lerner proposals. What set of prices will serve as an initial basis for allocative choices? If those prices do not yield an equilibrium, how can the single authority find price adjustments that take the economy toward equilibrium, in the way that occurs through the actions of self-interested individuals, as in a capitalist system? What incentives can be found that can guarantee that individual managers will, in fact, work to maximize the returns on the operations under their control, and how, in fact, can it be known that those returns are being maximized? These are all consequential issues; and unless they can be satisfactorily resolved, the prospects for market socialism (as the Lange-Lerner proposals are called) are not bright.

To a large extent, these obstacles to the smooth working of a socialist economic order are caused by faulty or incomplete assignments of *property rights*. State planners are in effect given the rights to control the use of productive equipment and resources, but they are not given the rights to reap the full gain that stems from using that equipment in best response to consumer preference: they do not keep the profits or bear the losses that stem from their resource-use decisions. Who does get the profits or bear the losses? Nobody: they are dissipated throughout the society by the manner in which production is organized.

The issues confronting market socialism, then, are of two types. The first type is computational and centers on the problem of moving quickly from an initial to an equilibrium set of prices. Even given command over massive batteries of advanced electronic computers, the job of reckoning price adjustments for a representatively complete array of goods from something like reasonably accurate cost and demand relations is beyond reach at the present time. The second type of issue is institutional; the problem is to describe a set of rules that will induce decision-makers to respond in the desired way to the price and wage signals that are sent out.

Market socialism, then, is a theoretical system in which government owns and controls the society's productive resources and attempts to allocate those resources in a way that controls the pace and direction of economic development and enhances the satisfaction and happiness of the individual members of society. In this respect, market socialism is similar to such other actions by government as intervention to control the use of monopoly power, intervention to rationalize externalities, and intervention to redistribute income. In the discussion of those topics it was noted that the prospects are by no means certain that government will find measures that lead to an improvement in economic performance: a decision by government to take action certainly does not convey automatic assurance that performance will improve. The recourse to market socialism would (at least in theory) eliminate any need for those piecemeal interventions in response to specific problems, but it would also mean that government has taken on the very large task of planning all economic activity.

Suppose that market socialism *could* be turned into a smoothly functioning system of allocation. A society choosing between market socialism and capitalism would be making a decision regarding the appropriate role of private ownership of productive resources. (Capitalism may be faced with problems of monopoly, externalities, and the maldistribution of income; but if those problems can be solved under a regime of market socialism, they should be solvable by the same methods under capitalism.) The choice boils down to whether public or private ownership of productive resources is desired. Is it certain that incentives to efficient performance will survive if private ownership in capital is abolished? If bureaucrats are put in command of society's capital, what set of signals or incentives will lead them to use those resources effectively? In short, are the gains in efficiency and equity sufficiently large to warrant so major an abrogation of liberty as is implied by abolishing private capital ownership? These questions will be answered differently by subscribers to different ideologies. And because no good *scientific* answers to the first two questions are available, the issue remains an ideological one.

It may turn out fifty years hence, when there is a clearer perspective on the theory of socialism, that the topic of market socialism is a dead end. The ideas of market socialism may be seen, at that future date, to be based on a naive view of the objectives of a socialist society. A basis for this suggestion is to be found in observing existing socialist economies, and in recent writings on the theory of socialism, particularly in the important work of J. Drewnowski, a Polish economist and planner, to which we now turn.[1]

18.3. STATE PREFERENCES AND THE ZONE OF STATE INFLUENCE

18.3.1. Drewnowski's Framework

Drewnowski's contribution to our understanding of socialist economies is in the way that he builds upon the fact that every modern society allocates its resources by two mechanisms: there are individually controlled mechanisms (principally and most importantly, markets); and there are collectively controlled, or State-operated mechanisms. As he points out, *these two mechanisms operate in response to two entirely different sets of control signals and objectives.* Mechanisms that operate within the *zone of individual influence* respond to the actions of individuals. A market, for example, responds to control signals generated by individual supply and demand decisions; and the objective of market action is to serve the preferences of individuals and to resolve unavoidable conflict among those preferences. Other mechanisms operate entirely within the *zone of State influence.* They are controlled by signals from the bureaucracy of the State, and the objective served in operating those mechanisms is the *preferences of the State's planners.* An example of such a mechanism can be found in the military establishment of the U.S., which commands the use of large capital and labor resources in the service of goals which it has to a large extent defined for itself. A similar example is to be found

---

[1]J. Drewnowski, "The Economic Theory of Socialism: A Suggestion for Reconsideration," *Journal of Political Economy* 69(August 1961).

in the entire heavy manufacturing sector of the economy of the USSR; large
quantities of resources are directed in the service of governmentally defined
objectives. The principal allocative mechanism in the ''zone of State influence''
is command, backed up by the threat of force.[2]

Finally, Drewnowski suggests the possibility of a ''zone of dual influence'' in
which ''State and individual preferences meet.'' An example of allocation in the
dual-influence zone is a State-owned and State-controlled enterprise which deals
directly with society's individuals and which takes their preferences into account
in making its operating decisions.

Socialism can be clearly distinguished from capitalism in terms of the
importance of different zones of influence, and hence, in terms of the
preferences that are served in the allocation of society's resources. A capitalist
economy, Drewnowski asserts, is one with a large zone of private influence and
no zone of State influence. A socialist economy is one with a large zone of State
influence and no zone of private influence.[3] There are, of course, substantial
zones of dual influence in both types of society.

Having thus outlined Drewnowski's framework for classifying economic
systems, it remains to consider two questions: (1) What are the various possible
forms that socialism can take? (2) Given the heavy emphasis that is placed upon
planners' preferences, how are individual humans likely to fare under socialism?

18.3.2. Degrees of Market Allocation under Socialism

We can easily envision a range of possible organizational forms for socialist
states. At the collectivist extreme, the entire national economy is in the State
zone of influence. Output rates and input mixes for all goods are controlled by
the State. Consumers' preferences have no effect on what is produced, or how.
Workers have no choice of occupation, and every individual as a consumer is
given an allocation of consumable goods.

This collectivist extreme describes no economy, past or present; it is simply
the beginning point of a discussion. First, and at the very least, the State will
allow exchange among individuals from their goods allocations. Relative prices
among consumer goods, reflecting the preferences of the individual consumers,
will be determined by that exchange process. However, those relative prices will
not affect output decisions: individuals may reveal that they want more shoes
and fewer belts by bidding a high price for leather in the form of shoes and a low
price for leather in the form of belts; but the production control authority has no
particular reason to view the outcome of that bidding as significant. Second, the

---

[2]Thus, in Boulding's terminology (Chapter 2, Section 2.1), allocation in the zone of individual
influence is principally through exchange relationships; in the zone of State influence allocation is
done by status, backed by threat.

[3]Thus, according to Drewnowski's definitions, the U.S. cannot be called purely capitalist
(consider the military establishment); nor can the USSR be called purely socialist (for reasons that
will be clear after the Soviet economy is discussed in Section 18.4).

State also might permit some choice of occupation to individuals; and wages might be set to induce people to enter categories of employment that are held to be important. At one time in its history, the economy of the Soviet Union offered little more than these first and second modifications as departures from the model of extreme collectivism. With a market for consumer goods, but no response in production to individual preferences, we have what Drewnowski calls a "first-degree market economy," a system that described the Soviet Russia of 1921 to 1965.

Socialism can respond more fully to individual preferences. Market-determined prices of consumer goods can serve to guide the production of those goods. The planners may continue to allocate new capital to individual production facilities for use in the production of specific goods; planners may in addition stipulate the total quantities of other inputs, such as labor and mineral resources, to be used for consumer goods production. But within that framework, "variable inputs" can be transferred from one line of consumer goods production to another in response to consumer demand, with the goal being to earn the highest realizable returns overall. That arrangement, with the total allocation of capital resources to consumer-goods production under the control of planners but with the mix of consumer-goods output that is obtained from those resources being determined wholly or partly by market signals, the picture is very much like the one seen in the Soviet Union after the adoption of planning reforms that were instituted in the middle 1960s. Such limited response, with no change in the quota of resources allocated to consumer-goods production, is in Drewnowski's terminology a "second-degree market economy."

The "third-degree market economy" is reached when total new investment in consumer-goods production remains under State control; but the allocation of new capital among plants that produce consumer goods of different types is responsive to consumer demands for finished products. The allocation of investment in consumer-goods industries is transferred from the State zone to the zone of dual influence. In this "third-degree market economy," it is conceivable that managers of facilities that produce consumer goods might, by bidding high prices for productive resources, be able to persuade the State to transfer some additional resources, which it planned to use for other purposes, into consumer-goods production.

18.3.3. Socialism and Individual Welfare

What, then, of the treatment of individuals under a socialist regime? It is not necessary that socialism be authoritarian or dictatorial. The ideal envisioned in the theory of market socialism is an individualistically based order; the "evil" of privately owned productive resources is to be abolished, but in all other respects the system resembles an ideal of competitive market capitalism. With a regime in which State preferences direct resource use to a large extent, the economic order will not be individualistic, but it need not be nondemocratic. The State can allocate resources in a way that fulfills the desires of a large majority of the population:

> The economic objectives that an individual has as a member of a nation, class, party or group . . . and also a number of long-term consumers' objectives, can be achieved only by [collective action]. If an individual wants the economy to grow at a faster rate . . . or the advancement of science, better working conditions, or cheaper public utilities, he cannot achieve these by individual action. He . . . has to vote at the election to bring to power a government that would have this sort of policy.[4]

State preferences, then, can conform more or less closely to the objectives of individuals. State action, when it serves objectives that are ignored or are inadequately served by the processes of individual allocation, can be guided by citizens at the polls.[5]

The same idea of expressing preferences through the political process can find application in a capitalist society, where (for example) the redistribution of income or the rationalization of externalities may be seen to require action by the State and may meet with the enthusiastic approval of a large majority of the population. Socialists are not unique in perceiving the possibility of going beyond market action, nor is their economic system *necessarily* more rigidly authoritarian than the capitalist system. Yet authority seems to be heavily used by the State in socialist societies. The widespread belief that there are many high-priority economic objectives that are beyond the reach of individual action does not suffice to explain why public ownership of all productive resources is necessary, for example.

Until Drewnowski's paper appeared, the controversy between supporters of socialism and capitalism centered on the familiar issues of equity and efficiency. The socialist contention has always been that capitalism is inequitable. Karl Marx and his followers predicted that capitalist society would become increasingly stratified by class, with the rich capitalists (owners of capital) becoming even richer and the poor workers becoming ever more miserable. (That prediction certainly has been proven inaccurate in the U.S. and Western Europe.) Some socialists further believe that capitalism, because it operates without the benefit of any central guiding intelligence, must be irrational, wasteful, and inefficient. (That second criticism of the capitalist order derives from the rationalist-individualist tradition of the French Enlightenment as discussed in Chapter 3 and is encountered today with particular frequency among *technocrats,* believers in

---

[4]Drewnowski, "Economic Theory of Socialism," *op. cit.* p. 343.

[5]The processes of State allocation are subject to an important conceptual drawback, insofar as anyone who adheres to individualist criteria is concerned. An important theorem, proved by K. J. Arrow, shows that an ordering of outcomes by the mechanism of State allocation must be *dictatorial* (one person's preferences being served without consideration of others); or it must fail to satisfy one of several properties (such as transitivity), which normally are required of an ordering that we are willing to consider as being representative of preferences. K. J. Arrow, *Social Choice and Individual Values,* New York: Wiley, 1951.

an engineering approach to all of society's problems.) On the other side of the controversy, the first capitalists to criticize the socialist alternative focused on the difficulty of running an economy directly in such a way that individual preferences are served reasonably well. The fundamental individualist proposition that any economic order must be judged on its ability to deliver desired goods and services to all members of society was not questioned on either side. Drewnowski's contribution to the discussion, then, was to point out that over a fairly wide range of allocative decisions in a socialist economy, no important direct role is assigned to the satisfaction of individual preferences.

The "unresponsiveness" of some governmental and corporate decisions to the desires of the citizenry is a frequently voiced criticism of today's American economy; if Drewnowski's view is correct and government allocation processes serve planners' preferences, then we should expect to find that many decisions by government will be unresponsive to individual tastes, regardless of whether the economy is organized along capitalist or socialist lines. Because the "zone of State influence" is greatly expanded under socialism, the problem of unresponsiveness is almost surely more pressing "there" than here.

18.4. SOCIALISM IN PRACTICE

18.4.1. Soviet Russia

In the Soviet Union before 1965, virtually all important decisions regarding the allocation of resources came from "the top." A central planning bureau, which operated nationwide, closely observed economic performance in the operation of numerous major industries that were designated as "important." This bureau chose rates of production and determined the acquisition of new plants and equipment for those industries. To aid in the task of managing production and investment, output schedules and forecasts of input requirements were prepared for these important industries. For "unimportant" industries, planning was carried out in a less detailed way. Performance was judged on the basis of the total "value" of production in these industries, and targets for total value of output from an industry were set; but in measuring the value of output, prices of the different goods produced were set by the State, not by market action. Input material quotas were allocated to these "unimportant" industries by the central planning bureau, but the industry's output mix, and the allocation of its inputs among various plants, was not supervised directly by the bureau. It was up to the ministries of production or the individual plant managers to devise output schedules which reconciled the output value targets with the availability of materials. That task was a very complicated one, because during the period when a new plan was being implemented, the unimportant industries served as "buffers"; unforeseen materials shortages were taken out of the allocations to those industries. Resulting shortages of output from those industries were met by a system of allocation according to governmentally established priority among individual consumers.

The central planning bureau gathered information from, and transmitted its instructions through, various ministries of production. There was a ministry of production in all "important" industries and in many of the unimportant ones. These ministries of production saw to it that output targets as set by the central planning bureau were realistic; they assigned production quotas and new investment to the various different individual plants that produced in their industries, and made sure that output plans were met in the individual plants.

Even today, planning for "important" industries is stratified in the described manner. The central planning bureau has broad responsibility for setting output quotas in those industries and for making sure that these quotas are feasible and consistent. The ministries of production in the various industries are consulted regarding the attainability of proposed outputs; these ministries then are responsible for dividing the output quotas among participating plants and for seeing to it that the quotas are met.

This type of system worked well, judged from the viewpoint of the State and its objectives. If the State wanted more rapid growth in capacity to produce aluminum, the necessary resources could be made available by directive. The Soviet economy was able to perform on virtually even terms with the much larger and more advanced American economy in selected areas, such as production of war goods and space technology. If the desires of individual consumers had been more heavily weighted, those accomplishments might not have been possible. But with the given structure and objectives, the performance of the Soviet economy in the delivery of goods to the average citizen was not good. The use of arbitrary output values to measure performance in "unimportant" industries (and most consumer industries were so classified) led to what we would regard as abuses: stories of shoe factories that produce only one size and style of shoe, or lamp factories that produce only massive and unsaleable (but very expensive) chandeliers, were widespread and no doubt true.

Criticism of the Soviet economy's performance in delivering goods for consumption led to changes in policy and method of operation in agriculture and the "unimportant" industries. Agriculture, which despite the creation of collectives in the 1920s remained one of the most glaringly inefficient sectors of the economy, was reformed by granting individual peasants the right to manage their own small plots of land, to sell the output from those plots at market-clearing prices in urban markets, and to keep the proceeds. Beginning in 1962, proposals for reform of the consumer goods sector were advanced by Yevsei Libermann, an economist. Libermann suggested, in effect, that "second-degree market allocation" be adopted. Resources should be allocated in the production of consumer goods by processes that have a distinctly capitalist or market socialist flavor. Planning should be structured "from the bottom up," with individual plants proposing profitability and output targets to the central planning bureau, instead of vice versa. The criterion of good performance in the plant should be rate of return on capital held: the ratio of profits to value of capital. This criterion would, in a rough way, assure that society obtained a desirable and hence usable output from the capital allocated to the plant. Finally, plans should be made and performance judged over long periods of time, so as to create incentives for the introduction of new productivity-increasing techniques. With performance judged on a short-term basis, there was actually an incentive *against* the introduction of such techniques because they drastically reduced total output during the periods in which they were introduced.

In addition to the formal reforms, the Soviet State has reportedly become more tolerant of attempts by individual citizens to obtain and provide goods or services without going through the cumbersome officially prescribed procedures. State-employed repairmen and artisans, for example, reportedly engage in extensive "moonlighting"—selling their services privately during off-hours at rates higher than are charged by the State. This enables a householder with a balky furnace to make a choice—let the State repairman fix the furnace next summer at a low charge or hire the State's repairman to come next Sunday to do the job and pay him three or ten times the State rate.

Even after these reforms and changes, the Soviet State is subject to the criticism that it is unresponsive to individual desires in its resource-allocation decisions. In America, too, the government has some important leeway in deciding upon programs that have not been subjected to the market test; however, we may well doubt that the American populace would have tolerated the degree of deprivation and austerity that the Soviet Russia citizenry bore while its government busied itself in acquiring the capability to wage modern war and to do high-level, high-quality scientific research. The burdens of living in a world power rest far more lightly (if not more easily) on the shoulders of the average American than on his Soviet counterpart.

18.4.2. Personal Income Distribution: Is the USSR "More Equal"?

It is widely and erroneously believed that income equality is a dominant goal of government policy in the Soviet Union. The Soviet government has always concealed information about what its citizens earn, but the few smidgens of factual knowledge that we have indicates that in Russia, the incentive effects of income differences are quite clearly recognized and acted upon. In fact, in the early years of Soviet socialism, the state-controlled press denounced income egalitarians as sentimental and romantic enemies of the people.[6]

In 1960, the U.S. Department of Labor published a collection of impressionistic salary ranges for different jobs in the Soviet Union.[7] A plant manager report-

---

[6]See Murray Yanowich, "The Soviet Income Revolution" in M. Bornstein and D. Fusfeld, eds., *The Soviet Economy: A Book of Readings* (Homewood, Ill.: Irwin), 1966.

[7]The B. L. S. data are cited by G. L. Bach, *Economics,* 7th ed. (Englewood Cliffs, N.J.: Prentice-Hall, 1971), p. 684.

edly earned 300–1000 rubles per month; an unskilled worker, 27–50 rubles per month. The ratio of monetary compensation, based on those figures, is between 11 and 20. In the U.S. today, a plant manager earns $25,000–$60,000 per year, and unskilled workers between $2.50 and $4 per hour; the ratio of compensation here today is between 5 and 8.[8]

Comparisons of this type must be hedged and qualified. In Russia, both the plant manager and the unskilled worker pay very low rents, and get their medical care from the State. Direct subsidies of that sort tend to make their living standards more equal than the raw salary data indicate. On the other hand, in the United States, the plant manager pays a higher percentage of his salary in income tax than does the unskilled worker; that, too, has an equalizing effect. But the U.S. plant manager is much more likely to obtain significant interest income and income in kind from owned property than is the unskilled worker, while in Russia, significant income from owned property is unheard of. And so it goes.

In 1971, two British scholars did a heroic piece of detective work on the USSR income distribution.[9] They had at their disposal only a few scattered facts, including a survey of incomes in an unnamed region of the USSR, taken by an unknown person or authority in an unknown "recent" period, and a "miserable diagram" (as they called it) which depicted the frequency distribution of wages and salaries in that country in 1946 and 1966. The survey reported only three income ratios from the distribution, and the diagram was badly drawn (lines that should be perpendicular, weren't), and the axes were not explicitly scaled; but by careful measurement and educated guesswork, the scholars were able to compute various ranges of wage and salary incomes for the USSR.

Let us define the quartile ratio of incomes:

$$\frac{\text{Lowest income of the top quarter of income earners}}{\text{Highest income of the bottom quarter of income earners}}$$

Similarly the decile ratio is

$$\frac{\text{Lowest income, top tenth}}{\text{Highest income, bottom tenth}}$$

and the semi-decile ratio is

$$\frac{\text{Lowest income, top twentieth}}{\text{Highest income, bottom twentieth}}$$

For the U.S., data from the U.S. Census Bureau is used to estimate these various ratios; for the USSR, estimates are based on the anonymous survey mentioned earlier. The ratios thus calculated are given in Table 18.1.

---

[8] These figures are informed estimates by a qualified observer—me.

[9] P. J. D. Wiles and Stefan Markowski, "Income Distribution Under Communism and Capitalism: Some Facts About Poland, the UK, the USA, and the USSR," *Soviet Studies* 22, Part I, January 1971, Part II, April 1971. These articles can be read profitably by a person with little economics background, and are fascinating.

TABLE 18.1. Income Distribution, U.S. and USSR, as presented by Wiles and Markowski

Ratio	U.S., 1968	USSR
Quartile	2.64 ($1,310–$3,462)	1.80
Decile	6.90 (794– 5,460)	3.85
Semi-decile	13.65 (519– 7,093)	6.20

Families ranked by *per capita* income per member.

Apart from the obvious questions of Soviet data reliability, the fact that those data come from a regional survey may make them non-comparable to nationwide U.S. data. For consider the differences between regional and nationwide distribution in the U.S.: the ratios in the distribution of family money income in the whole U.S. and in the northeastern U.S. (the New England states, plus New York, New Jersey, and Pennsylvania) for 1960 are displayed in Table 18.2.

TABLE 18.2. Nationwide and Regional Income Distribution, U.S., 1960*

Ratio	USA	Northeast
Quartile	2.67 ($3,336–$ 8,930)	2.18 ($5,100–$11,125)
Decile	8.74 (1,375– 12,029)	5.08 (2,900– 14,750)
Semi-decile	14.39 (1,000– 14,387)	Not calculable

Source: U.S. Bureau of the Census, *Statistical Abstract of the United States, 1970* (Washington, D.C.: Government Printing Office, 1970), Tables 500, 502.

*Note that the data base of this table differs from Table 18.1. However, even had the *per capita* correction of Table 18.1 been made, the nationwide vs. regional differences should be striking, and similar in magnitude to the differences shown here.

There remains property income to discuss. In the Soviet Union the government decides how capital shall be used. The mechanism that we see in the United States, whereby individuals who wish to start or expand businesses can borrow the savings of other people, is absent in Russia. The prospect of earning a substantial return in a new line of activity is always attractive in a capitalist society; it may be much less so under socialism. The socialist government may be motivated differently—instead of producing more and better personal deodorants, it can decide to build housing for the people. Or the State can decide to accumulate weapons. On numerous occasions the State has provided "necessities" to people, irrespective of their incomes. In the capitalist regime private individuals do a great deal of the investing. This investing is done in response to expectations of return; if those expectations are fulfilled, then something that is valued by people is being provided.

Most observers who are fascinated by income distribution feel that income "ought" to be distributed more equally. Intercultural comparisons of income inequality permit us to draw only very tentative conclusions with regard to the important issues of how much inequality we can hope to eliminate, and the types of inequality that might be eliminated under a different type of economic organization. Property income would substantially vanish under a strict socialist regime; with it would vanish some measure of efficiency in satisfying the tastes and preferences of individuals. Some of the inequality in wage incomes might disappear under socialism; on the other hand, inequality in wages might increase. There is no clear evidence from what we know about Russia that a large proportion of the existing inequality in the U.S. can be eliminated without imposing efficiency costs on the whole society.

18.4.3. Socialism in Other Countries

Other nations with socialist economies have departed markedly from the Russian model. Yugoslavia is famous for tolerating small-scale free enterprise and for granting workers in State-owned enterprises a measure of control over their conditions of work. China has had a stormy economic history in recent years. The years immediately following the success of Mao's communist armies saw an extremely rapid growth in agricultural output and industrial capacity: one of the most phenomenal performances ever recorded, in fact. In 1964 with the advent of the cultural revolution, the emphasis in China shifted; and a period of economic crisis ensued. Under the prodding of the intensely ideological Red Guard, the Chinese experimented with an abandonment of specialization and expertise. University scientists were sent to work on farms and farmers into steel mills. The broadening and humbling virtue that would result from having every man do many different tasks was stressed. Roles were deliberately played down in an effort to destroy role consciousness. In an unsuccessful experiment, individual households were encouraged to start up and operate small-scale "backyard" steel mills. In recent years the Chinese dislike of role consciousness has not abated, but there reportedly has been a return to specialization. A population of widely expert individuals remains a canon of Chinese ideology; apparently it is no longer so actively pursued as a target of Chinese policy. As in the Soviet Union, Chinese agriculture is encountering difficulty in the enforcement of collectivization. As in Russia, individual farmers have small private tracts that they can cultivate for personal profit; and there are complaints that too little attention is given to the cultivation of collectively owned lands, and too much to private lands.

18.4.4. The Program of Socialism for America

Many of the most vociferous critics of the American economy and of American society look upon socialism as the answer to our national problems. Socialism, we are told, will end poverty, pollution, sexism, and racial conflict; it will make us charitable instead of selfish; it will put an end to unemployment, the drudgery and alienating aspects of labor, and the waste of a consumption-oriented, advertising-controlled economy. In a world of socialism, war and imperialism would cease overnight. Production would be for use, not for profit.[10]

If socialism could, in fact, succeed where capitalism has failed with regard to those social and economic problems, it would indeed deserve to be instituted. But, as we have seen, socialism involves only two important changes from capitalism: productive resources are owned by the People (collectively) instead of by people (privately); and decision-making with regard to the uses of those resources is accomplished by the mechanism of government, rather than through private arrangements among individual owners. It is difficult to see how these changes can terminate racism, sexism, or individual "selfish" interest. Conflict among socialist countries (Hungary, 1956; Czechoslovakia, 1968) hardly supports the view of socialism as a system in which the use of force between nations is renounced: imperialism is as much a curse in the communist world as it is outside. Insofar as alienation and drudgery are concerned, we see in the novels of Solzhenitsyn a picture of life as different from the ideal depicted in socialist propaganda as life in a Gary steel mill or on an Alabama tenant farm are from the "American dream." Nor, apparently, is socialist society typically markedly less unequal in the compensations paid to workers than we find in America: the idea that men of low skill somehow fare relatively better in Russia than in America is, apparently, simply false. Finally, social mobility between generations may be no more of an avenue to full equality in Russia than here.[11]

This leaves us with a few important problems, allegedly solvable under the socialist alternative, to consider and to comment on. As far as pollution is concerned, we saw in Chapter 15 that state intervention of some type is necessary to combat many kinds of pollution in a capitalist society. This, however, does not mean that in a socialist economy the problems of pollution will automatically be confronted and successfully overcome. Pollution control must have sufficient weight in the State's list of preferences, or it will be neglected. Lake Baikal, the largest fresh-water lake in the world (in volume), is Russian—and it reportedly is becoming increasingly polluted.

The problem of unemployment is a pressing one in capitalist society. Were it possible to create low-wage, low-skill jobs, many nonworkers could be taken off the unemployment roles. But their productivity would not be high and their prospects for gain through time would not be bright. In America, "makework" schemes for low-skilled individuals have been resisted on the ground, perhaps mistaken, that such programs are "demeaning." More important, private employers have been given powerful incentives *not* to hire low-productivity workers through minimum wage laws, compulsory insurance plans, and other

[10]These remarks were made during a Los Angeles radio broadcast by a Socialist Party candidate for national public office during the 1972 election. I don't know who the candidate was, or what office she was seeking, but her speech was great.

[11]S. M. Lipset, "Social Mobility and Equal Opportunity," *The Public Interest*, no. 29, (Fall 1972).

programs that increase the costs of employment sufficiently to rule out low-productivity workers. There is no doubt that much progress needs to be made on the problem of unemployment under capitalism; but much of that need is due to government programs which make it uneconomical to hire persons of low skill and to an elitist view of street-sweeping and other unskilled maintenance tasks as "unfit" occupations for human beings.

It is a fact that America has a problem of poverty, and some of the poor suffer disproportionately from malnutrition and disease. Those problems can be solved as soon as we, as a society, decide that we want to see them solved. Less wealthy capitalist societies have solved them without all-out commitment to socialism as a necessary precondition. Is it plausible that we *must* turn to socialism before we can solve the problem of poverty? Is it assured that *if we do* turn to socialism, the problem of poverty will be solved?

Will a socialist society be a less consumption-oriented society? To the extent that the State wishes to divert resources out of consumption into uses that satisfy State preferences, it will be in the interest of the State to make us less consumption oriented—whether we want to be or not. In a socialist society of abundance in which personal income is on the average high, the government (or the planning bureau) might find advertising to be a very useful method for assuring the sale of consumer goods so as to maintain full employment. Would government advertising be a better way to stimulate consumption than corporate advertising? Clearly this is an issue of taste; but if we fear that advertising has the power to *coerce* consumers, then the fear of monolithic government advertising will probably be stronger than the fear of pluralistic and conflicting corporation advertising.

Most of the arguments for socialism, then, are of dubious quality: they amount to nothing more than low-order ideological posturing. Similarly, many of the arguments that are presented *against* socialism are ideologically based: we are shown pictures of the labor camps of Stalin's Siberia and told that there is where we all will be soon after the socialists take over.

One comfortable view of the socialist-capitalist controversy goes something like this: the whole business is a little bit hysterical and beside the point—after all, people of intelligence and good will can make *either* system work properly. But the crucial point that must be made with regard to that view is that socialism, to a much greater extent than capitalism, calls for people of great ability and good will to run the show properly. Under socialism those people are vested with enormous power. By contrast, consider once again the outlook on the problem of economic organization that Hayek imputes to Adam Smith:

> Smith's chief concern was not so much with what man might occasionally achieve when he was at his best but that he should have as little opportunity as possible to do harm when he was at his worst. . . . The main merit of the individualism which Smith advocated is that it is a system under which bad men can do least harm. It is a social

system which does not depend on our finding good men for running it, or on all men becoming better than they now are, but which makes use of men in all their given variety and complexity. . . .[12]

It is precisely the chief virtue of competitive capitalism that men of good will are *not* needed to make the system work well. We do not need to search, with Diogenes' lamp, for a panel of honest men to run a properly structured capitalist society: with the proper system of laws, and limitations on the power of individuals and government, and with a reasonably equitable distribution of wealth, everyone participates in the making of society's economic decisions in a way that serves "the public interest," as the individual members of society themselves perceive it.

It is no doubt true that today the powers of control over society's resources that are possessed by some private capitalists far exceed anything envisioned by Adam Smith. It is also true that in most of today's socialist societies, the top dozen or twenty planners and politicians make our five hundred leading capitalists look like pretty small potatoes in terms of the power that they wield. Moreover, there is substantial overt and continuing conflict of interest among our capitalists, which serves to limit the effective use of their power: they tend to cancel each other out as each one seeks greater advantage, even though the processes of market competition may be far from perfect. There is no reason to suppose that in a socialist order, planners and politicians will resolve their intergroup conflicts in ways that limit the impact of their exercise of power on the lives of "ordinary citizens."

Such observations as these may make it easier to understand how some people find it possible to resist the salesmanship of socialism's advocates. The socialist ideal is attractive: it appeals to man's nobler impulses and instincts. But the capitalist ideal in its own way is attractive, too: each man is given the incentive to make the most of his own talents in the service of his fellow man. The fact that capitalist reality is flawed and blemished is not a sufficient reason to embrace socialism—not, at least, without first examining and comparing the flawed and blemished reality of socialism as it now exists in much of the world. To compare the ideal model of the "good" system with the actual performance of the "bad" one is a dishonest game, no matter which side you choose as the good one.

APPLICATIONS AND EXTENSIONS

1. The importance of properly structured incentives for managers is illustrated by an occurrence in a large U.S. chain of clothing and department stores. In the 1930s, it was the founder's custom to grant a bonus to the manager of branch stores if sales in

[12]F. A. Hayek, *Individualism and Economic Order* (Chicago: University of Chicago Press, 1948), pp. 11, 12.

the current year exceeded sales in the preceding year. The size of the bonus was not systematically related to the amount of the sales gain. If you were a store manager, how would you respond to this bonus system, keeping in mind that your current sales can affect not only whether you get a bonus this year, but also whether you get a bonus next year?

2. Modern socialist societies are often applauded because of their freedom from advertising. Yet photographs taken in Moscow show numerous billboards and placards exalting the party leadership; and broadcasts on Radio Havana exhort workers to volunteer in the cane fields to help with the sugar harvest. Are such messages a form of advertising? If not, what are they? Are the advertisers likely to have greater or less power over consumers in socialist or capitalist societies?

3. Invention and innovation are, respectively, the discovery of new goods or processes of production and the introduction of new goods or production processes into use. What are the rewards and incentives to invent and innovate in a competitive capitalist society? In a socialist society?

4. "The right to own property or to start a business is meaningless. What is important are *civil* rights like freedom of speech and the press and freedom to vote." In a one-party socialist state, how can an individual support himself if he exercises freedom of speech and in so doing offends the state bureaucracy? Is a state monopoly in running newspapers likely to influence the content of a "free" press in such a state?

    Can civil liberties survive at all in the absence of private property and free exchange?

BIBLIOGRAPHICAL NOTE

Leo Huberman and Paul Sweezy, *An Introduction to Socialism* (New York: Monthly Review Press, 1963) although a rather disappointing book, is perhaps the best concise statement of socialist ideology. Benjamin Ward, *The Socialist Economy* (New York: Random House, 1967) contains a summary of the debate over "socialist calculation"— the problem of attaining efficient operation in a socialist economy.

Human Action, by Ludwig von Mises (Chicago: Henry Regnery, 1966), is a good source of anti-socialist argument. Information on socialist economies (principally the Soviet Union) can be found in Marshall Goldman, *Comparative Economic Systems: A Reader,* 2nd ed. (New York: Random House, 1971).

A useful general text on economic systems, which does a good job of comparing capitalism, "command" socialism, and market socialism both to each other and to their respective ideal models, is Gary M. and Joyce E. Pickersgill, *Contemporary Economic Systems* (Englewood Cliffs, N.J.: Prentice-Hall, 1974).

CHAPTER NINETEEN

Intervention

The country needs . . . bold, persistent experimentation. It is
common sense to take a method and try it. If it fails,
admit it frankly and try another. But keep trying.

FRANKLIN D. ROOSEVELT (1932)

In the United States, it is almost inconceivable what rubbish a
public man has to utter today if he is to keep respectable.

JOHN MAYNARD KEYNES (1932)

19.1. SOME CASES AND EXAMPLES

Socialism has not been the only widely popular political-economic movement
that has arisen in this century. A second movement, *welfare liberalism,* has been
widely subscribed to throughout Western Europe and the Americas for more than
forty years. To attain its goals, welfare liberalism relies heavily on intervention
by government into what had previously been private economic activity. During
periods when welfare liberal sentiments are running high and strong, a call is
issued for remedial government programs whenever a "problem" is popularly
perceived to exist in society; and more than one politician, journalist, or
intellectual has found it possible to enjoy a good career simply by activating
those perceptions.

Intervention, it will be argued here, is not without pitfalls. Occasionally the outcomes of government action are not only unforeseen, they are perverse; their consequences work out to be contrary to the intent of policy-makers. Frequently, it is possible for the trained economist to predict *in advance* by simple application of supply and demand analysis that consequences of a particular policy will be quite different from and far less fortunate than those intended. And if the analyst permits himself the luxury of hindsight, he often can quite easily discover why a particular policy action produced an outcome far from the intended one. In examining the record of experience with interventionist impulses, there are lessons to be learned about the power and direct effectiveness of economic incentives. When policies work out contrary to intent, it is usually because incentives that they create have been overlooked.

19.1.1. Airport and Airspace Congestion

Few industries have exempted themselves from the discipline of the market as consistently and with such dismaying results as have the transportation industries. Rails, canals and waterways, highway freight, and the airlines all have been the beneficiaries of governmental largesse in one form or another; and together they have been rewarded enormously by subsidies of various kinds from various levels of government. The airline industry is an interesting case to study for the unanticipated side effects that can mar a well-intended attempt to foster "rational economic progress."

Apart from the threat of highjacking, perhaps the most pressing problem associated with airline transportation at this time is congestion. Congestion leads to delays in takeoff, delays in landing, delays in baggage delivery. Congestion leads to increased risk of collision in midair. These risks and delays all are costly—costly to the airlines, who must pay higher fuel bills and higher insurance premiums, and costly to the passengers, who must pay high costs of unplanned waiting and of higher-than-necessary risk of death.

Despite the costs associated with risks and delays, the total cost of air travel is lower to the passenger than it would be in the absence of government subsidies; and returns to the airlines are higher than they would be without subsidies. The subsidies take several forms: the federal government subsidizes the development of new aircraft (yesterday, the 747, tomorrow, the SST?); the federal government underwrites a part of the operating expenses of some airlines by subsidizing the delivery of air mail; the federal government bears the high costs of controlling air traffic. Meanwhile, local governments subsidize the construction of landing and terminal facilities, thereby giving the airlines very cheap access to local communities.

The net effect of these subsidies is to increase the supply of air travel. The greater level of activity leads to congestion. If the airlines paid the full cost of their own operations, including the cost of providing and maintaining airport facilities and controlling the traffic, then air travel would be reduced below its present level and congestion would be less troublesome. Much of the concern over the perceived "need" to find additional airport sites for major metropolitan areas like New York and Los Angeles would disappear—if airline ticket purchasers had to cover the costs of the facilities now available, those facilities might be uncongested. The pricing of the ground facilities could be refined in recognition that a 6:00 P.M. takeoff time is a more valuable resource than a 7:30 P.M. takeoff time. If the "peak load" hours were higher priced than the "off peak" hours, the airports would give the airlines a direct incentive to schedule their traffic more uniformly through the day. Some of that incentive would predictably be passed on to passengers, with the result that the passenger flow would be more uniform during the day. Reliance on the price system could, and very likely would, make a more orderly and pleasant experience out of air travel —and it would lead to a more rational allocation of resources to and within the airline industry.

The price system would also make air travel more expensive—to the traveler. The subsidies paid to the airlines are a nice example of a small tribute, taken from everyone, so that a large bonus can be bestowed on a few individuals. In this case, the bonus takes the form of much lower airline fares than otherwise would be possible. Who benefits from the subsidies? The traveler, the airline corporation stockholder, the businessman whose profits are tied to travel (the Florida tourist industry being a good example). Who loses? To a small extent, every taxpayer loses—directly, out-of-pocket in support of the subsidy program, and indirectly, in many little ways: noisier and dirtier skies, degraded airport neighborhoods or paved-over countryside, higher prices for automobile fuel.

As long as the costs are diffuse and the benefits are tangible to a group with political muscle, the game will probably not change. However, it's good to understand what's going on, even if the prospects for effective change are limited.

19.1.2. Pesticides in California

The excitement over "environmental problems" in the U.S. that surfaced so dramatically to the headlines around 1970 has caused more than a small tremor of response in political circles. One of the villains indicted by the ecology movement is the chemical pesticide DDT, an inexpensive compound that was hailed as the answer to most public health and agricultural problems when it was introduced into use during World War Two. DDT did, in fact, lead to remarkable, even revolutionary progress in obtaining higher crop yields and reducing insect-borne diseases. Compared to equally effective pesticides, DDT is extremely cheap to produce, long-lasting in effect and hence cheap to use, and relatively safe for human beings to handle.

DDT's durability, or resistance to chemical breakdown, turned out to be a mixed blessing. On the one hand, infrequent applications sufficed to control most insect problems for long periods of time. On the other hand, because it is durable, DDT has accumulated in significant quantity in the fatty tissues of the bodies of animals (including human beings) and has disseminated throughout the atmosphere and ground water system. Traces of DDT have been found in the fatty tissues of the Antarctic penguin; and it is suspected to threaten the survival of a number of species, notably fish-eating birds such as the pelican and osprey. No health problems have ever been found to stem from human consumption of DDT, but there is a significant and not wholly irrational concern over imaginable possibilities.

Concern over those suspected and unknown effects of DDT accumulation has led several states to ban its use. Michigan, in 1970, found that DDT had accumulated in the salmon population of the Great Lakes in concentrations that exceeded the state-imposed maximum levels for commercial foods. Faced with the loss of its newly founded commercial salmon fishery (salmon were brought in from the Pacific in 1967), Michigan forthrightly responded by (a) raising the allowable concentrations of DDT in commercial foods, and (b) banning the further sale of DDT for home gardening or for agricultural use, thereby solving both the short-run problem of how to dispose of this year's catch and the long-run problem of how to protect future catches.

California, in the same year, undertook to reduce the use of DDT. Elaborate rules were developed that defined conditions under which the pesticide could or could not be used. The thrust of the legislation is apparently quite simple: if technically feasible substitutes for DDT are available for use on a particular crop, then DDT cannot be used; where no substitutes are available, then DDT can be used. The incentives created by this system are interesting and bear analysis. First, because DDT is considerably cheaper than any comparable pesticide, commodities that must use the substitute pesticides will experience a relative increase in price compared to the ones on which DDT can continue to be used. This, of course, encourages consumers to substitute DDT-intensive products for those on which no DDT is used, and thereby to continue eating DDT. Second, the rules discourage the development of new substitute pesticides for DDT—as long as cheap DDT can be used without restriction on some crops, nobody benefits economically from the development of more expensive insecticides to use on those crops.

There are other issues that can be raised: are the shorter-lived chemical compounds truly less toxic and safer for humans to handle? Do they truly do less damage to wildlife? Do they do as good a job of pest control? These all are questions that were left unanswered in the haste to legislate on behalf of pelicans, ospreys, and "threatened" humanity.

The use of DDT in both Michigan and California could have been discouraged, the unwanted and counterproductive incentive effects could have been avoided, the revenues could have been raised to subsidize research on alternative pesticides, if it had been taxed rather than prohibited. Farmers who must pay a high tax on every pound of DDT purchased will use DDT sparingly and will constantly be looking out for cheaper substitutes. The desire for substitutes among farmers gives chemical companies an incentive to develop alternatives. Relative prices of farm products will not shift in favor of goods that use DDT. Revenues will be generated by taxes; if those revenues are devoted to pesticide research, then the more DDT that is used, the greater the volume of research that can be supported, and the more rapid (presumably) the progress in finding substitutes. In this instance, and in many like it, we can safely predict that well-intentioned legislation, by failing to acknowledge man's capacity to economize, will fall short of producing a desired outcome.

19.1.3. The Rationing of Necessities during Periods of Shortage

An undercurrent of feeling persists in a market economy and surfaces whenever some sort of an emergency arises. The feeling is that an undirected, unsystematic process like market allocation can't possibly work very well; and the search begins for an orderly, rationalized, planned, centrally directed process. A common response to emergency conditions, then, is abandonment of the market system in favor of a system of direct controls.

A conspicuous example is to be found in the U.S. during the time of World War Two, when many strategic foodstuffs and commodities were *rationed*. Rationing is a response to scarcity that has a great deal of popular appeal, because it implies "share and share alike." When the production or availability of food is reduced, for example, market allocation can lead to outcomes like everyone's favorite example of social abuse—milk may be made available for the rich man's dog, while none is available for the poor man's child. Rationing, then, is attractive as a direct way to prevent socially undesirable allocations of that type: the poor man's child and the rich man alike can each be given a coupon entitling the bearer to purchase a quart of milk; then if the rich man wants his dog to have milk, he must give up some of his own.

We can probe more deeply by asking why, if rationing is a socially desirable and effective response in wartime, should it not be used in *nonemergency* situations to remedy the allocative problems that stem from unequal incomes? Similarly, are there superior alternatives to rationing in response to emergencies like wartime production cutbacks ("shortages")?

First, are there any immediately apparent superior alternatives to rationing? Rationing destroys the effectiveness of money prices as signals to resource flows. Under nonemergency conditions, it is better to overcome a shortage in part by increased output, and not entirely by reduced consumption, if we believe in the satisfaction of individual tastes and preferences as a goal. Thus, it is the common view among economists that market allocation, perhaps supplemented by income transfers, works quite well when there is no emergency to contend with.

But suppose the shortage is the result of a massive redirection of resources, and not the result of changes in tastes and preferences. A war effort is a good example. We can compare hypothetical sequences of events without rationing and with rationing in an effort to find out if rationing is necessary to obtain a smooth redirection of resources when an emergency of the magnitude of a war arises.

Without rationing, the government could simply bid up market prices of the resources required to maintain the war effort. The market system would then signal an increase in production of the goods most heavily demanded—those goods that rise most in relative price. This process can result in higher prices for "necessities" like food, of course—either because the government bids for the food directly, to feed the army, or because it bids for the resources such as labor and machinery that are used in food production, and thereby increases the cost of food production. Higher food prices affect the rich much less than the poor, but that may not be a problem. As a consequence of heavier demand for some goods to sustain the war effort, the demand for productive resources will increase; and this predictably will lead to higher wages and incomes. Whether the incomes of the rich man and the poor man grow more equal as a result of general wage increases depends in part on the value of the productive services that each man can render and in part on the extent to which the poor man was poor because he was not fully employed before the demand for labor increased.

If rationing is used to allocate resources, instead of market prices, both men, poor and rich, are deprived of the opportunity to satisfy their preferences: both are constrained in the consumption of specific goods. Hence, the unimpeded price system has advantages to offer, even in times of emergency. If incomes become more unequal as a result of the emergency, and if the increased inequality offends a widely shared sense of justice, then laws can be passed to transfer income from rich to poor. There is no reason to believe that a wartime emergency leads to greater income inequality than is experienced in normal times; and income transfers, which are the most effective and direct remedies for income inequality, can be employed during emergencies, as well as during normal periods.

It appears, then, that rationing and the central control of resource allocation are not demonstrably superior as emergency responses to the normal alternative of market allocation; and in fact they may be quite unnecessary. The market alternative permits a freer exercise of preferences; and the recourse to rationing paves the way for *illegal* markets, called "black markets," in which people who desire more of certain goods obtain them by paying higher prices without acknowledging the rationing rules.

The central objection to rationing, then, is that it is a clumsy response to the problem of inequality in income distribution: clumsy because it eradicates the signal system which transfers resources from less to more highly valued uses. In Germany during World War Two the market system was relied upon heavily; and the market rapidly brought food, medical supplies, and other desired goods and services forth after such catastrophes as the Hamburg fire-bombing raids of 1943. By tolerating very high prices in the "market period," a rapid and responsive flow of the right kinds of goods to relieve misery was obtained in the short run.

19.1.4. Regulatory Activity: The Case of Pharmaceuticals

In 1961 and 1962, the births of a number of severely deformed children were associated with prenatal use by the mothers of a German tranquilizer called thalidomide. Thalidomide's negative consequences occurred only when it was taken in a particular time interval of early pregnancy; otherwise, it was a remarkably effective and benign drug. A physician employed by the Food and Drug Administration discovered the appalling side effects of thalidomide, and its sale was banned immediately in the U.S.—not just to pregnant women, or to women of child-bearing age, but to everyone.[1]

Thalidomide symbolizes the nightmare of the regulatory agent charged with monitoring drug safety. Despite every reasonable precaution, an unsafe drug comes into use; and hundreds of lives are maimed as a consequence. Headlines are made, and the entire population recoils in horror.

In 1969, a contrasting story made the headlines. Sodium and potassium cyclamate, widely used artificial sweeteners, were found by the laboratory chemists of a large manufacturer to cause bladder cancers in rats when those chemicals were administered in massive quantities. A ban on the sale of cyclamates was imposed immediately and has been kept in effect despite substantial evidence that the tests could not have isolated the cyclamates as causative agents (in fact, it has been suggested—perhaps waggishly—that saccharin, a sweetener still in widespread use five years later, may have been the cause, since it was administered with the cyclamates).

The consequence of the ban on cyclamates has been (1) the destruction of hundreds of millions of dollars worth of capital in the food industry with soft drinks being a conspicuously heavy loser; and (2) an annoying hardship imposed on diabetics and overweight people who were deprived of the only palatable artificial sweetener known. We can never know how many people the FDA saved from death by bladder cancer through the ban; nor, conversely, can we ever know how many overweight people the FDA sentenced to death by heart attack as a consequence of being forced back to fattening sweeteners.

This second instance—the ban on cyclamates—is a more typical, and more interesting, example of the FDA at work than was the thalidomide case. It is

---

[1]Thalidomide was never offered for sale in the U.S. The quantities that were used were dispensed directly by physicians to patients to "try out."

more typical because it is a denial of market access to a substance that is not known to be unsafe, and in fact is known to be highly beneficial, rather than a grant of permission to use a substance that is incorrectly thought to be safe. It is more interesting because the effects of the cyclamate ban are diffuse, hard to measure, and "out of sight, out of mind," whereas the effects of thalidomide use were just the opposite.

There are, then, two potential sources of loss to society which stem from the decision processes of the Food and Drug Administration: the Administration can accept an unsafe substance; or it can defer acceptance of a safe substance. If the FDA makes the first type of error and admits an unsafe drug, a thalidomide-style headline news story may result. If it makes the second type of error, and delays the use of a potentially beneficial drug, hardly anyone is the wiser. It would seem that the FDA has a strong incentive to avoid the first type of error and little or no incentive to avoid the second. Thus, predictably, the costs to society associated with "type two error" will be very high. It is entirely conceivable that the costs to society of drugs withheld from market for prolonged periods of time because of unproven safety far exceeds the cost of any potential hazard from their earlier public use. We have no direct information on the magnitudes of these costs; but a closely related problem has been studied, with illuminating results.

The Food, Drug and Cosmetics Act was amended in 1962 to provide that manufacturers would subsequently have to prove any claims of effectiveness made on behalf of new drugs. In effect, the FDA took steps to assure not only that drugs are *safe* but that they also are truthfully advertised. The effect of that change in policy was studied about ten years later by Sam Peltzman, a former UCLA economist.[2] Peltzman found that:

1. The amendment substantially curtailed the rate of introduction of new drugs.
2. Accompanying that reduction in the rate of introduction, there was a reduction in demand for drugs by consumers.
3. New competitors were prevented from entering the drug market, and as a result the price of drugs was higher than it would have been in the absence of the amendment, despite the reduction in demand.

Peltzman estimates the loss to consumers that results from the reduced rate of introduction of new drugs at about $350 to $450 million annually. The gain stemming from having prevented the waste of money on drugs that do not perform as advertised is estimated at $100 to $150 million. Thus the enforcement of the 1962 amendment by the FDA costs drug users some $200 to $350 million per year, not counting the direct cost of maintaining a staff and monitoring manufacturers' claims, paid for out of taxes. Those costs which Peltzman estimated stem from the efforts to enforce truth; they do not touch upon the costs from enforcement of safety.

[2]Sam Peltzman, "An Evaluation of Consumer Protection Legislation: The 1962 Drug Amendments," *Journal of Political Economy*, 81(September–October 1973).

19.2. EVENTS AND THE IMPULSE TO INTERVENE

19.2.1. The Growth in Interventionism's Popularity

Almost any collection of examples of how intervention has worked, like those presented in the preceding section, can be used to cast doubt on the idea that intervention is a sure way to social betterment. Why, then, has intervention become an automatic response to any perceived social problem in the capitalist economies of the West? One way to approach that question is to look upon intervention as a contending *ideological movement*. This section explores the events out of which that ideological movement has grown.

Before chronicling those events, we want to define more precisely what an *ideology* is. An ideology is a *system of belief about the social order* that is (a) *prescientific*—i.e., not based on the systematic consideration of evidence; (b) strongly *program-oriented* or action-oriented; and (c) firmly, unquestioningly, and *widely believed*.

A century ago, when *laissez faire* was the dominant ideology of the English-speaking world, the relations between competitive market allocation and social welfare, as we understand them today, were only partially grasped by scholars of political economy; but it was the popular view that private property and market allocation assured efficient resource use (where efficiency is defined in accord with the individualist criteria discussed in Chapter 3). Some writers of that time went so far as to suggest that even private charity would undermine the efficiency of the market mechanism (see the Appendix to this chapter).

We can point to three major developments that have occurred since (roughly) World War One which have shaken the capitalist order and have led to the call for decisive change or reform. These developments, listed in the likely order of their importance, are:

1. The major world depressions of 1929–1938 and 1920–1921.
2. The establishment of socialist economies in the Soviet Union and (after World War Two) elsewhere.
3. The increasing tendency among intellectuals to define liberalism as a program that stresses equality and security rather than liberty; and to elevate equality to a place near the top among social priorities and objectives, at least insofar as the content of ideological pronouncements is concerned.

These happenings were accompanied, and in some measure stimulated, by four widely circulated criticisms of the capitalist order: (1) Capitalism is prone to crisis, depression, and widespread unemployment. (2) Capitalism tends to concentrate power in the hands of an elite, whose members, by monopolization and collusive control of crucial industries, increase their personal wealth at the expense of the general welfare. (3) Capitalism systematically deprives the public of an important array of public goods which can be provided in adequate volume only through the mechanism of collective action; capitalism also leaves unrationalized a host of external economies and diseconomies which can be balanced off only through collective action. (4) Capitalism tends systematically to widen the gap between rich and poor.

The first criticism, that capitalism breeds instability, requires the development of additional analytic methods which lie beyond the scope of this book; but the bases for each of the remaining three criticisms were explored in Part Two. In each case it was concluded that an unregulated capitalist order is indeed susceptible to the difficulties indicated by the critics. It was also suggested that in many instances the act of intervention creates problems that are no less difficult to handle than the ones they are supposed to overcome, frequently without "solving" the original "problem."

In the modern welfare states of Western Europe, intervention has gone far beyond the scope of what can be justified theoretically by those criticisms. There have been systematic efforts taken to provide, through the mechanism of the State, virtually everything affecting the health, safety, and comfort of the individual. Health care, housing, transportation, communications, entertainment, education—in Scandinavia, all or most of each of these goods and services are provided by the State; and in Britain, the State plays a major or exclusive role in the provision of each. Thus, some observers perceive a trend in Western societies: the processes of intervention, once unleashed in response to widespread perception of "major social problems," have grown and spread far beyond the scope of what can be justified theoretically by those criticisms. There have been systematic efforts to provide, through the mechanism of the state, services that had been performed traditionally (and often badly) by the extended family, or when the family was unable, by the church parish or local governmental authority.

19.2.2. Bureaucracy and the Impulse to Intervene

The mechanism of interventionist action is a cumulative one. A bureaucracy is created out of widespread desire to solve a problem or a set of problems; the bureaucracy soon becomes an interested party in the processes of decision-making within the society, identifying new problems and defining for itself new tasks which lead to growth in size and importance. Examples of the way a bureaucracy grows and perpetuates itself are easy to find.

The U.S. Army Corps of Engineers, created to provide the Army with construction capability in time of war, became an important force in changing the landscape of America. Literally thousands of major dams have been constructed by this agency; fly across any western state on a clear day and its handiwork is visible everywhere. The engineers have been charged with the ruthless use of political power in getting their projects approved; and indeed, they show an unusual adeptness for and understanding of the legislative allocation processes called "logrolling" and "porkbarreling."

The Department of Health, Education and Welfare, a federal agency created around 1950, began life under its first secretary with a budget of some $2½ billion. In twenty-two years that budget multiplied to about thirty times its original size. (Incidentally, this offers a good opportunity to issue a warning. Beware of concluding more than is justified when you read comparisons of the type just presented. The growth in the budget of HEW proves nothing, except that the agency has grown. As long as the marginal social benefit of HEW expenditures is greater than the benefits that could be obtained from alternative use of those resources, that growth in size is good, not bad. The reader will have to judge for himself, from evidence that he gathers himself, whether those marginal benefits have indeed exceeded their opportunity costs.) The growth in budget was in some part due to the lobbying activity of the HEW bureaucracy, which sought new responsibilities and duties, and hence a more important role for its members.

19.3. LEGISLATIVE AND BUREAUCRATIC ALLOCATION: WHEN DOES IT WORK WELL?

The question in our section heading has consistently been a puzzle that deserves the attention of competent theoretical and empirical social scientific inquiry. There are two extreme positions on this issue: the reflexive welfare liberal one, which never stops to question the prospects of success of a program of governmental allocation; and the reflexive libertarian one, which is prepared to recite a litany of failed programs and to assert an "impossibility theorem" regarding success in any venture.[3] Neither group is right. For there have been interventionist programs that must be judged conspicuously successful, both in terms of attaining a stated purpose and in terms of attaining broad-based popular support, as well as numerous costly failures.

One puzzling fact is that we have examples of programs that have succeeded in one locale and failed in another. Public housing is one example: in Britain, council homes have enjoyed universal robust popularity, while in America our public housing programs as often as not create "instant slums." Urban renewal and air-pollution control offer other examples of programs that have enjoyed some success in Britain but have either failed outright or have suffered heavy loss of support here.

Numerous considerations will be found to impinge on why a legislative allocation program is successful as judged by the value of the benefits realized per dollar of budgetary outlay. Among the more important may be these interrelated factors:

[3]Some "purer" libertarians hold that the basis of governmental failure as an allocative mechanism is rooted in something like natural law. They do not base their pessimism on mere experience; rather, they purport to understand certain "principles of human nature" or "principles of social organization" which counterindicate governmental success (efficiency, justice) in allocation.

1. *The program's basis of support.* A program that is easily seen to be gravy for a clearly identifiable special interest probably cannot hope to maintain popularity; and unpopular programs seldom are successful. There is a further factor: a program whose support is widespread because its benefits are wide-reaching may be easier to terminate if it becomes cost-ineffective, because the group that is paying for the program overlaps in a large way with the group that is benefiting.

2. *The amount of intelligence exercised in its design.* Here the relation amounts to much more than just "success is evidence of good design." There will be many conflicting interests that must be weighed and balanced in any program (physician versus patient interest in the Medicare program, not to mention the interests of the public at large). A program need not be well-designed to be popular, but good design will probably take into account the need to avoid unpopularity.

3. *Restraint* by parties with a vested interest in the program in their exercise of pressure to institute, expand, or modify it. The Economic Opportunity programs of the Johnson Administration were among the most conspicuously unsuccessful efforts at social melioration in human history, because they violated conditions (1) and (2) as a result of excessive pressure on their behalf. By contrast, council housing in Britain was instituted without mobilizing the poor in support of it; the law was in effect a gift from the nation to its less advantaged citizens. Few council estates in Britain have the feel of ghetto or prison that can be observed in typical American public housing tracts, which may in part be due to the fact that those who helped to pay for the British tracts did not resent pressures brought to bear on behalf of those who would live in them.

4. *The extent to which the program requires special skill or training to administer.* Bureaucrats quickly acquire a personal interest in programs that require specialized talents; if the group of bureaucratic specialists is sufficiently large, and if their skills are hard to apply elsewhere, then there is virtually no hope of closing down a program, no matter how poorly it may be functioning. The more interchangeable the administrators, the more easily a program can be staffed; and if the program works out poorly, interchangeability makes it easier to close it down.

We know a great deal more about the factors that make for successful market allocation than we do about how successful political programs are shaped. Whatever the forces that separate successful programs from unsuccessful ones, those that have been unsuccessful, such as those instituted by the Office of Economic Opportunity during the late 1960s, seem to have violated several of the four principles or conditions for success that are listed here.

19.4. WILL INTERVENTION SAVE ORANGE COUNTY?

In the headnotes of Chapters 14 and 15, President Theodore Roosevelt nicely summarized the overwhelming majority opinion with regard to economic development. Through the course of this book we have studied how decentralized market processes work. We have seen instances in which they work imperfectly—in regard to questions of land use, the most important imperfections are probably externalities (considered in Chapter 15). Externalities and other imperfections create instances in which intervention by government can be beneficial; yet we find many instances of intervention, such as those discussed in Chapter 4 and earlier in this chapter, which turn out to be ineffective, or worse, to be perverse in their effect.

Our Chapter 14 headnote from TR embodies the ideal of conservationism (or as we call it today, environmentalism); the Chapter 15 headnote is an expression of egalitarian sentiment. How well founded are those statements? If we view them from a broad historical perspective, do they raise issues of substance; and if so, do they suggest constructive ways of dealing with issues?

To find a possible answer, let's project ourselves back to 1907, and take a look at one of the many land-use activities that might have aroused our conservationist's ire, and our President's.

The forests were under heavy attack during 1907 in the upper Great Lakes region; by that date, many square miles of Michigan and Wisconsin had been transformed into stump lot. The land appeared to be ruined: hopelessly unsuitable for agriculture because of thin soil and uncertain growing season, what could be done with it? At the time Roosevelt spoke, nobody knew what was to become of that land; but earlier experience should have suggested that a reasonable answer would be forthcoming. For a century earlier, farther to the south and east, even more outrageous abuse of the land and forest had been evident in the Western Reserve of Ohio, where homesteaders practiced the kind of agriculture described in our quote from Weissmilch (page 276). From the perspective of Roosevelt's day, it should have been clear to persons of training and discernment, if not to the President or to most of the population at large, that the agricultural practices of the pioneers reflected an extremely enlightened conservationist attitude: they sought to conserve the scarcest resource in their productive arsenal, human labor. In the Germany of 1800, labor was plentiful, farmlands and forests were scarce. German farmers lovingly husbanded every square foot of field, and gathered the deadfall from every acre of forest for fuel. But in America, the labor that would have been necessary to practice German-style cultivation was simply not available.

By economizing on labor, by not harvesting logs and stacking them carefully for future use, those pioneers were able first and foremost to survive; and second to begin the process of capital formation in the new area. The capital they formed was cleared and habitable (albeit temporarily depleted) land, and transportation networks. It would have been hard for Roosevelt to argue that his generation (the great-grandchildren of the early landbusters) suffered as a consequence of the impatience, and capital formation decisions, of those forebears.

Similarly, when Roosevelt's generation was in the saddle, the same sort of conservation was being practiced in the forests of Michigan and Wisconsin. Those forests were being turned into towns, farmhouses, barns, railway lines, mills, and mines at a rapid rate. The society's labor and managerial skill went into those forms of capital, rather than into the administration of less destructive tree harvesting techniques, or the planting of new tree farms, or any other activities directed at softening the visible impact of timbering on the landscape of the upper Midwest. Did they in fact skin and exhaust the land, as the President's untutored perceptions suggested? Today, if you visit Benzie or Leelanau Counties in Michigan or Door County in Wisconsin, you will find a land of clear water, blue sky, and delightful second- and third-growth forest, truly one of the prime recreational assets of America. Who foresaw that the stump lots of 1907 would be thus transformed? Not the few hardy souls who tried farming and then gave up, nor Roosevelt himself. But the evidence from an earlier time was there for everyone to read: it was but necessary to observe the historical development of such areas as the Western Reserve. As in the Western Reserve, the upper Midwest region was *not* subjected to comprehensive study, nor to the scrutiny of planners or regional development experts; no new federal Department of Stumplot Restoration poured tens or hundreds of millions into a search for "socially optimal" new uses. And as in the Western Reserve, the decentralized mechanism of the market produced an outcome, which, had it in fact been produced by bureaucratic control, would have been hailed as a triumph.

How in fact did good things eventuate from the apparent ruin created by the Ohio agriculture of 1800 and the Michigan lumbering of 1900? The outcome emerged out of the interactions of hundreds of thousands of individuals, each seeking his own advantage, using his property in the "pillaged" areas in ways that he hoped would increase his wealth. In Michigan, some sought to farm, and failed; others turned to orchards, and survived; still others fostered tourism, and prospered eventually. There was hardship for those who failed; very low incomes could be relieved perhaps only by migration to Grand Rapids or Detroit to work in factories. But the sum total of that hardship was quite possibly no greater than would have eventuated had a moderately well-chosen, centrally administered plan been put into effect, for the speed with which landowners adapted to realistic possibilities was surely greater.

Today in America, numerous developmental activities are comparable in their impact upon the conservationist psyche to the tree-cutting in Michigan and Wisconsin in the early 1900s. We strip-mine the coal fields of Kentucky, West Virginia, Illinois, and Utah; we deposit uranium mine tailings in Colorado and Wyoming; we relentlessly cut down all but the most monumental of the coastal redwoods; we build nuclear power plants, divert entire river systems, denude whole mountains to create ski slopes; we pave over the choice citrus groves of Orange County to create suburban tract housing. But if we look at the history of our development, we see that the market-directed activities of one generation, which cause such dismay to many of the best educated and most sensitive members of that generation, usually also convey great benefit to successor generations.

The Chapter 15 quote from Roosevelt embodies a strong egalitarian element. Egalitarian sentiments have always been powerful instruments for control, regulation, or legislation in American society. Roosevelt appeals to those sentiments with his plea for the "public welfare," a term which invokes all of us little men struggling for our rights against the rich and powerful owners.

The irony of such appeals is that frequently egalitarian sentiments are used as weapons against change, in situations where change would be of enormous benefit for the worst-off members of the society. Examples involving land use are easy to find: scorn is directed at such purveyors of low-cost convenience as mobile home parks, fast food outlets, coin-operated laundries, small auto repair garages and discount furniture warehouses; and every effort is made in most communities to localize, isolate and control the spread of such establishments (and thereby to raise the cost of patronizing them). In addition, and more seriously, egalitarian sentiment has been brought to bear against housing development, both in the subdivision of new areas, and the higher-density redevelopment of many older areas. The impact of that type of control is to slow down the rate at which previously occupied older housing of higher quality becomes available to low-income individuals.

Despite persistently incorrect predictions of environmental disaster, and unfulfilled objectives of greater equality, people today more than ever appear to be convinced that land use controls are necessary for noble purposes of conservation and equalization. Why?

One answer contains two major components or dimensions. First, people are mistrustful of unadministered mechanisms. It is the miracle of social order that occasionally unplanned and unadministered institutions evolve spontaneously, with great net benefit to nearly everyone. The most important of these institutions is the market; but it is hard to convince any typical or average bystander that good things emerge from unimpeded market action, particularly where the use of land is involved. There is no way, most observers feel, that a decent outcome can eventuate from the workings of selfish motives through an undisciplined mechanism. In short, there is considerable ignorance; and it is in the interest of academics, intellectuals, and politicians to foster mistrust and ignorance regarding uncontrolled institutions like markets: they, after all, are the potential controllers.

Second, much of mankind apparently is very "conservative" (in the sense of nostalgic, or resistant to change). Much of the apparent larger concern for the environment or for the fate of the poor which is raised against plans for development is a simple rationalization of resistance to change in familiar surroundings.

What does all of this bode for the development of areas like Orange County? At this writing, attempts are under way (via the creation of a California Coastal Commission) to protect the entire California coastline from "unplanned, chaotic, ruinous" development. Myriad interests are to be served by the coastal controllers. Conflicting interests among residential, agricultural, conservationist, and recreational claims are to be resolved in the public interest. Wetlands are to be preserved in the interest of fostering numerous lesser animal and plant species; and cleanliness, beauty, and accessibility for use are to be preserved for future generations.

Is such a plan workable? Experience elsewhere with zoning and other far less ambitious control programs suggests that (a) the bureaucracy which will be founded will add to the cost of doing business in, or simply of living in, the zone of the Commission's control; persons of limited vision and understanding (albeit of the best will) will be put in charge of disposing of matters and issues that they barely comprehend; (b) individuals will be encouraged to mount support among other individuals in coming before the Commission with plans for use of the coast of benefit to themselves, and the overriding consideration in determining whether they will be successful is the number of the right kinds of votes that they represent; and (c) *at best,* the visible effects of the Commission, compared to what would have happened in its absence, will be negligible.

But what about the poor? Won't the efforts of the Commission to prevent urban sprawl, preserve farm land, and extend recreational opportunity help them? It appears, in fact, that the poor are the group least helped (or most injured) by such control programs. The imposition of land use controls, and the erection of barriers of bureaucratic harassment to developers, slows down the rate of increase in the supply of housing, and leads to a higher price that the poor must pay for this important good. (It matters little that the coastal zone housing typically is costly, and hence requires high income for occupancy. Persons moving into new coastal housing vacate housing elsewhere, which is occupied by others who vacate housing; and so on, until low income people are given a wider array of more affordable choices.) Controls also slow down the rate at which more demanding and better-paying jobs are created. In short, to the extent that such intervention is impelled by egalitarian sentiment, it is misguided.

The record of past experience, then, makes it appear that large-scale intervention in land use, motivated by concern over the impact of developmental ''destruction'' on the environment and on the poorer members of the society, will retard the creation of privately owned wealth without distributing existing wealth more equally; and it is also likely to delay or even to prevent finding the best patterns of resource use for the future in the protected areas.

We can, of course, make planning and control more palatable and successful by agreeing that it is planners' preferences and not individual preferences that should be served; once that has been achieved, it will remain only to eliminate all competition and dissent among planners, and tranquillity, harmony, and the maximum of social welfare will be ours. *Any* problem can be thus defined right out of existence, by a citizenry willing to pay a high enough price.

19.5. INTERVENTION'S LONG-RUN PROSPECTS

In the early programs of government intervention into the economy, concern for the individual remained the uppermost consideration. The view was expressed that the individual could achieve a fulfilling life only if relieved of such heavy economic concerns as fear of medical disaster or fear of starvation. Regarding the collective insurance schemes, it was held that we all owe it to each other to spread those major risks of health and fortune so as to prevent their burden from becoming intolerable to any individual or small group of people.

With the passage of time, however, that view began to change. Many interventionist programs were proposed that reflected the outlook that the State must spread its benefits evenly and fairly; if one group receives a great deal of benefit from one program, then some other group is justified in claiming compensating equivalent benefits through another program. The process becomes one not of finding *generally* beneficial programs, but rather of designing special programs, each one beneficial to a narrow array of interests. Housing, educational and vocational programs, rural electrification, mortgage insurance, and other innovations in Britain and America embodied this approach. The outcome seems to have been an increasing fragmentation and alignment in accord with group interest within the society. Labor unions foster worker solidarity, to the extent of encouraging hostile acts against property, or engaging in mindless rhetoric about the injustice of profit. "Minority" groups (including women) pursue legislation which in effect requires that minority-group members be hired *in preference* to white males. Other special-interest groups, including the aged, have organized hastily and have become increasingly vocal in protection of their members' "rights."

All these developments have occurred in response to the increasing role that has been assigned to government in the allocation of resources. To a limited degree, group pressures can be brought to bear through the market process; but government allocation is far more responsive to the interest of voter blocs.

But just as the once-dominant *laissez-faire* ideology was revised under the pressure of internal and external political and economic forces, so it appears that the currently dominant welfare liberal doctrines are subject to revision. The chief pressure toward revision is economic efficiency. In recent years, dissatisfaction has been growing in both Britain and America over the economic performance of interventionist politicians and bureaucrats. Because the success of welfare liberalism depends on satisfying government's various clientele groups, we well may wonder whether interventionist ideology will be able to persist in something recognizably close to its present form.

The presently existing and growing dissatisfaction with the performance of government can find at least three possible outlets. If individualist values are restored to something like their earlier primacy, then the movement may be toward an economic structure with government's role in the economy very strictly limited to tasks (like the provision of public goods) which are handled awkwardly at best by private arrangements. Alternatively, there may be a de-emphasis of class, group, or political clientele interests; and a welfare state resembling the apparently efficient models of Scandinavia's homogeneous societies may evolve. And finally, if the emergency created by government allocation in response to group pressure becomes sufficiently acute (as may be close to happening in Britain), the appeal of holistic values (p. 47) will predictably become stronger; and a move to collectivism or some other politically centralizing doctrine could follow.

In part, the present unsettled state of both Britain and America is attributable to the deficiencies of welfare liberalism *as an ideology*. It is simply lacking in the kind of unifying and galvanizing and rallying impact that some of its predecessors and alternatives convey. In a society with a well-established, widely subscribed, and spiritually nurturing political ethic (like the liberal individualism of *The Federalist* or the holism of present-day China), any program must pass scrutiny for its contribution to ''the common good.'' A severe and searching discussion of costs and benefits (in large part ideologically defined) is inevitable. Without the guidance of a clearcut ethic, social policy can and does drift dangerously. It becomes a trading game; and a new and powerful trader, the bureaucracy, emerges during the process of play. The bureaucracy has a life and interests of its own, and programs can become established or be perpetuated to serve its ends.

Neither present-day Britain nor America seems to possess a coherent and unifying political credo. The values proclaimed to reside in welfare liberalism by its intellectual proponents are not widely perceived—to the ordinary citizen it is an exasperating system in which the squeaky wheel gets greased, and the wheel that doesn't squeak has its grease taken away.

As a consequence, commonly shared values have disappeared and class or political affinity group interests have come to dominate in both societies, more in Britain than here. The costs and benefits of interventionist programs are weighed not by reference to a transcendent and universal ethic, but rather by reference to the political power of their supporters and detractors. In that evaluation process much bad can be overlooked.

In the foreseeable future, then, the capitalist institutions of property and markets may emerge to attain an importance that they have not enjoyed for nearly a hundred years; or they may be vilified, abrogated, and regulated. Those events will depend purely on the crystallization of ideology in the English-speaking nations.

But ideology, however strongly held, cannot repeal the deeper regularities that are the subjects of scientific inquiry. We have the such knowledge of deeper regularities in the realm of economics. We know that *properly organized, property and markets are efficiency-increasing institutions*. Replacements for those institutions have been sought, but never discovered; and they will probably continue to be important components of social organization for as long as there is human society.

*APPENDIX I
PRIVATE CHARITY IN NINETEENTH-CENTURY BRITAIN

A major analyst of the intellectual history of economics, George Stigler, cites an interesting problem first noticed by Mountifort Longfield of Dublin in the 1840s. The poor of England subsisted largely on wheat flour at that time; and in years of bad wheat

*The material in this section may be too advanced for some introductory coverage.

harvest, great hardship was inflicted on the lower classes. As an act of private charity, wealthy Englishmen occasionally bought wheat at the market price and resold it to the poor at half price. Longfield chided the wealthy benefactors for their actions, asserting that the artificially reduced price to poor people stimulated demand for wheat to such an extent that the benefits of the charitable act were largely dissipated, the price of wheat was nearly doubled, and the grain-growers were given a large subsidy by the misguided rich who thought they were "aiding" the poor. Longfield's analysis can be represented in Figure 19.1. The demand of the poor in the absence of any action by the rich benefactors is given by the segment DD^1. Now suppose that at prices above p^0 the rich stand ready to buy up grain and resell it to the poor at half-price. The amount that the rich will provide, let us assume, equals the amount that the poor wish to buy. When the subsidy scheme is enforced, the demand curve "jumps" at p^0 in such a way that the quantity demanded at every market price above p^0 equals the quantity demand at *half* the market price along the schedule DD^1. The reason for this is obvious: when the market price of wheat is P_{sub}, the poor consumers pay only one-half P_{sub}, or P (Figure 19.1). The demand curve, under the subsidy scheme, then, is the heavy broken line that traces the path $D^1D^2D^3D^4$. With a bad harvest the supply S_{low} is available, in contrast to S_{normal} of most years. The full amount of wheat available will be consumed, with or without subsidy. If the supply of wheat is *inelastic* (that is, if quantity supplied does not vary much in response to price changes, as drawn in Figure 19.1, and as may be true of the supplies of most agricultural commodities between harvests), then the price will be P_{sub} instead of P. The charitable act of purchase and resale (in the case of zero elastic supply) leads to a *doubling* of wheat prices, with *no* reduction in price to the poor consumers!

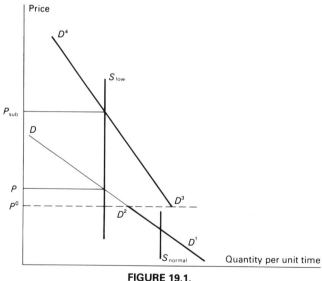

FIGURE 19.1.

Longfield's analysis requires three conditions to sustain the predicted outcome of higher prices to farmers and very little gain by the subsidized poor. First, it is assumed that *only* the poor consume wheat. At least, there is no provision in the analysis for unsubsidized wheat demand. Second, the wealthy supporters of the subsidy scheme are assumed to meet *all* demands that arise at the subsidized price. Finally, the supply curve is assumed to be zero-elastic (vertical). If any one of these conditions is relaxed, the analysis loses some of its bite. Changes in the second and third conditions can be worked out easily in Figure 19.1. To relax the second condition, the demand curve is not moved up as much above p^0; and to relax the third condition, the S_{low} curve is drawn with a less than vertical positive slope. It remains to see what happens when the first condition is relaxed, that is, when there is demand from groups other than the subsidized poor.

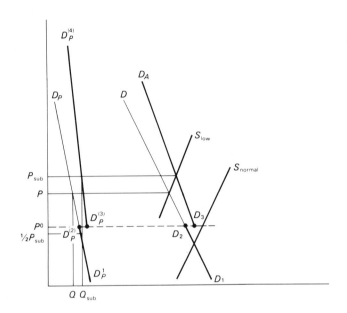

FIGURE 19.2.

In Figure 19.2, $D_p D_p^1$ and DD^1 are respectively the demand curves of poor consumers who are eligible for subsidy, and of the entire society. $D_p^1 D_p^2 D_p^3 D_p^4$ heavily drawn in Figure 19.2, is the demand curve of the poor group with the described subsidy scheme at prices higher than p^0. $D_1 D_2 D_3 D_A$ is the demand curve of the entire society, also heavily drawn, with the assumption that the subsidy scheme does not affect the price paid by nonpoor consumers. In the absence of the subsidy, the poor would consume Q at the price of P. With the subsidy, the market price is P_{sub}; the poor consume Q_{sub} and they pay a price $P_{sub}/2$. Clearly, the poor are greatly benefited by the subsidy, since Q_{sub} exceeds Q, and P exceeds $P_{sub}/2$. The benefit that shows up in Figure 19.2 but not in Figure 19.1 is the result of the fact that in Figure 19.2 there is a group of unsubsidized consumers from whom the wheat can be bid away; this has the same effect in preventing extreme price rises as elastic supply has. To accentuate the difference between Figures 19.2 and 19.1, the supply curves in Figure 19.2 are drawn to show some responsiveness of quantity sold to price (they are more than zero-elastic).

APPLICATIONS AND EXTENSIONS

1. In 1975 the Sierra Club proposed that the government put limits on the amount of lumber sold abroad (principally to Japan) because the rate of sale was viewed as a threat to supplies of wood (and the size of our nation's forest acreage).

   As the price of lumber rises, do you expect the rate of tree harvest to increase or decrease? Do you expect the acreage devoted to tree production to increase or decrease? If the worldwide demand for lumber is permanently higher, will our children's children have larger or smaller forests in which to play?

2. In 1975 the editor of *Backpacker* magazine proposed that fees be levied on users of wilderness back country. He argued that (a) direct payment will give wilderness lovers a stronger voice in political determination of such questions as use and development of wilderness and (b) necessary services will be paid for anyway out of general tax revenues; by footing the bill through fees, wilderness users can obtain credit for paying their own way. Do you find his arguments persuasive? Are there any important differences between fees to cover the cost of maintaining wild lands for people to roam in, and tuition fees to cover the cost of maintaining universities for people to study in?

3. In 1954, the country was vigorously debating legislation that would make federal funds available to public school systems. The opponents of "federal aid to education" held that federal support would imply federal control. What evidence can be seen today that substantiates their view?

4. In 1972 a Chicago lawyer did a study of land use in Houston, Texas. Houston has no zoning laws. Did he find gas stations being built in expensive residential areas, or a chaotic hodgepodge of vacant land, residential land and commercial land intermixed randomly? No. He found that land use in Houston is hardly distinguishable from land use in cities which have zoning laws. Which of the following assertions are consistent with his findings?

   "Bureaucrats on zoning boards are too easy to corrupt by people with money who want to use land their way."

   "Economic forces, and not zoning maps, determine the viability of commercial enterprises in different locations; and without the prospect of viability there will be no commercial development."

   "Private covenants and other voluntary or contractual usage restraints can operate effectively where they are needed."

   (See B. H. Siegan, *Land Use Without Zoning,* Lexington, Mass.: D. C. Heath, 1972.)

BIBLIOGRAPHICAL NOTE

The benefits of government intervention are widely celebrated. An influential writer in the British interventionist movement was the sociologist Leonard Trelawney Hobhouse; his little book, *Liberalism,* reprinted editions (New York: Oxford University Press, 1966), is perhaps the best single source on the topic.

Contemporary attitudes are steeped in the interventionist outlook. Virtually every newspaper in the USA and Great Britain contains, in its editorials and news columns, daily reports of social problems, the efforts of various study commissions and govern-ment agencies to solve those problems, and the need for greater effort. Of late, we have begun to see occasional pessimistic commentary in the news media regarding the effec-tiveness of interventionist efforts. The popular writer Tom Wolfe published, in 1970, a book that may have been the most influential anti-interventionist document ever to appear: *Radical Chic and Mau-Mauing the Flak-Catchers* (in paperback by Bantam Books, New York). Wolfe is justly famous for his style and humor.

The most comprehensive interventionist testimonial is Paul Samuelson's widely used *Economics* (New York: McGraw-Hill, nine editions). This is the twentieth century's most successful textbook and one of the century's half-dozen most influential books in economics; it is also a thousand-page valentine to the interventionist outlook and record of accomplishment.

Friedrich Hayek is probably the most thoughtful critic of intervention. *The Con-stitution of Liberty* (Chicago: University of Chicago Press, 1960) analyzes the dangers of interventionism and raises philosophical objections. His *Capitalism and the Historians* (Chicago: University of Chicago Press, 1954) examines the evolution of attitudes in favor of intervention.

George Stigler points out the issue discussed in the Appendix to this chapter in *The Theory of Price*, 3rd ed. (New York: Macmillan, 1966).

Name Index

Subject Index